Archaeological Investigations of the Maldives in the Medieval Islamic Period

This book presents pioneering research on the Indian Ocean archipelago of the Maldives in the medieval period. Primarily archaeological, the book has an interdisciplinary slant, examining the material culture, history, and environment of the islands.

Featuring contributions by leading archaeologists and material culture researchers, the book is the first systematic archaeological monograph devoted to the Maldives. Offering an archaeological account of this island-nation from the beginnings of the Islamic period, it complements and nuances the picture presented by external historical data, which identify the Maldives as a key player in global networks. The book describes excavations and surveys at a medieval site on the island of Kinolhas. It offers a comprehensive analysis of finds of pottery, glass, and cowries, relating them to regional assemblages to add valuable new data to an under-researched field. The artefacts suggest links with India, Sri Lanka, the Middle East, Arabia, central Asia, southeast Asia, and China, offering tangible evidence of wider connections. The research also evidences diet, crafts, and funerary practices. The rigorous presentation of the primary material is framed by chapters setting the context, conceptual approaches, and historical interpretation, placing the Maldives within broader dynamics of Islamic and Indian Ocean history and opening the research results to a wide readership.

The book is aimed at students and researchers interested in the archaeology and history of the Indian Ocean, Islamic studies, island and coastal communities, maritime networks, and the medieval period, with special relevance for the 'Global Middle Ages'. It will appeal to art historians, archaeologists, museologists, and heritage and material culture studies researchers with related interests.

Anne Haour is Professor in the Arts and Archaeology of Africa and Director of the Centre for African Art and Archaeology (CfAAA) at the University of East Anglia, United Kingdom.

Annalisa Christie is Assistant Professor in Cultural Heritage at University College Dublin, Ireland.

British Institute in Eastern Africa Memoir
Series editor: Stephanie Wynne-Jones

I am delighted to introduce this revitalised memoir series, published as a collaboration between the British Institute in Eastern Africa (BIEA) and Routledge. Since the 1960s, the BIEA Memoir series has published monographs on landmark research projects from across the region. The series began with a survey of Islamic architecture along the East African coast and has included excavations at Kilwa, Manda and Shanga (Swahili coast), Aksum (Ethiopian Highlands), Soba (Sudan), and Nyanga (Zimbabwe).

The new series will build on that tradition of outstanding research, providing the definitive guide to significant projects with substantive datasets, providing space and opportunity to present data for the long-term use of scholars in the region. The books will also showcase the ways in which scholarship on the region has changed over time—notably through an emphasis on interdisciplinarity and collaboration.

The British Institute in Eastern Africa is one of the British International Research Institutes supported by the British Academy. Founded in 1959 as the British Institute of History and Archaeology in East Africa, the BIEA has a strong tradition of interdisciplinary research, and recent projects have embraced political, environmental, and development studies, geography, public health, art, and performance.

Archaeological Investigations of the Maldives in the Medieval Islamic Period
Ibn Battuta's Island
Edited by Anne Haour and Annalisa Christie

For more information about this series, please visit: https://www.routledge.com/British-Institute-in-Eastern-Africa-Memoir/book-series/BIEAM

Archaeological Investigations of the Maldives in the Medieval Islamic Period

Ibn Battuta's Island

Edited by
Anne Haour and Annalisa Christie

Routledge
Taylor & Francis Group

LONDON AND NEW YORK

Cover image: Excavations under way at Kinolhas Trench 631. Note an additional rectilinear structure to the left of the image; several further structures exist, hidden by vegetation. Drone photography by Annalisa Christie, Aslam Abubakuru and Ali Riffath.

First published 2022
by Routledge
2 Park Square, Milton Park, Abingdon, Oxon OX14 4RN

and by Routledge
605 Third Avenue, New York, NY 10158

Routledge is an imprint of the Taylor & Francis Group, an informa business

© 2022 selection and editorial matter, Anne Haour and Annalisa Christie; individual chapters, the contributors.

The right of Anne Haour and Annalisa Christie to be identified as the authors of the editorial material, and of the authors for their individual chapters, has been asserted in accordance with sections 77 and 78 of the Copyright, Designs and Patents Act 1988.

British Library Cataloguing-in-Publication Data
A catalogue record for this book is available from the British Library

Library of Congress Cataloging-in-Publication Data
A catalog record has been requested for this book

ISBN: 978-0-367-76269-8 (hbk)
ISBN: 978-0-367-76276-6 (pbk)
ISBN: 978-1-003-16622-1 (ebk)

DOI: 10.4324/9781003166221

Typeset in Times New Roman
by Apex CoVantage, LLC

Contents

Illustrations

Figures

Tables

Box

Contributors

Annalisa Christie is Assistant Professor in Cultural Heritage at University College Dublin (Ireland) where she coordinates the MSc in World Heritage Conservation (online) programme and co-coordinates the MSc in World Heritage Management and Conservation. Her research interests include interpretation, presentation and value of cultural heritage, African archaeology, maritime archaeology, and cowrie shell analysis. During the 'Cowrie Shells: An Early Global Commodity' project, her focus was on analysing the cowrie assemblages and conducting an anthropological assessment of Maldivian maritime practices. She is currently working with colleagues to examine the relationship between heritage values and sustainable development in the Mafia Archipelago, Tanzania.

Laure Dussubieux is a chemist specialising in the determination of the compositions of ancient artefacts made from synthesised or natural glass, metals, and stones. Her research directly informs hypotheses about ancient and modern trade and exchange, technology, and their relationship to the development of social complexity around the world. She has published extensively about the circulation of ancient glass around the Indian Ocean. Since 2004, she has managed the Elemental Analysis Facility (EAF) at the Field Museum in Chicago (USA), and her current title is Research Scientist.

Anne Haour is Professor in the Arts and Archaeology of Africa and Director of the Centre for African Art and Archaeology (CfAAA) at the University of East Anglia (UK). An anthropologically trained archaeologist, she has worked mainly in Niger, the Maldives, and Benin. She has particular expertise in the analysis of ceramics and cowrie shells, and her core interests concern the way in which an interdisciplinary dialogue, centred on archaeology, can shed light on the relationships between people, objects, and political entities in the medieval period.

Shiura Jaufar is an archaeologist at the Department of Heritage, Republic of Maldives, with degrees from La Trobe University (Australia), Durham University (UK), and the University of East Anglia (UK). Research interests include the archaeology and heritage of the Maldives and the wider Asia–Pacific region, Islamic archaeology, archaeological mitigation, and ceramic analysis.

St John Simpson is an archaeologist and senior curator at the Department of the Middle East at the British Museum (UK). He has excavated extensively in the Middle East and Central Asia and curated major exhibitions relating to Yemen, Afghanistan, and Siberia. His core research concerns Sasanian and early Islamic material culture from Iraq, Iran, the Persian Gulf, and Central Asia, but he has published widely on topics ranging from ancient South Arabia to smoking in the Ottoman empire.

David Vigoureux is a graduate of archaeology and anthropology at the University of Oxford (UK), where he specialised in prehistory with a thesis on the bone technology of Upper Palaeolithic Sri Lanka. His research interests lie in the intersection of heritage and development, and he has most recently completed an internship at the Division of Creativity, Culture Sector of UNESCO, where he helped efforts to measure and articulate culture's contribution to the Sustainable Development Goals.

Marilee Wood is an honorary research associate in the School of Geology, Archaeology, and Environmental Studies at the University of the Witwatersrand (South Africa). She received a master's degree from that university and a PhD from Uppsala University (Sweden). She specialises in glass beads that were traded into Africa in the Islamic period, with an emphasis on Indian Ocean trade.

Ran Zhang is a research associate in the Department of Archaeology, Durham University (UK). His research is concerned with how Chinese trade affected the maritime economy of the Indian Ocean and Europe from the eighth to the nineteenth centuries, with an interest in the values of various commodities in ancient trade. He has expertise in the identification and dating of Chinese ceramics as well as archaeological field experience in the United Arab Emirates, India, Sri Lanka, Qatar, and China.

Acknowledgements

This book, as most books, reflects a collaborative endeavour, and it is a great pleasure to thank those who made possible, or contributed to, the work reported here.

We begin with the funders, the Leverhulme Trust [RPG-2014–359], with additional support from the Sainsbury Research Unit, the University of East Anglia, and (for the glass analysis) the Ministry of Education, Culture Sports, Science and Technology/Japanese Society for the Promotion of Science: Grants in Aid for Scientific Research Grants [18K12566 and 20H01372].

Needless to say, none of the research would have been possible without our partners in the Maldives. We are grateful for the unstinting support of Hon. Yumna Maumoon, Hauwwa Nazla, and Asiyath Mohammed. The President of the Academy of Dhivehi Language, Ashraf Ali, and Director of the Academy of Dhivehi Language, Aminath Abbasa, received us warmly. Naseema Mohammed, Jadhullo Saleem, and Richard, Lucas and Charlotte Doyle were there at the very start.

At the Department of Heritage (now National Center for Cultural Heritage) in Male, we thank Ibrahim Mujah and Ahmad Zameer.

In Kinolhas, we were kindly received by members of the Kinolhas Council (especially Council President Ahmed Hussain, Faisal Ibrahim, and council member Zubair Hussein). For their work at the site, we are grateful to Ibrahim Shaahir, Abdhul Sathaaru, Hassan Junaidh, Abdul Muhaimin, Hassan Nabeel, Zaidh Zubair, Hussain Zaidh Zubair, Hamid Ali, and AbuBakuru Easa. Our hosts, Ramla Easa, Abdul Hameed, and Abdul Sathaar, played a vital part in the success of the fieldwork.

The 2016 fieldwork depended on the assistance of a number of people: local councils, and specifically, at Utheemu, Ahmed Ikram and the two Hussains, Agirou, and colleagues Shyam, Latif, and Latifa at Utheemu Department of Heritage. In Male', Mizon and Hussein, and in Veyvah, Abil, Simon, and Ali. At Maamigili, we thank Hassan Niyaz.

For the ethnographic strand of work, we thank Shehezine Fathimath, our colleague and interpreter in this project, and the councils of the many islands visited as part of our survey and ethnographic research, in addition to those cited earlier: Mulah in Meemu; Alifushi, Rasgetheemu, Angolitheemu, Meedhoo, Inguraidhoo, Fainu, and Vaadhoo in Raa; Gan, Fonadhoo, Ishdhoo, Kalaidhoo, Dhanbidhoo, Mundhoo, and Hithadhoo in Laamu; Fenfushi, Diggurah, Maamigili, Kunburudhoo, Haggnaameedhoo, and Omadhoo in Alifu Dhaalu; Maalhos in Alif Alif; Maamendho, Nilandhoo, and Dhaandhoo in Gaafu Alifu.

Many people played a role in the post-fieldwork analysis of results and in the ultimate production of this book. We are grateful to colleagues and friends for comments on chapters and on finds: Abdulrazzaq Alrromehi (King Abdulaziz Foundation for Research and Archives, KSA), Julian Andrews (University of East Anglia), Paul Dennis (University of East Anglia), Michael Feener (Center for Southeast Asian Studies, Kyoto University), Wang Guangyao (Deputy Director of the Institute of Archaeology, Beijing Palace Museum), Timothy Insoll (University of Exeter), Derek Kennet (Durham University), Paul Lane (University of Cambridge), Mark Littlewood (AOC Archaeology) John Mack (University of East Anglia), Marcos Martinón-Torres (at the time University College London), Conor McDermott (University College Dublin), Peter Mitchell (University of Oxford), Abigail Moffett (University of East Anglia), Caroline Robion-Brunner (Université Toulouse II Jean Jaurès), and Nigel Wood (University of Oxford).

Alastair Grant (University of East Anglia) provided help and advice throughout the project on the marine biology aspects and was a wonderful co-investigator.

For access to Maldivian collections in the UK, we are grateful to Sushma Jansari (Tabor Foundation Curator: South Asia), Xanthe Shrestha and Lowri Jones at the British Museum; and Alessandra Cereda, Sarah Mitchell, and Aimée Payton at the Ashmolean Museum.

For finds analysis, Yoshinari Abe and St John Simpson acknowledge the helpful support by Mr. Ryuji Shikaku of Okayama Orient Museum. Debbie Harris, Senior Conservator, and Helen Rush, Conservation Co-ordinator, both at Norfolk Museums Service, analysed and conserved the octagonal metal find in Chapter 9, and we are grateful to Maria Ledinskaya, Sainsbury Centre for Visual Arts, for the initial appraisal.

The analysis of the earthenware rims in Chapter 5 was carried out by the authors and by doctoral research student at the University of East Anglia, and freelance specialist in post-excavation analysis Susan Anderson.

We are grateful to Maria Ledinskaya, Conor McDermott, Giulia Nazzaro, Nicolas Nikis, and Bolaji Owoseni for drawings and illustrations, and to the owner and operator of the drone at Kinolhas, Aslam Abubakuru and Ali Riffath. Margit Thøfner and Lynne Crossland proofed and edited sections of the text and improved them. We are grateful to Kate Fornadel and her team at ApexCoVantage, Matthew Gibbons at Taylor & Francis, and BIEA Series Editor Stephanie Wynne-Jones for their help during the final stages of the production of the book. Thanks also to Ann and David for their unfailing support throughout. Lastly, our thanks to various reviewers along the life of this project.

1 Introduction

An archaeological study of a Maldivian island

Anne Haour

Introduction

The Maldives, a coralline archipelago lying in the Indian Ocean, off the tip of India (Figure 1.1), is probably best known to the casual reader for its travel industry. Until recently, its key promotional messages focused on the natural beauty of the islands and the opportunity they offer to travellers to seclude and remove themselves from the hectic pace of modern life. This island-nation is, in fact, more sea than land, covering an area of 90000 km² yet with a land-mass of less than 250 km².

In this marketing exercise, little space has been given to the historical and cultural depth of the Maldives. Historians, especially those who worked on Indian Ocean trade networks, took a different view. In particular, the trade in the shells of the cowries that occur in considerable numbers on these reefs has guaranteed the Maldives a place in writings on global connectivity since at least the fourteenth century, with the account of North African traveller ibn Battuta. In terms of early archaeological research, the early twentieth-century work of H. C. P. Bell, British civil servant and the first Commissioner of Archaeology of the then-Ceylon (now Sri Lanka), and the later enquiries of Thor Heyerdahl in the 1980s, documented major standing remains suggestive of the Buddhist past of these islands. Oral traditions, which set the initial occupation of the archipelago by communities from Sri Lanka or India to about 2000–2500 years ago, were broadly confirmed by this work. Brief surveys of epigraphic and ceramic materials dating to the Islamic period (its beginnings conventionally set at AD 1153, date at which oral traditions suggest the rulers of the Maldives converted to Islam) followed. However, the first systematic archaeological work occurred just 30 years ago, at the Buddhist site of Kaashidhoo, as part of a study of global cowrie trading networks (Mikkelsen 2000).

A major gap remained. No archaeological research had been undertaken on the medieval period, despite the repeated assertion that the Maldives played a key role in Indian Ocean networks at the time. The aim of the work presented in the present volume, conducted primarily in 2017 but with important context-setting research in 2013, 2016, and 2019, was to begin to address that question. It was carried out as part of a project funded by the Leverhulme Trust [RPG-2014–359] with the broader aim of improving understanding of both the West African and Maldivian ends of the medieval cowrie trade.[1] As part of this, archaeological survey and excavations took place in 2017 at the island of Kinolhas, in Raa atoll, which is famous for being the landing-place of ibn Battuta during his visit, probably in December 1343. This work provided the first archaeological overview of the island, adding to the insights obtained by the same team the year before, which had involved test excavations around the Maldives and placed on the record a number of Islamic-period sites (Jaufar 2019, Chapter 9, this volume).

The subject of the present book is the work conducted at Kinolhas. This chapter begins with a brief presentation of the geography and environment of the Maldives, then presents an overview of the trade networks which extended westwards to the East African coast and Arabia, and from there to the Mediterranean and West Africa; and east- and northeast-wards, into the Indian subcontinent, China, and southeast Asia. The aim here is not to rehearse the very extensive literature on medieval trade networks in those areas, but instead to highlight key aspects that can inform a Maldivian perspective, with a focus on the period AD 1100–1600. Indeed, the Maldives offer a compelling case study of medieval connectivity, due to their geographical position and their role in provisioning maritime shipping. Historical sources show that they occupied centre stage in some travellers' minds. Two individuals, ibn Battuta and Zheng He, illustrate this. Born three generations and a quarter of a world apart, in Tangier (present-day Morocco) in 1304 and in Kunming (Yunnan, present-day China) in 1371, the two men have achieved long-lasting international renown. Both are closely associated with visits to the Maldives.

The Maldives: an introduction

The Republic of Maldives consists of a double chain of coral islands, running roughly north–south, and made up of over 2000 coral reefs that form 26 natural atolls (Figure 1.2). The growth of these atolls—small shallow-water carbonate platforms some tens of kilometres in diameter—is plastic in relation to prevailing winds and wave action, and they rarely approach the diagrammatic circular form; for example, Raa atoll, in which Kinolhas is situated, is roughly oval. The reef flat is usually broken by channels allowing the internal lagoon to fill and drain at each tidal cycle, and one principal entrance often dominates (Longhurst and Pauly 1987). This will have had considerable historical significance

DOI: 10.4324/9781003166221-1

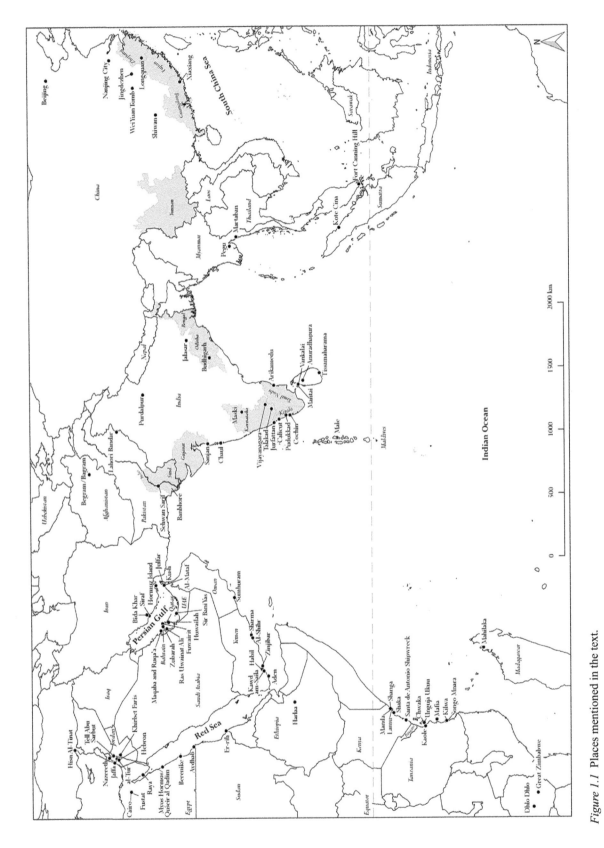

Figure 1.1 Places mentioned in the text.

Source: Map by Annalisa Christie, created using Natural Earth.

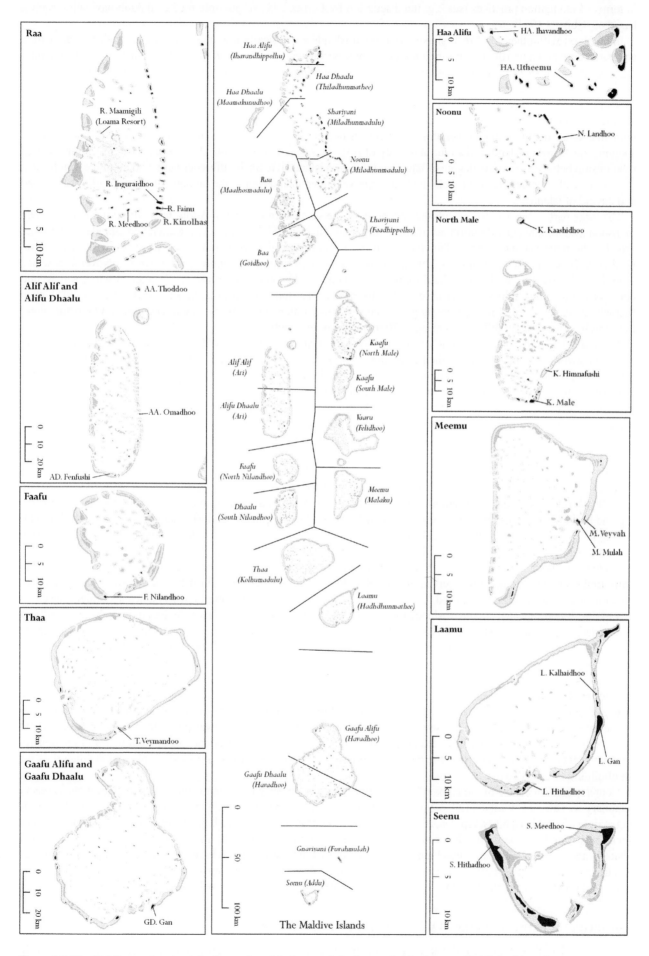

Figure 1.2 The Maldives—showing islands mentioned in the text (islands sampled by the team highlighted in red).

Source: Map by Annalisa Christie. Basemap from GADM.org.

in terms of navigation practices (see e.g. the discussion by Forbes 1981 of possible medieval Arab navigation routes, based on Tibbetts 1971).

In common with other coral reef islands, Maldivian islands are typically low in elevation and small in area, with a vegetated core and a narrow beach running around their perimeter. In fact, of the 1192 islands making up the country, less than 3% exceed 1 km² in area, and most social and economic activity occurs on land that is less than 1.3 m above the highest astronomical tide (Edwards n.d., p. 4; Maps 2016, p. 8). Within this general picture, considerable variation exists in the structure and development of islands and atolls—as might be expected, given that the Maldives stretch over almost 900 km north to south. Lagoon depth, for instance, is highly variable; while Raa atoll is among the shallowest, with an average depth of 26 m, other atolls are twice as deep (Vecsei 2000, p. 218, Risk and Sluka 2000). This may be a significant factor in island formation: in a study of ring reefs (*faro*) in Baa atoll, Perry et al. (2013) identified a clear relationship between *faro* size, degree of lagoonal infill, and island size. Such differences are evident in the Maldives at the coarse scale, where shallower atolls include large vegetated islands while the lagoons of deeper atolls are unfilled and devoid of islands.

The large part of the Maldives, with the exception of the southernmost atoll of Addu, falls within the Indian Ocean monsoon system. Succinct descriptions are offered by e.g. Risk and Sluka (2000) and Kench and Brander (2006), but broadly, the northeast monsoon, in Dhivehi *iruvai*, lasts from December to March, when winds blow from the east–northeast. These are the drier months. During the southwest monsoon, the *hulhangu*, from April to November, winds blow from the west to northwest. Island shorelines respond to short-term and seasonal changes in wind, waves, and currents, making them inherently dynamic landforms; based on a study in Baa atoll, Kench and Brander (2006) showed that islands undergo substantial morphological change between monsoon seasons, due to accretion and erosion along the shoreline, resulting in differences of up to 50 meters in beach width.

The provision of fresh water is one of the significant contributions of the Maldives in historical accounts relating to trade networks. On many islands, the percolation of rain into the subsoil creates a freshwater lens which effectively floats on top of the seawater permeating the porous coral rock, sand, and rubble that constitute the islands. In the northern atolls, where the effects of the dry northeast monsoon are felt most strongly, many wells become brackish towards the end of this monsoon but produce good water during the wet southwest monsoon. Edwards (n.d.) reports that on Male' island the groundwater level is generally less than 1.2 m below the surface, a situation confirmed by archaeological excavations in the palace gardens carried out by Carswell (1975–1977), as well as by the present author's team at locations across the Maldives. Square wells built of stone blocks, some said to be of some antiquity, are a recurrent feature on Maldivian islands (including Kinolhas; see Chapter 3, this volume).

In terms of stone, the islands themselves are limited to consolidated coral sand ('sandstone', in Dhivehi *veligaa*) and coral. Until relatively recent restrictions, coral was widely used for construction; madrepore coral, the finest for carving and building purposes, is termed locally *hirigaa* (Forbes 1983, Ragupathy and Mohamed 2008, p. 41). Bell (1924, p. 295, fn. 6) writes, 'Máldivians divide the madrepore of their Atols into three main classes: *hiri-gá*, *veli-gá*, *rat-gá*, the two latter being coral-sandstone (*hiri* "white;" *veli* "sand," *rat* "red;" *gá* "stone")'.

Archaeological standing remains certainly offered a ready source of building material. Upon visiting Gan in Addu atoll, Bell (2002 [1940], p. 120) observed that the Buddhist structures there had 'furnished to the Muslim Islanders . . . a continuous supply, still unexhausted, of coral slabs, ready dressed, for building their Mosques and chief houses', a process he found repeated on other islands (Forbes 1983, pp. 48–51). This has been documented archaeologically at some sites, for example at Nilandhoo (Litster 2016). However, while stone was used for public buildings, the domestic structures of the Maldives consisted largely of perishable materials such as wood and thatch, difficult to identify in the archaeological record.

In terms of vegetation, Maldivian islands are marked by a clear-cut zonation of tree species from pioneers colonising littoral forests to much denser vegetation with larger and long-lived species towards the landward side. In the case of islands with larger land area, a succession of shrubby vegetation starting on the coast builds up to a thick and dense forest growth. In fact, an early seventeenth-century source claimed that it was possible to jump from one island to the other using the branches of overhanging trees, given the proximity of islands to one another and the density of their vegetation; it also describes the coconut palm as a key resource, furnishing food, drink, and the materials for shipbuilding (Bertius 1618).

Contemporary accounts of the fauna of the Maldives build upon early twentieth-century regional accounts. A recent summary was offered by Litster (2016, pp. 164–166, and references therein). Terrestrial fauna is very restricted, consisting mainly of fruit bats, birds, reptiles, commensals such as rats and shrews, a rich invertebrate fauna, and domesticates such as cats, rabbits, goats, and chickens. Avifauna is largely limited to seabirds and shorebirds, the majority seasonal visitors, and small numbers of amphibians. In contrast to this limited terrestrial fauna, the Maldives host an abundant and diverse marine fauna, both vertebrates and invertebrates. As well as supplying a major source of subsistence, some of these, in particular the shells of turtles and cowries, were also important in global trade networks.

The medieval networks of the Maldives and the Indian Ocean

The medieval Indian Ocean world has played a central role in theoretical debates on early globalisation. The world systems theory as defined by Wallerstein (1974) has been well discussed, particularly as regards the timing and nature of 'world systems' and connections with capitalism (see e.g. Denemark et al. 2000, Stein 2002). The model remains popular with archaeologists, in part because of its focus on the creation and circulation of goods and wealth, but also due to its contention that the unit of analysis should not be just a single state or society but rather the larger integrated system.

While the Maldives have typically been mentioned in passing in Indian Ocean studies, the archipelago has not really been integrated into them, largely due to the lack of archaeological information. An early attempt to use artefacts to link the Maldives into much wider global patterns was made by John Carswell, based on an unsystematic collection of surface ceramic material in the streets of Male'. This suggested to him (Carswell 1975–1977, pp. 139–140, also in Hourani 1995 [1951], p. 145) that the Maldives were a stopover for westbound rather than eastbound travel. Two doctoral theses have recently moved the discussion forward, based on more substantial assemblages from the Maldives: Litster (2016) and Jaufar (2019) both discuss variants of world systems and globalisation theories, with specific reference to the archipelago.

One major unknown is the inception of the Maldives' connection with the global world. Indeed, the date of the initial settlement of the archipelago remains unclear; it is certainly possible that some islands were populated considerably earlier than the early centuries AD, which is the date of the earliest archaeological evidence (at the site of Nilandhoo; Chapter 2). In terms of historical accounts, the first plausible mention of the Maldives occurs in Indian and Sri Lankan semi-legendary sources dating to about 2000 years ago. These are followed by a handful of later accounts, including by the mid-first-century Greek writer of the *Periplus of the Erythrean Sea*, the fifth-century Chinese traveller and scholar Fa Hsien, the mid-sixth-century Greek writer Cosmas Indicopleustes, and the ninth-century 'Suleiman The Traveller' (full references in Chapter 2, this volume, but key here are Carswell 1975–1977, Forbes 1980, 1981, Mohamed 2008, 2014a, 2014b). These are subject to debate, since it is difficult to ascertain whether they are referring to the Maldives or to other islands lying off the Indian peninsula. Confusion with the Laccadives is a particular issue, not resolved until the eleventh century with the account by Al-Biruni. Nevertheless, generally speaking, the sheer range of these sources testifies to the cosmopolitanism of this part of the world already in the first millennium AD. Later historical records certainly confirm that by the fourteenth century the Maldives' networks extended westwards to East Africa and Arabia and east and northeast into the Indian subcontinent, China, and southeast Asia.

One driving force behind these networks was the exchange of material items. On this front, historical sources vary in resolution and detail and can be difficult to integrate with the archaeological data. Texts from the early second millennium AD onwards typically mention cowrie shells, coir (fibre from the outer husk of the coconut), and fish as the dominant exports of the Maldives. A Portuguese report from 1503, describing the seizing of four Maldivian ships off the Indian coast of Kerala, situates the Maldives as the place 'at which is made the *cairo* [*coir*] rope which serves the ships of all India for cables and shrouds, besides being of great use on shore' (Vogel and Hieronymus 1993, p. 224). Coconuts themselves, which, when young, can serve as a portable source of water, were probably also fundamental; a tenth-century source suggests the intentional cultivation by Buddhist monks of the coconut palm in the Maldives, in order to serve as a water supply (Lambourn 2018a, pp. 176–177). Freshwater was certainly an equally valuable, though perhaps less newsworthy, commodity that could be picked up in the Maldives by Indian Ocean seafarers; its availability is noted explicitly in nautical charts, for example (e.g. Moresby et al. 1838–1839). The obvious issue, from an archaeological perspective, is that most of the export goods mentioned in historical sources have little archaeological visibility—a notable exception being the shells of cowries, and their global significance has been well discussed (key references among a vast literature include Hogendorn and Johnson 2003 [1986] and Yang 2019). The Maldivian cowrie trade apparently flowed in two streams: eastbound to southeast Asia and China, and westbound to the Red Sea, the Persian Gulf, and East Africa, and from there, it is hypothesised, to the Mediterranean and West Africa. Clearly this trade must have been accompanied by the exchange of other commodities, but these unfortunately did not captivate historical writers to the same extent.

Unusually, the Maldives were reliant on imports for most key items; the islands lack clay and iron ore, for example. As the nearest landmass, India is of key significance here. Indeed, the ceramics of Indian origin that occur in Maldivian archaeological assemblages—including at Kinolhas—serve not just as evidence for the direct contacts maintained between regions but also as proxy indicators of the archipelago's wider engagement with the Indian Ocean world. An Indian origin for some of the earthenwares recovered at sites on the coast of Arabia, and on the Indian Ocean and Red Sea coastlines of Africa, has long been suggested: such ceramics have been recovered at numerous sites in East Africa, with the main published accounts coming from Manda, Shanga (both in Kenya), and Kilwa (in Tanzania) (Chittick 1974, 1984, Horton et al. 1996, Chapter 5, this volume). This type of material ranges in date from the seventh through to the fifteenth centuries, but the bulk falls in the eleventh to fourteenth centuries. Most is utilitarian, including water jars, bowls, and cooking vessels.

Traditionally, such material attracted less archaeological interest than did other imports such as glazed ceramics of Far Eastern or Islamic origin. There is now growing realisation that it is precisely such 'ordinary' material that might inform us on past identities and trading communities. Some may have been destined for carrying water for the voyage across the ocean, while others may have been owned by Indian communities living and working in East Africa. The idea of specialist trade diasporas, well known in West African and trans-Saharan contexts (Haour 2013, 2017, Forrest and Haour 2018), is of course also amply debated in discussions of Indian Ocean connections. There, it has been given a renewed impetus by some of the remarkable historical records which offer insights into the lived experience of this trade. Among these are the texts of the Cairo *geniza* (mainly of eleventh-century date). These have been studied by a range of scholars, but one example of the opportunities presented by this material is the work by Lambourn (2018a) on a document containing a list of personal possessions carried by the North African Jewish trader Abraham Ben Yiju, who traded between Aden and the Malabar coast of India in the 1130s and 1140s. This analysis highlights the importance of domestic materiality, and the efforts which mobile people deployed, via multiple networks and systems of exchange, to maintain 'an everyday normal' in their translocation. The list's material world includes not only objects but also food-stuffs, and in fact by far the greatest share of household items can be grouped under the umbrella of 'food culture': raw and processed foodstuffs, spice condiments, and objects associated with the storage, preparation, and consumption of food (Lambourn 2018a, p. 98). A recurrent item is the *mazza*, identified as a Yemeni term for what is probably an earthen vessel (Lambourn 2018a, p. 78, note t, citing Goitein and Friedman 2008: 561, n. 49).

Another example is presented by an archive of Arabic documents uncovered at the Islamic site of Quseir al-Qadim, on the Egyptian Red Sea, shedding light on the activities and operations of a family shipping business in the thirteenth century. This set of discarded personal documents illuminates one trader's family, 'their social ties, and their attitudes towards life, illness, death, and God' (Guo 2004, p. 90). More widely, the texts shed light on domestic policies and business customs in Ayyubid and Mamluk Egypt and, to a lesser extent, on the Arabian shore of the Red Sea and Yemen. Aside from grains, the documents discuss a variety of goods, chiefly foodstuffs, domestic items such as bottles, cups, and pottery, textiles, and, less frequently, livestock and sailing equipment such as ropes. Traffic in enslaved people is rarely mentioned, and nor are spices, despite their well-known importance in Indian Ocean trade. Coral, semi-precious stone, and beads are alluded to but, unfortunately, no mention is made of cowries or, more broadly, of shell of any kind.

Westwards from the Maldives to Yemen, the Red Sea, and the Persian Gulf

Oral and written historical traditions suggest the relevance of Red Sea connections linking through to the Mediterranean. A North African Muslim is credited by some traditions, reported by ibn Battuta, with the conversion of the ruler of the Maldives to Islam in the mid-twelfth century (Chapter 2, this volume). In the late sixteenth century, the Shafi'i school of jurisprudence was introduced from southern Arabia, and the adherence of Maldivians to this school links them with communities of the western Indian Ocean littoral such as those of the East African coast. Its prevalence may also suggest that Islamic belief spread to the Maldives directly across the Arabian sea from Yemen and the south Arabian region of Hadramawt, rather than from mainland India (Forbes 1981, 1983).

The literature relating to connections along the Red Sea is enormous (see Power 2012, Cooper 2014 for recent summaries) and draws on a range of literary and archaeological evidence. One point to insist on for the present study is the apparent increase in international traffic with the emergence and growth of the Fatimid Caliphate centred in Fustat from the late tenth century (Old Cairo). At that time, a shift in the maritime trade of the Indian Ocean saw goods increasingly routed to the port city of Aden and to ports of the Red Sea rather than to the Persian Gulf (Hrbek 1977, Bramoullé 2012, Chakravarti 2015). In fact, Bramoullé (2012, p. 135) has described the Red Sea as essential to the very survival of the Fatimid dynasty in the twelfth century. The Red Sea port of Aydhab—today at the border of Egypt and Sudan—has been best discussed historically, although it remains little studied archaeologically. By the 1050s, it was the major port on the Hajj route, judging by the account of a Persian traveller on his way from Egypt to Mecca, who also mentions that it was visited by ships coming from Abyssinia, Zanzibar, and Yemen (Cooper 2014, p. 243).

The documents of the Cairo *geniza* are of relevance in these developments and shed indirect light on the networks in which the Maldives were involved. The twin city Cairo–Fustat formed the terminal for both the Mediterranean and the India trade and served as a distribution centre for the goods of both (Goitein 1973, p. 23). A key role was played by Aden, in present-day Yemen, which connected traffic between India, the Red Sea ports, and the East African coast and served as a major hub for the Jewish 'India traders' (Pouwels 2002, Margariti 2007). The importance of Aden, initiated under the Fatimids, continued under the Ayyubids; perhaps the most powerful incentive for their interest, remarks Margariti (2007) in her study of the *geniza* documents, was Yemen's importance in the collection of revenue from the India trade, and Aden's huge revenue-generating potential. From the mid-eleventh century, it was also a crucial stepping-stone for religious missions fanning out across South Asia (Forbes 1981, Lambourn 2018b). Slightly later, in the fourteenth century, ibn Battuta specifically mentions Yemen—by which he probably means Aden—as a place with which Maldivians conducted trade in cowries, the people of Yemen using them as ballast in their ships. In fact, Yemen is the only Arab country mentioned by ibn Battuta (Forbes 1981, p. 70).

The allusion to cowries is important. In his reading of the *geniza* documents, and with reference to ibn Battuta's statement, Iroko (1987, p. 43) suggests that

> Arabes et Juifs du Yemen ainsi que ceux d'Egypte tiraient de ce commerce des cauris qui n'est jamais le seul objet transporté, deux avantages : d'abord, de par leur poids, les cauris constituent dans leurs navires un excellent lest à la place du sable qu'ils utilisaient auparavant . . . Ensuite, leur valeur marchande, une fois déchargés en Arabie ou en Egypte, leur procure de substantiels profits.

Unfortunately, cowries feature little in medieval records. The *geniza* documents do include a letter written in Aydhab, probably in May 1141, by one Nahray b. Allan, who is about to set sail for India and is writing to his son in Alexandria to inform his family of his plans. Among the goods he is forwarding to Fustat from Aden are 'two bales of cowrie shells, measuring 1 *mudd*' (Goitein 1973 , p. 199).[2]

Perhaps, he speculates, the cowries might best be sold in Spain, where they would presumably be used as amulets, ornaments, and/or, in pulverised form, for eye powder (Goitein 1973, p. 200, n. 20).

The role of Cairo presents a problem. Because the evidence on trade routes generally, and on those routes dealing with cowries specifically, is so sparse, it seems to be more an assumption than a demonstrated fact that the city constituted a major medieval market for cowries. Bovill (1958, p. 127, n.), commenting on a passage by sixteenth-century chronicler Leo Africanus, observes that cowries were imported to West Africa through Cairo, a statement repeated verbatim and without explanation in the second edition (1968, p. 148, n.). Presumably this assessment derives from the fact that Cairo was a known medieval economic centre; for example, Bovill (1968, p. 206) identifies it as the chief market for ivory. Hogendorn and Johnson (2003 [1986], p. 15) sound a more cautious note, acknowledging that although a major market likely existed for cowries in medieval Cairo, this is circumstantial and uncertain. Their argument primarily rests on Cairo's strategic position and proximity to trade routes, and on the lack of convincing alternatives (Hogendorn and Johnson 2003 [1986], pp. 26, 164, n. 67). On the other hand, Hrbek (1977, p. 92) finds the evidence to be too meagre to justify the idea that the main flow of cowries to sub-Saharan Africa passed through Egypt prior to the fifteenth century.

These questions, which have yet to be resolved, have major ramifications. It is known through the archaeological record that cowries from Indo-Pacific or at the very least Red Sea sources were reaching West Africa from as early as the seventh century AD (Haour and Christie 2019). The potential role of the Red Sea not just as a transit zone for, but also as a source of supply of, cowries to West Africa in medieval times has recently been proposed by Insoll (2021), based on data from excavations of eleventh- to early fifteenth- century deposits in eastern Ethiopia. Data on the natural distribution of various species of cowrie within the Red Sea are insufficient at present state of knowledge and, as noted by Insoll (2021), provenancing studies of archaeological material through oxygen isotope analysis will be fundamental. This said, it certainly appears that some of the cowries traded to West Africa originated in the Maldives. In particular, a recent re-analysis of cowries from the eleventh- or twelfth- century caravan load recovered from the Ma'den Ijafen (or Blad al-Wuda) site in the Mauritanian Sahara strongly suggests that they originated in the Maldives, based on the shell species and sizes represented and the high proportion of unmodified shells (Christie and Haour 2018a).

As well as Red Sea networks, Persian Gulf routes were probably also relevant to the Maldives; Abd-er-Razzak, a Persian emissary to India, reports seeing Maldivians at the emporium of Hormuz in 1442. This may point to regular shipments of Maldivian coir, fish, cowries, ambergris, and tortoise shell to Arabia (Vogel and Hieronymus 1993, p. 224). Al Mas'udi, who visited Sri Lanka in the early tenth century, reported that traders from Oman and Siraf (at the northern end of the Persian Gulf) had made the trip to the Maldives (Carswell 1975-1977, p. 135), although Forbes (1981, p. 69), believes the Laccadives may be meant here. Connectivity is also suggested by the shared use of the *larin*, a short doubled-up length of silver wire likely first made around the beginning of the sixteenth century at Lar, formerly an important point on the caravan route from the Persian Gulf, and the use of which spread down the west coast of India to Sri Lanka and the Maldives (Allan 1912, Quiggin 1949).

Much has also been made of a comment by sixteenth-century writer Leo Africanus, who stated that the coinage of Timbuktu was of plain gold but that in matters of small value 'certaine shels brought hither out of the kingdom of Persia' were used (cited in Hiskett 1966, p. 347, Einzig 1949, p. 141). Most seem to agree that Persia was a staging point on maritime or overland routes, rather than a primary source (Quiggin 1949, Hiskett 1966, Johnson 1970, Hogendorn and Johnson 2003 [1986]). In any case, the terminology is vague: at the time at which Leo Africanus wrote, the territory covered by Persia extended from the Black Sea to present-day Pakistan.

Westwards connections to East Africa

Archaeological data demonstrate the presence of goods from China, the Indian subcontinent, and southeast Asia on the East African shoreline from the mid-first millennium AD. The Maldives sit at an obvious midpoint for some of these connections, but allusions to direct maritime links between the archipelago and East Africa are fleeting, difficult to evaluate, and for the most part postdate the medieval period. It has been postulated by Shepherd (1982) that Austronesians came via the Maldives to Madagascar and East Africa two millennia ago, a proposition difficult to substantiate (Duarte 1993, who however accepts a direct Austronesian route between the Maldives and Madagascar a thousand years later (his Map 2)).

The existence of direct links between the Maldives and East Africa and its islands in the second millennium AD, on the other hand, is well accepted. Historical sources penned by Central Asian scholars are a key resource here. Al-Biruni speaks of islanders trading in shells, travelling with their coconut palms, and using coir to build boats, which Pouwels (2002) considers to be a report of Maldivian travel to East Africa, while Abul Hassan describes boats leaving the Maldives carrying dried fish, tortoise shells, and cowries to Africa (Maloney 2013), although it is not clear which specific region is meant. Both authors were active in the eleventh century. Pouwels (2002, pp. 400–401) has proposed that the growing significance of a route linking India to the East African coast via the Maldives largely accounted for the increased importance of a coastal network which, under the hegemony of Kilwa, included Pemba, Zanzibar, Mafia, Mozambique, the Comoros, and Madagascar in the thirteenth and fourteenth centuries. Further evidence comes from cartographic data. Beaujard (2007) has suggested that Arabic nautical charts of the fifteenth and sixteenth centuries, as well as archaeological data in the form of Chinese imports, suggest prolonged contacts of northern Madagascar with southeast Asia via the Maldives, while a map dating to the second or third quarter of the sixteenth century, possibly based on Zheng He's voyages, shows routes departing the Maldives for East Africa as well as Arabia and India (Carswell 1975–1977, Figure 7, Forbes 1981, pp. 77–78).

These possible maritime connections are difficult to evaluate. Forbes (1981, pp. 72–75), drawing on Tibbetts' readings of fifteenth century Ahmad ibn Majid, suggests that 'the important route linking Malabar with the Kilwa sultanate on the Swahili Coast of East Africa' bypassed the Maldives to the north. The issue is not helped by the perennial confusion in medieval historical sources between the Maldives and the Laccadives. A further obstacle is that the southwestern Indian Ocean routes, in which the Maldives potentially participated, remain less well researched than those forming part of the better-known monsoon system operating north of the Equator. The different currents and winds prevailing on the southern part of the East African coast distinguish it from regions farther north. The monsoon winds weaken at a point roughly south of the Pangani River in the north of present-day Tanzania, and strong contrary seasonal currents in the Mozambique Channel have historically forced ships sailing across the Indian Ocean bound for Kilwa, Mozambique, the Comoros, and Madagascar to 'winter' in East Africa and await better conditions for a less turbulent return.

Although such southern routes are less discussed, they were clearly in use. James Horsburgh's nineteenth-century *India Directory* states, for example, that in July and August only the so-called southern passage was available for ships leaving India for the Persian Gulf: they went westward to Africa below the Equator, and back northeast along the coasts of Africa and Arabia (Seland 2011, p. 401). It seems that these southerly routes were also in use during the medieval period, although the evidence for this is purely archaeological. Historical sources tend to focus on specific segments of wider networks: for example, the Cairo *geniza* documents as a whole contain few references to shipping down the African coast, suggesting the trade between Aden and East Africa constituted a discrete segment of the maritime Indian Ocean world that lay outside the reach of those traders (Margariti 2007). Cooper (2014, p. 179) remarks that for navigators leaving Egypt and aiming for East Africa, 'the medieval accounts have little or nothing to say'. Archaeological glass bead evidence for its part hints at significantly different trade patterns between the northern and southern portions of the East African coastline. The contacts of the former included Sri Lanka, the Persian Gulf, India (particularly the northwest), Egypt, the eastern Mediterranean, and perhaps Thailand; the southern shoreline of East Africa, on the other hand, evidences almost no links north of the mouth of the Red Sea, but strong connections with the Persian Gulf before the second millennium, and with India (particularly its southern regions) afterwards (Wood 2015). Al-Mas'udi, who is thought to have visited the northern offshore islands of present-day Tanzania in the early tenth century on a return voyage from China and India aboard a Persian ship, recorded that the coast of modern-day Mozambique was the furthest limit of the land, and the end of the voyages made from Oman and Siraf (Wood 2015; see also Duarte 2012).

Some of the connections between the Maldives and East Africa proposed through material culture remain to be substantiated. For example, Carswell (1975–1977, p. 154) identified in his collections from Male' fragments of Chinese pottery which he suggests exactly matched a bowl excavated at Dhlo Dhlo (Danangombe) in Zimbabwe, which, he advanced, 'provides incidental proof of the Maldives being on the route for Chinese porcelain bound for East Africa'. However, all that such finds demonstrate is membership of shared networks and practices of exotics consumption. A similar point may be made of the parallels between the Maldives and East Africa that draw on architectural comparisons. Along the Swahili coast, architectural technologies for building elite houses and public buildings, including mosques, employed mortared blocks of reef coral. This represents a point of commonality with the Maldives; indeed, Jameel and Ahmad (2016, p. 49), alluding to the cases of Kilwa Kisiwani, Songo Mnara, or Shanga on the Swahili coast (but also Er-rih on the Red Sea coast of Sudan), propose that the Maldives and coastal East Africa offer the best extant examples of such architecture today. However, while both traditions employed coral stone set in lime mortar, plastered and lime washed, and shared carving styles, Maldivian masons used coral stone carpentry, a technique involving interlocking blocks that is 'not found in any other part of the world' (Jameel and Ahmad 2016, p. 50).

Oft-repeated claims of connections through population movements and intangible heritage remain debateable. Some traditions speak of the—often forced—movement of people. Accounts suggest that enslaved Africans were brought to the Maldives by royals and nobles after their pilgrimage to Mecca (Jaufar 2019, p. 18 and references therein), but this fails to specify the origin of the victims. While it is known that even before the Islamic era enslaved Africans were taken to the Middle East and India, the terms used are so vague that they could indicate an origin anywhere in eastern Africa, including the Red Sea region (see e.g. discussion in Pouwels 2002, p. 395). Swahili traditions holding that a people called 'Debuli' or 'Diba' played a part in the origin of several coastal settlements, in Zanzibar, Pemba, Kilwa, and Lamu, have been interpreted as relating to people from the Maldives, but an identification with the port of Daybul in India, probably the site of Banbhore near Karachi (Whitehouse and Williamson 1973, Collinet 2010, Wood 2015), is much more likely (Horton 2004, n. 29). Maldivian *Bodu beeru* drumming, usually involving three double-headed drums, percussion, a lead singer, and a chorus, is suggested to have originated in East Africa, with Swahili terms featuring in its songs (Jameel and Ahmad 2016, p. 33), but the timeline for this proposed introduction is not clear.

A final word might be said again about Yemen. Connections between the East African coast and Arabia have of course long been known, and the topic has formed a long-standing issue of debate in the archaeology of the Swahili coast (for a recent review of a vast literature, see Fleisher et al. 2015). These connections come into sharp focus in the Yemeni archaeological and historical record. According to thirteenth-century writer ibn al-Mujawir, who spent time in Aden and reported on its people and history, African immigrants were the first to build palm-frond houses there, and such huts filled an entire section of the city in his day (Margariti 2007, p. 102). A later source, Abu Makhrama, insists on the role of enslaved Africans in operating the stone quarries that he suggests were in operation by the twelfth century (Margariti 2007, p. 47, n. 55). Again, however, the specific origin of these individuals is uncertain.

The archaeological evidence offers a clearer illustration of the connection between East Africa and the Yemeni coast, in the form of data from the site of Sharma. Mentioned in tenth- and twelfth- century historical accounts, this port in Hadramawt, as documented archaeologically, seems to have been a short-lived transit entrepôt devoted to maritime trade between around AD 980 and the second half of the twelfth century. Copal, a tree resin, was identified in some quantities, mainly as blocks of raw material; copal trees do not grow in the Arabian peninsula, and the resin appears to have been in transit at Sharma, originating in East Africa or Madagascar and on its way to Asian ports (Regert et al. 2015). East African pottery is present from the earliest occupation; the types recovered match ceramics known from the Swahili coast, and it is suggested their great number may indicate an importation by a Swahili diaspora (Martin and Rougeulle 2015, p. 175). This occurrence of East African ceramics, mainly globular vessels, here but also elsewhere on the Yemen and Oman coastlines, speaks for the intensity of eastern African trade by the eleventh century and may indicate the presence of African inhabitants or travellers (Horton 2004, Fleisher et al. 2015, p. 107). Some of these sites also contain pottery of likely Indian origin, again signifying the relevance of a framework of study that integrates a wide geographical scope through a consideration of trade diasporas.

Eastwards from the Maldives

Historical evidence exists for the Maldives' connections to the east and northeast, namely to India, southeast Asia, and China. There are historical mentions of trade connections and payments of gifts between rulers of the Maldives and China, and the fourteenth-century account of Zheng He's travels includes a chapter on the Maldives and Laccadives (Carswell 1975–1977). However, the best evidence of connections between the Maldives and its Asian neighbours concerns the trade in cowrie shells, particularly the well-documented export to the Bengal market, with possible connections further to Myanmar, Thailand, and perhaps China.

Bengal, in northeast India, is specifically mentioned by ibn Battuta as a trade partner for the Maldives. Already in the thirteenth century, the principal circulating medium appears to have been the cowrie, and the Muslim Bengal sultanate went on to establish a dual monetary system of cowries and silver coins, a practice continuing for the better part of four centuries (Quiggin 1949, Deyell 2010). Fourteenth-century Chinese authors such as Wang Ta-yüan and Fei-shin (the latter of whom served under the command of Zheng He) mention this use of locally minted silver coinage and cowries for small purchases, and in the late fifteenth century the Portuguese found cowries in use as currency in many areas, especially Odisha and Bengal (Egami 1974, pp. 31–32, Hogendorn and Johnson 2003 [1986], p. 14). Majumdar and Chatterjee (2014a, 2014b) have even proposed earlier, epigraphic evidence for cowrie dealers in twelfth-century Odisha.

The dual use of cowries and silver in Bengal raises questions, since neither item occurs locally. The shoreline of Bengal is not propitious to the natural occurrence of cowries; to summarise Longhurst and Pauly (1987, p. 13), it is almost totally covered in Gangetic muds and entirely lacks corals. Moreover, Bengal has no indigenous sources of silver; putative sources are the mining regions of northeastern Myanmar or neighbouring Yunnan, in China. Thus, 'while Bengal's monetary system was structured to meet the needs of a large domestic economy, it clearly depended for its existence on sustained linkages, both overland and maritime, with the broader Asian/Indian Ocean trading networks' (Deyell 2010, p. 64). Similarly, Majumdar and Chatterjee (2014a) propose that eastern India formed part of a much wider regional network of cowrie exchange, spanning the Maldives to China.

The existence of land routes heading eastwards from Bengal into Yunnan and the high-altitude regions of the present-day Thai–Myanmar–Laos borderlands is documented by nineteenth- and twentieth-century accounts, and Forbes (1987; see also Forbes and Henley 2011) has suggested that these may date back to the seventh to tenth centuries, or earlier. Vogel and Hieronymus (1993, p. 240) consider this backwards projection 'partly acceptable' and suggest more stress should be put on Yunnan silver exports and cowrie imports in the period before the sixteenth century. In fact, as well as being rich in deposits of gold, silver, and other precious metals (see e.g. Higham 1996, Figure 3.4) and geographically central, Yunnan also has a long history of using cowries. Hundreds of thousands of these shells have been recovered from graves, mainly at the site of Shizhaishan, on a hill on the broad lacustrine plain surrounding Lake Dian (von Dewall 1967, Higham 1996, Yao 2010, Yang 2019). Cowries continued to be current in Yunnan over an extended period; their use for adornment purposes is documented by ninth-century secretary Fan Chou, who was based in what is now northern Vietnam, and their function as currency is reported in the eleventh century, by Marco Polo in the late thirteenth century, and up into the Ming period (Hogendorn and Johnson 2003 [1986], Vogel and Hieronymus 1993, Yang 2019).

The point here is that the Maldives' involvement with Bengal is well demonstrated for the medieval period, and that this may have connected the archipelago further with routes extending into mainland Asia. Overland trading routes may not have caught historical chroniclers' attention in the way that maritime routes did. Based on the spatial distribution of epigraphic, textual, and archaeological references to cowries, on the supposed deep antiquity of the land route between India and Yunnan, and on Yunnan's landlocked location and lack of long stretches of navigable rivers, Vogel and Hieronymus (1993) and Yang (2004, 2019) have suggested that some or all of the cowries used in Yunnan originated in the Maldives.

Structure of the book

This introductory chapter has offered a survey of the movement of people and things from and to the Maldives, as described in historical and archaeological data and drawing on regions around the Indian Ocean and into mainland Asia and Africa. The aim has been to situate the Maldives within these spheres, and to highlight the cosmopolitan character of the sources relating to the archipelago. Evidence for goods likely to have originated in the Maldives was also scrutinised, as it offers valuable proxy data for the islands' involvement in global networks where they are not explicitly mentioned in historical testimonies.

Chapter 2 reviews historical and archaeological work carried out in the Maldives to date. Historical sources are varied in detail and in quality and come from a wide range of authors—Indian, Sri Lankan, Mediterranean, Chinese, Persian, Arab, and European. Archaeological work has, in contrast, been extremely limited. What little research has been accomplished has focused on the Buddhist period and remains quite descriptive or incompletely published.

The remaining chapters present the backbone of the work. Chapter 3 outlines the survey and excavation strategies deployed at the site of Kinolhas. It presents the results of pedestrian and shovel test pit surveys and explains how these data helped refine the selection of areas for further investigation through larger-scale excavations. These excavations are then detailed in Chapter 4, which provides contextual information on the seven trenches excavated at Kinolhas, describing the deposits, stratigraphy, and chronology. These include four 2 x 2 m units, two 2 x 1 m units and one 6 x 4.5 m unit, the latter encompassing a mortuary complex.

The following four chapters describe the finds recovered—the pottery, fauna, and small finds (largely glass and metal). Chapters 5 (earthenwares) and 6 (glazed pottery), the first ever study of a stratified, large ceramic assemblage from the Maldives, offer an overview of previous work and characterise the materials recovered to provide a typology of medieval ceramics on the archipelago. The Maldives present an unusual case study: since this archipelago lacks clay, all pottery recovered must be considered imported. These two chapters relate the finds to other regional assemblages and identify directions for future research. As part of this account, Chapter 5 draws on works dealing with low-fired earthenwares from the wider western Indian Ocean, particularly Sri Lanka, India, Yemen, and Pakistan, and prominent within the assemblage are 'Indian' or 'Indian-type' wares. Chapter 6 presents the glazed ceramics, which include Chinese and southeast Asian material dated from between the fourteenth and nineteenth centuries, as well as a smaller quantity of material originating in the Middle East. The Kinolhas assemblage is compared to that recovered from over 100 archaeological sites of the western Indian Ocean, to discuss the networks of which the Maldives formed a part and any changes over time, including the reality of the so-called 'Ming Gap'. Chapter 7 considers the marine and terrestrial bones and the marine shells recovered from the excavations at Kinolhas, examining any variation across the site and providing insight into patterns of resource exploitation. Chapter 8 discusses the various classes of portable material culture recovered. Data presented here include the results of visual and elemental analyses on eight glass beads recovered from stratified contexts, most of which encountered as a cache, typological and chemical work on glass bangles and fragments, and visual analyses on the metal, ceramic, and stone objects.

Lastly, two synthetic chapters situate the research at Kinolhas within wider geographical contexts. Chapter 9 surveys the historical, archaeological, and environmental data presented in previous chapters and considers these results in light of data from earlier, small-scale excavations at the Maldivian sites of Utheemu, Veyvah, and Male' (Jaufar 2019). Chapter 10 closes the volume with a summary overview of the work conducted, considering its contribution to a better understanding of the Maldives' role in the medieval Indian Ocean world.

Notes

1 For other publications issuing from the project, see Haour et al. (2016), Haour et al. (2017), Christie and Haour (2018a, 2018b), Christie et al. (2019), Jaufar (2017b, 2017c, 2019).
2 Goitein (1973, p. 199, n. 14) suggests that this cannot be the regular Egyptian *mudd*, which comprised about 2.5 litres (see e.g. Guo 2004 for examples of this measurement), but was probably similar to the Jerusalem *mudd*, containing about 100 litres.

2 An overview of previous historical and archaeological work in the Maldives

Shiura Jaufar and Anne Haour

Introduction

The earliest history of the Máldive Islands is buried in complete obscurity. This has naturally resulted from their geographical isolation and the comparative insignificance they have ever possessed in the eyes of leading outside nations.... Even at this day, in the Twentieth Century, the world still knows little of the history of the Máldive Islands, and the manner of men who inhabit them.

(Bell 2002 [1940], p. 16)

Bell's comment is surprisingly downbeat, especially coming from a leading authority on the history of the Maldives. While it is certainly true that primary sources concerning this history are varied in detail and in quality, they come from an outstanding range of sources: Indian, Sri Lankan, Mediterranean, Chinese, Persian, Middle Eastern, and European. The most important are the accounts of the fourteenth-century Moroccan traveller ibn Battuta (Gibb 1929, Husain 1976, Luthufee 1991) and that of the seventeenth-century French traveller François Pyrard de Laval (Didi 1995, Gray and Bell 1887). Both spent several months, even years, in the Maldives. These and others have been relatively well discussed (see for example Carswell 1975–1977, Forbes 1980, Mohamed 2008, Yang 2019). Others, in particular Maldivian sources, have received rather less attention. They include written chronicles such as those known as *Ta'rikh*, probably begun in the early eighteenth century (Bell 2002 [1940], pp. 201–204, Tajuddin et al. 1981, Forbes 1983, pp. 47–48, Luthufee 1998a, 1998b, 1998c, Tajuddin 2010), and the *Radavalhi* (Bell 2002 [1940], pp. 198–200, National Centre for Linguistic and Historical Research 1979).

As well as historical documents, available data include inscriptions and grave epitaphs (Bell 2002 [1940], pp. 179–186, 1924, pp. 283–303, Forbes 1983, Carswell 1975–1977, pp. 26–30, Kalus and Guillot 2005, Ahmad and Jameel 2012); place-name analysis (Mohamed and Ragupathy 2005); grants and legal documents inscribed on copper plates, known as *loamaafaanu*, typically relating to the endowment of religious institutions (Bell 1931, pp. 539–578, 2002 [1940], pp. 179–186, Maniku and Wijayawardhana 1986, Mohamed 2002, pp. 2–4, Lambourn 2008); grants on paper or vellum bearing a royal seal (Bell 2002 [1940], pp. 187–198); and finally numismatics (Allan 1912, Bell 2002 [1940], pp. 75–86, Heimann 1980, Hogendorn and Johnson 2003 [1986]).

Unfortunately, both the date and origin of the settlement of the Maldives remain unknown. Historical accounts and tradition suggest that they were first inhabited over 2500 years ago by groups coming from the Indian subcontinent (Bell 1883, p. 21, Mohamed 2005, 2008, 2014a, Riyan 2011, Maloney 2013). The strong similarities between the Maldivian and Sinhalese languages (Bell 1883, p. 21, Mohamed 2005, Maloney 2013) and some *loamaafaanu* (copper-plate inscriptions) support this idea. Based on Sri Lankan chronicles and on the Jatakas, which are popular stories of the former lives of Buddha, Maloney (2013, pp. 38–40) suggests that the Maldives were settled centuries before the Christian era and that early cultural contact came not just from Sri Lanka, but also from Gujarat. As well as elements derived from Sinhalese, the Maldivian language includes influences from Urdu, Arabic, English, and Hindi and shares features with languages spoken in north India and southeast Asia, demonstrating multiple cultural interactions (Fritz, cited in Yang 2019, p. 22). Bell (1883, p. 21) suggested that individuals originally from Arabia and Africa came to live in the Maldives through these islands' contact with the Indian coast, particularly with Muslim communities in Malabar. Thus, the history of the peopling of the Maldives appears complex.

It has been suggested that Maldivians practiced both Hinduism and Buddhism prior to Islam. The evidence for the former is largely linguistic (Maloney 1980, pp. 48–51). The evidence for Buddhist practice is varied, being both linguistic (Bell 1883, p. 75, Mohamed and Ragupathy 2005, Maloney 2013) and archaeological (Bell 2002 [1940], Forbes 1983, Skjølsvold 1991, Mikkelsen 2000, National Centre for Linguistic and Historical Research 2002, 2004, Jaufar 2017a, Feener 2018). The archaeological evidence includes the standing remains which will be discussed later in this chapter—for example, the extraordinary sites of Kaashidhoo and Nilandhoo—as well as occasional chance finds. These include a gold leaf from Veymandoo in Thaa atoll, and a coral stone casket from Nilandhoo in Faafu atoll, both of which reference royalty according to Mohamed and Ragupathy (2005). In recent years, the inventories carried out by the Maldives Heritage Survey have led to the recording of remarkable chance finds made over the years by communities during construction projects and curated locally that are suggestive of Buddhist affinities.[1]

DOI: 10.4324/9781003166221-2

A shift from Buddhism to Islam appears to have occurred in the twelfth century. The date and cause for this conversion are the subject of conflicting traditions. A fourteenth-century wooden inscription from the Friday mosque in Male', recovered in the roof cavity during renovations in 1964, places the conversion at AD 1153, a date now widely accepted in international scholarship and Maldivian national consciousness. According to this inscription, reported by ibn Battuta and many later writers (Bell 1883, 2002 [1940], Husain 1976, National Centre for Linguistic and Historical Research 1979, 2004, Forbes 1981, 1983, Luthufee 1991, Kalus and Guillot 2005, pp. 27–35), the conversion was the result of a visit by one Abu al-Barakat al-Barbari, who overcame a demonic spirit. However, an alternative version presented by the Maldivian Ta'rikh suggests that conversion to Islam was mediated by a Persian traveller named Yusuf Shams al-Din of Tabriz (Bell 2002 [1940], Carswell 1975–1977, Forbes 1981, 1983, Tajuddin et al. 1981, Luthufee 1991, 1998a, 1998b, 1998c, Kalus and Guillot 2005, Tajuddin 2010). To this can be added the evidence from the *loamaafaanu*, suggesting that the Islamisation of the Maldives was abrupt. They suggest that the rulers of the Maldives ordered people to convert, abolishing the institutions of Buddhist monastic orders, demolishing monasteries and destroying religious images, and confiscating monastic lands and reallocating their revenue to the support of new mosques. The date suggested for these events appears to be the late twelfth century, a little later than the traditionally accepted date of AD 1153 (Feener 2021).

Whatever the case may be, these narratives are probably at least partly symbolic. The process of conversion to Islam is unlikely to have involved a neatly unfolding movement and will have involved multiple levels: political, economic, and individual. Moreover, Islam, which was introduced to the Malabar coast of India during the seventh century AD, must have made an initial impact on the Maldives earlier than the twelfth-century date reported (Forbes 1981, 1983).

The rest of this chapter will consider first written, then archaeological, sources relating to the Maldives.

The written sources

The first plausible mention of the Maldives is found in Indian and Sri Lankan Buddhist sources: the Buddhist Jatakas (500–250 BC) and Sinhalese historical records, the source of many accounts of the ancient history of Sri Lanka and India (Maloney 1980, 2013, pp. 38–47, Skjølsvold 1991, p. 11). In particular, the Dipavamsa, believed to have been compiled in the third/fourth centuries AD, describes the exile of the aboriginal inhabitants of Sri Lanka, dispelled as inferior beings, a legend also reported in the Mahavamsa, a slightly later and more comprehensive epic poem which likely drew on the Dipavamsa. Maloney (2013, pp. 41–47) has suggested this place of exile was the Maldives:

> the island where the 'non-humans' went seems, on several counts, to represent the Maldives. Certainly the Maldives are a 'low land' and they are 'in the great and deep ocean, in the midst of the water at sea', and certainly 'waves always break' there, for no place in the Maldives is beyond the sound of the sea. The Maldives is 'like the plain of Lanka' in many respects—in the vegetation, which is 'pleasing, green and cool', with groves, forests, trees with fruit and flowers, grass, food and corn, and even lakes. Also, there was 'no master'. The Island of Giri had rivers according to the legend, and while the Maldives have no rivers, the compassionate Buddha could probably not be imagined to send even 'non-humans' to a land without rivers, for the 'excellent Giridipa' was said to be even 'superior to this land of Lanka'.
>
> (Maloney 2013, p. 43)

There are several other possible mentions of the Maldives in the first millennium AD. These include reports by the Greco-Roman polymath Ptolemy in the second century and by the Greek merchant and hermit Cosmas Indicopleustes who, in the mid-sixth century, described a number of islands lying close to one another, possessing fresh water and coconut palms (Carswell 1975–1977, p. 133, Heimann 1980, n. 9–11, Forbes 1981, p. 65, n. 49, Skjølsvold 1991, p. 11, Mohamed 2008, p. 69, 2014b, p. 11, Kovács 2008, p. 113). The *Periplus of the Erythrean Sea* (c. AD 120) mentions tortoise shells from islands which may be the Maldives (Forbes 1980, p. 75, 1984, Mohamed 2014b, p. 11). Roman historian Ammianus Marcellinus records ambassadors from Sri Lanka, and possibly the Maldives, visiting the Roman emperor Julian in AD 362 (Gray in Gray and Bell 1887, pp. 426–427, Forbes 1984, p. 57, Skjølsvold 1991, p. 11, Mohamed 2008, p. 70, 2014b, p. 11). Chinese sources form another relevant corpus. The Buddhist monk and translator Fa Hsien, who travelled by foot from China to India and spent several years there at the beginning of the fifth century, supposedly mentions islands near Sri Lanka. Records of the Tang dynasty of China (seventh to tenth centuries) suggest diplomatic connections with the Maldives and allude to the production of salt in the Maldives and its trade to India (Forbes 1980, Mohamed 2008, p. 70, 2014a, p. 80, 2014b, p. 20). However, some of these references seem tenuous, and many occur as later editorial comment.

One major problem surrounds the precise identification of the various islands referred to by early accounts. In the mid-ninth century, one 'Suleiman the Merchant' discusses the fishing of cowries using coconut fronds, and the existence of a queen who kept vast stores of cowries in her treasury. Unfortunately, he makes no distinction between the Maldives and the Laccadives, which lie to the north, off the coast of Kerala (Forbes 1981, pp. 65, 69; Hogendorn and Johnson 2003 [1986], p. 23). Arab historian and geographer al-Mas'udi, who visited India—especially its western coast—and perhaps Sri Lanka, in the early tenth century, closely follows Suleiman's account, to the extent that Yang (2019, p. 26) suggests that he may have copied it. Al-Mas'udi reports that cowries were sun-dried on beaches, during which time their flesh rotted, leaving behind empty shells (Hogendorn and Johnson 2003 [1986], p. 82). Al-Biruni, a century later, is the first to make a clear distinction between the Maldives and the Laccadives, identifying the former as a specialised producer of cowries and the latter as producers of coir (Carswell 1975–1977, Heimann 1980, Forbes 1981, Hogendorn and Johnson 2003 [1986], Majumdar and Chatterjee 2014a, Yang 2019). Persian traveller Abul Hassan (ca. AD 1030) also describes the islands, speaking of them as being divided into two classes according to their principal production (cowrie shells or coconut coir) and writing that 'the ships from these islands transport dried fish, tortoise shells, and white cowries to Africa and a large oyster-shell is sent to Italy where they make cameos of it' (Maloney 2013, p. 419, Mohamed 2014b, p. 11). A twelfth-century letter in the Cairo *geniza* mentions a ship departing Karnataka for Aden and calling at *al-Dyyb* to take on coir and coconuts, but rather than the Maldives as suggested by Goitein and Friedman, Lambourn (2018b) suggests that the Laccadives are meant. At a similar time, al-Idrisi—who did not travel outside the Mediterranean and therefore relies on informants—closely follows earlier authors, covering nearly all particulars detailed by his predecessors (Bell 2002 [1940], p. 17, Forbes 1981, p. 69, Hogendorn and Johnson 2003 [1986], pp. 24–25). He talks of the royal control of cowrie stocks and their collection using pieces of coconut wood as bait, but fails to make the distinction between the Laccadives and the Maldives. He lists tortoise shells as a major product, as well as other items such as coconut, coir rope, ambergris, and sperm whale oil (Carswell 1975–1977, p. 136, Mohamed 2014b, p. 11). In one problematic passage he describes the port of Jurfattan, in Kerala, as being the nearest mainland to 'Sarandib'. This term is typically understood as referring to Sri Lanka, but the description would then make little sense, and Lambourn (2018b, p. 74) suggests that he may in fact be using the term to refer to all of South Asia's offshore islands, including the Maldives and the Laccadives.

This, then, is the situation up to the twelfth century. In the mid-fourteenth century comes the most detailed extant medieval source: the account by Moroccan traveller ibn Battuta, who visited the Maldives (*al-Dib*; *Dhibat al-Mahal*) twice between AD 1343 and 1346. He stayed for about 18 months during his first visit, acting as a judge and taking four Maldivian wives and several concubines (Gibb 1929, Husain 1976, Luthufee 1991). His is the first detailed account of the islands, their culture, politics, and economy, and it gives details of internal and external trade activities and commodities. In an oft-cited account, he reports:

> The money of the islanders consists of wada'. This is the name of a mollusc, collected in the sea and placed in pits dug out on the beach. Its flesh decays and only the white shell remains. A hundred of them is called *siya*, and 700 *fál*; 12,000 are called *kotta*, and 100,000 *bostú*. Bargains are struck through the medium of these shells, at the rate of four *bostú* [400,000 cowries] to a dínár of gold. Often they are of less value, such as twelve *bostú* [1,200,000] to a dínár. The islanders sell them for rice to the people of Bengal, where also they are used for money They are sold in the same way to the people of Yemen, who use them for ballast in their ships in place of sand. These shells serve also as a medium of exchange with the negroes in their native country I have seen them sold, at Máli and at Jújú, at the rate of 1,150 to a dínár.

> (Vogel and Hieronymus 1993, pp. 223–224)

Crucially to the topic of this book, he makes a direct mention of the island of Kinolhas: 'When I arrived at these islands I disembarked on one of them called Kannalus, a fine island containing many mosques, and I put up at the house of one of the pious persons there' (Gibb 1929, p. 245).

Ibn Battuta's mention of the technique of burying cowries in pits differs from earlier accounts, and this method was said to be superior as it retained the shine of the shells (Hogendorn and Johnson 2003 [1986], p. 82). The account also shows that he exchanged some jewels for cowries in order to hire a boat to Bengal, though he was then ultimately prevented from departing (Yang 2019, p. 27). Mentions of India, Yemen, and China pepper his description of the Maldives, again highlighting the archipelago's wide connections.

Chinese accounts are also important at this time. Wang Ta-yüan visited the Maldives for several months over AD 1330–1331 and was informed that its cowries were exported to Pegu (in modern-day Myanmar) and to Bengal (Yang 2019). Eight or nine decades later, the fleet of mariner Zheng He visited the Maldives on three occasions (see Chapter 6, this volume). Ma Huan, an interpreter and scribe on Zheng He's fourth and sixth expeditions, provided details of the geography, environment, and culture of the archipelago (Egami 1974, Carswell 1975–1977, p. 137, Forbes 1980, p. 75, Hogendorn and Johnson 2003 [1986], p. 25, Maloney 2013, p. 44, Mohamed 2014a, pp. 80–87). He stated that people collected cowries (*hai-pa*) and piled them into mountain-like heaps, discussed the trade of cowrie shells as currency to Thailand and Bengal, and mentioned dried fish and coconut ropes and the fact that Chinese ships would occasionally visit to purchase ambergris (Carswell 1975–1977, p. 137; Hogendorn and Johnson 2003 [1986], p. 25). Yang (2019, p. 30) quite reasonably suggests that the Chinese ships likely also took on cowries.

The Maldives were most likely visited by sailors from the Arab world. Tibbetts (1971, pp. 460–462), in his translation of the writings of fifteenth-century navigator ibn Majid, provides an overview of the places described, offering possible identifications with specific islands in the Maldives. As far as can be determined, the locations relate to islands and atolls to the eastern side of the double chain of atolls that make up the Maldives, which incidentally may offer a confirmation of the hypothesis advanced by Carswell (1975–1977, pp. 139–140, and in Hourani 1995 [1951], p. 145) that the Maldives were a stopover for westbound rather than eastbound travel.

The fullest account of the Maldives comes from the early seventeenth century and was written by François Pyrard de Laval, a French castaway detained in Male' between AD 1602 and 1607 (Gray and Bell 1887, Carswell 1975–1977, Didi 1995). He learned Dhivehi and set down a remarkably detailed 'ethnographic' account of life at the time. In common with ibn Battuta and other visitors, he described the production, use, and trade of cowrie shells to Bengal, as well as the exploitation and trade of tortoise shells to India. Meals were taken on faïence 'fashioned in the native style, and imported from Cambaye; or else it is of China porcelain, which is very common, and used by almost all' (Carswell 1975–1977, p. 140).

The archaeological data

The earliest, and still one of the most important, contributions to Maldivian archaeology is the work of H. C. P. Bell who, as a British civil servant in Sri Lanka, first visited the Maldives in 1879. His initial purpose was to investigate the wreck of a British ship, but his interest in the Maldives continued until his death in 1937. During his first visit, Bell suggested that an archaeological survey would help to document the Maldives' Buddhist past; subsequent visits, in 1920 and 1922, allowed him to carry out extensive research and surveys on local art, religion, linguistics, archaeology, and geography (Bell 1883, 1925, 2002 [1940]). During the 1920 trip, reports were gathered about known past sites, and in the 1922 archaeological expedition 12 islands were visited. The work involved recording and small-scale excavations, with a study of Buddhist remains in Hithadhoo (Seenu atoll, the southernmost of the Maldives), locations in Laamu atoll (including a large mound on Gan island, Figure 2.1) and at Fuvahmulah, a lone island situated in the Equatorial Channel. A range of portable artefacts relating to the Maldives' Buddhist past were also recorded. The structures were all, at this point, in a state of decay, some too damaged to enable any typological study, but Bell proposed that mouldings and architectural style suggested links with Sri Lanka and a tentative date of the late first millennium AD (Forbes 1983).

Poorly contextualised chance finds shed light on the connections between the Maldives and other parts of the world; such as the case of the gold leaf and casket discussed previously. Another curious find is that of a Roman Republican *denarius* minted in Rome in either 90 or 89 BC (Forbes 1984), recovered within a Buddhist *stupa* on Thoddoo (Alif Alif atoll). The coin was pierced and had evidently been used as an ornament; its state of wear is consistent with a long period of circulation (Forbes 1984, Mohamed 2008, p. 76).

Material indications of the connections between the Maldives and other parts of the world are also evident through ceramics. Intrigued by finds of Chinese pottery in Syria dating to the Yuan and Ming periods (late thirteenth to mid-seventeenth centuries), John Carswell sought to identify the routes whereby this material had travelled, and directed his attention to the Maldives. During a month-long visit in 1974, he and his colleagues collected potsherds from the (at

Figure 2.1 The Havitta on Gan island, Laamu atoll.

that time unpaved) streets of Male', where 'the sand was studded with sherds of porcelain' and 'each monsoon shower revealed a fresh crop' (Carswell 1975–1977, p. 144). Pottery was also collected by excavating two trenches on either side of the reported line of the walls of the former Sultan's palace, based on a 1921 map by H. C. P. Bell. Trench B was abandoned as it hit tree roots. But Trench A, a 2 x 1 m unit terminating at 1 m below surface, uncovered a wall two courses high and a small ceramic assemblage in the lower third of the excavation (Carswell 1975–1977, Figure 11, Plate 59b). Lastly, permission was also obtained to sift the topsoil being removed from cemeteries as part of a move to increase available building land, and a distinct assemblage from the Hadibi mosque was thereby obtained (Carswell 1975–1977, Figure 10). The assemblage issued from this work consisted of some 800 potsherds and vessels[2] with origins in China, the Middle East, and possibly Sri Lanka.

The earliest material recovered appeared to date to the late Song period (conventionally dated AD 960–1279): finds include 'fragments of small bowls and dishes . . . the majority of hard grey ware with grey or greenish glazes, some with combed and/or incised decoration . . . and one with carved petal panels' (Carswell 1975–1977, p. 152). Fragments of probable Ming date (conventionally dated AD 1368–1644), a rare example of Islamic pottery (buff with turquoise glaze), eight Persian dishes, and one Chinese 'Swatow' dish were also recovered. Three sherds matched a bowl excavated in 1929 at the site of Dhlo Dhlo (Danangombe, in present-day Zimbabwe) (Carswell 1975–1977, p. 154, Plates 62c, 64b, 67a). Overall, the material of Chinese origin recovered through the various investigations fell largely in the twelfth to eighteenth centuries. Moreover, certain excavated sherds resembled material known to Carswell from Vankalai in northwest Sri Lanka, suggesting a possible connection between the two places (Carswell 1975–1977, pp. 158–160).

Test excavations were carried out in 1983 and 1984 as a joint project between the Kon-Tiki Museum (Oslo) and the Maldivian government (Heyerdahl 1986, Skjølsvold 1991, overview in Litster 2016, pp. 85–88). The purpose was to understand the character of the pre-Islamic archaeology of the Maldives, and the work focused on the mounds termed 'Havittas', a name used locally to refer to what appear to be ancient Buddhist stupas.[3] Investigations were limited to trenching and test excavations on a mound and its vicinity on the island of Nilandhoo (Faafu atoll) for a total of ten days, Bodu Havitta on Gan (in Gaafu Dhaalu atoll) for a total of nine days, and Dhadimagi Havitta on Fuvahmulah island, previously examined by H. C. P. Bell (Skjølsvold 1991, pp. 11–16, Litster 2016). These three sites will be further discussed in Chapter 5, since one part of the pottery they yielded was discussed in a later doctoral thesis by Mirani Litster (2016). Some of the other structures previously exposed by Bell were re-examined.

Archaeological work at Nilandhoo Foamathi, on the east side of the island of Nilandhoo, generated the most substantial results (Skjølsvold 1991, pp. 16–43). Work concentrated on the Havitta, a mound 2.5 m high and 13.5 m in diameter. This Havitta, termed 'Structure I', proved to be part of a former temple area that included a present-day mosque and other structures. Once sectioned, it revealed the remains of a stone base made of cut and fitted stone blocks; a construction about 10 x 10 m in size, with the remains of a staircase and a pathway leading to it on the west side, was identified (Skjølsvold 1991, Figure 16). Artefacts recovered included stupa-like stone figures, worked stone blocks (some, such as Cat. Figure 34, of Buddhist style), a dozen undiagnostic potsherds, a bone fragment, and fragmentary shell, among which two cowries (Skjølsvold 1991, pp. 30–31, 74–79, 91–92, 98–116, 160–165). The remains were interpreted as the foundation walls of a structure subsequently torn down, while the cross-section of the Havitta suggested its interior consisted of fill material; the artefacts may be intrusive, although the fact they were concentrated may indicate intentional deposition (Skjølsvold 1991, p. 32). Investigation of a mound 10–15 m west of the Havitta, dubbed Structure II, amounted to little more than the 'mere uncovering of finds already located by the natives' (Skjølsvold 1991, p. 33). These consisted largely of miniature stupas and other stone pieces, as well as two potsherds, apparently in a secondary context.

The trench was left open following the 1983 season and was tampered with by a group of filmmakers, who exposed part of a stone structure which the Heyerdahl team reinvestigated during the following season. This was roughly 8 x 8 m in size, with protruding quadrangular chambers. A row of stones, possibly robbed from the Havitta, was uncovered east of it, and a double wall, Structure IV, to its north. These segments appeared to connect and were thought to represent a temple boundary. The particular interest of the excavation of Structure IV, by means of a 9.4 x 1 m trench, is that it uncovered a refuse area and yielded a stratified pottery assemblage: the first—and, until the work reported in the present book, the only—such occurrence in the Maldives. This material, which was subsequently studied by Mikkelsen (1991) and Litster (2016), will be further discussed in Chapter 5. Glass fragments, cowries, a bead and a copper piece were among the other artefacts recovered. Although most of the remains relate to a Buddhist temple, the upper layers of the trench seem to belong to the time after the introduction of Islam in the twelfth century (Mikkelsen 1991, pp. 200–201). Indeed, tradition holds that Nilandhoo was the second island of the Maldives—after Male'—to be provided with a mosque (Skjølsvold 1991, p. 16).

Further dates as well as a detailed description of the excavations of the various structures (there termed 'features') at Nilandhoo were subsequently provided by Litster (2016, pp. 105–124). They include several new radiocarbon dates on charcoal, including the earliest known date from a Maldivian site, 1717 ± 30 bp [Wk 30394] from the refuse deposit in Structure IV. Significantly, the two dates from the site originally run on shell were recalibrated. In particular, the date of 1230 ± 70 bp [T 5575] on one of the shells retrieved at the base of the Havitta fill, calibrated at the time to AD 650–850 (Skjølsvold 1991, p. 32), was corrected to AD 1170–1423 (Litster 2016, p. 136, Table 5.9).[4] This suggests that the Havitta was covered sometime between the twelfth and fifteenth centuries; as this is slightly later than the traditional date for the national conversion to Islam, this is taken to indicate the transition from Buddhism may not have been synchronous across all parts of the Maldives (Litster 2016, p. 250). However, the work also suggested post-depositional movement of charcoal and taphonomic issues, attributed to intentional reburial of the site and the disturbance associated with vegetation growth (Litster 2016, p. 121).

The Heyerdahl team also undertook work over a total of nine days in 1983 and 1984 on Gan island, in Gaafu Dhaalu atoll in the southern Maldives. This focused on a large, 9 m high, mound, Bodu Havitta, 'the big mound', and dealt mainly with architectural concerns, but the objects recovered included a stone figure of a lion, miniature stupas, and shaped stone blocks. Trenches opened close to the Havitta yielded potsherds, a coral bead and human remains in poor condition, and survey around the Havitta identified the remains of several other structures (Skjølsvold 1991, pp. 43–66, 80–86, 93–97, 117–145, 165–182). At Fuvahmulah, work was brief and was limited to the clearing of structures (Skjølsvold 1991, pp. 14–16, 90). These two sites were not dated.

Overall, the sites are attributed to the Buddhist occupation period, and the excavations evidenced multiple building phases in addition to later use during the Islamic period (Litster 2016, pp. 135–136). The work provides little data on the medieval material culture of the Maldives. The catalogue of finds from these investigations (Skjølsvold 1991, pp. 74–182) concentrates on architectural fragments; the images provided of beads and potsherds recovered are uninformative (Skjølsvold 1991, Figures 6, 7, 150) or missing (Skjølsvold 1991, Figure 152). The separate report on the ceramics from Feature IV (Mikkelsen 1991, revisited by Litster 2016) is, however, helpful and will be discussed in detail in Chapter 5.

In 1987, a team from the Archaeological Survey of India visited Landhoo (Noonu atoll) to document a mound. The work confirmed that this represented a Buddhist religious centre; the stupa evidenced at the site was the largest structure in the area, the remainder having been destroyed (Archaeological Survey of India 1910–1911, National Centre for Linguistic and Historical Research 2004, Jaufar 2017a). The team also recovered an engraved coral stone block with inscriptions in the style of the South Indian Pallava dynasty, thought to date to the sixth century and thus the oldest known written inscription from the Maldives (National Centre for Linguistic and Historical Research 2004, Mohamed and Ragupathy 2005, Jaufar 2017a).

The first thorough and systematic excavations to be conducted in the Maldives came in the 1990s, carried out by Egil Mikkelsen and his team from the Museum of Medieval Stockholm and the University of Oslo, in collaboration with the National Centre for Linguistic and Historical Research in Male'. The impetus of this research was an interest in the trade in cowrie shells into northern Europe in the first millennium AD, and the role of Buddhism in this trade. The site chosen for investigation was Kaashidhoo, in Kaafu atoll. The area examined, termed Kuruhinna Tharaagadu, was known as a Buddhist site, monastery, and house of worship. The research, which involved three excavation seasons from 1996 to 1998, has been only summarily published so far (Mikkelsen 2000) but is further described by Litster (2016) in the context of a doctoral thesis revisiting the findings.

The site was situated outside of Kaashidhoo village in a coconut, papaya, and banana tree plantation and evidenced slight elevations, approximately 1.5 m high, and coral stones visible on the surface. Over the three excavation seasons, an area of 1880 m^2 and 64 structures were investigated, revealing part of a building identified as a monastery. A partial site plan is provided by Litster (2016, Figure 5.4). The structures were mainly built of coarse coral stone, with lime plastering and mouldings on the outer faces; the inside was generally filled with sand or stones. Their size and shape varied: they ranged from 1 m to 11.5 m in size, and were square, rectangular, circular (some with semi-circular extensions), and in one case 16-sided. Some bell-shaped structures were interpreted as miniature stupas. Most of these features constitute platforms of various kinds which probably served to support light buildings of wood, used for reliquaries or statues; only the lowermost sections (30–40 cm high) had typically survived, the rest having been mined for building material over the years. Notable finds included a pit of 62000 cowrie shells, dated to AD 700–990 after calibration (1690 ± 65bp [T 12495], date on shell), as well as further cowrie and clam shell deposits, four human graves, a bronze bowl, the bones of a giant tortoise, small terrestrial and sea turtles, a Chinese bronze coin, bronze rings, iron fragments, potsherds, and beads of several colours (Mikkelsen 2000).

The charcoal, bone, and shell radiocarbon dates from the site and the proposed sequence of building were recently summarised by Litster (2016, pp. 94–104). The earliest date obtained on a structure came from a posthole (1505 ± 60 bp [TUa 1884], calibrated to AD 345–604, date on charcoal) and occupation continued through to the eleventh/early thirteenth centuries (1430 ± 45 bp [T 13666], calibrated to AD 1024–1223, date on shell, presented with caution) (Litster 2016, p. 98). Four phases of construction are proposed, following, with some chronological modifications, the original model presented by Mikkelsen (2000, Litster 2016, Table 5.5). An initial building phase in the middle third of the first millennium AD was followed by an occupation during which large deposits of cowries were made. A second building period is suggested in the closing two centuries of the millennium, with a possible ritual use of turtles, then a northwards extension of the structure, and a number of human burials, in the fourth and final phase (Litster 2016, p. 104).

Recent work at Kaashidhoo by the Maldives Heritage Survey team (see later in this chapter) has involved clearing of the accumulated overgrowth on the site and the creation of a comprehensive new set of visual records using drone flyovers, photogrammetry, and 3D laser scanning (Feener 2019).

One of the present authors (SJ) carried out test pitting at different locations around the Maldives. These included investigations of a bathing tank on Utheemu and a stone structure on Ihavandhoo, both islands situated in Haa Alifu atoll (Jaufar 2012, 2015b, 2016). The excavation at Utheemu revealed that the stepped sandstone bathing tank was built on top of cut timber blocks, which were well preserved under water. The excavation at Ihavandhoo, for its part, brought to light carved coral stone blocks resembling those used in the construction of ancient mosques, suggesting the site may have been a stone cutting workshop (Jaufar 2016). Another strand of investigation occurred as part of the process of preparing the nomination to the UNESCO World Heritage List of six historically and architecturally significant coral stone mosques (Ahmad and Jameel 2012, UNESCO 2013). Test excavations at four of the sites revealed the mosques were built on a combination of sand and coral stone foundations, and features such as postholes were recognised in one case (Jaufar 2013, 2014, 2015a).

In recent years, two separate research projects have demonstrated further the growing international interest in the archaeology and built heritage of the Maldives. In 2017, survey and test excavations were carried out at two mosque complexes to investigate the relationship between pre-Islamic and Islamic phases, and to contribute new data to the ongoing UNESCO World Heritage List nomination (Pradines n.d., 2018). The two sites investigated were the Fandiyaaru compound on the island of Meedhoo, in the far southern atoll of Seenu (Addu), and the Old Friday mosque at Fenfushi island in Alifu Dhaalu atoll. While the Fandiyaaru compound is the largest in the Maldives, consisting of four mosques, 15 mausolea, and 500 tombstones, Fenfushi Old Friday mosque, said to date to the early eighteenth century, is reputed as one of the finest examples of a Maldivian coral stone mosque (Ahmad and Jameel 2012). The test excavations challenged accepted datings and identifications and concluded, albeit on limited evidence, that neither mosque was built precisely on the site of Buddhist temples.

Extensive survey and mapping work has been underway since 2018 by the team of the Maldives Heritage Survey, aiming to systematically inventory and document the endangered tangible cultural heritage of the Maldives, including 'mosques, Muslim grave markers, the remains of Buddhist ritual sites, and other historical structures and physical objects . . . through digital photography, 3D terrestrial scanning, and GIS to create an open-access online heritage database' (Feener and Daly 2018). Work has involved several field seasons and extensive mapping at four atolls: Laamu, Fuvamulah, Seenu, and Haa Alifu and preliminary work has begun in Haa Dhaalu and Kaafu (Male') atolls. Up until 2020, when field operations were suspended due to the COVID-19 pandemic, the project had completed a comprehensive survey of 152 islands across six atolls (Feener et al. 2021a). Taking the example of Laamu atoll, occurrences include coral stone mosques, cemeteries, small pre-Islamic statues, and three large Buddhist ritual complexes (Feener 2018, Jaufar 2018). The surrounds of the Havitta examined a century ago by H. C. P. Bell on Gan island, in that atoll (see Figure 2.1), were comprehensively mapped and the mound placed within its wider landscape, which included dozens of additional structures and earthworks, suggesting a major Buddhist ritual complex (Feener et al. 2021, Figure 3). In early 2018, at Fuvahmulah the team unearthed what appeared to be a large statue base, underneath which was a coral stone casket containing cowrie shells interpreted as a devotional deposit (Yang 2019, p. 31). Research is ongoing and data are continually uploaded (Feener 2018), including datasets for LiDAR scans of sites and structures (Open Heritage 3D).

Conclusion

Although the origins of the settlement of the Maldives are unclear, it appears that the islands have been occupied for over 2500 years, possibly originally as the result of migration from India and Sri Lanka. Major religious changes include a shift from (possibly) Hinduism and (certainly) Buddhism to Islam. Due to their location, the Maldives played a part in a number of different networks and outside visitors have penned accounts of the Maldives for at least the past 1000 years, and perhaps far longer. While the nature and intensity of political and social connections will have varied over time, continuities are marked, among these the recurrent mention of Maldivian exports such as the products of the coconut palm (notably coir), fish, and diverse other marine products like cowrie shells, ambergris, and tortoise shells. Early sources remain quite nebulous, but much more detailed information is available in the later writings of ibn Battuta and François Pyrard, which begin to provide more 'ethnographic' and unambiguous accounts of the culture, politics, economy, and trade relations of the Maldives.

Until the research presented in this book, relatively little archaeological work had been undertaken in the Maldives, and it was limited to preliminary surveys, archaeological test pitting and amateur excavations and a single scientific excavation, at the Buddhist site of Kaashidhoo. It is against this background that the took place investigations at the island of Kinolhas, the focus of the present book.

Notes

1 These include items such as a seated Buddha and a female torso from Kalhaidhoo, in Laamu atoll (https://sketchfab.com/3d-models/lam-ikd-1-so1-9459f8461f8347e6b30c3ee4cced5629, https://sketchfab.com/3d-models/lam-ikd-1-so2-059fa9af7ec34 0edb34ae31b6f05f7c6), or two zoomorphic lamps from Fuvahmulah (https://sketchfab.com/3d-models/gni-had-6-so12-663f27 667d2f403786a2fde6d11b196f, https://sketchfab.com/3d-models/gni-had-6-so1-f92aa03680be4b4386a039b38d452847).
2 The assemblage was subsequently donated as a study collection to the Ashmolean Museum in Oxford (Chapter 5).
3 Forbes (1983, p. 44) observes that the Dhivehi term 'havitta' resembles the Sinhalese 'chaitya' (referring to a shrine, sanctuary, temple, or prayer hall), perhaps confirming the idea of a Buddhist association for the remains.
4 The other date on shell, T 5576 from Structure II, was also corrected to be four to five centuries younger than initially reported (Mikkelsen 1991, p. 200 vs. Litster 2016, Table 5.9).

3   Approaching the heritage and archaeology of Kinolhas

Annalisa Christie

Introduction

This chapter presents the survey strategies adopted to characterise the archaeological landscapes of the island of Kinolhas. We describe the sites recorded during pedestrian surveys, highlighting significant features worthy of investigating, including a possible harbour attributed by the local community as being 'ibn Battua's harbour'; Buddhist features including a bathing tank; and as yet un-investigated stone structures. Further, we outline the analysis of the ceramics and fauna recovered during systematic shovel test pit (STP) excavations as these data helped to refine the selection of areas for further larger scale excavation. Outcomes of the larger-scale excavations will be detailed in Chapter 4.

Comprising an area of 54.3 hectares, in 2014 Kinolhas was reported to have a population of 473 people (Maps 2016), which in 2017 we were told was closer to 600 people. According to Ragupathy and Mohamed (2008, p. 59), the etymology of the name is 'the island of Lhos trees at the corner', where the 'corner' refers to the island's position at the southeast corner of Raa atoll. Vegetation remains dense at the extremities of the island, with the modern settlement limited to its central part.

Preliminary surveys—2016

During the 2016 field season, we briefly visited Kinolhas as part of a wider survey of Raa atoll. That survey aimed to revisit and assess the condition of Islamic period sites listed in an existing UNESCO-funded inventory for the Maldivian Department of Heritage (Riyan 2011) and partly discussed by Kalus and Guillot (2005, pp. 47–51), and to identify other areas of archaeological interest.

Existing data suggested the existence of notable heritage sites on the island. Kalus and Guillot (2005) had published several inscriptions visible in Male', including a funerary headstone which had been removed from Kinolhas to the National Museum in 1987. This headstone bore the date of AD 1480 and named the deceased as one Abu Bakran; his precise identity remains unknown, but the fact he was known as Shaykh Djunayri suggests he originated from Djunayr/Junnar, today in western India, at the time part of the influential Bahmani sultanate (Kalus and Guillot 2005, p. 51). The white marble and the overall style of the Kinolhas gravestone connect it to Cambay, India; it is part of a group of such inscriptions—including a mihrab in a mosque in Male', dated to AD 1322—serving as a witness of commercial and cultural links from Gujarat to maritime southeast Asia via the Maldives (Kalus and Guillot 2005, pp. 26, 51, Figure 2, 7).

While the headstone had been removed from Kinolhas to Male', the uninscribed footstone was left in situ. Kalus and Guillot did not themselves visit Kinolhas during their research trip to the Maldives but instead relied on information from the National Council for Linguistic and Historical Research in Male'. They describe the Kinolhas gravestone as coming within a cemetery, used for several centuries, and close to a ruined shrine. The name of the deceased had been added at the time the stone was carved, but it was not clear whether the nearby shrine was dedicated to him or whether he was a visiting pilgrim (Kalus and Guillot 2005). The shrine, however, is said by the UNESCO Cultural Resources inventory (Riyan 2011) to be devoted to one Uthman Thakurufaanu.

We revisited the site, assigning it the number KIN16–01; it lies close to the southwestern extent of the modern settlement, which is rapidly encroaching on it (Figures 3.1 and 3.2). We saw the gravestone, which currently lies prone, and sought further information from the local community. We were told that a now disappeared shrine and mosque had been constructed from cut *hirigaa* (coral stone). The mosque, referred to as Furqaan mosque, was renovated in the 1970s to include a lime plaster roof but was subsequently taken down in the 1980s to construct a road. The mosque was set within a boundary wall, which would have encompassed two other rectilinear features, interpreted as wells. The fallen remains of the eastern and western sides of the boundary wall are still visible, though the northern section of the western wall was truncated in 2017 after the removal of a large tree nearby. Although the physical remains of the shrine are no longer visible, there is a clear depression approximately 6 ft from the remaining marble tombstone.

Several tombstones were observed to the east of the site close to another large tree; while a mound of corals stones was noted to the west of the boundary wall, thought to have been created in the clearance of the road. Other surface remains in the area included pot sherds and cowrie shells as well as fragments of a larger vessel.

KIN16–02 is situated close to the modern harbour on the north side of Kinolhas (Figure 3.1). Here we observed the remains of a low coral stone and mortar wall enclosure that stands approximately 40 cm high. The wall encompassed an

DOI: 10.4324/9781003166221-3

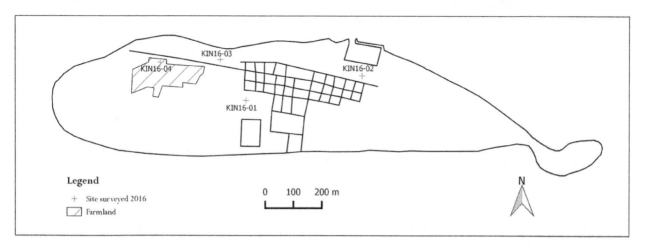

Figure 3.1 Map of Kinolhas.

Figure 3.2 KIN 16–01. Gravestone can be seen lying prone front right. Kinolhas, taken February 2016.

area of dense vegetation and modern refuse as well as the fallen remains of a dozen gravestones. To the east and south side of the enclosure were various piles of stones and evidence of recent digging, including two wells. A line of stone continues across a modern road, possibly representing the footprint of a former mosque. Community members reported that the mosque was taken down because it stood in the way of a planned road.

Situated to the west of the harbour on the north coast (Figure 3.1), KIN16–03 represents the remains of a quadrilinear structure associated with several mounds of stones, scattered pottery, and cowrie shells. The structure overlooks two offshore markers that are reported to indicate a cut through the fringing reef. Small mounds of structural debris line the shoreline, some clearly modern, but others may be old. Visibility is good, as this part of the shoreline lies within the modern settlement and has been cleared of vegetation.

Informants reported that an area to the west of the present-day settlement had been the likely location of medieval occupation; it included places they referred to as ibn Battuta's house and a past harbour (Figure 3.1). The area was visited by one of us (ACH) and pottery (both earthenwares and glazed), cowrie shells, and stone blocks suggestive of past structural remains were observed. The site was recorded as KIN16–04. Many of the stone blocks and pottery remains were clearly not in situ and appeared, together with modern refuse, in the spoil created as a result of cultivation: this area is marked by a series of fenced-off gardens where crops such as watermelon are grown. It appeared clear that these had disturbed an archaeological deposit. Just to the west, however, lay an area of low shrubs and grasses with poor visibility, and sporadic patches of relatively bare soil with creepers. Previous experience of similar creepers at a sites excavated in Utheemu in 2016, discussed in Chapter 8, suggested vegetation this may be indicative of buried remains, an impression confirmed by the dark, powdery soil. Given the quantities of archaeological materials observed, their probable date, and the prospect of undisturbed deposits, we elected to return and conduct further investigations in the uncultivated area.

The 2017 intensive surveys

As discussed in Chapter 2, there had been no previous archaeological study of a medieval settlement of the Maldives. While a small number of surface remains (in the form of pottery scatters and isolated structural debris) were initially observed during the 2016 survey of Kinolhas (KIN16–04), the nature of sub-surface archaeology in that area remained completely unknown.

As such, during our second visit to the island in 2017, we used a two-pronged approach combining targeted pedestrian surveys across the whole uncultivated area and shovel test pits (STP) in a smaller STP Study Area within this. These surveys aimed to

- Document the extent of any archaeological deposit(s)
- Contextualise data from the STP excavations by recording features in the wider landscape, including other standing remains and surface features
- Identify areas for larger scale excavations

The STP surveys revealed a stratigraphically similar layer across most of the site, which consistently yielded cultural remains. Archaeological materials such as earthenware and glazed ceramics, bone, and shell were recovered in varying densities, with particularly high frequency in the southwestern extent of the STP Study Area. Pedestrian surveys in the STP Study Area and wider landscape revealed several isolated worked stones, as well as low-lying rectilinear features. Detailed analysis of the materials recovered and the features identified are discussed later in this chapter.

The shovel test pits: methodology

The systematic excavation of STPs across a landscape is an established approach in East Africa and other parts of the world (e.g. Nance and Bell 1986, Lightfoot 1989, Fleisher and LaViolette 1999, among others) used to map the nature and extent of sub-surface remains. Having identified the area to the west of the present-day settlement at Kinolhas as being of potential archaeology interest, it was first necessary to characterise and map the extent of the potential archaeological deposit to provide more specific areas for open-area excavation. STP surveys enabled us to achieve this.

The westernmost side of the island is characterised by a patchwork of open areas covered in grass and creepers; dense vegetation made up of species such as *Hibiscus tiliaceus* (Dhigga), *Calophyllum inophyllum* (Funa), and *Guettarda speciosa* (Ooni); and stands of larger trees including species exploited for snacks and seasoning, such as *Pandanus tectorus* (Boa Kashikeyo) and *Terminalia catappa* (country almond; Midhili), as well as coconut groves and, close to the western endpoint of the island, merging into mangrove and swampy land.

The uncultivated landscape covers an area of approximately 0.05 km². Visibility in the more densely forested areas was very low, and the trees were often so close together that open area excavations would have been difficult without significant clearance. During our 2016 field season, we conducted test excavations on the island of Veyvah, in Meemu atoll, in similar conditions. The deposits in these test pits showed significant root disturbance, and excavation was challenging. Drawing on these experiences, and to minimise the potential of finding archaeological deposits heavily disturbed by tree roots during our work on Kinolhas, the shovel test pit survey area was therefore primarily situated in the eastern–central space.

Prior to the field season, one of us (ACC) used QGIS to create a 10 x 10 m grid overlaying the uncultivated area, with a 100 x 100 m section of the grid covering the more open area selected as the initial focus for the excavations. Initial expectations were that we would excavate 11 north–south transects (spaced 10 m apart), with test pits positioned at 10 m intervals across the STP survey area. On arrival in the field, however, the vegetation was much denser than had been apparent in the aerial photographs (likely taken at a different time of year). As such, the sampling strategy was adjusted with the interval between transects and test pits increased to 20 m.

While the STP excavations were underway (as described later), pedestrian surveys were conducted in the more densely forested areas to the south and west of the STP survey area, accompanied by community leaders and members. During these surveys, the team (ACH and SJ) were shown two rectilinear stone features and a bathing tank in the area immediately south of the area initially selected for STP excavation. These rectilinear features were said to have been possible domestic structures, and in a part of the island where 'the wealthy are said to have lived in ibn Battuta's time'. We therefore elected to extend our original STP survey area to determine whether they were associated with any sub-surface remains. The extended survey universe (Figure 3.3) covered an area of 100 m (east–west) and 150 m (north–south) and contained 45 test pits. It is hereafter referred to as the STP Study Area.

Test pit locations were marked out using a handheld GPS, compasses, and tapes. These were excavated by shovel[1] until sterile sand (*dhonveli*) was reached. Material removed was hand sifted: pottery, bone, and shell were recovered. Each STP was photographed and the dimensions and depth, including the depth at which the sterile layer was encountered, were recorded. This provided insight into the depth of the archaeological deposits.

Figure 3.3 Kinolhas survey universe showing all test pits. Depth of test pits shown below test pit numbers.

The pottery and fauna collected during the STP survey were counted and analysed. These data were used to create a density heat map across the STP Study Area, enabling us to refine the selection of our open-area excavation areas by identifying potential areas of higher anthropogenic activity. The results of the STP surveys are outlined in the next section.

The shovel test pits: results

The depths of the STPs excavated ranged from 30 cm to 1 m, with an average of 57 cm; sterile deposits (easily identifiable due to the colour and nature of the sediment, *dhonveli*) were reached between 30 cm and 77 cm. Measurements of the depth at which *dhonveli* was first encountered were plotted on QGIS. Polygons were created around STPs of similar depth in order to create a low-resolution isopach allowing us to evaluate potential anthropogenic topography.

Pottery

From 36 of the 45 shovel test pits excavated, 836 sherds of pottery were recovered in varying densities. These comprised 766 sherds of earthenware and 70 sherds of exotic ceramics (Table 3.1). With the exception of STP416, most of the test pits devoid of pottery were located at the northernmost edge of the site, with higher densities of pottery recovered in the central part of the STP Study Area. STP544 returned the highest quantities of both earthenware and exotic ceramics. The high density of earthenware from STP478 reflects the recovery of a broken but articulated ceramic vessel (Figure 5.12).

Only the STP material associated with the seven subsequently excavated trenches was subjected to detailed analysis. This is a total of 399 sherds, of which most (60%) were earthenwares of small size that were simply counted and discarded (Table 5.1). The remainder are discussed in Tables 5.4–5.6 (for the 370 earthenware sherds) and 6.1 (for the 29 glazed sherds).

Fauna

From 33 of the STPs excavated (Table 3.2), 601 shell and bone fragments were recovered, 85% (n=509) of which were identifiable to species, family, or taxa. While the shells were identified to species or family where possible, the bones were categorised into the following groups:

- Marine fauna comprising fish cranial elements and fish post-cranial elements (vertebra and fin spines)
- Terrestrial fauna comprising bird bones (likely chicken), ungulate remains (cow and sheep or goat), and rodent bones
- Unknown fragments

Table 3.1 Densities of ceramics from each STP. P=total pottery; E=number of which glazed imports.

Transect 1			Transect 2			Transect 3			Transect 4			Transect 5			Transect 6		
STP	P	E	STP	P	E	STP	P	E	STP	P	E	STP	P	E	STP	P	E
112	0	0	174	0	0	139	0	0	168	0	0	197	0	0	257	14	0
174	3	1	234	8	0	201	0	0	230	1	0	259	17	2	319	11	0
236	15	1	296	28	0	263	15	2	292	6	2	321	23	7	381	25	2
298	25	2	358	5	1	325	62	6	354	19	2	383	11	2	443	8	3
360	49	0	420	17	2	387	3	0	416	0	0	445	3	2	505	13	1
422	19	1	482	11	1	449	33	4	478	58	2	507	13	0	567	7	0
484	6	2	544	159	18	511	28	1	540	28	1	569	0	0	629	4	1
						573	7	0	602	1	0	631	11	1			

Table 3.2 NISP shell and bone from each STP.

Test pit	Molluscs						Bones						Total
	Monetaria moneta	Cypraea Sp.	Atactodea glabrata	Unknown gastropod	Unknown bivalve	Nerita Sp	Fish bone cranial	Fish bone vertebra	Bird	Rodent	Ungulate	Unknown	
Transect 1													
112	0	0	0	0	0	0	0	0	0	0	0	0	0
174	0	0	0	0	0	0	0	0	0	0	0	0	0
236	1	0	0	1	1	1	1	0	0	0	0	0	5
298	1	0	1	1	0	0	0	4	1	0	0	0	8
360	56	1	0	0	0	0	5	3	0	0	0	2	67
422	2	0	0	0	0	0	2	1	0	0	0	0	5
484	0	0	1	0	2	1	0	0	0	0	0	0	3

(*Continued*)

Table 3.2 (Continued)

Test pit	Molluscs						Bones						Total
	Monetaria moneta	Cypraea Sp.	Atactodea glabrata	Unknown gastropod	Unknown bivalve	Nerita Sp	Fish bone cranial	Fish bone vertebra	Bird	Rodent	Ungulate	Unknown	
Transect 2													
172	0	0	0	0	0	0	0	0	0	0	0	0	0
234	4	0	0	0	0	0	3	6	4	0	0	4	21
296	8	0	1	0	0	0	1	1	1	0	0	0	12
358	0	0	0	0	0	0	0	3	0	0	0	1	4
420	0	0	1	0	0	0	1	2	0	0	0	1	5
482	2	0	0	1	0	0	0	0	0	0	1	0	4
544	8	2	0	0	0	0	27	93	10	2	3	49	194
Transect 3													
139	0	0	0	0	0	0	0	0	0	0	0	0	0
201	0	0	0	0	0	0	0	0	0	0	0	0	0
263	0	0	0	0	0	0	0	0	0	0	0	0	0
325	1	2	2	0	0	0	4	5	3	3	0	11	31
387	0	0	0	0	0	0	0	0	0	0	0	0	0
449	14	1	0	0	0	0	4	12	3	1	0	4	39
511	4	0	0	0	1	0	5	8	0	0	0	2	20
573	1	0	0	0	0	0	0	0	0	0	0	0	1
Transect 4													
168	0	0	0	0	0	0	0	0	0	0	0	0	0
230	0	0	0	0	0	0	0	0	0	0	0	0	0
292	1	0	0	0	0	0	0	0	3	0	0	0	4
354	2	0	0	0	1	0	0	3	0	0	0	3	9
416	0	1	0	1	0	2	0	0	0	0	0	0	4
478	2	0	0	0	0	0	2	5	1	0	0	0	10
540	0	0	0	0	0	0	1	1	0	0	0	0	2
602	0	0	0	0	0	0	0	0	0	0	0	0	0
Transect 5													
197	0	0	0	0	0	0	0	0	0	0	0	0	0
259	1	0	0	0	1	0	0	0	0	0	0	0	2
321	1	1	0	0	1	0	0	0	0	0	0	0	3
383	2	0	0	0	0	0	1	1	0	0	0	0	4
445	1	0	0	0	0	0	0	0	0	0	0	0	1
507	98	1	1	1	0	0	3	2	0	2	0	0	108
569	0	0	0	0	0	0	0	0	0	0	0	0	0
631	0	1	0	1	0	0	0	0	0	0	0	0	2
Transect 6													
257	0	1	0	0	0	0	0	0	0	0	0	0	1
319	8	0	0	1	0	0	0	1	0	0	0	1	11
381	9	2	0	0	0	0	0	0	0	0	0	0	11
443	3	0	0	0	0	0	0	0	0	0	0		3
505	5	0	0	0	0	0	0	0	0	0	0	0	5
567	1	0	0	0	0	0	0	0	0	0	0	0	1
629	0	0	0	0	0	0	0	0	0	0	0	0	0

In addition to counts, the remains were examined to identify any evidence of human activity. For shells, this included any evidence of deliberate modification (e.g. removal of the dorsum for cowries) and evidence for burning; in the case of bones, this also included any evidence of butchery such as cut marks, chop marks, or scraping.

As far as molluscs are concerned, 274 shells were recovered. The following species were recorded: *Monetaria moneta* (Linnaeus, 1758) (n=236), *Atactodea glabrata* (Gmelin, 1791) (n=7), *Cypraea Sp* (Linnaeus, 1758) (n=13), and *Nerita sp* (Linnaeus, 1758) (n=4). A further 14 specimens could not be identified to species or family—comprising seven bivalves and seven gastropods (Table 3.2).

The dominance of *Monetaria moneta* and other cowrie species in the overall assemblage compared with other mollusc species may reflect sampling bias: other molluscs may have been overlooked as presumed beach deposits. However, the proportions of these different species is largely similar to those issuing from the open area excavations (discussed in Chapter 7). The majority of the cowrie shells recovered issue from two STPs: STP507 (98 cowries) and STP360 (56 cowries).

The shells were mostly intact. Fragmentation was only observed in 3% (n=8) of the remains, all of which were cowries. Evidence of burning was also limited to cowries; this was observed on 30 specimens spread across five STPS (STP507–n=15; STP360–n=11; STP511–n=2 and STP381 and STP505–n=1 each). It is unclear whether this was the result of deliberate action. None of the cowries showed any other evidence of deliberate modification in the form of perforation or removal of the dorsum.

In terms of fish and animal bones, 327 individual fragments were recovered during the excavations. Of these, 24% (n=78) could not be identified to species, family, or taxa. Marine fauna made up 64% (n=211) of the assemblage—with the majority of these (n=151) being vertebrae. The remaining 12% (n=38) of the bones were from terrestrial fauna, 68% (n=26) of which were bird bones (likely chicken) (Table 3.2).

While shells were recovered from 27 of the 45 STPs excavated, bones were only recovered from 20 STPs (Table 3.2). They were particularly abundant in STP544, which returned 56% (n=184) of the total bone assemblage from the STP excavations. This test pit also accounted for 75% (n=3) of the ungulate remains.

Most of the bones from the STP assemblage were fragmentary and, apart from one exception (a burnt fish vertebra from STP511), showed no evidence of anthropogenic modification.

The pedestrian surveys

Thirty-four sites were recorded as part of the surveys comprising 17 isolated *veligaa* or *hirigaa* stones, seven scatters of several worked *veligaa* and *hirigaa* stones; three rectilinear stone features, one rectilinear stone structure; four wells; one bathing tank; and one mound (Table 3.3, Figure 3.4).

Table 3.3 Description of sites identified by pedestrian surveys.

Site no.	Site type	Dimensions	Description	Interpretation
KIN17–01	Isolated stone	0.41 x 0.41 x 0.11 m	Single loose *veligaa* block that has been shaped. Probably not in situ	
KIN17–02	Stone scatter		Sporadic *veligaa* and *hirigaa* blocks associated with a depression in the ground, approx. 4 m in diameter. Poor visibility, though close to another concentration (KIN17–05) that is near a *Pandanus tectorus* tree	Possible bathing tank
KIN17–03	Isolated stone		Isolated *veligaa*.	
KIN17–04	Isolated Stone		*Veligaa* stone close to T544	
KIN17–05	Stone scatter		A dozen *hirigaa* and *veligaa* stone blocks near a screwpine, situated approx. 60 m away from STP544	Unknown
KIN17–06	Stone scatter		Concentration of *hirigaa* and *veligaa* stone blocks around a *Terminalia catappa* tree. Unclear whether the stones are in situ but disturbed by the growth of the tree; or whether they have been placed around the tree during field clearance	Unknown
KIN17–07	Isolated stone			
KIN17–08	Isolated stone	0.4 x 0.65 x 0.12 m	Single worked *veligaa* stone standing approx. 40 cm from the ground	
KIN17–09	Stone scatter	0.42 x 0.13 m	Single block of *veligaa* standing up approx. 4–5 cm from the surface. The top of the stone has 4–5 parallel striations and a crack in the middle. It is surrounded by other, smaller *veligaa* stones	
KIN17–10	Isolated stone	0.45 x 0.26 m	Upright circular *veligaa* stone standing at a slant approx. 26 cm proud of the surface. 45 cm at base, and approx. 10 cm thick. Fragmented	
KIN17–11	Stone scatter	3 x 1 m	Linear stone arrangement comprising a mix of medium sized *fotigaa* (broken table coral), *veligaa*, and *hirigaa* stones. Appears in situ, though some of the stones are loose. Located in a densely vegetated area with *Hibiscus tilaceus* trees	
KIN17–12	Isolated stone			
KIN17–13	Stone scatter	0.75 x 0.55 x 0.15 m	Two fragments of a single worked *veligaa* stone one piece of which has been rotated 180° and stacked on the other. The underside of this part of the stone is very uneven with shells embedded in it	
KIN17–14	Mound	1 m diameter	Low compact mound of loose *veligaa* and *hirigaa* stones and rubble including gravestone fragments. Likely created as a result of clearing for cultivation which has occurred in the vicinity in living memory	Clearance mound
KIN17–15	Isolated stone		*Veligaa* stone probably not in situ	
KIN17–16	Isolated stone	0.4 x 0.5 m	Single *hirigaa* block, shaped and broken on the eastern side	
KIN17–17	Well	0.73 x 0.77 m	Well-preserved rectilinear feature, that is more defined around the northwestern corner. Feature comprise five *veligaa* stones	Well

(*Continued*)

Table 3.3 (Continued)

Site no.	Site type	Dimensions	Description	Interpretation
KIN17–18	Well	1.04 x 1.04 m	Well-preserved square feature with all four sides visible. The north side wall is approx. 12 cm diameter, which is slightly thicker than the other walls (approx. 6–7 cm diameter)	Well
KIN17–19	Well		West and south sides of a square *veligaa* structure comprising 3 stones. Thought to be a well. The west side stands 5 cm higher than the south side, which has a pair of parallel stones, the outer of which might represent collapse	Well
KIN17–20	Isolated stone			
KIN17–21	Rectilinear feature	2.5 x 1.7 m	Situated in a densely forested area, the rectilinear structure comprises a series of *veligaa* blocks approximately 20–30 cm long by 10 cm wide. Located close to T631	Based on location and similarity for feature excavated in T631, this is likely a mortuary structure
KIN17–22	Rectilinear feature	2.2 x 1.8 m approx.	Situated in a slightly more open area; surrounded by a number of *veligaa* and *hirigaa* stones. Council president suggests the remains are 'very very old'—associated with those who came before. He noted that the location had almost been forgotten	Situated adjacent to STP631 and subsequently excavated. Mortuary structure containing the remains of one individual. Surrounding stones represented collapsed structure and the tops of other grave markers
KIN17–23	Stone scatter		Four stones located between STP631 and STP443. The first located 5–6 m north of the second is a square stone with broken corners. The second is a standing *veligaa* stone with a rounded top—situated 5–6 m west of a *veligaa* and *hirigaa* stone alignment—both of which were fragmented	
KIN17–24	Isolated stone			
KIN17–25	Bathing Tank	8 x 8 m approx.	Roughly circular stone structure thought to be the remains of a bathing tank with an entrance to the east which is now covered with *Pandanus tectorus* trees. The structure has local associations with a bodhi tree (*Ficus religiosa*) and local elders suggested it was a bathing tank	Bathing tank
KIN17–26	Isolated stone	0.4 x 0.4 m	Shaped *veligaa* block in a dense concentration of *Scaveola taccada* trees, measuring approx. 40 x 40 cm	
KIN17–27	Isolated Stone			
KIN17–28	Isolated stone			
KIN17–29	Rectilinear structure	24 m east—west; 16 m north–south	Rectilinear structure with longer wall on northern edge. Local traditions suggest this represents the collapsed boundary wall of a palace known as *Boe falu ganduvaru*. Encompasses the remains of S2, S3, and Well 4. The area is heavily vegetated with *Pandanus tectorus, Scaveola taccada, Calophyllum inophyllum* and *Terminalia catappa* trees. The structure is surrounded by several depressions to the east	
KIN17–30	Well	1.2 x 1.2 m	Feature comprising 3 large *veligaa* blocks placed on their sides to form an incomplete square (missing the northern edge). Standing stones are surrounded by coral stone rubble	Well
KIN17–31	Rectilinear feature	5 x 3 m	Rectangular structure comprising *veligaa* stone and at least two worked *hirigaa* stones which have a groove. Most of the blocks have been worked and shaped	
KIN17–32	Isolated stone			
KIN17–33	Isolated stone		*Fotigaa* stone	
KIN17–34	Isolated stone		Single block of coarse *veligaa* in a clearing in the forested area. Close to another worked stone	

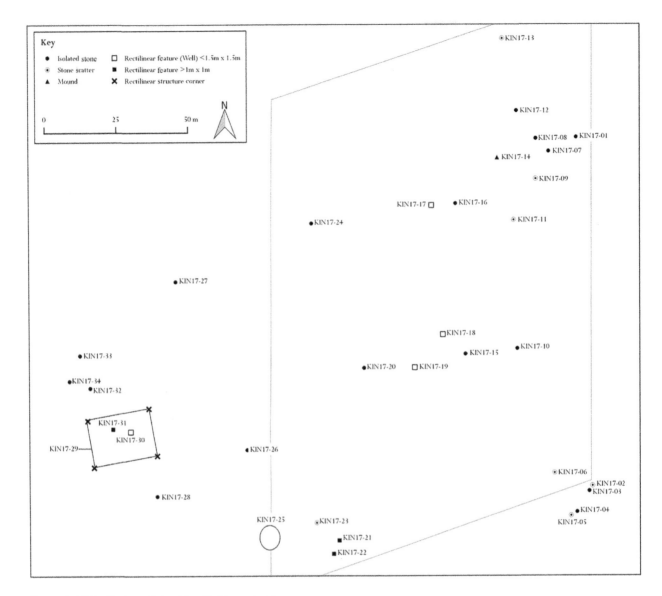

Figure 3.4 Distribution of sites identified by pedestrian surveys.

Discussion

The distribution of material culture recovered from the STP excavation was plotted in GIS to create a heatmap (Figure 3.5). This was plotted using both raw numbers from each STP and a ranking of material culture (pottery and fauna) recovered per m³—with the latter calculated using the dimensions and depths of the STPs.

When the depth of deposit in the test pits is examined, the data suggest an undulating land surface with two or three raised areas where deposits appear to have accumulated (Figure 3.5 left). There is an area of deeper deposit (68—69 cm) running across the transects approximately 40 m south of the northern extent of the STP Study Area. While one might expect that the deeper STP would produce higher quantities of material culture, there appears to be no correlation between the depth of deposit and the finds recovered from these STPs.

The distribution of pottery and faunal remains, on the other hand, evidence similar patterns (Figure 3.5 centre, right). One notable feature is the comparative absence of fauna and ceramics recovered from the northern areas. The most productive STPs are in the south, central, and eastern parts of the STP Study Area. This was particularly clear from the high densities of both pottery and fauna in STP544, which could suggest the presence of a midden in this area.

This pattern is mirrored by the distribution of sites identified during the pedestrian surveys—with most of the surface remains recorded to the south, central, and eastern areas (KIN17–01, KIN17–08, KIN17–09, KIN17–10, KIN17–12, KIN17–14, KIN17–15, KIN17–16, KIN17–17, KIN17–18, KIN17–19, KIN17–20, and KIN17–24). Further surface remains were also recorded to the south of STP544 as part of the pedestrian surveys (KIN17–02, KIN17–03, KIN17–04, and KIN17–05), including pottery, *veligaa* stones, and apparent structural debris, including a possible bathing tank. Only one site is located close to the northern extent (KIN17–13). This is an isolated *veligaa* which showed some evidence of having been disturbed, and thus may not be in situ.

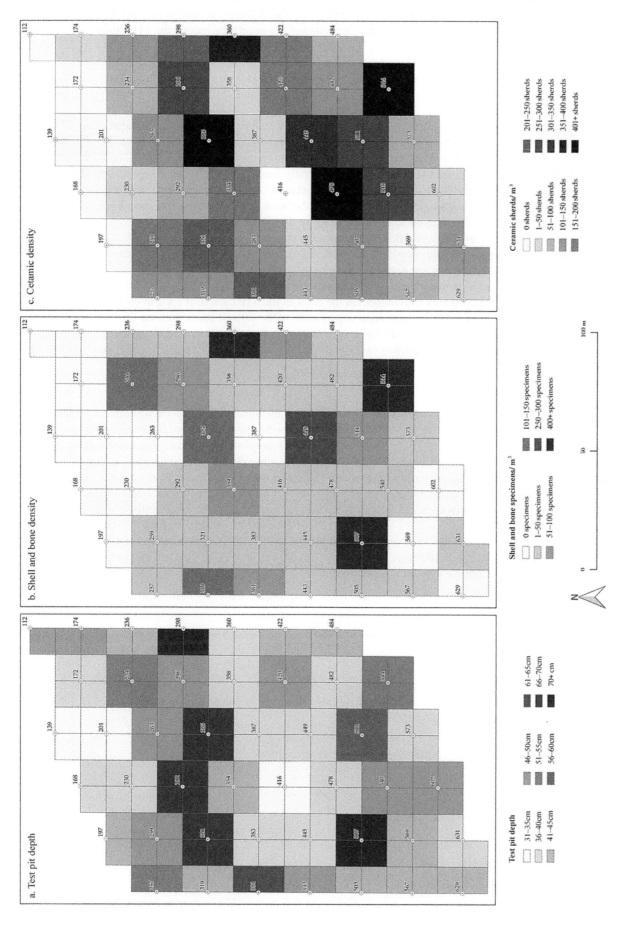

Figure 3.5 Heatmaps showing (a) depths of the STPs, (b) densities of shell and bone, and (c) densities of ceramics.

On this basis, we would suggest that the core archaeological areas start to the south, approximately 75–100 m inland from the northern coast. This is not to exclude the possibility of recovering material in the 50 m strip between the edge of the STP Study Area and the coast—nor does it suggest this area was definitely unused in the past. It could have been used for activities that leave less archaeological trace. The nature of the vegetation around the STP Study Area may also be hindering the visibility of other remains.

Pottery and faunal remains were recovered from STPs in the southwestern extent of the site (except STP569, which was sterile), but were less frequent than other areas. This is likely to reflect the fact that most of the test pits in this area were likely located within a mortuary space that included fallen funerary structures as well as a bathing tank.

Our surveys within the wider landscape suggests that the archaeological area also extends to the west of the STP Study Area. Although this area was characterised by dense vegetation, felt quite damp, and appeared lower lying than the rest of the site, it was also very rich in standing archaeology. These sites (KIN17–26, KIN17–28, KIN17–29, KIN17–30, KIN17–31, KIN17–32, KIN17–33, and KIN17–34) were generally better preserved than others identified by the surveys, with any disturbances generally associated with the vegetation cover. This combined with the local traditions which speak of the presence of a palace structure in this area—the boundary wall believed to have been represented by the rectilinear structure KIN17–29—make it an ideal location for further investigation.

At present, it is not possible to infer whether the settlement would have extended to either the west or the south coast of the island without further sub-surface investigation—either through remote sensing or STP excavation—as the visibility of non-structural surface scatters was severely hindered by the vegetation.

To increase confidence in recovering archaeological deposits, data from the heatmaps generated as a result of the STPs were used to identify areas for open area excavation. On the basis of the STP data, four 2 x 2 m units were opened over STP321, STP325, STP449, and STP544 as these represented some of the densest concentrations of material culture. An additional two 1 x 2 m units we opened over STP360 and STP443 to define the eastern and western edges of the survey universe respectively. A larger 6 x 4.5 m unit was excavated adjacent to STP631 to examine surface remains close by.

Excavation methodology

The work took place between 22 January and 16 February 2017. Our team included nine local workmen, and their assistance, and that of the island council, was invaluable. The trenches were excavated stratigraphically following natural layers—the only exception to this was in T631, where natural layers were also divided spatially to differentiate between different areas in the trench. In all cases, contexts were recorded following the Museum of London *Archaeological Site Manual* (Museum of London 1994), describing the nature of the deposit and frequency of natural and cultural inclusions as well cross-reference to plans, sections, samples, and other comments. All deposits were sieved unless otherwise stated, and environmental samples were taken from key deposits for flotation. On reaching sterile—consistently identified as soft white sand with no inclusions—a further 10 cm was excavated to ensure no further material culture was present. Where features were identified, they were planned at a scale of 1:20. Section drawings of all four sides of the trench were completed at a scale of 1:10 before closing.

The following chapters will discuss the finds recovered.

Note

1 However, one test pit, STP478, was excavated by trowel as a near-complete carinated vessel was recovered in it (Figure 5.12).

4 Kinolhas
The trenches and stratigraphy

Introduction

Anne Haour

We approached the island of Kinolhas as a *terra incognita*, since no Maldivian medieval site had been previously investigated. Through a comprehensive survey and a programme of shovel test pitting along six transects (see Chapter 3), we obtained a first insight into the nature of the sub-surface remains across a sizable area. This evidenced the existence of a continuous archaeological deposit and highlighted varying densities of material, particularly ceramics and fauna. This guided the placement of larger-scale excavation units.

The present chapter outlines the results of the excavation of these seven units.[1] Overall, four 2 x 2 m units were opened over areas which shovel test pits (STPs) had shown to contain some of the densest concentrations of material culture. Two additional 1 x 2 m units were opened at the eastern and western edges of the survey universe, on Transects 1 and 6, with a view to sampling these areas which had returned fewer finds and, presumably, represented the edge of the site. Finally, a larger 6 x 4.5 m unit was excavated to examine some substantial surface remains identified during the pedestrian surveys. These various trenches sampled points in an area roughly 100 x 150 m in extent (Figure 3.3).

In considering the deposits and stratigraphy of these seven trenches, useful Dhivehi terms include *veligaa, hirigaa, fotigaa*, and *kaashiveli*—namely, consolidated coral sand ('sandstone'), madrepore coral, broken table coral, and decayed 'sandstone'. These features, especially the first two, were frequently encountered during fieldwork and were of crucial importance in guiding the process of excavation and the interpretation of finds. *Dhonveli*—fine, white sand—was another recurrent feature of major significance, as it signalled the end of the archaeological layer. Key features recorded in the section drawings are illustrated in Figure 4.1.

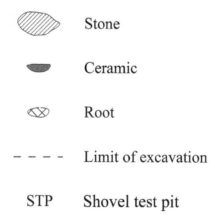

     Stone

     Ceramic

     Root

– – – –   Limit of excavation

STP   Shovel test pit

Figure 4.1 Key for section drawings.

Trench 321

David Vigoureux

Introduction

Trench 321 was set up as a 2 x 2 m unit, which encompassed the corresponding shovel test pit in its southwest corner. This location was selected for excavation as STP321 had yielded a good number of ceramics, including glazed wares (Table 3.1), thus offering good prospects of sampling the variety of material culture which we had observed in the spoil heaps of nearby fields. Trench 321 was located on Transect 5, with Trench 631 situated 100 m to the south.

DOI: 10.4324/9781003166221-4

Stratigraphy

Table 4.1 lists the deposits encountered. Three distinct archaeological layers were uncovered in the excavation of this unit: a topsoil consisting of loose brown soil and two layers of lighter grey soil, labelled Contexts 2a and 2b. The distinction between 2a and 2b was only noted when drawing the final sections, so artefacts bagged during excavation were simply labelled as being from 'Context 2', and are entered as such in the tables accompanying Chapters 5 to 8 in the rest of this volume.

Context 2a began between 20 and 30 cm from the surface and exhibited a high frequency of large stones. These were planned and carefully checked for possible associated charcoal or artefacts, but they were in no apparent order and were mainly unworked (Figure 4.2). These included local *veligaa* and *hirigaa*, but also many stones identified as foreign to

Table 4.1 Description of excavated deposits, Trench 321.

Context	Description	Associated material culture	Level at base of context (*unless specified: NW, NE, SW, SE)	Sieved (Y/N)/mesh size
1	Dark brown humus layer, few archaeological finds	Pottery, shell, lithic, slag	25, 23, 29, 29	25% at 1 cm, 75% at 5 mm
2a	Thin grey-brown coarse layer, some roots. Coral inclusions, large, foreign stones	Abundant pottery, slag, lithic, bone, metal, shell, glass, charcoal	37, 37, 37, 40	Y—1 cm
2b	Loose, grey soil. Less coral, far fewer inclusions than 2a. Possibly a transitional context created by the seepage of Context 2a downwards	Pottery, shell	47, 47, 54, 52	Y—1 cm
3	Cut of a pit going into southern section wall		Pit with very narrow base, 94	
4	Fill of Context 3. Dark brown soil. Lots of charcoal, some pottery	Pottery, bone, lithic, charcoal Two radiocarbon dates: Beta 461519 and 461520	Pit with very narrow base, 94	Y—1 cm
5	Three-stone arrangement at southeast side of the trench. It includes one 'Type C' stone. There were no other stones at that level. Yellow-brown soil	Pottery	40 at centre	Y—1 cm
6	Sterile, sandy layer. Sporadic roots growing vertically	None	69, 65, 66, 64	Y—1 cm
7	Cut of pit in the middle section of the trench		59 at centre	
8	Fill of Context 7. Diffuse, dark sand	None	59 at centre	Y—5 mm
9	Small round cut in centre of trench		58 at centre	
10	Fill of Context 9. Slightly darker sand than surrounding context	None	58 at centre	Y—5 mm
11	Small oval cut near the south side of the trench		59 at centre	
12	Fill of Context 11. Darker soil. Potentially connected to Pit 4	None	59 at centre	Y—5 mm
13	Very small circular cut near the middle of the trench		57 at centre	
14	Fill of Context 13. Very dark soil. Appeared to contain root matter	None	57 at centre	Y—5 mm
15	Very small and shallow circular cut in the northern part of the trench		56 at centre	
16	Fill of Context 15. Dark soil	None	56 at centre	Y—5 mm
17	Small oval cut near middle of the trench		59 at centre	
18	Fill of Context 17. Very shallow, slightly darker soil. Numerous white flecks	None	59 at centre	Y—5 mm
19	Small, circular cut in the western side of the trench		59 at centre	
20	Fill of Context 19. Very shallow, slightly darker soil. Numerous white flecks	None	59 at centre	Y—5 mm
21	Large semi-circular cut into the western section of trench		59 at centre	
22	Fill of Context 21. Quite loose, dark yellow-brown soil. Lots of coral flecks. No archaeological material. Not visible in section drawing. Possibly related to proximity of shovel test pit	Shell	59 at centre	Y—1 cm
23	Group of stones near eastern edge of trench. Dark yellow brown soil. No archaeological material	None	48 at top of stones, 53 at base	

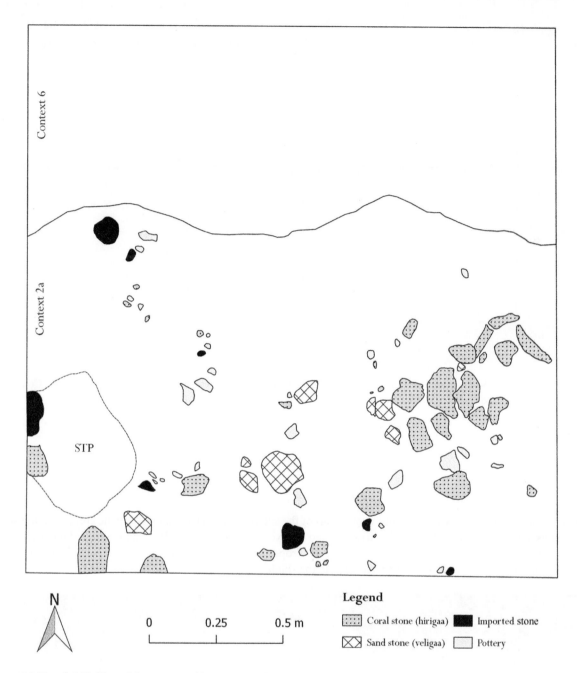

Figure 4.2 Trench 321. Plan of the context of large stones, Context 2a.

Source: Drawn by Annalisa Christie.

the Maldives. These included a dozen pieces of a limestone and at least 18 examples of the red-brown stone of Type C, which appears to be a type of microcrystalline quartz with impurities, formed under the influence of hydrothermal circulation; the presence of 'desert varnish' on some surfaces suggested it has come from the surface of a desert pavement (Paul Dennis and Alastair Grant, University of East Anglia, pers. comm.). There was a high concentration of these in the southwest corner of the excavation. Context 2a yielded metal slag and an abundance of pottery.

Layer 2b, 35–40 cm from the surface, was greyer and looser and contained far fewer archaeological and coral inclusions. A large conical cut, Context 3, dug into it. Its fill (Context 4) consisted of coarse dark brown soil transitioning gradually into lighter-coloured and increasingly damp soil, with a near cement-like consistency at the base of the pit, at 94 cm BD (below datum), where a few potsherds were recovered and water was reached.

Several small circular or near-circular cuts were investigated to determine whether they might be post holes. However, most were shallow and/or diffuse and at least one (Context 14) contained decaying root matter. They are interpreted as a result of root action.

Context 6 was sterile. It was excavated in two parts: first the northern half of the trench, then the southern. Figure 4.3 shows the south section at completion; the pit, Context 4, is visible here.

An unusual feature of Trench 321 is that it yielded almost 1.2 kg of metal slag.

There are two dates from Trench 321, both from the pit (Context 4).

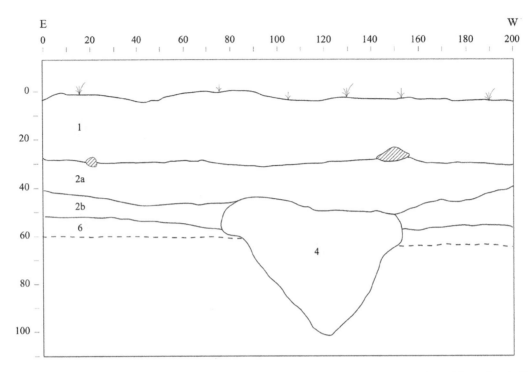

Figure 4.3 Trench 321. South section at completion. Two dates, Beta 461519 and Beta 461520, are issued from the pit, Context 4.

Source: Drawn by Nicolas Nikis.

Trench 325

Shiura Jaufar

Introduction

Trench 325 was set up as a 2 x 2 m unit in a central part of the site (Figure 4.4), encompassing the corresponding shovel test pit in its southeast corner. This location was selected for excavation because STP325 had indicated this was an area with plentiful ceramics, including a comparatively high proportion of glazed materials (Table 3.1). This unit was on Transect 3, the same as Trench 449, which lay 40 m to the south.

Figure 4.4 Drone shot, with T325 visible at bottom centre; T321 can be seen to lower right, T449 to top, and T360, with the group of standing people, at left.

Stratigraphy

The contexts encountered in Trench 325 are shown in Table 4.2. The excavation uncovered six contexts and reached sterile at 50–60 cm. The topsoil was a damp humic layer with many roots, overlaying a very gritty layer, Context 2, which contained many coral inclusions and was difficult to trowel. This layer was first identified at the eastern side of the unit and was subsequently encountered at various depths throughout the unit, most concentrated at its north and south edges. A diffuse ashy patch was noted at the southwest corner. Following this was a similar layer, Context 3, with fewer finds but many small coral flakes.

Three possible pits (Contexts 4, 5, and 6) cut from the level of Context 3 into sterile (Context 7). The most convincing of these was Context 5, about 55 x 25 cm in size, abutting the north section. Context 4 for its part lay just off the northern side of the shovel test pit, so may reflect this disturbance, but it was differentiated from the surrounding soil by its colour and the fact it yielded artefacts (albeit only 6 unremarkable potsherds). Lastly, Context 6 was roughly 30 x 50 cm in size in the northeast corner of the unit.

As had first been observed at the time STP 325 was excavated, sterile occurred at varying levels within the unit. This was initially thought to indicate past disturbance, but to this must be added the fact that some of the upper layers, as well as the land surface, are on a slight slope, with the southern part 7–10 cm higher than the northern part. Figure 4.5 shows the west section at completion, with Pit 5 visible at the northwest corner of the unit.

Table 4.2 Description of excavated deposits, Trench 325.

Context	Description	Associated material culture	Level at base of context (*unless specified: NW, NE, SW, SE)	Sieved (Y/N)/ mesh size
1	Dark brown humus layer, loose and fine-grained, many roots and dead leaves, occasional pottery and shell	Pottery, bone, shell, charcoal	?, 31,?, 29	25% at 1 cm, 75% at 5 mm
2	Greyish brown coarse-grained loose sand, fewer roots, many coral inclusions, many stones of which some large, diffuse ash patch at southwest corner, much pottery and shell, few bones	Pottery, bone, shell, metal, grindstone fragment, glass, possible ceramic spindle whorl [SF 22], slag, charcoal Radiocarbon date: Beta 461517	47, 49, 44, 39	Y—1 cm
3	Greyish brown coarse-grained loose sand, fewer roots, very many coral inclusions, occasional pottery, bone and shell but less than in Context 2	Pottery, bone, ?glass	63, 60, 56, 47	Y—1 cm
4	Greyish brown fine-grained sand, many coral flakes, little pottery, bone, and shell. Fill of Context 8	Pottery, bone, shell	85 at centre	Y—1 cm
5	Dark brown loose fine sand, little pottery, charcoal. Fill of Context 9	Pottery, ?glass, charcoal Radiocarbon date: Beta 461518	85 at centre	Y—1 cm
6	Light greyish brown coarse-grained loose sand, many coral flecks. Fill of Context 10	Pottery	100 at centre	Y—1 cm
7	Yellowish white fine sand, very few roots. Sterile	None	77 at centre	Y—1 cm
8	Cut of Context 4		85 at centre	
9	Cut of Context 5		85 at centre	
10	Cut of Context 6		100 at centre	

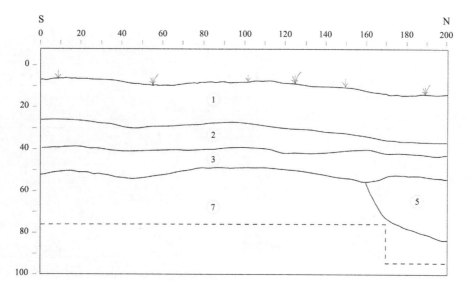

Figure 4.5 T325. West section at completion.

Source: Drawn by Nicolas Nikis.

Trench 360

Annalisa Christie

Introduction

Trench 360 was a 1 x 2 m unit oriented with the long edge on the east–west axis, encompassing the corresponding shovel test pit in its southeast corner. This location was selected for excavation in order to investigate the southeastern extent of the site. Transect 1, on which this unit lay, was close to the gardens and fields adjacent to the modern village (Figure 4.6, Figure 4.7). This shovel test pit returned the highest quantity of archaeological remains of all the shovel test pits on this transect, in terms of earthenwares, *Monetaria moneta* cowrie shells, and marine and terrestrial fauna (Tables 3.1 and 3.2).

Figure 4.6 Drone shot, showing location of T360.

Figure 4.7 T360 during excavation.

Table 4.3 Description of excavated deposits, Trench 360.

Context	Description	Associated material culture	Level (cm) at base of context (*unless specified: NW, NE, SW, SE)	Sieved (Y/N)/mesh size
1	Loose, coarse, and flecked light brown humic layer with many roots	Pottery, bone, shell	19, 20, 21, 19	N
2	Loose, coarse light brown sand with frequent shell and coral inclusions creating white flecking. Fewer roots than Context 1. Dense in pottery, bone, and shell, with infrequent stone	Pottery, bone, shell, stone, charcoal, glass	29, 29, 28, 25	Y—5 mm
3	Loose, coarse brown sand with yellow flecks, lighter in colour than Context 4 and thus excavated separately. Restricted to the western 1 x 1 m end of the trench. Fair pottery, bone, and shell, becoming less frequent to the base of the context	Pottery, bone, shell	50, 51, 52, 52	Y—5 mm
4	Compact, coarse, dark brown sand with yellow flecking. Restricted to the eastern 1 x 1 m. Initial deposit contained darker lenses interpreted as result of root action. Fair pottery, bone, and shell, returning fewer remains than Context 2	Pottery, bone, shell, glass	50, 51, 53, 52	Y—5 mm
5	Loose, fine dark brown sand representing the fill of a possible oval pit that cut through Contexts 4 and 7 (eastern side of trench). Charcoal and bone were only recovered from the sieve, not by hand	Charcoal, bone	59 (at centre of cut)	Y—5 mm
6	Loose, fine dark brown sand with yellowish white flecks representing the fill of a possible circular pit cut through Contexts 3 and 7 (western side of trench). Few finds	No record made	59 (at centre of cut)	Y—5 mm
7	Yellow-white fine sand with few coral inclusions. Sterile	None	58, 58, 58, 58	Y—5 mm
8	Cut of Context 5		59 (at centre of cut)	
9	Cut of Context 6		59 (at centre of cut)	

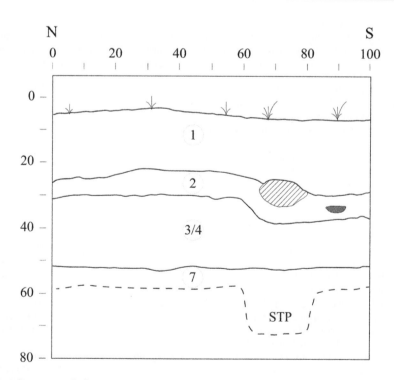

Figure 4.8 T360. East section at completion.

Source: Drawn by Nicolas Nikis.

Stratigraphy

Seven contexts were recognised in Trench 360. Sterile was reached at 53 cm. Excavated deposits comprised a layer of topsoil (Context 1), three archaeological deposits (Contexts 2, 3, and 4), and two possible single context pit fills (Context 5 and 6)—of which only one (Context 5) returned archaeological remains. Context 7 was sterile. Table 4.3 describes the deposits encountered and Figure 4.8 shows the east section at completion.

Differences between contexts were minimal. While a slight colour difference was noted between Contexts 3 and 4, this became less defined after a couple of centimetres, and on closer inspection it is likely these contexts represented the same deposit. Archaeological remains diminished as excavation progressed into this deposit, which was subsequently found to lie over sterile fine yellowish white *dhonveli* sand. Although the lenses of loose, fine dark brown sand in Contexts 5 and 6 were initially both interpreted as possible pits, Context 6 is likely natural.

Trench 443

Annalisa Christie

Introduction

Trench 443 was a 1 x 2 m unit, oriented with the long edge on the north–south axis. It was laid out south of its corresponding shovel test pit. This area was selected for excavation as it appeared, based on the results of survey and shovel test pit trials, to represent the southwestern-most extent of the site. Although other shovel test pits farther north along this transect, Transect 6, featured higher densities of archaeological remains (Table 3.1, Table 3.2), we decided to avoid these as they were located close to other excavations (in particular Trench 321) and would not offer the broader view of the site that we aimed for.

Stratigraphy

Fifteen contexts were recognised in Trench 443. Sterile was reached at a depth of 62 cm. Excavated deposits comprised a layer of topsoil (Context 1), three archaeological deposits (Context 2, 5 and 14), and five possible single context

Table 4.4 Description of excavated deposits, Trench 443.

Context	Description	Associated material culture	Level (cm) at base of context (*unless specified: NW, NE, SW, SE)	Sieved | (Y/N)
1	Loose, coarse brown sand with many roots. Some isolated coral stone inclusions, considered natural	No finds	17, 16.5, 18, 17	N
2	Coarse brown sand with fewer roots. Coral and shell inclusions creating white flecking. Fair pottery, including glazed. Some bones and shell (mostly cowries). Context overlaid stones—3 *veligaa*, 1 *fotigaa*, 1 *hirigaa*, one an unknown red rock of likely foreign origin	Pottery, shell, marine and terrestrial bone, sandstone, coral stone, imported stone, charcoal	28, 38, 28, 28 (top of stones) 42, 41, 29, 42 (Context base)	Y—5 mm
3	Circular cut with sharp edged break at the top and non-perceptible break at the base, bottoming out to a rounded point at 25 cm. Filled by Context 4		73 (to centre of excavated cut)	
4	Grey-brown coarse sand, more compacted than Context 5	Pottery, shells, marine and terrestrial bone, charcoal	73	Y—5 mm
5	Compact-loose whitish brown coarse sand with three sub-circular ashy charred lenses at north of trench, namely Contexts 7, 9, and 11. Deposit still returning archaeological material	Pottery, shells, marine and terrestrial bone	49, 50, 49, 49	Y—5 mm
6	Sub-circular cut with sharp edge break at top and non-perceptible break at the base, bottoming out to a concave base at 10 cm. Filled by Context 7		59 (to centre of excavated cut)	
7	Charcoal and loose coarse black-grey sand. No finds	None	59	Y—5 mm
8	Sub-circular cut with sharp edge break at top and non-perceptible break at the base, bottoming out to a concave base at 9 cm. Filled by Context 9		58 (to centre of excavated cut)	
9	Charcoal and loose coarse black-grey sand. No finds	None	58	Y—5 mm
10	Ovate cut with sharp edge break at top and non-perceptible break at the base, bottoming out to a concave base at 12 cm. Filled by Context 11		61 (to centre of excavated cut)	
11	Loose coarse black-grey sand. Some pottery and bone	Pottery, bone, charcoal	61	Y—5 mm
12	Circular cut truncated to the south and west by the edges of the trench. Sharp edge break at top and non-perceptible break at the base, bottoming out to a concave base at 12 cm. Filled by Context 13		61 (to centre of excavated cut)	
13	Hard, fine grey-black sand which was removed in clumps. No finds. Sticky	None	61	Y—5 mm
14	Coarse white-grey sand with few finds (mostly pottery and bone). Deposit wetter to base	Pottery, bone, charcoal, shell	70, 71, 66, 70	
15	Sterile white fine sand		83, 82, 82, 83 Limit of Excavation	N

pit fills (and associated cuts), only two of which (Contexts 4 and 11) returned archaeological remains. Contexts are described in Table 4.4.

This unit revealed a stratigraphy comparable to that of the other trenches excavated. The loose coarse brown sand of Context 2 was the richest deposit in terms of archaeological material. As in the other trenches, density of archaeological material was much less in subsequent layers. The presence of blocks of stone (*veligaa*, *hirigaa*, and *fotigaa*) in Context 2 was, however, an unusual feature of this unit. These appeared to have been shaped and may have been in situ (Figure 4.9). Given the proximity of Trench 631 and the burial and structures brought to light there, the blocks in T443 were initially thought to have possible funerary associations. However, subsequent investigation revealed that these remains were of much smaller scale than those from T631.

The coarse whitish brown deposit of Context 5 returned a series of darker ashy/charcoal-rich lenses. Though these were initially interpreted as possible pits, upon investigation it seems more likely that, with the exceptions of Contexts 4 and 11, which returned archaeological remains, these features were natural. Figure 4.10 shows the west section at completion.

Figure 4.9 Shaped stone blocks from T443.

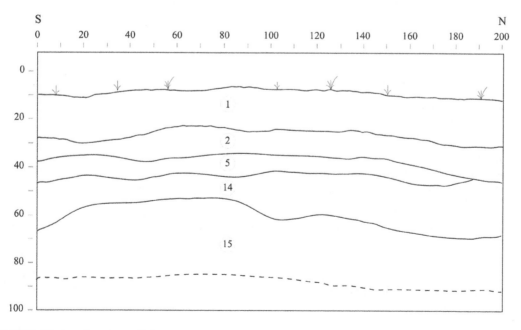

Figure 4.10 T443. West section at completion.

Source: Drawn by Nicolas Nikis.

Trench 449

David Vigoureux

Introduction

Trench 449, a 2 x 2 m unit, encompassed the corresponding test pit in its southwestern corner. It was selected for excavation because STP449 had revealed the presence of plentiful ceramics and molluscs as well as some fauna (Table 3.1, Table 3.2). This unit was on Transect 3, the same as Trench 325, 40 m to its north.

Stratigraphy

Excavation revealed three distinct layers. Context 1, reaching a depth of 15–20 cm, consisted of a light brown topsoil, with very few roots and evidence of animal activity. Below this lay Context 2, a thin (10 cm) layer of a lighter brown and yellow colour with coral flecks, which was rich in archaeological material, including charcoal, bone, shell, pottery,

Table 4.5 Description of excavated deposits, Trench 449.

Context	Description	Associated material culture	Level at base of context (*unless specified: NW, NE, SW, SE)	Sieved (Y/N)/ mesh size
1	Light brown humus layer, slightly damp, a little coarse, very loose at top 5 cm (spongy), very few roots and finds, evidence of animal action	Pottery, bone	23, 25, 21, 18	None
2	Light brown, yellow flecked, slightly coarse but finer than Context 1, with coral inclusions, frequent pottery and charcoal, very frequent bone	Pottery, bone, charcoal, metal, shell, glass, fired earth, 1 bead (SF 45)	33, 32, 34, 33	Y—5 mm
3	Light brown, transitioning to yellow-brown, loose, coarse soil with occasional small flecks of coral, roots, very few finds	Pottery, bone, charcoal, metal, shell	58, 58, 56, 56	Y—5 mm
4	Cut of Context 5		40 at centre	
5	Near centre of trench. Dark/very dark brown coarse soil, flecked, with charred material, somewhat loose, forming a wide, shallow deposit, 33 x 33 cm in size	Charcoal	40 at centre	Y—5 mm
6	Cut of Context 7		66 at centre	
7	Near northwest corner of trench. Dark brown, loose, rather coarse, flecked, few inclusions, lots of fibrous charcoal, some roots, transitions to yellower soil, 22 x 16 cm in size	Metal, charcoal	66 at centre	Y—5 mm
8	Cut of Context 9		68 at centre	
9	In southwest quadrant of trench, very dark brown coarse soil, flecked, lots of charcoal, compact, evidence of root action, 33 x 28 cm in size	Pottery, charcoal Radiocarbon date: Beta 461527	68 at centre	Y—5 mm
10	Cut of Context 11		43 at centre	
11	Abutting east section of trench, very dark brown, coarse, small flecks, some bone, quite loose and somewhat wet, some root action, 20 x 15 cm in size	Bone, charcoal Radiocarbon date: Beta 461528	43 at centre	
12	Eastern section, extending between 32 and 50 cm from northeast corner. Mass of 17 cowries	Cowries	34	
13	In northwest quadrant of trench. Mass of 99 cowrie shells and small glazed ceramic vessel (SF 81)	Pottery, cowries	50	Y—5 mm
14	Light yellow-brown soil, few pieces coral, quite compact, slightly wet	Charcoal	50	Y—5 mm
15	Cut of Context 16		83	
16	In east side of trench. Dark brown, fine soil, loose, some small flecks, roots, few other inclusions	Pottery, glass, charcoal Radiocarbon date: Beta 461529	83	Y—50% at 5 mm
17	Yellow-white, loose coarse soil, little amount of coral and roots	Sterile	57	Y—5 mm
18	Dark brown coarse flecked soil, loose, coral inclusions. This context was defined during section drawing		54	Y—5 mm
19	Cut of Context 18		54	
20	Fill of small pot SF81	Electrum pendant, 6 beads (SF 82b–g)	N/A	Handpicked with 10x lens

and glass. Context 3 consisted of light brown to yellower soil, with few coral inclusions and very little archaeological material. Various soil features cut into it; these were mostly shallow and diffuse, although three of them (Contexts 5, 7, and 9) contained charred material, some resembling burnt coconut fibres. A much larger pit (Context 16, some 60 cm wide at its summit) cut into the east section; it contained few archaeological remains, but despite signs of root action was the most convincing pit in this trench (Figure 4.12). Context 11, a loose, possible pit feature, sat just above it. Another potential pit, Context 18, was only recognised during the final drawing of the south section; it had been missed as the soil was very similar to that of Context 2, but somewhat darker. The contexts encountered are described in Table 4.5 and Figure 4.12 shows the east section at completion.

Two caches of cowrie shells were recovered, both within Context 3. Context 12 was a mass of 17 cowrie shells abutting the east section at a depth of c. 30 cm. A discrete feature (Context 13) consisting of 99 cowrie shells arranged around a small glazed ceramic vessel (SF 81) was recovered at 40–50 cm depth (Figure 4.11). Upon sieving the fill inside the pot (Context 20), a small yellow artefact and several beads were found (SF 82a–g; see Chapter 8, Figures 8.1.1, 8.3.1, 8.3.5).

Figure 4.11 Trench 449, Context 13/14. Cowrie cache and small glazed ceramic vessel (Small Find 81) at the time of discovery.

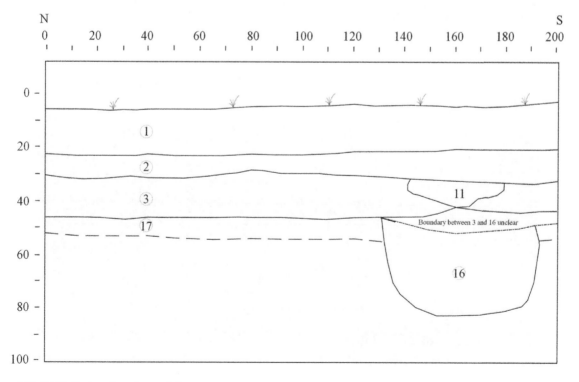

Figure 4.12 T449. East section at completion.

Source: Drawn by Nicolas Nikis.

Trench 544

Shiura Jaufar

Introduction

Trench 544 was a 2 x 2 m unit located in a heavily vegetated area (Figure 4.13), encompassing the corresponding shovel test pit in its southeast corner. It was chosen for excavation because this shovel test pit, which lay on Transect 2, had revealed an extremely high density of finds, particularly fauna and ceramics (Table 3.1, Table 3.2).

Stratigraphy

The unit recovered four contexts above the sterile soil, which was reached at a depth of 60–65 cm. The deposits excavated are described in Table 4.6. The land surface was sloping, with the northern end of the trench some 18–20 cm higher that the southern end (a gradient of about 1:10) (Figure 4.14).

Table 4.6 Description of excavated deposits, Trench 544.

Context	Description	Associated material culture	Level (cm) at base of context (*unless specified: NW, NE, SW, SE)	Sieved (Y/N)
1	Dark brown humic layer, with many roots, some of which thick. No finds in first few buckets but then begin on northern end of unit	Very abundant pottery and bones, shell, some stones, metal, glass, and charcoal	28, 27, 45, 38	Y—1 cm
2	Dark greyish brown, coarse-grained loose soil, lots of coral, stones	Abundant pottery and bones, shell, occasional charcoal, glass, metal (some possibly cuprous), grindstone, ?whetstone (SF 60) Radiocarbon date: Beta 461525	51, 47, 56, 50	Y—5 mm
3	Greyish brown, coarse-grained loose soil, few roots and little coral, some stones. Mottled with diffuse ashy and darker patches	Abundant pottery and bones, little shell, occasional charcoal and glass	57, 55, 63, 57	Y—5 mm
4	Greyish brown, coarse-grained loose soil, some stones, numerous ashy patches	Occasional pottery, very abundant bones, little charcoal and metal, glass, 1 bead (SF 90) Radiocarbon date: Beta 461526	67, 64, 71, 67	Y—5 mm
5	Light yellow	Charcoal; otherwise sterile	62	Y—5 mm
6	Greyish brown ashy feature, 21 x 26 cm, at southern end of unit	Few bones, charcoal	89 at centre	Y—5 mm
7	Cut of Context 6		89 at centre	

Figure 4.13 Trench 544. A watermelon break. Context 2 under excavation.

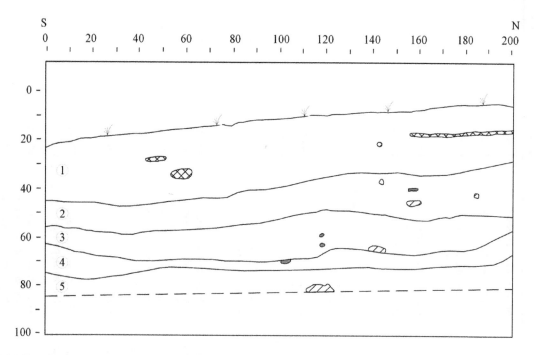

Figure 4.14 Trench 544. West section at completion.

Source: Drawn by Nicolas Nikis.

The topsoil was a fine, humic layer with an extremely dense network of roots. As such, it was difficult to trowel and was excavated by hoe, with due caution given the density of finds. A huge amount of pottery and bones were recovered. Patches of charred material occurred in the northeast and centre of the trench. Artefacts were mostly concentrated on the northern side of the unit, with particularly rich deposits in the northeast corner.

Context 2, excavated by trowel, was a dense deposit of coral rubble, stone fragments of varying size, and roots. This deposit yielded many finds, including abundant bones and large pottery fragments. Context 3 was similar, but with fewer roots, large stones, and finds and some diffuse ashy patches. These ashy patches became very visible in Context 4, a layer of greyish ashy soil, with the occurrence of some much darker patches. The most remarkable feature was the large number of bones it contained. It also yielded a bead (SF 90; see Chapter 8). The lower limit of Context 4 was diffuse and merged gradually into Context 5, light yellow sterile sand, cut only by a decayed root (Context 6),which appeared during the cleaning of the unit for final photographs.

The east and west sections evidenced a pronounced sloping, following the lay of the land surface which, as stated earlier, was more elevated at the north.

Trench 631

Annalisa Christie

Introduction

Trench 631 was laid out to the west of the corresponding shovel test pit, at the southernmost extent of Transect 5, which itself lay in the southwest corner of the survey area. It lay 100 m south of Trench 321. Although the shovel test pit had returned a comparatively low density of material culture (Table 3.1, Table 3.2), it was located within a part of the survey area that included a number of linear and rectilinear stone features. During preliminary discussions with the community, it was initially hypothesised that some might represent the remains of a house or domestic structure. A now overgrown stone bathing tank also lay nearby.

Stratigraphy

Trench 631 comprised 28 contexts, including 24 deposits and 4 features. The unit reached a maximum depth of 36 cm in most of the trench, though it extended deeper, up to 66 cm, around a set of human remains recovered during excavation. The deposits encountered in Trench 631 are listed in Table 4.7. Some contexts were designed to improve spatial control: they specify locations within what may be essentially the same deposit. All deposits were sieved through a 1 cm mesh unless otherwise stated (see Table 4.7).

Table 4.7 Description of excavated deposits, Trench 631.

Context	Description	Associated material culture	Levels at base of context-	Associated context (s)
1	Coarse, loosely compacted brown sand with few roots. The deposit was excavated by hoe and contained few stone fragments. 10% of deposit unsieved as no finds recovered	Small stone fragments	5 cm	
2	Coarse, loosely compacted brown sand with few roots. The deposit was excavated by trowel and contained few stone fragments	Small stone fragments, charcoal	5 cm	
3	Coarse, loosely compacted brown sand with few roots. The deposit was excavated by hoe initially, then trowel as larger *hirigaa* tombstones and *veligaa* stones were observed. Deposit around the stones contained a mix of exotic and earthenware pottery, smaller stone rubble (*hirigaa* and *veligaa*), and a few shell fragments	Pottery, shell, large *veligaa* stones, tombstones	13 cm	
4	Coarse, loosely compacted brown sand with few roots. The deposit was excavated by hoe. Possibly a continuation of Context 1, but with more pottery. Excavated to maximum depth of Context 3	Pottery, stone, charcoal	13 cm	2, 3
5	Coarse, loosely compacted brown sand with few roots. A series of large unworked *hirigaa* stones were recorded adjacent to the southern edge of the rectilinear feature. These overlaid a small deposit of *kaashiveli* which included glazed pottery	Pottery, loose *hirigaa* stones	17 cm	1, 3
6	Coarse, loosely compacted brown sand with white flecks and lots of roots. Excavated by hoe initially and trowel once *hirigaa* slabs and *veligaa* stones were uncovered. The slabs and stones were interspersed with pottery	Pottery, *hirigaa* slabs, and *veligaa* stones	14 cm	1,2
7	Coarse, loosely compacted yellowish brown sand with white flecks and lenses. Excavated by hoe. Although there were no roots, there were some small coral stone inclusions. Little pottery and no large *veligaa* or *hirigaa* stones	Pottery	37 cm	1,2
8	Coarse, loosely compacted brown sand with white flecks and few roots. Very little pottery compared with the rest of the trench. Excavated by trowel. Covers the area within Structure 1	Little pottery	14 cm	
9	Coarse, loosely compacted brown sand with white flecks and some roots. Very little pottery compared with the rest of the trench. Excavated by hoe. Covers the area to the east and south of Structure 1	Little pottery	15 cm	
10	Coarse, loosely compacted brown sand with few roots excavated by trowel. Same as Context 6 but with more *veligaa* stone (attributed to Context 15) so given a different context number. Numerous large potsherds including almost entire pots. These occurred throughout the context, with particular concentrations close to the northwest corner of Structure 1 and adjacent to this on the northern edge of the trench (Figure 4.17)	Pottery, charcoal Radiocarbon date: Beta 461521	30 cm	12, 16
11	Main concentration of *veligaa, hirigaa,* and *fotigaa* stones in the area north of Structure 1. These stones of varying size are surrounded by Context 12. The distribution of these stones is shown in (Figure 4.17). Spatial continuation of stones in Context 15	*Veligaa, hirigaa,* and *fotigaa* stones, shaped fragment of gravestone	30 cm	15
12	Coarse, loosely compacted brown sand with few roots excavated by trowel. The deposit surrounded the stones in Context 11. Deposit is the same as Context 10 but situated between the northern edge of Structure 1 and the northern edge of the trench (Figure 4.17). Many large pottery sherds including glazed; however, these are in more discrete concentrations than those in Context 10	Pottery, charcoal Radiocarbon date: Beta 461522	30 cm	10, 16
13	Fine, loosely compacted brown sand with grey flecks. Few roots. Excavated by trowel. Covers the area within Structure 1. Some small patches of *kaashiveli* underneath few medium-sized *veligaa* and *fotigaa* stones— possibly decayed stone	Pottery	16 cm	
14	Moderately coarse, loosely compacted brown sand with white flecks. Many large *veligaa, hirigaa* and *fotigaa* stones particularly in the southwest corner. Some limited pottery glazed. Broken tombstone identified in southwest corner adjacent to Slab A, interpreted as a footstone. Covers the area within Structure 1	Grave footstone maker (*hirigaa*), pottery	17 cm	
15	Main concentration of *veligaa, hirigaa,* and *fotigaa* stones in the area northwest of Structure 1. These stones of varying size are surrounded by Context 10. The distribution of these stones is shown in Figure (4.17). Spatial continuation of stones in Context 11	*Veligaa, hirigaa,* and *fotigaa* stones, inscribed fragment of gravestone	24 cm	11

	Description	Finds	Depth/Level	
16	Coarse, loosely compacted brown sand with white flecking. Whiter colour than Context 9, and contained more *veligaa*, *hirigaa*, and *fotigaa* stones Excavated by trowel. Covers the area to the east and south of the of Structure 1, with the densest concentration of pottery recovered from the east side of Structure 1	*Veligaa, hirigaa* and *fotigaa* stones, charcoal, pottery, glass Radiocarbon date: Beta 461523	24 cm	**10, 12**
17	Coarse, loosely compacted yellowish brown sand with white flecking including some small *fotigaa* stones overlaying *kaashiveli*. Excavated by trowel. Covers the area within Structure 1. Similar to Context 4 and 14 in terms of deposit—but was allocated a new context number. Human skull encountered in northwest corner of the deposit	Low frequency of pottery. Human skull	NW=27 cm NE=26 cm SW=22 cm SE=23 cm	
18	Human skeleton excavated with wooden pick and brushes. The legs and body were 20 cm below the top of the skull which was disarticulated and upside down. The legs extended beneath Structure 1. To fully expose the remains, the north and west edges of the structure were dismantled. Loose bone fragments were retained in separate bags, but the skeleton was left in situ and was reburied at the end of the excavation, together with loose fragments of bone	No finds were associated with the remains	Levels on top of the skeleton as follows: Skull—27 cm Feet—47 cm Pelvis—47 cm Elbow—42 cm Shoulder—42 cm	
19	Coarse, loosely compacted yellowish brown sand with white shell flecks situated beneath the fill and stones in Context 10 and 15. Excavated by trowel and hoe. Frequent pottery recovered, but smaller in size than material in Contexts 10 and 12. Some pedestals were left to support the standing tombstones	Pottery, shell	31 cm	**20**
20	Coarse, loosely compacted yellowish brown sand with white shell flecks situated beneath the stones and fill of Contexts 11 and 12. Excavated by trowel and hoe. Frequent pottery recovered, but smaller in size than material in Contexts 10 and 12. Infrequent shell. Some pedestals were left to support the standing tombstones	Pottery, shell	28 cm	**19**
21	Coarse, loosely compacted grey-brown sand associated with human remains (Context 18). Not likely a grave fill per se—no discernible difference to earlier contexts (Context 14 and 17). Poorly defined. Finds—which consist of non-diagnostic potsherds (Tables 5.1, 5.4)—may have come from section straightening rather than associated with the human remains themselves	Pottery	66 cm	
22	Coarse, loosely compact yellowish brown sand with infrequent pottery and shell. Covers the area to the north of Structure 1 excluding a small area adjacent to Standing Tombstone 27b (Context 24)	Pottery, cowries, charcoal	36 cm	**7, 26**
23	Coarse, loosely compact brown and yellowish brown sand. Excavated by trowel when the north and west sides of Structure 1 were dismantled. Contained limited pottery and quite a few roots	Pottery, *veligaa* stones, charcoal Radiocarbon date: Beta 461524	Not available	
24	Coarse, loosely compact yellowish brown sand with infrequent pot and few roots. Arbitrary area approx. 30 x 40 cm adjacent to Standing Tombstone 27b on the south side.	Pottery	36 cm	**22**
25	Small cache of 10–15 *Monetaria moneta* recovered from Context 24. No cut observed	Cowries	36 cm	**24**
26	Coarse, loosely compacted brown and yellowish brown sand excavated by trowel and hoe. Covers the area to the south and east of Structure 1. Returned some small *fotigaa* stones overlaying *kaashiveli*	*Fotigaa* stones	36 cm	**22, 7**
27	Standing *hirigaa* tombstones—individually classified. See text for further details	N/A	N/A	N/A
28	13 *veligaa* stones which form a 2.6 x 2 m rectilinear features. See text for further details	N/A	N/A	N/A

In the initial stage of excavation, a 3 x 3 m unit was set out, aligning with and bisecting the corner of one of the rectilinear features adjacent to STP 631 (as such, Trench 631 was not aligned to the cardinal points). It was hoped this would provide insight into different uses of domestic space by including areas interpreted as being 'inside', 'outside', and 'possibly outside'. These areas were excavated as separate contexts: Context 2 was the space delimited to the north and west by the stone blocks of the rectilinear feature, Context 1 (presumed to be 'outside') was the area to the west of this, while the northern part of the excavation unit was termed Context 3 ('possibly outside') (Figure 4.15).

As excavation progressed, we observed that while the stones forming the rectilinear structure were unworked sandstone (*veligaa*), two of them were made from coral stone (*hirigaa*) (referred to as Slab A and Slab B) also occurred (Figure 4.16). These were subsequently identified as part of a group of tombstones and were recorded collectively as Context 27 (Table 4.9).

While Contexts 1 and 2 contained a very low density of material culture (primarily small pieces of stone rubble with infrequent pottery), several other larger *hirigaa* and *veligaa* stones became visible during the excavation of Context 3. These were interspersed with moderate quantities of pottery. Once fully exposed, we noted that one of the *hirigaa* stones had a curved top reaching a shaped apex, suggestive of a tombstone. At this point, it became clear that rather than dealing with a domestic space as initially presumed, we may be faced with a mortuary space. Excavation was therefore suspended while advice was sought from the council and mosque representatives. Permission was granted to continue excavation with the objective of identifying and understanding the relationship between the rectilinear structure—henceforth Structure 1—and the *veligaa* and *hirigaa* stones identified in Context 3. To achieve this, the trench was

Figure 4.15 Trench 631. Initial excavation area—Context 1 ('Outside') is under excavation, Context 2 ('Inside') is to the left, and Context 3 ('possibly outside') is the area at the bottom of the image. Structural remains bounding Context 2 represent what later came to be defined as the northwest corner of 'Structure 1'.

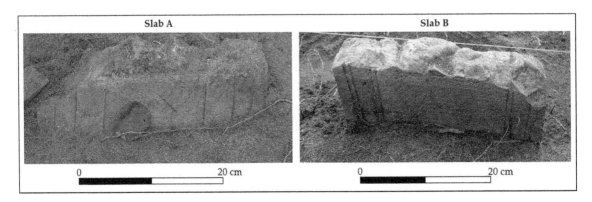

Figure 4.16 Trench 631: Incised hirigaa slabs A and B.

expanded by 1.5 m to the north, south, and east of the original footprint, resulting in a 6 x 4.5 m excavation area (Figure 4.17). This expansion encompassed Structure 1 and enlarged the area of Context 3.

Structure 1 was situated in the southeast corner of the trench (Figure 4.17). Prior to excavation, the tops of four of the *veligaa* stones and one of the *hirigaa* stones had been visible, protruding approximately 20 cm above the surface deposits. These became exposed during the excavation of Context 2 and when the trench was extended Context 2 was equally extended, working to the east and south limits of the new excavation area until the edges of the structure were identified.

It was determined that Structure 1 was 260 cm long and 200 cm wide and comprised a single course of 14 *veligaa* stones (Figure 4.17, Figure 4.18, Table 4.8). There were three stones on each of the short sides, running east–west, and

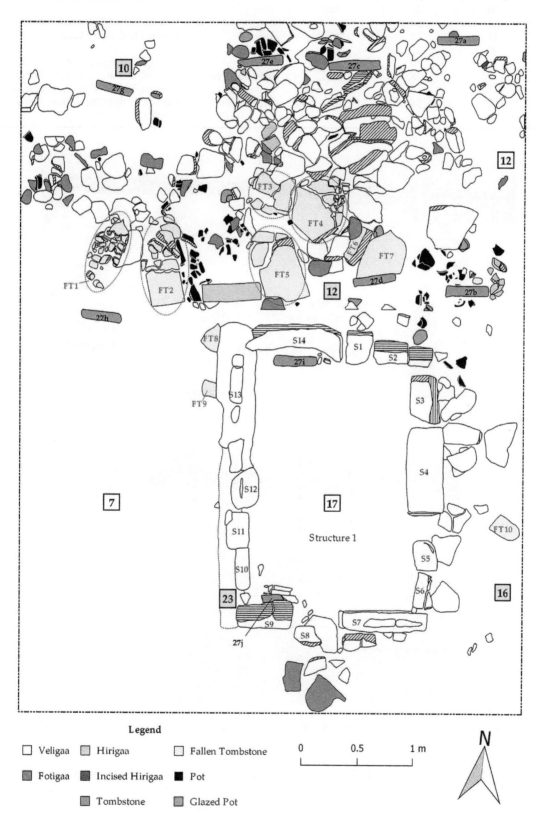

Figure 4.17 Trench 631, showing original trench boundaries.

Table 4.8 Dimensions of core *veligaa* stones in the rectilinear structure.

Stone #	Length (cm)	Width (cm)	Height (cm)	Alignment	Notes
1	30	27	12	Upright	
2	32	28	11	Upright	
3	28	39	12	Outward slope	
4	75	40	12	Outward slope	
5	26	28	9	Outward slope	
6	33	24	19		Top visible from the surface
7	70	42	16		
8	42	34	9		
9	52	32	15		Top visible from the surface
10	45	23	12		
11	4	30	10		Removed during excavation
12	63	28	14	Outward slope	Top visible from the surface. Broken in three places. Removed during excavation
13	102	36	13	Outward slope	Top visible from the surface. Removed during excavation

Figure 4.18 Trench 631. Structure 1 after exposure. North is to left of image.

Figure 4.19 Partially excavated Slab C to the south of the rectilinear structure showing damage. Note the similarity in decoration to Slab A (Figure 4.16).

four on the long sides, running north–south. These stones were allocated to Context 28. With the exception of Stone 10, which appeared to have been cut square, the stones were unworked. There was no evidence that they had been placed within a cut, and they instead rested on a coarse brown sandy deposit. There was no trace of the use of mortar.

Two *hirigaa* stones were recorded at either end of the western side of the structure. The northern one – Slab A – had been visible above the soil surface prior to excavation (Figure 4.16). During excavation, a third *hirigaa* slab (Slab C) was noted in the south western corner of Structure 1 (Figure 4.19). As it was fragmentary, it was not fully exposed.

Figure 4.20 Overall view of Trench 631, looking southwards.

Noteably, its top was decorated in a similar way to Slab A. These two were identified as gravestones, Slab A representing the headstone and Slab C the footstone.

Four deposits (Contexts 8, 13, 14, and 17) were excavated within Structure 1. They primarily comprised coarse, yellowish brown sand with white flecking and infrequent patches of *kaashiveli*, observed beneath smaller *fotigaa* stones. Very little material culture was recovered, when compared with the deposits outside Structure 1: only a few small potsherds were recovered.

Human remains were encountered during the excavation of Context 17. Permission was granted by local authorities to undertake cleaning, so long as the burial was not disturbed. This process revealed a skull and associated skeleton, which were labelled Context 18, with the deposit from the surrounding area given a separate number (Context 21). There was, however, no evidence of a grave cut, and Context 21 should be considered simply as an arbitrary division to ensure any materials associated with the burial were treated separately. The cranium and mandible were encountered initially, immediately adjacent to the base of Slab B (Figure 4.16), and post-cranial elements identified subsequently.

The cranium and mandible were disarticulated, damaged, and disturbed. The skull was face down, approximately 20 cm above the rest of the skeleton, positioned approximately over the arm, at a depth of 21 cm. The mandible was embedded in the deposit around the cranium overlying the eye sockets. Apart from the distal end of the right fibula and the right foot, which had been disturbed, the rest of the post-cranial remains were articulated and intact. The individual was lying on the right side, with knees slightly flexed. The position, oriented north–south and facing west, is consistent with an Islamic burial.

The distal ends of both radii, ulnae, tibiae, and fibulae and of the left femur extended beneath the stones forming the western edge of Structure 1. The proximal ends of the humeri as well as a number of the cervical vertebrae, including the atlas and axis, extended beneath Slab B and the stones forming the northern edge of the structure.

In order to expose the burial fully, Stones 11, 12, 13, and 14 (Table 4.8, Figure 4.17) were removed along with Slab A and a small trench was then opened within the larger area (Figure 4.20).

Fully exposed, the skeleton measured 147 cm from shoulder to toe and 133 cm from shoulder to distal tibia. The cranium had a diameter of 14 cm and the long bones were measured as follows:

Left femur: 44 cm
Left humerus: 29 cm
Right tibia: 35 cm
Right fibula: 33 cm
Right femur: 42 cm

The measurement on the left femur was considered the more accurate based on the level of exposure.

The excavation of Trench 631 also exposed a substantial area of debris and fallen stones. *Veligaa*, *hirigaa*, and *fotigaa* fragments extended approximately 3.5 m north of Structure 1, forming a roughly circular mound (Figure 4.21). This was allocated two context numbers based on spatial location—Context 15 on the west side of the trench and Context 11 on the east. The fill between the stones within each area was also allocated different contexts, mainly for consistency. Context 10 was the deposit surrounding the stones of Context 15, and Context 12 the fill of the stones of Context 11. It is probable that the stones in Contexts 15 and 11 were deposited at the same time; indeed, the compaction, colour, and composition of deposits surrounding these stones was very similar throughout the feature. The rate of deposition around the stones was unclear, however. The mound itself occupied a height of about 14–16 cm within the overall depth of 36 cm reached by the trench. The stones were interspersed with large fragments of glazed ceramics, some of which were near-intact vessels, and concentrations of fragmented sherds. Subsequent analysis showed that, despite our initial expectations, these originated from different vessels which for the most part did not reconstruct (see Chapter 6).

Ten fallen/broken tombstones were found during the excavations. These are described in Table 4.9. While most of these were observed in the mound, two (FT8 and 9) were found beneath Stone 13 in Structure 1, while FT10 was recovered to the east of Structure 1 (see Figure 4.17). One, FT5, was inscribed (Figure 4.22).

Figure 4.21 Drone image of T631. North is to the right. The mound of *veligaa, herigaa,* and *fotigaa* rubble is clearly visible, interspersed with fragments of pottery.

Table 4.9 In situ (Context 27) and fallen tombstones recovered during the excavations.

ID	Measurements (cm): length x width x thickness	Description/Condition	Decoration	Associated feature (if applicable)
FT1	N/A	26 articulated but broken *hirigaa* fragments showing a curved top culminating in apex, suggesting they may be female. Community members suggested this stone could have marked the grave of a child. This is supported by the fact that the refitted fragments create a small tombstone, comparable in size to FT8, 9 and 10	None visible; stone too fragmented	
FT2	N/A x 30	*Hirigaa* slab comprising 11 pieces, the largest of which is the base	None	
FT3	N/A	*Hirigaa* slab comprising five fragments of varying size	Evidence of two parallel raised linear features on either side of the stone—with a 3 cm-wide gap between them—similar to decoration on Slab A	
FT4	N/A	*Hirigaa* slab comprising 1 large section and 14 smaller fragments. The large section has a curved top culminating in apex that is suggestive of a female tombstone	None	

(Continued)

Table 4.9 (Continued)

ID	Measurements (cm): length x width x thickness	Description/Condition	Decoration	Associated feature (if applicable)
FT5	50 x 37	*Hirigaa* slab associated with four smaller fragments that articulate to form a curved top. Well preserved. Two lines of inscription at top of stone, written in Arabic script beginning with the 'I' (Abdulrazzaq Alrromehi, pers. comm.) (Figure 4.22, top left)	Two parallel ridges around the unbroken edges of the stone commencing 15 cm from the base with a 2 cm gap between them	
FT6	N/A x 30	Well preserved *hirigaa* fragment with curved top. Initially thought to be associated with FT8 below, but on removal, its shape and size was inconsistent with it	None	
FT7	N/A x 40	*Hirigaa* slab with curved top culminating in a distinctive apex suggestive of a female tombstone. Base of the slab is broken	1.5 cm-wide groove running 1 cm inset from and parallel to the unbroken edges of the tombstone	
FT8	23 x 11.5	Near-intact *hirigaa* slab with rounded top. Community members suggest this is the tombstone of a child, based on its size	None	
FT9	25 x 13	Almost intact *hirigaa* slab with a pointed top. Community members suggest this is the tombstone of a child, based on its size	None	
FT10	25 x 14	Almost intact *hirigaa* slab with rounded top. Community members suggest this is the tombstone of a child, based on its size	None	
27a	30 x 40 x 9	Headstone, inscribed at the top on the south face (Figure 4.22, right). The inscription is written in Persian calligraphy first evidenced in the fourteenth century CE. The script was commonly used in Persia, Transoxiana, Sind and India (Abdulrazzaq Alrromehi, pers. comm.) Both faces were pitted and cracked, likely due to root action	Undecorated	27b
27b	44 x 40 x 11	Foot stone, tilted to the east. Both faces were very pitted	Undecorated	27a
27c	45 x 45 (narrowing to 43) x 8 (narrowing to 7)	Headstone. Partially broken, the top is well weathered, as it was exposed prior to excavation	South face decorated with two 1 cm-wide incised grooves that run parallel to the eastern and western sides of the stone, approximately 1 cm from the edge. North face is undecorated	27d
27d	39 x 42 x 5	Foot stone, tilted to the east. Top of the stone weathered as it was exposed prior to excavation	North face decorated with a 1 cm-wide incised groove that runs parallel to the eastern side of the stone, approximately 1 cm from the edge. Possible evidence of similar groove on the western side now eroded. South face is undecorated	27c
27e	38 x 42 x 8	Headstone, inscribed on the south face (Figure 4.22 left bottom). The inscription is likely to be in Indian script; however, the text contains more than one font and language (Dr Abdulrazzaq Alrromehi, King Abdulaziz Foundation for Research and Archives (Darah) pers. comm. to ACC student). Poorly preserved with several areas broken or worn down. Much of the inscription is illegible	South face decorated with two 3 cm-wide incised grooves that run parallel to the eastern and western sides of the sone, approximately 1.5 cm from the edge.	None
27f		Partner tombstone for 27e is missing		

Table 4.9 (Continued)

ID	Measurements (cm): length x width x thickness	Description/Condition	Decoration	Associated feature (if applicable)
27g	33 x 35 (narrowing to 33) x 8	Headstone. Well preserved	North and south faces decorated with two pairs of parallel incisions on the eastern and western sides of the stone. The first pair are spaced about 1 cm apart, inset 2 cm from each edge. The second pair of incised lines are 2 cm in the first set, at the same spacing. The incisions run from the top of the stone to 10 cm above the Limit of Excavation	27h
27h	51 x 37 (narrowing to 33) x 7	Footstone—initially recorded as Slab B. Well preserved. Two circular holes were observed: one on the west side, 42 cm from the base, and the other just east of the central line, 30 cm from the base	North and south faces are both decorated with two pairs of parallel incisions on the eastern and western sides of the stone. The first pair are spaced about 1 cm apart, inset 2 cm from each edge. The second pair of incised lines are 2 cm within the first set, at the same spacing (Figure 4.16). The incisions run from the top of the stone to 17 cm from its base	27g
27i		Headstone—initially recorded as Slab A. Situated in the northwest corner of Structure 1	Well finished. South face of Slab A had two parallel raised linear features on either side of the stone—with a 3 cm-wide gap between them (Figure 4.16)	27j
27j		Footstone—initially recorded as Slab C, recovered from the southwest corner of Structure 1. Quite fragmented. Not removed during excavation	North face featured two parallel raised linear features on either side of the stone—with a 3 cm-wide gap between them (Figure 4.19)	27i

Figure 4.22 Inscribed tombstones (Left top: Fallen Tombstone FT5, Left bottom Tombstone 27e; and right, Tombstone 27a).

Once the *veligaa* rubble and associated deposits had been fully excavated and recorded, the fallen stones were systematically removed and the deposit beneath them excavated to level the trench. This was again allocated two different context numbers based on spatial location (Context 19 to the west and Context 20 to the east). The removal of the fallen debris clarified the layout of seven standing *herigaa* tombstones, which were recorded collectively as Context 27 and are described in Table 4.9. Of the nine tombstones, two were inscribed (Tombstones 27a and 27e, Figure 4.22) and seven were decorated (Tombstones 27c, d, e, g, h, i and j).

The design traditionally followed in the Maldives has been that gravestones are peaked at the top for men and rounded for women (Bell 2002 [1940], Forbes 1983). While the preservation of the standing stones in Trench 631 was generally very good, their tops had sustained damage to varying degrees. As such, it is not clear how they were shaped, making it difficult to determine whether they were male or female grave markers.

Discussion

Based on the presence of the tombstones and burial, Structure 1 is interpreted as a mausoleum, and this, combined with the presence of the standing tombstones to its north, suggests that at one point this area was part of a cemetery. Mausolea and built shrines which house the remains of important people have also been observed in other parts of the Maldives—for instance, the *ziyaarat* on Laamu Hithadhoo (LAM-HTD-3) or the *kuda ziyaarat on* Kaafu Himnafushi (KFA-HMF-1) were recorded as part of the Maldives Heritage Survey (Feener 2021b, 2021c).

The mausoleum and associated cemetery are particularly interesting given its proximity to the possible bathing tank identified to us by the community. Such bathing tanks have been associated with coral stone mosques and cemeteries in other parts of the Maldives, including Kan'dhuvalu mosque, on the island of Utheemu in Haa Alifu atoll (Jaufar 2019, p. 76), and Genmiskiyy on the island of Fuvahmulah, Gnaviyani atoll (MHS 2020), among others.

As stones from Structure 1 overlay parts of the skeletal remains, it appears probable that the individual was buried first, and the structure built subsequently. The location of the structure in relation to the burial is odd. During our excavations of another inhumation in Trench 5 at Utheemu island, Haa Alifu atoll (Haour et al. 2016, pp. 74, 76; and Chapter 9, this volume), which was also interpreted as an Islamic burial, it was noted that the remains, positioned on the right side facing west, were close to the western edge of the grave cut. Thus, it is possible to envisage how the western edge of Structure 1 might have partly overlain the skeleton, particularly considering subsequent damage. However, the northern edge of Structure 1 was positioned over a significant portion of the upper torso. There is also the question of the cranium, which was clearly disturbed, with significant damage to the cranium and mandible and disarticulation from the rest of the skeleton. Given that the cranium was encountered at a much shallower depth than post-cranial remains, it is possible that it was disturbed and subsequently redeposited adjacent to the headstone.

It is likely that the *veligaa* stones in Contexts 11 and 15 would have once formed part of Structure 1. As the main concentration of *veligaa* rubble lies solely to the north of the structure, we would argue that their removal was the result of deliberate action rather than natural collapse. This is supported by the presence of broken tombstones and pottery fragments within this mound.

The distribution of the standing tombstones suggests there may have been four other burials to the north of Structure 1, though there was no evidence of any grave cuts. Interestingly, there was no evidence for other burials to the west of Structure 1, and this area also returned very little by way of material culture.

Overview: stratigraphy and dating

Anne Haour

The seven trenches investigated: general comments

Six 2 x 2 or 2 x 1 m trenches were excavated at Kinolhas, totalling 20 m². Their stratigraphies were broadly similar: below the topsoil came a thin, archaeologically rich deposit followed by levels with decreasing numbers of finds, finally fading into a sandy sterile layer, easily recognised as fine yellowish white *dhonveli* sand. Typically, the archaeological layer presented as loose, coarse light brown sand with coralline inclusions, rich in pottery and bone and yielding occasional small finds such as glass or metal. So similar were the stratigraphic sequences in several pits that this archaeological layer ended up with the same denomination, Context 2, in all units. Layers were generally fairly horizontal and they blended gradually into one another, with few marked discontinuities. Stratigraphies were shallow, sterile being reached at 45–50 cm, a little deeper (55–70 cm) in Trenches 443 and 544. The greatest depth reached was 1 m, in the excavation of a pit, Context 4, in Trench 321, at which point groundwater was encountered.

Structural remains—or even definite in situ materials—were rare, being limited to ill-defined arrangements of stones. When these stones were either locally occurring but shaped, or identified by their geology as being not native to the Maldives, they were clearly indicative of human action. In addition, pits were identified in several trenches. Most significant here were a large tapering pit (Context 4) cut from the base of Context 2a in Trench 321 (Figure 4.3); Context 5 in Trench 325 (Figure 4.5); Contexts 4 and 11 in Trench 443; and Contexts 11 and 16 in Trench 449 (Figure 4.12). Finds from these features included charcoal, and four samples were dated, as outlined later. Unfortunately, artefacts were scarce in these features, and ceramic finds typically undiagnostic, rendering them of little use in untangling the chronology of the site.

Although the general character of the six units was comparable, several general points can be made. First, although the stratigraphies of Trenches 325, 449, and 544 followed the rule of a thin, archaeologically rich layer followed by a less distinct context fading into a sandy sterile layer, their interpretation is not straightforward. Trenches 325 and 544 were on a slope, while Trench 449 yielded unusual finds, including a buried cache consisting of cowries and a small glazed vessel containing six beads, as well as some inconsistent radiocarbon dates. Second, although small finds were generally homogeneous, Trench 321 was notable for yielding almost 1.2 kg of metal slag, otherwise extremely rare on the site. Another characteristic of Trench 321 was the presence of a large number of stones, at times in dense scatters, some of which must have been imported to the Maldives.

In addition to these six units, a much larger horizontal exposure was opened at the southwestern side of the area studied. Termed Trench 631, this was designed to investigate the architectural remains visible on the site surface but, in the event, the excavation exposed a remarkable funerary context. Although Trench 631 was not excavated to any great depth due to the specificity of the remains encountered, sterile was reached in most parts. The main event evidenced involved the construction and dismantlement of a sizeable sandstone structure, Structure 1. Material culture was particularly abundant within an area of stone rubble forming a mound covering approximately 2.5 x 2.5 m.

Dating

A total of 13 dates were run on charcoal samples from the excavations, coming from five trenches: four dates from Trench 631; three from Trench 449; and two from each of Trenches 321, 325, and 544 (Table 4.10). The samples were taken as much as possible from discrete, significant locations, either in pit fills or in association with artefacts or stone collapse. Dates were run by Beta Analytic, who performed the calibration at two sigma using INTCAL 13 (Talma and Vogel 1993, Reimer et al. 2013). This section will discuss the results, focusing primarily on stratigraphic questions but referring, where helpful, to the artefacts recovered—in particular, to the glazed ceramics, which offer some dating evidence and will be discussed in more detail in Chapter 6.

Both samples from Trench 321 issued from the pit, Context 4. They returned similar dates (600 ± 30 bp, Beta 461519, and 530 ± 30 bp, Beta 461520) which, after calibration, cover the long fourteenth century. The pit had been excavated from the base of Context 2a, a level which featured a great number of haphazardly arranged stones and ceramic fragments, including large rims, and it was probably dug at the time of this occupation, or very shortly beforehand. As such, the archaeological layer in Trench 321 can be attributed to the fourteenth century or early fifteenth century. Having said this, the datable glazed ceramics (N=33) from this layer span the fourteenth to seventeenth centuries (Chapter 6).

Two dates were run from Trench 325. One sample came from a pit, while the other was recovered during section cleaning at the level of Context 2, the archaeological layer. The calibration curve at this point allows a precise reading for the Context 2 date (510 ± 30 bp, Beta 461517), namely AD 1400–1440. The pit, Context 5, was cut from the base of Context 3, a layer that yielded some archaeological materials, into the sterile soil beneath. This date (550 ± 30bp, Beta 461518) calibrates to either a period comparable to that from Context 2, or to several decades earlier, in the first half of the fourteenth century. An early fifteenth date is most likely for both contexts even though, once again, some of the datable glazed ceramics run into the Late Ming period (Chapter 6).

Three dates were run from Trench 449, two from pits (Contexts 11 and 16) and the third from a shallow, charcoal-rich feature termed Context 9. These had been cut into (in the case of Contexts 9 and 11) or from (in the case of Context 16) Context 3, which itself underlay the main archaeological level. The three dates are, however, widely spread. While that from Context 9 (570 ± 30 bp, Beta 461527) falls in the long fourteenth century, in line with the Trench 321 and 325 samples, the other two are younger, though the vagaries of the calibration curve complicate the reading. The date issued from Context 16, the most convincing of the pit features (340 ± 30bp, Beta 461529), runs AD 1455–1645 after

Table 4.10 Radiocarbon dates from Kinolhas.

Sample #	Trench	Context	Notes	Lab #	Bp	±	Calibration at two sigma—AD
12	T 321	4	Associated with pottery at base of the pit, Context 4	461519	600	30	1295–1410
13	T 321	4	From within the fill of the pit, Context 4	461520	530	30	1325–1345, 1395–1435
3	T 325	2	Section cleaning	461517	510	30	1400–1440
11	T 325	5		461518	550	30	1315–1355, 1390–1430
36	T 449	16		461529	340	30	1455–1645
34	T 449	11		461528	290	30	1500–1600, 1615–1660
33	T 449	9		461527	570	30	1305–1365, 1385–1420
38	T 544	4		461526	620	30	1290–1405
22	T 544	2		461525	560	30	1310–1360, 1385–1425
44	T 631	23	From the soil surrounding the blocks in north and west of Structure 1	461524	600	30	1295–1410
16	T 631	10		461521	420	30	1435–1490, 1605–1610
18	T 631	12	Associated with stone collapse north of Structure 1	461522	150	30	1665–1785, 1795–1890, 1905-Present
27	T 631	16		461523	560	30	1310–1360, 1385–1425

calibration. The date from Context 11, a loose, possible pit feature sitting just above Context 16 (290 ± 30bp, Beta 461528), essentially runs AD 1500–1660.

Beyond this divergence in radiocarbon readings, spanning three and a half centuries, the stratigraphy of Trench 449 itself presents some problems. Due to evidence of animal burrowing and root action, it was suspected during excavation that past disturbance had occurred. This is also suggested by the finds, which include atypical artefacts resembling Indian Red Polished ware and one rouletted sherd (*sensu* Carswell 1975–1977 and Litster 2016), a fragment of modern glass (SF 43, see Chapter 8.2.2), and what appear to be in situ votive depositions consisting of two cowrie caches, one of which associated with a small ceramic vessel. The later dates may therefore represent contamination. The datable glazed ceramics recovered in Trench 449 do not resolve these issues, as they span the fourteenth to the seventeenth centuries, albeit with a bias towards the earlier periods; of the 30 sherds from this unit, 25 are younger than the sixteenth century, in contrast to T321 and T325.

Two samples were run from Trench 544 (620 ± 30 bp, Beta 461526, and 560 ± 30 bp, Beta 461525), returning dates in the long fourteenth century. Both were taken from contexts extremely rich in pottery and bone which, in combination with the pronounced sloping of the layers, suggests this unit sampled a midden. The fourteenth-century date for these deposits suggested by the two radiocarbon readings is in line with the results from other trenches. However, the very large assemblage of datable glazed sherds from Trench 544 nuances this picture. Of the 214 datable sherds, which as in other units run from the fourteenth to the seventeenth centuries, the largest part (N=94, 43.9%) date to the fifteenth century, with N=38 (17.8%) assigned to the fourteenth century and N=60 and N=22 (28% and 10.3%) to the sixteenth and seventeenth centuries respectively.

Four samples were run from Trench 631, the funerary complex. One, from Context 23 (600 ± 30 bp, Beta 461524), came from the soil in which sat the blocks making up the north and west sides of Structure 1, and it yielded a date in the long fourteenth century. The three other samples were recovered from contexts around Structure 1 which were in all respects similar, consisting of coarse, loosely compacted brown sand that carried fragments of sandstone and coral stone, as well as abundant and often large pottery fragments. However, the three charcoal samples returned divergent results. One date, issued from the mound to the north of Structure 1, is essentially modern, postdating the late seventeenth century (150 ± 30 bp, Beta 461522). Another, from a slightly different part of the same mound (420 ± 30 bp, Beta 461521), returned a date spanning AD 1435–1610. The third issued from debris to the east and south of Structure 1 (560 ± 30 bp, Beta 461523) and returned a date of the long fourteenth century.

While some of these datings from Trench 631 are in line with the evidence from other units, they also point to more recent disruption. The variations suggest extensive reworking of this part of the site, consistent with the destruction of what seems to have been a funerary structure, and the building up of a large mound of stone debris, broken tombstones, and pottery. Charcoal from a later date may have migrated into the deposits, particularly as a product of land clearance, which could have entailed adding stones to the existing rubble mound. The datable pottery fragments (N=61) are, for the most part, once again in the fourteenth- to seventeenth- century range (with a majority, N=35, 57.4%, in the fifteenth century) but a ninth/tenth century Islamic bowl was also recovered (Chapter 6). If not representative of a violent episode, this mound of debris is, at the very least, indicative of heavy-handed reworking of the material remains. The mound was likely created at a time when the burial ground had been either forgotten or was no longer respected, but prior to the span of present memory given that the presence of a burial ground in this location appeared unknown to the community.

Considering the 13 radiocarbon dates globally, it is significant that nine of them, coming from all five trenches sampled, fall sometime between AD 1290 and 1440. They suggest that the main occupation of this part of Kinolhas—both habitation and funerary components—can be placed in the fourteenth and early fifteenth centuries. A similar date can be suggested for the construction of Structure 1 in Trench 631. Its date of destruction is not clear from the three samples recovered from the mound of rubble, but a period later than the early fifteenth century and prior to the eighteenth seems credible.

The occupation at this western end of the island of Kinolhas, however, must be considered within a much longer-term habitation of the island. The earlier end of the spectrum is represented by standing remains associated by the local community with Buddhist practice (Chapter 3) and some of the artefactual material from Trenches 449 and 631. Equally, a later occupation is suggested by the fact that Trenches 449 and 631 each yielded two dates that may be more recent—although calibration poses some issues and all but one of these later dates may in fact fall in a period that is only slightly after the span indicated by the other dates. Beyond this, small amounts of Late Ming blue and white porcelain produced between the 1570s and the 1620s ('CBW2-3' pottery; Chapter 6, this volume) made their way into most of the trenches excavated. Agricultural and horticultural activities through the centuries have likely caused some movement of artefacts and disturbance of layers—a situation also described at the site of Nilandhoo, for example (Litster 2016). This said, at Kinolhas the archaeological deposits were, for the most part, sealed beneath a topsoil very different in nature and containing few artefacts, thus arguing for the deposits' integrity. The thinness of the archaeological layer seems to be a significant factor in understanding the stratigraphy; it may suggest that the settlement shifted across different parts of the island against a background of longer-term occupation.

Note

1 A preliminary field report was published in Haour et al. (2017).

5 The earthenware pottery

Anne Haour and Shiura Jaufar

Introduction

This chapter deals with the earthenware, unglazed pottery recovered during excavations at Kinolhas, presenting the assemblage and relating it to other regional evidence. A few points should be highlighted at the outset to situate the approach taken. First is the fact that prior to the present work very little research had been carried out on archaeological ceramics in the Maldives. Earlier studies by John Carswell, Egil Mikkelsen, and Mirani Litster offered some guidance, but none considered a stratified, large assemblage of the sort recovered at Kinolhas, and it therefore proved necessary to consult broader works dealing with ceramic assemblages from the wider western Indian Ocean. The assemblages from Arikamedu (Tamil Nadu, southern India, second century BC to medieval—Wheeler et al. 1946, Begley 1996, 2004), Vijayanagara (southern India, fourteenth to seventeenth centuries AD—Sinopoli 1993), Sharma (Yemen, late tenth/twelfth century—Rougeulle et al. 2015), Tissamaharama (Sri Lanka, mid-first millennium BC-late first millennium AD—Schenk 2015), Mantai (Sri Lanka, first millennium AD—Graham 2013), and Sehwān Šarīf (Pakistan, eighth to eighteenth centuries AD—Collinet 2010) in particular proved valuable. The fact that the low-fired earthenware of the type which formed the bulk of the Kinolhas assemblage remains a poorly understood subgroup of western Indian Ocean ceramics presented an obstacle. Prominence has often been given to glazed wares, considered to be diagnostic imports, and earthenware dismissed as local production. However, the Maldives offer an unusual case study in ceramics analysis, since the archipelago lacks clay. As such, all pottery recovered, including the humble earthenwares, are to be considered imports.

This last point presents both opportunities and challenges. Historically, trade in pottery containers has been documented over a range of periods. The Cairo *geniza* documents speak of vessels known as *mazza*, used to carry copper, gum, kohl, and vitriol (Collinet 2010, Lambourn 2018a). In the sixteenth and early seventeenth centuries, the Portuguese used ceramic vessels to export ghee from Sind (southeast Pakistan) to Hormuz, and Portuguese apothecary Tomé Pires (ca. 1512–15) stated that 'coarse pottery', 'like that from Seville', was shipped from Gujarat to eastern Africa (Horton 2004, p. 67, Collinet 2010, p. 9). Ibn Battuta mentions that the people of the Maldives bought cooking pots from visiting boats against five or six chickens and François Pyrard de Laval stated that meals in the Maldives were taken on dishes in the local style imported from Cambay or from China (Carswell 1975–1977, pp. 140, 160).

The Indian subcontinent occupies a major position in debates on the circulation of ceramics within the western Indian Ocean. For instance, on the East African coast, Chittick (1984, p. 101, Plates 54, 55) suggested with 'some confidence' an Indian origin for some of the pottery recovered at Manda (Kenya), which consisted almost entirely of water-pots (or 'chatties'). This suggestion was based on the fact that this material, although unglazed, was distinct from locally produced pottery in both form and fabric, and that it resembled modern vessels made in India. However, these potentially Indian items generated less archaeological interest than did other imports, such as those of Chinese origin (Hawkes and Wynne-Jones 2015). This situation is not unique to the East African coast; coarser, 'household' wares such as these have generally attracted less attention than glazed imports. Moreover, the context of medieval pottery production in India remains unclear. In one of the first systematic studies of a medieval assemblage in India, from the site of Vijayanagara, Sinopoli (1993) remarked on the general lack of interest in ceramics, due partly to the wide range of other types of evidence available, such as literary texts, inscriptions, or artworks. Echoing this sentiment, Collinet (2010) noted that architectural studies have predominated, and that the material—especially the ceramic material—of Islamic-period sites remained largely unpublished; the question of specific area of origin (with possible sources in Sind, Gujarat, Karnataka, or Kerala) is hardly mentioned, proportions within assemblages rarely considered, and chrono-typological studies not systematically carried out.

In fact, archaeological knowledge of the early medieval period of India generally remains hazy; much of the available evidence comes from sites with earlier foundations (see Hawkes 2014 for a critical discussion). Chakravarti (2015, p. 27) observed that only two phases of the protracted past of India's involvement in the Indian Ocean maritime trade have received sustained scrutiny from historians: the Roman trade of the first few centuries AD, and the period between AD 1500 and 1800 which witnessed the advent of European adventurers and trading companies. The first half of the second millennium—critically relevant to the data from Kinolhas—has received marginal attention. Given that India represents a potential source for the ceramics recovered in the Maldives, this is an important caveat.

Having considered all of this, the priority in the analysis of the Kinolhas material was to create a ceramics description that was systematic and as objective as possible, recording sherds individually by attribute rather than defining wares. Also, rather than describing a decoration purely by its visual appearance, a concerted effort was made to understand the tools used, thus giving an insight into the potters' gestures.

DOI: 10.4324/9781003166221-5

This chapter begins with a brief overview of previous work on archaeological ceramic assemblages from the Maldives, then characterises the materials recovered at Kinolhas. It presents the various decorative types and main forms encountered to sketch out the first comprehensive typology of medieval, Islamic ceramics on the archipelago. The chapter concludes by identifying areas for future research.

Previous work on Maldivian ceramics

During a month-long visit in 1974, John Carswell and colleagues collected several hundred potsherds in Male'. These were picked up in the streets, recovered by sifting the topsoil of a cemetery and a mosque, and found during excavation of two trial trenches inside and outside the reported line of the walls of the old Sultan's palace. General findings are detailed in Chapter 2 of this volume. In September 2015, the present authors made a visit to the Ashmolean Museum in Oxford to examine the Carswell archive.[1] A great deal of this material has been published, in illustrated detail, by Carswell (1975–1977), so close to 800 sherds are recorded in the literature,[2] but the opportunity to handle the sherds and to study the associated photographic folder and comments was invaluable. The great majority of the collection consists of glazed wares, and they mainly issue from surface contexts, but a small group excavated in Sultan's Park offered important insights. The lowest layer of Trench A yielded 12 sherds, of which 8 were earthenware apparently deriving from vessels with ribbed forms, often sharply carinated, and with overhanging rims (Carswell 1975–1977, p. 158, Plate 65a and Figure 13).[3]

A significant later study of archaeological ceramics was carried out by Mikkelsen (1991, pp. 185–186, 192–193) on an assemblage issued from excavations by Thor Heyerdahl's team at 'Structure IV' at the site of Nilandhoo (Skjølsvold 1991, Figure 4; see Chapter 2, this volume, for discussion). The trench had sampled a refuse area, which provided the first stratigraphically documented artefact sequence in the Maldives. This assemblage consisted of 1063 sherds, comprising 118 decorated sherds (including 17 glazed items) and 945 undecorated sherds (Mikkelsen 1991, Tables IV and V). Although the majority of the structural remains from Nilandhoo relate to a Buddhist complex, the stratigraphy is confused and some of the Structure IV material appears to postdate the supposed introduction of Islam in the twelfth century. Most of the assemblage consists of thin-walled brown pottery, most commonly decorated with lines, while 'waffle pattern' and 'net pattern' also occur (Mikkelsen 1991, p. 200, Table IV). The publication includes several plates of line drawings (Mikkelsen 1991, Figures 6–8), but the illustrations are not cross-referenced with the decoration names employed in the tables, so that descriptors such as 'lines' or 'net pattern' remain ill-defined. However, judging by the drawings, the material from Nilandhoo manifests clear parallels to the finds from Kinolhas, notably in terms of linear and checkerboard paddle impressions. Mikkelsen (1991, pp. 200–201) assigns this pottery to a likely origin in India and Sri Lanka and suggests the type was used over a long period of time and is therefore of little help in suggesting chronology.

In recent years, the two most important contributions to Maldivian ceramic analysis have arisen from doctoral research.

Litster (2016) provides an analysis of pottery assemblages issued from four previously excavated sites across the Maldives, investigated in 1983–1984 by a team led by Skjølsvold and Heyerdahl, and in 1996–1998 in work directed by Mikkelsen's team.[4] The sites concerned are Kuruhinna Tharaagadu (Kaashidhoo island), Nilandhoo Foamathi (on Nilandhoo island), Bodu Havitta (on Gan island in Gaafu Dhaalu atoll), and Dhadimagi Havitta (on Fuvahmulah).[5] The ceramic corpus studied consists of 1669 sherds. Some of the assemblages are very small; for example, owing to time constraints and access restrictions, only 18 sherds from Kaashidhoo were studied, amounting to 740 grams from an estimated total of 30 kilos of ceramics recovered. In fact, the majority of the material examined—71%—issued from the excavations at Structure IV at Nilandhoo, which, as discussed above, offered the first stratigraphically documented artefact sequence in the Maldives (Mikkelsen 1991). With 1180 sherds, the collection studied by Litster is slightly larger than Mikkelsen's reported 1063, as it includes some material beyond that of Structure IV itself (Litster 2016, Table 6.7, 151).

Across the various sites examined, Litster (2016, Table 6.1) identifies four ware families, based on presumed origin and the attributes set out by Kennet (2004) and Saunders (2013) for western Indian Ocean assemblages. One of these four families is 'Unknown', and the remaining three are divided into types: Longquan celadon in the 'Far Eastern' family; Paddle Impressed, Northern Black Polished, and Indian Red Polished in the 'South Asian' family; and finally, Sasanian-Islamic from the Persian Gulf and Red Sea in the 'Western Asian' family (Litster 2016, Table 6.2). The present chapter is concerned largely with items in the 'South Asian' group; a comment on the materials that would fall into 'Far Eastern' and 'Western Asian' categories is provided in Chapter 6.

As mentioned previously, most of the material derived from the site of Nilandhoo. There, over 98% of items (N=1164) belonged to the South Asian family (Litster 2016, Table 6.12). These included 'fine wares' such as Northern Black Polished and Indian Red Polished wares, as well as paddle-impressed sherds and other decorated sherds not identified to type (Litster 2016, p. 156). Numbers of sherds are not given, but the text suggests that only six examples of the two 'fine' wares were identified, implying that the vast majority fell within the 'paddle impressed' and 'unidentified' groups. The rim shapes indicate that most take the form of *handi*—a general name used in parts of India to designate vessels used for containing and cooking foodstuffs. Their storage and cooking role is further supported by the vessels' high porosity and sooting on the exterior, and their prevalence in the assemblage suggests a high turnover. Only two decoration styles were identified, present throughout contexts: the first cord-impressed, the second evoking the paddle-impressed wares found in southern India and reported over a considerable time, from the first millennium AD through to the present day (Litster 2016, p. 156). Absolute numbers of these two decorations are not given.

The three other sites considered by Litster also point to the importance of earthenware. Thirty-eight undecorated earthenware sherds were recovered from Bodu Havitta on Gan island (out of a total of 40), and 420 (out of 423) sherds belonging overwhelmingly to undecorated *handis* are reported from Dhadimagi Havitta on Fuvahmulah island (Litster 2016, Tables 6.15, 6.17). Lastly, five sherds of paddle-impressed ware, all from surface collection, were identified at the site of Kaashidhoo, from a total of 18 studied across different contexts.

In summary, South Asian ceramics were recovered from all four sites investigated. These were typically of the *handi* type, with soot evident on a large proportion of the vessels, confirming their use for cooking. Other, less common South Asian material included Northern Black Polished and Indian Red Polished wares made of fine, well-levigated clay and a broader range of forms, including sprinklers and lamps (Litster 2016, p. 161, Figure 6.6). However, Litster's results are difficult to use because few quantitative data and illustrations are provided within the text.

The doctoral research by one of the present authors (SJ) also considered ceramic material from a range of locations across the Maldives, excavated in 2016 by a team on which she herself was present and with a focus on the Islamic period. A total of 2132 sherds from three sites (Utheemu, Male', and Veyvah) were studied, almost all from stratigraphically secure layers. Seven radiocarbon dates underpin the chronology of the three sites, falling between the late twelfth and the seventeenth centuries (see Chapter 9, this volume). Most of the ceramics (90.5%) consisted of earthenware sherds, of which approximately half were decorated. Impressed sherds were the most common form of decoration, falling into five types, of which linear paddled impressions were the most frequent (Jaufar 2019, Table 24 and Figure 81). 'Waffle'—a term adopted from Mikkelsen (1991)—and 'linear paddle' decorations were defined at this point (Jaufar 2019, pp. 179–180), and these terms are used with the same meaning in the present chapter. Incised and slipped sherds were also common. Sixteen types of rim were identified, mainly suggesting large storage/cooking vessels. The earthenware assemblage also included fragments of a spouted vessel and of a shallow dish or pot lid, and carinated body sherds. Some of the decoration types, particularly the paddle-impressed decorations and cable applications, were compared to material from Arikamedu and Sharma (Jaufar 2019, pp. 182–194, citing Begley 1996, 2004, Selvakumar 2011, Rougeulle et al. 2015).

In summary, prior to the work presented in this chapter, four studies over the past 45 years had offered descriptions of some 4600 archaeological sherds from locations in the Maldives. These varied in scope and detail; the assemblages studied were generally relatively small and concerned surface, or poorly dated, materials. Moreover, analyses often focused on glazed wares (Carswell 1975–1977) and, except for the material from Nilandhoo considered by Mikkelsen (1991) and then Litster (2016), mainly dealt with materials connected to Buddhist structures. As such, comparative materials for the Kinolhas assemblage were rather limited. The following section details the methodology used to study the collection of over 7700 sherds recovered from excavations and shovel test pits at the site.

The Kinolhas assemblage: methodology and overview

Most of the ceramic material recovered at Kinolhas was fragmentary. The need for a thorough description of the materials from a previously un-researched region and time period had to be balanced against what was achievable within the time available. A major practical consideration here was the stringent baggage allowance operated by Maldivian airlines, and for this reason, much of the material was analysed on site.

The initial stage was designed to be systematic and straightforward: any sherd smaller than 3 cm square was counted and discarded. This offered an objective means to reduce the amount of material for study, while incurring minimal loss of information since analysis of variables such as decoration can be very unreliable on smaller items. The total material discarded comprised 3495 sherds, 241 of which were from the shovel test pits (STPs) and the remainder from the various excavation units; there, Trenches 544 and 631 accounted for over 70% of the material, a dominance in line with subsequent analyses (Table 5.1). This discarded material will not be discussed further.

All retained material was then washed, and diagnostics (rims, bases, etc.) and body sherds treated separately. Body sherds that were undecorated or belonged to decoration types that could be reliably recognised were recorded on site and

Table 5.1 Pottery from Kinolhas: undersize sherds discarded.

Trench and context	No. of sherds	
T321 (Unspecified context)	1	
T321 (Context 1)	23	
T321 (Context 2)	286	
T321 (Context 4)	4	
Total trench 321		**314**
T325 (Unspecified context)	9	
T325 (Context 1)	33	
T325 (Context 2)	214	
T325 (Context 3)	21	
T325 (Context 4)	3	
T325 (Context 6)	1	
Total trench 325		**281**

(Continued)

Table 5.1 (Continued)

Trench and context	No. of sherds	
T360 (Context 1)	4	
T360 (Context 2)	45	
T360 (Context 3)	11	
T360 (Context 4)	4	
Total trench 360		**64**
T443 (Context 2)	78	
T443 (Context 4)	4	
T443 (Context 5)	2	
T443 (Context 12)	6	
T443 (Context 14)	1	
Total trench 443		**91**
T449 (Context 1)	4	
T449 (Context 2)	169	
T449 (Context 3)	32	
T449 (Context 9)	1	
T449 (Context 16)	4	
Total trench 449		**210**
T544 (Context 1)	275	
T544 (Context 2)	727	
T544 (Context 3)	186	
T544 (Context 4)	100	
Total trench 544		**1288**
T631 (Context 2)	1	
T631 (Context 3)	15	
T631 (Context 4)	35	
T631 (Context 5)	16	
T631 (Context 6)	12	
T631 (Context 7)	5	
T631 (Context 10)	203	
T631 (Context 12)	174	
T631 (Context 13)	9	
T631 (Context 14)	42	
T631 (Context 16)	31	
T631 (Context 19)	16	
T631 (Context 20)	281	
T631 (Context 21)	14	
T631 (Context 22)	80	
T631 (Context 23)	6	
T631 (Context 26)	56	
Total trench 631		**996**
TOTAL	**3254**	
Shovel test pits		
321	15	
325	41	
360	34	
443	8	
449	28	
544	109	
631	6	
TOTAL	**241**	
Grand total test pits and shovel test pits		3495

then reburied. Less straightforward items were exported to the University of East Anglia (UEA) on a temporary export permit. Diagnostic items were exported to UEA and subjected to detailed analysis, carried out by the present authors and by pottery analyst and UEA doctoral research student Susan Anderson.

All sherds were analysed individually attribute by attribute. Attributes recorded include sherd type (body, rim, base), surface treatment, and size. In the case of rims, shape, presence of burnish, slip, and, where possible, rim angle and vessel diameter were recorded. In total, 4229 sherds were studied, issued from shovel test pits and seven trenches. Of these, 3770 were body sherds, of which 1067 (28.3%) were decorated. The remaining 459 were diagnostic sherds (rims, spouts and bases), of which 264 (57.52%) were decorated. Occurrences of slip are classed as a decoration for the purposes of the present analysis.

Table 5.2 presents the distribution of material across units and shows that the largest assemblages were recovered from Trenches 544 and 631. They yielded a similar number of sherds in absolute terms (about 1500 items), but T544 represented a much smaller excavated volume and, as such, its sherd density neared 600 sherds per cubic metre—in fact, the figure is nearly 1060 sherds/m^3 if all the small, discarded material (Table 5.1) is included.

Table 5.2 Kinolhas: distribution of material across units.

Unit	L x W (m)	Depth (m)	Total volume excavated (m³)	N sherds		Thus sherd density
				Body	Diagnostic	
T544	2 x 2	0.70	2.8	1468	211	599.64
T631	6 x 4.5	0.36	9.72	1504	165	171.71
T321	2 x 2	0.40	1.6	221	20	150.63
T325	2 x 2	0.60	2.4	210	26	98.33
T449	2 x 1	0.50	1.0	92	5	97.00
T360	2 x 1	0.60	1.2	72	13	70.83
T443	2 x 2	0.55	2.2	94	8	46.36
				3661	**448**	
Shovel test pits				**109**	**11**	
GRAND TOTAL				**3770**	**459**	

The volume of pottery recovered within units is linked directly to the existence of the archaeological layer. In Trenches 321, 325, 360, 443, and 449, most pottery was recovered from Context 2, with relatively few items occurring from layers above or below. The exception to this rule was Trench 544 in which, although most material occurred in Context 2, a significant amount was recovered from Context 1, and finds continued below Context 2. Trench 631 offers a slightly different picture. The fill of a large mound of rubble (Contexts 10, 12; N=651 sherds) and the deposit on which this rested (Contexts 19, 20 and 22, N=556 sherds) yielded the greatest number.

The Kinolhas assemblage: decorations

Box 5.1 introduces the decorations encountered in the Kinolhas assemblage and the codes used to record them; this is intended to serve as a guide to reading Tables 5.3 and 5.4, which present the results of the analysis of body and rim sherds respectively. The main categories of decorations are impressed, incised/stabbed, and channels, and other types include painted, slipped, and appliquéd.

Box 5.1   Codes used for the decorations occurring in Kinolhas assemblage.

UND. Undecorated
INDIS. Indistinct

1) Impression

Carved paddle impression

WAF. Waffle—series of square/rectangular impressions in a checkerboard pattern; see Figure 5.1a
LP. Linear paddle—series of linear/near linear impressions (often overlapping)
LLP. Large linear paddle; see Figure 5.1b

Other impressions

CP1. Linear, ladder-like impressions, crisp, sometimes overlapping
CP2. Globular convex nodules separated by raised lines
CP3. Crisp, neat impressions in herringbone pattern
CP4. Sinuous or straight lines with sharply demarcated triangular shapes; see Figure 5.2, top row
CP5. Crisp ladder-like impressions, occasionally associated with globular convex nodules
CP6. Miscellaneous impressions consisting of a combination of CP decorations: different angled lines, arched lines, circular and sun-shaped globular nodules; see Figure 5.2, bottom row
UNK. Unknown impressed decoration

2) Incised and stabbed decor

Incised lines. With stylus or other similar single pointed tool; cross-section is a V; narrow. Subtypes:

INC. One incised line
MPI. Multiple parallel incised lines

MI. Multiple incisions

WCI. Wavy continuous incised line

ZCI. Triangular continuous incised line

LFI. Multiple parallel incisions, floral incisions, and wavy continuous incisions

M I-H. Miscellaneous multiple incisions (including parallel diagonal lines, creating diagonal squares) and multiple rows/cluster of shallow circular indentations within the squares and incised lines

MPI-W. Multiple parallel incisions (both horizontal and vertical)

ID int. Interior decorated—deeply incised lines on interior of sherds; some overlapping; crisp; rather haphazard

Stabbed and stamped. Single impression with end of single tool. Subtypes:

S1-L. Line of impressions of point of a round-ended tool, creating circular holes or depressions

S3. Impression of flat-sectioned tool, creating a rectangular indent

S3-V. Series of impressions of a flat-sectioned tool, in a line

S3-D. As above, but impressions arranged diagonally, in a line

S4. Impression of a tool creating impressions that are oval with pointed extremities

S4-L. Line of impressions of a tool creating impressions that are oval with pointed extremities—a horizontal alignment

S4-V. As above, but flipped 90 degrees, resulting in a vertical alignment

S5. Impression of point, creating triangular holes or depressions

S5-L. Line of impressions triangular holes or depressions

S6. Stamped circles

S6-L. Row of stamped circles

S7-L. Short parallel lines, likely made up of single impressions of a round-ended tool set close together

CW. Chattered ware (aka 'rouletted' ware). Concentric circles consisting of rows of small impressed lines

FING. Single impression of a fingernail, creating a crescent shape

3) Channels

Ch. Channel (cross-section is a U; relatively wide)—likely made with a finger or similar. Margins are raised due to displacement of clay

MC. Multiple channels

SQC. Relatively wide channel with a rectangular cross-section

Variant: SQCB—as SQC but includes raised middle band(s)

4) Paint

Painted decoration. RP, red paint; BP. brown paint

5) Slip

Refers to an overall colouration. RS. Red slip, BS. Brown slip

6) Appliqué

RB. Raised band—added linear strip of clay

Cab. Cable—an added strip of clay impressed with small impressions, perhaps finger marks

PA-1. Nubbins—rounded

PA-2. Nubbins—flattened

7) Notable fabric

FO. Fine orange

FG. Fine grey

8) Form attribute

CAR. Carinated

SIP. Brown slipped (ext), MPI and deeply pinched from the interior, leaving raised finger marks protruding from exterior

Table 5.3 Kinolhas assemblage: body sherds.

Trench 321

Cont.	#	D1	D2	D3	D4	D5	Remarks
321:1	1	CAR					
321:1	2	LP					
321:1	1	RS					
321:1	20	UND					
321:1	1	CP4					See Figure 5.2
321:1	1	CP5					
321:2	1	CP5					
321:2	1	UNK					
321:2	1	M I-H					Very fine light creamy fabric. See Figure 5.4
321:2	3	CP4					See Figure 5.2
321:2	6	CAR					
321:2	1	CAR	RB				
321:2	1	CH					
321:2	4	CP1					
321:2	1	CP3					
321:2	2	INDIS					
321:2	6	LP					
321:2	1	MI	RB	WAF	RB		
321:2	4	MPI					
321:2	4	RB					
321:2	1	RB	CH	CH	RB	RP	Red-brown paint lower
321:2	1	RB	SQC	RB	MI		
321:2	1	RB	WCI				
321:2	5	RS					
321:2	1	SQCB	S1-L				
321:2	137	UND					
321:2	8	WAF					
321:4	3	UND					
321:4	2	LP					
TOTAL	**221**						

Trench 325

Cont.	#	D1	D2	D3	D4	D5	Remarks
325:1	1	CAR					Greyish black
325:1	1	LP					
325:1	1	CP3					
325:1	1	CP4					
325:1	1	RS					
325:1	17	UND					
325:2	1	S6-L					
325:2	1	S6	S6	S6			See Figure 5.5
325:2	6	CAR					
325:2	1	CH	RB				
325:2	4	INDIS					
325:2	6	LP					
325:2	5	CP4					
325:2	1	RP	UND				One red line paint inside
325:2	2	RB					
325:2	1	CP3					
325:2	7	RS					
325:2	1	LP	S6	S6			See Figure 5.5
325:2	1	MI	RB	S3-D	MI	UND	
325:2	1	MI					
325:2	122	UND					
325:2	2	WAF					See Figure 5.1a
325:3	1	LP					
325:3	1	MPI					
325:3	1	CP1					
325:3	4	CP3					
325:3	12	UND					
325:3	3	WAF					

(Continued)

Table 5.3 (Continued)

Trench 325

Cont.	#	D1	D2	D3	D4	D5	Remarks
325:4	1	INDIS					
325:4	2	UND					
325:5	1	MI					Fine grey fabric
TOTAL	**210**						

Trench 360

Cont.	#	D1	D2	D3	D4	D5	D6	D7	D8	Remarks
360	1	S3-V	RB	S3-V	CAR					
360:1	1	MPI								
360:1	3	UND								
360:1	1	LFI								Fine buff fabric. See Figure 5.4
360:2	1	LFI								Fine buff fabric. See Figure 5.4
360:2	3	MPI-W								V fine light creamy fabric. See Figure 5.4
360:2	3	UND								V fine light creamy fabric. Refits MPI-W in line above. See Figure 5.4
360:2	1	CAR	LP							
360:2	1	CH								
360:2	1	CH	RB							
360:2	1	CP4								
360:2	3	INDIS								
360:2	1	MPI								
360:2	1	MPI	RS							
360:2	1	WAF								
360:2	1	WAF								
360:2	1	RB								Fine grey fabric
360:2	1	RS	UND	MI						V fine light brown fabric
360:2	1	UND								Fine grey fabric
360:2	1	UND	MI	LP						
360:2	1	UND	CAR	RB	UND	RB	CH	RB	RB	
360:2	32	UND								
360:2	1	WAF								
360:3	1	LP								
360:3	3	UND								
360:4	2	MPI								
360:4	4	UND								
TOTAL	**72**									

Trench 443

Cont.	#	D1	D2	D3	Remarks
443:2	1	WAF			
443:2	1	MC			
443:2	1	SQCB			
443:2	1	LP	CAR	UND	
443:2	1	SQC	MI		
443:2	1	MI	CAR		
443:2	4	CAR			
443:2	1	CH			
443:2	3	INDIS			
443:2	8	LP			
443:2	2	MPI			
443:2	2	RS			
443:2	66	UND			
443:2	1	CP6			See Figures 5.2, 5.3
443:4	1	UND			
TOTAL	**94**				

(Continued)

Table 5.3 (Continued)

Trench 449

Cont.	#	D1	D2	D3	Remarks
449	5	UND			
449:1	1	RB			
449:1	2	UND			
449:2	1	CAR			
449:2	1	CH			
449:2	1	CH	RB		
449:2	3	INDIS			
449:2	2	MC			
449:2	2	LP			
449:2	2	CP5			
449:2	1	UND			
449:2	3	WAF			
449:2	1	LP	MI		Burnish
449:2	7	LLP			
449:2	2	MPI	RB		
449:2	1	S1-L	S6		See Figure 5.5
449:2	1	MPI	RS		
449:2	4	RB			
449:2	3	RS			
449:2	32	UND			
449:2	3	WAF			
449:2	1	S6-L			
449:3	1	CAR			
449:3	1	LP			
449:3	1	LLP			
449:3	1	UNK			
449:3	5	UND			
449:9	1	UND			
449:16	3	MPI			Three refitting sherds. V fine orange ware. Not treated as a diagnostic as no rim lip, but dish, diam. 14 cm
TOTAL	**92**				

Trench 544

Cont.	#	D1	D2	D3	D4	D5	D6	D7	D8	D9	D10	D11	D12	Remarks
544:1	8	CAR												
544:1	1	CAR	MPI											
544:1	8	CP2												
544:1	1	INC	MI											
544:1	14	INDIS												
544:1	10	LP												
544:1	1	ID int												
544:1	3	MPI												
544:1	2	MPI	RS											
544:1	1	BP												One brown painted line
544:1	9	RB												
544:1	9	RS												
544:1	1	SQCB	SQCB											
544:1	1	S3-V	S3-V	UND										
544:1	201	UND												
544:1	1	UND	INC	S5-L	S1-L									
544:1	6	CP1												
544:1	1	WAF												
544:1	1	ZCI	MI											
544:1	1	UND	CP5											
544:2–4	1	CAB												
544:2–4	27	CAR												
544:2–4	3	CAR	LP											
544:2–4	1	CAR	MPI											
544:2–4	1	CAR	RS											
544:2–4	15	CAR												

(*Continued*)

Table 5.3 (Continued)

Trench 544

Cont.	#	D1	D2	D3	D4	D5	D6	D7	D8	D9	D10	D11	D12	Remarks
544:2–4	1	CAR	MC int											
544:2–4	3	CH	RB											
544:2–4	3	CH	RS											
544:2–4	29	CP1												
544:2–4	4	CP2												
544:2–4	1	CP3												
544:2–4	7	CP4												See Figures 5.2, 5.3
544:2–4	1	CP5												
544:2–4	2	CP6												See Figures 5.2, 5.3
544:2–4	1	ID int												
544:2–4	1	INC	RB	INC										
544:2–4	1	INC	RB	RB	UND									
544:2–4	1	INC	RB	S1-L										
544:2–4	1	INC	UND											
544:2–4	54	INDIS												
544:2–4	5	INDIS	RS											
544:2–4	10	UNK												
544:2–4	2	LLP												See Figure 5.1b
544:2–4	91	LP												
544:2–4	2	LP	MI	MI	MI	LP								Fine orange fabric
544:2–4	3	LP	CAR	LP										
544:2–4	2	M I-H												Very fine light creamy fabric. See Figure 5.4
544:2–4	1	MI	CAR											
544:2–4	1	MI	MI	MI	MI	MI	MI	MI	RB	CH	MI	MI	UND	INC in 7 and 2 rows
544:2–4	1	MI	RB	CAR										
544:2–4	1	MI	RB	INC										
544:2–4	1	MI	RB	RB	RB	CH	S3-V	CH	S3-V	UND				
544:2–4	1	MI	MI	MI	MI	MI	RB	CH						INC in 5 rows
544:2–4	3	MI	UND											
544:2–4	1	MI	UND	RB	RB	RB	RS int							Fine orange fabric
544:2–4	1	MI	UNK	UND										
544:2–4	1	MI	UND	RS										
544:2–4	21	MPI												
544:2–4	2	MPI	RB											Fine white clay, ?spout. See Figure 5.4
544:2–4	4	MPI	RS											
544:2–4	23	RB												
544:2–4	4	RB	RS											
544:2–4	1	RB	RB	SQCB	RB	CAR								
544:2–4	1	RB	RS											
544:2–4	1	RB	RB	CH	RB	CAR	UND							
544:2–4	36	RS												
544:2–4	1	S3-V	RB	S3-V	CAR	UND								
544:2–4	1	S4-L	UND	S4-L										
544:2–4	1	SIP	BS											Possibly moulded
544:2–4	1	SQC	UND											
544:2–4	1	UND	MPI	MPI	CP5									
544:2–4	788	UND												
544:2–4	1	UND	CAR	LP										
544:2–4	1	UND	INC	CAR	UND									
544:2–4	1	UND	MI	MI	MI	MI	S5-L	S5-L	UND					INC in 4 rows
544:2–4	1	UND	RB	RB	CAR									
544:2–4	1	UND	RB	SQCB	RB	CH	RB	RB	UND					
544:2–4	1	UND	RS											
544:2–4	1	UND	CAR	RB	CH	MI	RB	MI	UND					
544:2–4	10	WAF												
TOTAL	**1468**													

(*Continued*)

Table 5.3 (Continued)

Trench 631

Cont.	#	D1	D2	D3	D4	Remarks
1,2,3,5,6	2	CAR				
1,2,3,5,6	2	LP				
1,2,3,5,6	1	S6-L				Fine grey fabric. See Figure 5.5
1,2,3,5,6	38	UND				
1,2,3,5,6	1	RB				
1,2,3,5,6	1	CAR				
4&13	1	UNK				
4&13	2	CP1				
4&13	1	CAR				
4&13	1	CAR	LP			
4&13	1	LP				
4&13	1	MPI				
4&13	3	RB				
4&13	37	UND				
4&13	2	CAR	RB			
10&12	43	CAR				
10&12	1	CAR	S4	MI		
10&12	1	CAR	S4-V			
10&12	1	CAR	FING			
10&12	2	CH				
10&12	1	CH	RB			
10&12	1	CP3				
10&12	25	INDIS				
10&12	6	LLP				
10&12	1	LP	CAR			
10&12	1	LP	CAR	UND		
10&12	19	LP				
10&12	2	LP	CAR			
10&12	1	MC	RB	CAR		
10&12	3	MC	RB	CAR		
10&12	1	MC	RB			
10&12	4	MPI				
10&12	25	RB				
10&12	1	RB	MI	RB	MI	
10&12	1	S1-L	MCH			
10&12	1	S6	S7-L			
10&12	1	SQC	RB	MI		
10&12	1	SQCB	S1-L	MI		
10&12	502	UND				
10&12	6	WAF				
631:11	11	UND				
631:14	1	CH				
631:14	1	INDIS				
631:14	1	LP				
631:14	1	RB				
631:14	40	UND				
631:16	1	MI	RB			
631:16	2	CAR				
631:16	1	CP6				
631:16	1	CAR	INC			
631:16	1	CAR	S1-L	S1-L		S1-L in two rows
631:16	1	CAR	LP			
631:16	1	CAR	RB	RB	RB	
631:16	1	CH				
631:16	1	INDIS				
631:16	3	RB				
631:16	32	UND				
631:16	1	SQC	RB	SQCB	RB	
631:17	3	CAR				
631:17	2	INDIS				
631:17	1	LP				
631:17	14	UND				
19&20	2	CAB	CAR			
19&20	26	CAR				
19&20	1	CAR	MPI			

(Continued)

Table 5.3 (Continued)
Trench 631

Cont.	#	D1	D2	D3	D4	Remarks
19&20	1	CAR	RB			
19&20	1	CAR	RS			
19&20	5	CH				
19&20	1	CH	RB			
19&20	3	CP3				
19&20	1	CP6				
19&20	7	INDIS				
19&20	1	LLP				
19&20	16	LP				
19&20	1	MC	CAR			
19&20	1	MI	FING			
19&20	3	MPI				
19&20	1	MPI	RB			
19&20	9	RB				
19&20	1	RB	FING	MI		
19&20	1	RB	CAR	MI		
19&20	1	RB	MI			
19&20	1	RB	WAF			
19&20	2	S1-L	CAR			
19&20	1	S3-V	RB	S3-V	CAR	
19&20	1	S3-V	CAR			
19&20	1	S3-V	RB	S3-V	INC	
19&20	1	S3-V	CAR			
19&20	1	S4-V	CAR	INC		
19&20	327	UND				
19&20	3	WAF				
631:21	1	LP				
631:21	3	UND				
631:22	1	MI	S3-D			Fine grey fabric
631:22	1	RB	CAR			
631:22	7	CAR				
631:22	1	CAR	INDIS			
631:22	7	INDIS				
631:22	6	LP				
631:22	2	CP1				
631:22	1	CP4				
631:22	2	MPI				
631:22	5	RB				
631:22	1	RB	CAR			
631:22	101	UND				
631:23	1	MPI				
631:23	1	RB				
631:23	7	UND				
631:24	1	CAR				
631:24	1	MI	CAR			
631:24	1	MI	RB	MI		
631:24	4	UND				
631:26	1	CAR				
631:26	1	CAR	MPI			
631:26	2	CH				
631:26	1	INDIS				
631:26	7	LP				
631:26	1	MPI				
631:26	1	MPI	RB			
631:26	2	RB				
631:26	45	UND				
631:26	1	WAF				
TOTAL	**1504**					

Shovel test pits

Cont.	#	D1	D2	D3	D4	D5	Remarks
STP 321	1	INDIS					
STP 321	1	RB	MI				
STP 321	1	LP					

Table 5.3 (Continued)
Shovel test pits

Cont.	#	D1	D2	D3	D4	D5	Remarks
STP 321	2	UND					
STP 325	1	INDIS					
STP 325	1	LP					
STP 325	13	UND					
STP 325	4	WAF					
STP 360	1	CAR					
STP 360	4	INDIS					
STP 360	1	S3-V	RB	S3-V	CAR	UND	
STP 360	11	UND					
STP 443	1	CAR					
STP 443	1	UND					
STP 449	1	CW					See Figure 5.6
STP 449	1	LP					
STP 449	9	UND					
STP 544	1	CAR	RB				
STP 544	1	CP1					
STP 544	1	WAF					
STP 544	1	RS ext					
STP 544	1	RB	UND	INC			
STP 544	2	CP2					
STP 544	3	INDIS					
STP 544	1	LP					
STP 544	1	MPI					See Figure 5.5
STP 544	1	S6					See Figure 5.5
STP 544	1	RB					
STP 544	36	UND					
STP 544	1	WAF					
STP 631	1	CH	MPI				
STP 631	3	UND					
TOTAL	**109**						

Note: To aid legibility within this vast body of data, in the case of the very large assemblages (T544 and T631) contexts have been grouped where this is stratigraphically appropriate.

Table 5.4 Kinolhas assemblage: rim sherds. i = interior, e = exterior.

	Rim Type	<	Ø	Base type	Spout type	Burn. (i/e)	Slip (i/e)	D1	D2	D3	D4	D5	Remarks
321:1	1	2	31					SQCB	CAR				
321:1	36	3?	14										
321:1	?												Too eroded to analyse
321:2	?												Too eroded to analyse
321:2	?												Too eroded to analyse
321:2	6?	3	13										Flanged, pedestal base? fine white
321:2	9	2?	29					CH					V abraded, white
321:2	28	?	24					CH					
321:2	26	3?	22					RB					
321:2	18	?	18					INC					Incised line outer rim edge, v abraded
321:2	18	?	18					INC					Incised line outer rim edge, v abraded
321:2	13	1	24					LP?					
321:2	9	2	32					MI	RB	S3-D	RB		White
321:2	10	2?	24										Worn
321:2	16	?	21										
321:2	17	2?	30										
321:2	24	3?	22										V abraded
321:2	36	3?	30										Large vessel, large thick bead
321:2	40	4	13										
321:2					3?								End lost
Total 321–20													
325:1	2	2	20					INC	RB	RB	RB		Lip incised
325:1	?												Too eroded to analyse
325:2	?												Too eroded to analyse

Table 5.4 (Continued)

	Rim Type	<	Ø	Base type	Spout type	Burn. (i/e)	Slip (i/e)	D1	D2	D3	D4	D5	Remarks
325:2	?												Too eroded to analyse
325:2	?												Too eroded to analyse
325:2	?												Too eroded to analyse
325:2	?												Too eroded to analyse
325:2	2	2	24					RB	RB				Heavily worn
325:2	2	2	24					INC	RB	CAR			
325:2	25	2	38					INC					Groove ext. rim, slightly elongated bead
325:2	11	1	20					MC					
325:2	7	1	27			i.		MI	MI				
325:2	22	2	23					MI					2 grooves in top of rim
325:2								MI					FG
325:2							e.?	MI					FG, dark grey slip?
325:2							i.	S3-V?	MI				FG, black slip survives in incised lines (int.)
325:2	5	2	23										FG, abraded
325:2	8	?	25										White gritty
325:2	21	2	24										Slightly tapered thicker rim
325:2	34	3	12										FO
325:2	34	3	12										FO
325:2	35	2	20										Vesicular fabric
325:2	39	5	21										Poss lid? Grey vesicular
325:3	1	2	27					CAR					
325:3	?												Too eroded to analyse
325:3	22	?	29				i.?	INC					Groove in rim top, white fabric,?orange slip
Total 325–26													
360:1	5	2	21					CH?	CAR				Rim incised on top
360:2													FG body sherd, poss had spout attached?
360:2	13	1	26					LP?					
360:2	38	4	24					S3-D	S3-D	S3-D			FG
360:2	24	?	31										Pierced below rim
360:2	37	5	20										
360:2	37	5	20										
360:2	37	5	20										
360:2	37	5	20										
360:2	37	5	20										
360:2	37	5	20										
360:3	3	2	24					INC					
360:4	25	2	38					RB					Worn int
Total 360–13													
443:2	10	2	31										
443:2	14	2	22										
443:2	25	3	20					RB					
443:2							e.?	RB					Poss part of Type 3 spout? Brownish slip?
443:2	2	2	30					RB	CAR				
443:2	1	2	23					RB					
443:2	1	2	30					RB	RB	RB	RB	CAR	White/greyish clay
443:2	1	2	24					SQCB	CAR				
Total 443–8													
449:1	8	2	25					MI					White gritty, incised lines ext. rim
449:2	?												Too eroded to analyse
449:2	?												Too eroded to analyse
449:3	10	?	26										
449:3	11	2	14										FG
Total 449–5													
544:1	6	2	20			i & e	i & e	CH	MC				Black slip
544:1	1	2	24				RS i./e.	INC					
544:1	38	4	13					INC					Groove just below rim tip ext.
544:1	2	2	24					INC	INC	MPI	RB	CAR	Lip incised
544:1	2	2	20					INC	MPI	RB	RB	CAR	Lip incised

(*Continued*)

Table 5.4 (Continued)

	Rim Type	<	Ø	Base type	Spout type	Burn. (i/e)	Slip (i/e)	D1	D2	D3	D4	D5	Remarks
544:1	3	2	17					INC	MI				
544:1	?												Too eroded to analyse
544:1	?												Too eroded to analyse
544:1	?												Too eroded to analyse
544:1	?												Too eroded to analyse
544:1	?												Too eroded to analyse
544:1	?												Too eroded to analyse
544:1/ 3	?												Too eroded to analyse
544:1	1	2	28					MI					
544:1	1	2	31					MI	RB	CAR			
544:1	1	2	23					MI					
544:1	5	2	25					MI					White
544:1	5	2	25					MI					White
544:1	5	2	16					MI					
544:1	2	2	18					MPI	RB	RB	MPI	CAR	
544:1	23	2	23					PA-1					
544:1	23	2	29					PA-1					PA-1 in squares, impressed
544:1	1	2	29					RB					
544:1	1	2	28					RB	CAR				
544:1	1	2	26					SQCB	CAR				
544:1	1	2	33					SQCB	RB	CAR			
544:1	27	2	21										
544:1	35	2	20										Vesicular
544:1	37	4	32										
544:1	39	5	27										Poss lid? Grey sandy
544:1	40	4	16										
544:1	40	4	12										Vesicular
544:1					1								FG
544:1					1								
544:1	?43												V fine sandy sherd
544:1	10	2	23				i & e?						Orange slip?
544:1	22	1	24										
544:1	24	2	12				e?						Orange slip?
544:1	24	2	12				e?						Orange slip?
544:1	24	2	12				e?						Orange slip?
544:1	1	2	27										Undec, very eroded
544:1								UND	MI	UND	ZCI		FG, spout?
544:2	?												Too eroded to analyse
544:2	?												Too eroded to analyse
544:2	?												Too eroded to analyse
544:2	?												Too eroded to analyse
544:2	?												Too eroded to analyse
544:2	?												Too eroded to analyse
544:2	?												Too eroded to analyse
544:2	?												Too eroded to analyse
544:2	?												Too eroded to analyse
544:2	?												Too eroded to analyse
544:2	?												Too eroded to analyse
544:2	?												Too eroded to analyse
544:2	?												Too eroded to analyse
544:2	?												Too eroded to analyse
544:2	6	2	23					CH	S3-V	INC	S3-V	INC	Grooves on inner rim, v abraded
544:2	6	2	23					CH	S3-V	INC	S3-V	INC	Grooves on inner rim, v abraded
544:2	24	3	26					RB					
544:2	1	2	28					INC					
544:2	10	2	30				i. & e.	INC					Orange slip, incised line in rim edge
544:2	10	2	27				i. & e.	INC					Orange slip, incised line in rim edge
544:2	10	2	19				i. & e.	INC					Orange slip, incised line in rim edge
544:2	22	?	22					INC					Groove in top of rim
544:2	22	?	24					INC					Groove in top of rim
544:2	24	2	21					INC					Groove ext. rim
544:2	28	1	17			i. & e.		INC	MI				Groove in rim

(Continued)

Table 5.4 (Continued)

	Rim Type	<	Ø	Base type	Spout type	Burn. (i/e)	Slip (i/e)	D1	D2	D3	D4	D5	Remarks
544:2	29	1	15					INC	MI				Grooves in upper and outer edge of rim
544:2	33	1	13					INC					Groove ext. rim, orange gritty fabric
544:2	2	2	21					INC	INC	RB	RB	CAR	Lip incised
544:2	1	2	27				i./red e.	MI					Lip incised
544:2	8	2	16					LP					
544:2	11	1	20					MC					
544:2	19	?	30					MC					Channels in rim outer edge
544:2	19	?	30					MC					Channels in rim outer edge
544:2	1	2	26					MI	RB	CAR			
544:2	1	2	27					MI	RB				
544:2	11	1	22					MI					Vesicular fabric
544:2	20	2	24					MI	CAR				
544:2	20	2	24					MI	CAR				
544:2	31	1	17					MI					Coarse grey vesicular fabric, grooves in rim
544:2	41	4	8					MI					
544:2	41	3	6					MI	MI	PA-2?			
544:2	29	1	17					MI?					V abraded, grey vesicular?limestone-tempered
544:2	1	2	24				i./e. red	RB	CH	CAR			Lip incised
544:2	1	2	27					RB	CAR				
544:2	1	2	26					RB	RB				
544:2	23	2	33					S6					FG
544:2	23	2	33					S6					FG, prob same as previously
544:2	23	2	31					S6					FG, prob same as previously, but ?slightly smaller Ø
544:2	1	2	30					SQCB	CAR				
544:2	1	2	24					SQCB					
544:2	1	2	27					SQCB	CAR				
544:2	1	2	30				i./red e.	SQCB	CAR				Incision along lip
544:2	1	2	44				red i./e.	SQCB	CAR				Incision along lip
544:2	1	2	27				red e.	SQCB	CAR				
544:2	1	2	33					SQCB	CAR				
544:2	1	2	34					SQCB	CAR				
544:2	5	2	15					WCI					
544:2	1	2	26										Incision along lip
544:2	4	3	22										
544:2	4	3	24										
544:2	5	?	15										
544:2	10	2?	26										Abraded
544:2	10	2	30										
544:2	11	2	12										
544:2	12	2?	21				i.						Reddish slip, worn
544:2	12	2?	21				i.						Reddish slip, worn
544:2	12	2?	21				i.						Reddish slip, worn
544:2	12	2?	21				i.						Reddish slip, worn
544:2	12	2	23										
544:2	12	2	30										Heavily abraded grey ware
544:2	14	2	21										
544:2	17	2	24					CAR					
544:2	17	2	24					CAR					
544:2	17	2	24					CAR					
544:2	17	2	24					CAR					
544:2	19	2	30				i. & e.						Red slip, white fabric
544:2	19	?	21										
544:2	19	?	23										
544:2	20	2	18					CAR					
544:2	20	2	18					CAR					
544:2	20	2	18					CAR					
544:2	20	2	21										Grey vesicular fabric

(Continued)

Table 5.4 (Continued)

	Rim Type	<	Ø	Base type	Spout type	Burn. (i/e)	Slip (i/e)	D1	D2	D3	D4	D5	Remarks
544:2	20	2	21										Grey vesicular fabric
544:2	21	?	23										
544:2	21	2	26										
544:2	22	?	22										
544:2	23	2	24										Fine sandy w. red clay pellets, int surface lost in part
544:2	23	1	22										Everted tip is rounded wedge
544:2	24	2	22		e.								
544:2	26	1	18										Grey vesicular fabric, abraded
544:2	26	1	23										
544:2	26	1	23										
544:2	26	1	23										
544:2	26	1	23										
544:2	26	1	23										
544:2	27	2	23										
544:2	33	2	29										
544:2	35	2	22										Vesicular fabric
544:2	37	4	21										
544:2	37	4	21										
544:2	39	5	20										Poss lid? Grey vesicular
544:2	42	4	17				i.						Red slip
544:2	43	4	10										Odd, could be a lid or base? FG
544:2	43	4	10										Odd, could be a lid or base? FG
544:2	43	4	10										Odd, could be a lid or base? FG
544:2	43	4	10										Odd, could be a lid or base? FG
544:2	44	3?	6				e.						FO, white slip
544:2				3a									FG, wear suggests not part of a pedestal?
544:2				3a									FG, wear suggests not part of a pedestal?
544:2				4									FG,?lid knob, but sherd appears to be base angle
544:2				7		e.							Dark red fabric, may be edge of small lid?
544:2					2								FG, carinated spout
544:2					2								FG
544:2								RB	UND	RS			FO, spout?
544:2								UND	INC				FG, spout?
544:2								UND	MI	MI	MI	UND	INC in 3 rows, FG, spout?
544:2								UND	MI	UND			FG, spout?
544:2								UND	RB	RS i.			FO, spout?
544:3	?												Too eroded to analyse
544:3	?												Too eroded to analyse
544:3	?												Too eroded to analyse
544:3	?												Too eroded to analyse
544:3	?												Too eroded to analyse
544:3	?												Too eroded to analyse
544:3	1	2	27					SQCB	CAR				
544:3	5	2	22					CH	RB?				
544:3	9	3?	40					CH	RB				
544:3	35	2	26					CH					Vesicular fabric, 2 shallow channels in rim upper surface
544:3	25	2	28					RB					
544:3	8	2	27					INC					Vesicular, abraded
544:3	8	2	27					INC					Vesicular, abraded
544:3	8	2	27					INC					Vesicular, abraded
544:3	10	2	25				i & e?	INC					Orange slip?, incised line in rim edge, sooted
544:3	22	?	22					INC					Groove in top of rim
544:3	17	2	28					LP?					Only a small area of body survives
544:3	5	2	19					MI					Vesicular fabric, incised lines ext. rim
544:3	5	2	19					MI					Vesicular fabric, incised lines ext. rim
544:3	2	2	26				i./e.	MPI	RB	CAR			Red slipped
544:3	23	2	33					S6					FG, a group

(*Continued*)

Table 5.4 (Continued)

	Rim Type	<	Ø	Base type	Spout type	Burn. (i/e)	Slip (i/e)	D1	D2	D3	D4	D5	Remarks
544:3	23	2	33					S6					FG, a group
544:3	23	2	33					S6					FG, a group
544:3	23	2	33					S6					FG, a group
544:3	23	2	33					S6					FG, a group
544:3	23	2	33					S6					FG, a group
544:3	23	2	33					S6					FG, a group
544:3	23	2	33					S6					FG, a group
544:3	10	2	24					S3-V	S3-V	S3-V			White (may be white slip int??)
544:3	10	2?	26										Pale buff gritty
544:3	24	2	32					CAR					Abraded, bead has a straight lower edge
544:3	27	?	20										
544:3	38	3	8				i. & e.						White ware, red slip, could be a pedestal base?
544:3	39	5	25				i. & e.						Black slip, but mostly worn off, v fine pale grey fabric
544:3			7		?		e.						?lid with plain horizontal edge, central 'spout', incomplete, white slip
544:4	5	1	18										Worn exterior
544:4	9	?	23					CH					
544:4	20	2	23					RB	CAR				
544:4	5	2	19					INC					Vesicular fabric, incised line ext. rim
544:4	10	2	30				i. & e.	INC					Orange slip, incised line in rim edge
544:4	8	1	18					MI					Pink gritty, incised lines ext. rim
544:4	8	2?	19					MI					Pink gritty, incised lines ext. rim
544:4	8	1	22					MI					Pink gritty, incised lines ext. rim
544:4	41	3	7					MI					
544:4	7	2	24										White gritty
544:4	17	?	20										V abraded, vesicular fabric
544:4	27	?	22										
544:4	30	2	21										White powdery deposit ext.
544:4				3a?									FG
544:4	?												Too eroded to analyse
544:4				5									Fine whiteware, may be lid knob?
Total 544–211													
631:3	?												Too eroded to analyse
631:4	1	2	28					RB					
631:5	5	2	29										Buff
631:5	?												Too eroded to analyse
631:5	?												Too eroded to analyse
631:5	1	2	26					SQCB	CAR				
631:10	1	2	30					INC					
631:10	6	3	18					CH	S3-V?	S3-V?	CAR		V abraded
631:10	3	2	19					INC					
631:10	3	2	19					INC					
631:10	?												Too eroded to analyse
631:10	?												Too eroded to analyse
631:10	?												Too eroded to analyse
631:10	?												Too eroded to analyse
631:10	?												Too eroded to analyse
631:10	3	2	19					INC					
631:10	3	2	19					INC					
631:10	3	2	19					INC					
631:10	6	3	22					INC	S3-V	S3-V?	CAR		
631:10	9	2	19					INC					Groove in top of rim & ext. edge
631:10	26	1	17					INC					Groove in outer edge of rim
631:10	2	2	20					INC	MPI	RB	RB	CAR	Lip incised, also another raised bank on interior
631:10	2	2	21					INC	MPI	RB	RB	CAR	Lip incised
631:10	2	2	22					INC	INC	RB	CAR		Lip incised
631:10	5	2	35					MI					Pale buff
631:10	1	2	31					MPI	RB	RB	RB		Pinkish clay

(*Continued*)

Table 5.4 (Continued)

	Rim Type	<	Ø	Base type	Spout type	Burn. (i/e)	Slip (i/e)	D1	D2	D3	D4	D5	Remarks
631:10	1	2	27					RB					
631:10	1	2	25					RB	CAR				
631:10	1	2	36					RB	RB	RB	RB	CAR	White/greyish clay
631:10	2	2	20					RB	CAR				
631:10	1	2	25					RB	CAR				
631:10	1	2	36					RB	RB	RB	RB	CAR	White/greyish clay
631:10	1	2	28					SQCB					
631:10	1	2	31					SQCB	CAR				
631:10	1	2	25					SQCB	CAR				
631:10	1	2	33					SQCB	CAR				
631:10				1									Thick
631:10	13	1	22										
631:10	13	1	22										
631:10	13	1	22										
631:10	19	?	35										White gritty, larger vessel than others, thicker rim, could be subtype
631:10	19	?	35										White gritty, larger vessel than others, thicker rim, could be subtype
631:12	1	2	23					INC					
631:12	4	3	17					CH					
631:12	6	2	23					CH	MI	S1-L	MI		
631:12	6	2	23					CH	MI	S1-L	MI		
631:12	6	2	23					CH	MI	S1-L	MI		
631:12	6	2	24					CH	S3-V?				V abraded
631:12	5	2	20					CH?					V abraded
631:12	16	3	16					RB	CAR				
631:12								RB	INC				Part of spout or small cylindrical vessel??
631:12	1	2	25					INC					
631:12	2	2	18					INC	RB	MPI	RB	CAR	Lip incised
631:12	2	2	18					INC	MPI	RB	RB		Lip incised
631:12	2	2	24					INC	RB	CAR			
631:12	3	2	19					INC					
631:12	3	2	23					INC					
631:12	3	2	24					INC	MI				
631:12				2				INC	CAR				
631:12	19	2?	20					MC					Channels in rim outer edge
631:12	2	2	15					MPI	RB	CAR			
631:12	?												Too eroded to analyse
631:12	?												Too eroded to analyse
631:12	?												Too eroded to analyse
631:12	?												Too eroded to analyse
631:12	?												Too eroded to analyse
631:12	?												Too eroded to analyse
631:12	?												Too eroded to analyse
631:12/14	?												Too eroded to analyse
631:12	2	2	28					RB	RB	CAR			
631:12	4	3	30					S3-D	CAR				
631:12	4	3	30					S3-D	CAR				
631:12	4	3	28					S3-D	CAR				
631:12	1	2	35					SQCB	CAR				
631:12	1	2	25					SQCB	CAR				
631:12	1	2	24										
631:12	20	1	11										Buff with grey core, rounded end to rim
631:12	21	2	19										White
631:12	21	2	19										White
631:12				3a									FG
631:12					?								Body sherd with base of?spout
631:13	11	2	25					INC					Incised line ext. rim edge
631:14	9	2	40					MI/RB					Sup rim with grooves & RB
631:14	16	2	33										V abraded
631:14	18	?	30										
631:14	36	1	20										V abraded, vesicular fabric
631:16	3	2	19					CH	INC				

Table 5.4 (Continued)

	Rim Type	<	Ø	Base type	Spout type	Burn. (i/e)	Slip (i/e)	D1	D2	D3	D4	D5	Remarks
631:16	9	1	27					RB/groove	RB				
631:16	9	1	27					RB/groove	RB				
631:16	9	1	27					RB/groove	RB				
631:16	?												Too eroded to analyse
631:16	?												Too eroded to analyse
631:16	?												Too eroded to analyse
631:16	?												Too eroded to analyse
631:16	?												Too eroded to analyse
631:16	1	2	26					INC					
631:16	10	2	27					INC	MI	CAR			Incised line on rim edge, 2 at carination
631:16	10	2	27					INC	MI	CAR			Incised line on rim edge, 2 at carination
631:16	10	2	27					INC	MI	CAR			Incised line on rim edge, 2 at carination
631:16	10	2	27					INC	MI	CAR			Incised line on rim edge, 2 at carination
631:16	10	2	27					INC	MI	CAR			Incised line on rim edge, 2 at carination
631:16	10	2	27					INC	MI	CAR			Incised line on rim edge, 2 at carination
631:16	1	2	23					SQCB	CAR				
631:16				3									
631:20	6	2	28					CH	S3-V	S3-V			Pierced below rim
631:20	6	2	28					CH	S3-V	S3-V			Pierced below rim
631:20	6	2	24					CH	S3-V?				V abraded
631:20	1	2	28					INC					
631:20	2	2	24					INC	INC	RB	RB x 2	CAR	Lip incised
631:20	2	2	19					INC	MPI	RB	CAR		Lip incised
631:20	2	2	18					INC	MPI	RB	RB		Lip incised
631:20	2	2	22					INC	INC	RB	CAR		Lip incised
631:20	2	2	18					INC	INC	RB	CAR		Lip incised
631:20	6	2	24					INC	S3-V	S3-V			Surfaces mostly lost, dec may be diagonal
631:20	6	2?	23					INC					
631:20	22	1	21					INC	LP?				Rim top grooved, diag impressed lines on body
631:20	24	2	33					INC	MC?				Groove ext. rim
631:20	3	2	19					INC					
631:20	1	2	23					MI	RB	CAR			
631:20	3	2	20					MI					
631:20				6				MI					Concentric rings at centre and outside foot ring
631:20	?												Too eroded to analyse
631:20	?												Too eroded to analyse
631:20	?												Too eroded to analyse
631:20	?												Too eroded to analyse
631:20	?												Too eroded to analyse
631:20	?												Too eroded to analyse
631:12/20	?												Too eroded to analyse
631:20	24	1	13					MI?					Shallow lines at neck? Abraded
631:20	9	2?	26					MI/RB					Sup rim with grooves & RB
631:20	2	2	14					MPI	RB	CAR			
631:20	2	2	28					MPI	INC	MPI	RB		2 incisions lip
631:20	1	2	24					RB					
631:20	1	2	36					RB	RB	RB	CAR		White/greyish clay
631:20	2	2	22					RB	RB	CAR			
631:20	2	2	26					RB	RB	CAR			
631:20	2	2	22					RB	CAR				
631:20	2	2	24					RB	CAR				
631:20	2	2	21					RB	CAR				
631:20	2	2	26					RB	CAR				
631:20	4	3	24					S1-L	CAR				
631:20	4	3	25					S1-L	CAR				
631:20	1	2	27					SQCB	CAR				
631:20	1	2	27					SQCB	CAR				
631:20	1	2	32					SQCB	CAR				

(Continued)

Table 5.4 (Continued)

	Rim Type	<	Ø	Base type	Spout type	Burn. (i/e)	Slip (i/e)	D1	D2	D3	D4	D5	Remarks
631:20	4	3	23										
631:20	5	2	29										Buff
631:20	11	2?	22										Thick with tapered edge
631:20	18	?	30										
631:20	27	3	16										Abraded
631:20				1									Spots of greenish?glaze int, fine grey vesicular, large vessel
631:20				1									FG, v worn/abraded
631:20					3								FG, short, could be a tripod foot, but hollow
631:22	6	2	24					CH					V abraded
631:22	2	2	18					INC	RB	RB	RB		Lip incised
631:22	3	2	22					INC					
631:22	3	2	22					INC					
631:22	2	2	22					RB	CAR				
631:22	10	2	26			i & e?							Orange slip?
631:22	?												Too eroded to analyse
631:22	?												Too eroded to analyse
631:22	?												Too eroded to analyse
631:24	?												Too eroded to analyse
631:24	9	2	32					CH					
631:24	10	2	22			i & e?							Orange slip?
Total 631–165													

Shovel test pits

STP	Rim Type	<	Ø	Base type	Spout type	Burn. (i/e)	Slip (i/e)	D1	D2	D3	D4	Remarks
325	14	2	26									
325	2	2	18					I	RB	RB	RB	Lip incised
325	4	3	30					S1-L				Reduced
544				3								FG—note edge of base looks like flaring rim with squared end
544	43	6	14					MI				Odd, could be a lid or base? FG
544	43	6	14					MI				Odd, could be a lid or base? FG
544	43	6	14					MI				Odd, could be a lid or base? FG
544	43	6	14					MI				Odd, could be a lid or base? FG
544	1	2	35					MI	CAR			
544	1	2	26					RB	CAR			
631	2	2	19					I	I	RB	RB	Lip incised
Total STP—11												

Impressions were the most common type of decoration at Kinolhas. The most homogeneous and visually distinctive group consisted of paddle-impressed sherds, which constituted just over a quarter (25.87%) of the decorated body sherd assemblage. These sherds fall into two major types: the first consists of a series of square or rectangular impressions in a checkerboard pattern (WAF), and the second of a series of linear or near linear impressions, often with overlapping areas; these impressions are typically quite fine (LP), but a less common, larger variant, termed LLP, also exists (Figure 5.1). Only a handful of instances of paddle-impressed decorations were noted on rims, and these are mainly uncertain, suggesting that this type of decoration was restricted to body sherds.

A heterogeneous, much less common, and far less well understood set of impressed decorations included highly distinctive motifs possibly resulting from the use of moulds, carved paddles, or stamps; these will be discussed below. A small number of impressed or rolled impressions of indefinite origin was also recorded.

Incised and stabbed decorations were also frequent. Lines cut with a single pointed tool dragged over the clay result in a narrow line with a V-shaped cross-section. The simplest types are easy to describe, being either single (INC) or multiple (MI, or MPI if parallel) lines. More complicated designs, involving wavy or triangular continuous lines, also occurred, but were rare. A small number of sherds decorated with relatively complex incised patterns was characterised by a fine grey fabric, as will be discussed below.

When impressed singly—that is, stabbed or stamped—a tool creates a range of different decorations depending on the nature of its end (angular, circular, ovoid, triangular. . .) and a series of these may be placed in lines or curves. The coding

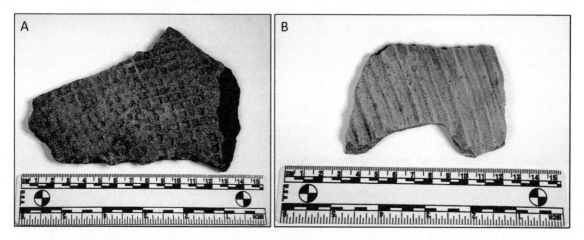

Figure 5.1 WAF (left) and large linear paddled (LLP) (right) paddle-impressed sherds from Kinolhas. Left: Unnumbered sherd (recorded in the field), Trench 325, Context 2; right: sherd #354, Trench 544, Context 2.

Source: Photo by Guilia Nazzaro.

system aimed to capture that variation. Stamped concentric circles (S6), resulting from the use of a specialised tool or perhaps a hollow reed, were very distinctive and unusual (Figure 5.5). Fingernail impressions also occurred, but rarely.

Lines made by dragging a broad object such as a finger or a square stylus across the clay create a relatively wide, U-shaped cross-section; margins are often raised due to the displacement of the clay. Such channels occurred both singly (CH) or severally (MC). A characteristic type consisted of a square channel with a relatively wide, rectangular cross-section, coded SQC, and a variant, SQCB, with a raised band or bands in the centre of the channel; whether this is intentional or not remains unclear, but it forms a distinctive design.

A few other decorations were identified. These included paint and slip, as well as appliqué, the latter in several forms, including raised band (RB), which involved the addition of a linear strip of clay, and cable (CAB), in which the added strip was marked with small impressions, perhaps finger marks. More rarely, nubbins were added, coded PA.

Parallels from other sites

Decorations similar to those described earlier have been documented in the published literature. Paddle-impressed wares, which were common in the Kinolhas assemblage and very distinctive, are considered first. As discussed previously, such wares had already been reported by earlier researchers in the Maldives (Mikkelsen 1991, Litster 2016, Jaufar 2019). Moreover, research has, in the last 25 years or so, improved understanding of the techniques involving in creating these decorations.

An early depiction of paddle-impressed wares, from Arikamedu, was provided by Wheeler et al. (1946, especially Plates XXVIIIb: 5, XXXIc: 2). These were described as designs impressed, either deliberately or accidentally, by mats or baskets (Wheeler et al. 1946, p. 51). Subsequent work at Arikamedu sought to improve understanding, aiming to tighten descriptions of these decorations and to pay closer attention to the tools involved in their creation (Begley 1996, Selvakumar 2004, 2011). It emerged that three different decorative techniques had indeed been used: impressing with woven objects such as baskets, pressing into a mould, and hammering with a textured paddle (Begley 1996, p. 202). Accordingly, in the study of the archaeological assemblage from Arikamedu, Begley (1996, p. 203, Figures 4.227–229) treated as a distinct category, 'Motif 6', '*only* those sherds which appear to have been decorated with impressions of paddles forming a continuous geometric motif'. Ethnographic parallels were sought and examples from a present-day potters' workshop in Kerala (Begley 1996, Figures 4.225, 4.226, 4.230) found to offer convincing parallels for the archaeological material.

Overall, impressed wares formed only a fraction of the total pottery recovered at Arikamedu, but it is present throughout the site, and the technique may have continued into medieval times (Begley 1996, p. 204, Selvakumar 2004, p. 620). It was found that the decoration occurred mostly on body sherds below the vessel neck (Selvakumar 2004, pp. 618, 620). This Arikamedu pottery offers good parallels for the 'waffle' decoration from Kinolhas, under the name 'impressed checkerboard' (Begley 1996, Figure 4.228, 2004, Figures 3.35–3.39), and for 'linear paddled' decoration (Begley 2004, Figures 3.32–3.33, Selvakumar 2011, Figure 9.2).

Arikamedu lies on the eastern coast of India, and it is now clear that paddle-impressed ceramics occur across a range of periods in nearby Sri Lanka. They are reported at the mid-first millennium BC to late first millennium AD site of Tissamaharama, and the technique of finishing the body of a pot with the help of a paddle and anvil continues today (Pavan and Schenk 2012, p. 197). Some of the paddle-impressed pottery from Tissamaharama fell within a rather heterogeneous 'fine grey' category, with a very fine paste (Schenk 2006, Figure 2j), dispelling the assumption that this decoration must be associated with coarse wares. At Mantai, paddled decoration was recurrent in deposits likely dating from the first/

second to the fifth/sixth centuries AD, though later intrusive material from the eighth century also appeared (Graham 2013, pp. 191, 192, Plate 11.1, and images on CD accompanying the volume, e.g. 1841, 1850, 1853). Different shapes, including a variety of bowls, storage jars, and lids, and with a wide range of fabrics, were reported.

Interestingly, paddle-impressed wares also have a much wider distribution, around the edges of the Indian Ocean and into the Persian Gulf and Red Sea. McKinnon (2015, see esp. Figure 20) reports a motif comparable to the Kinolhas 'waffle' decoration in northern Sumatra (Indonesia), putatively linked to the presence of merchants of Indian origin in medieval times. At Sharma, Yemen, where some 20% of the diagnostic earthenware is thought to have originated in the Indian subcontinent, a group of impressed decorations, described as likely paddle-impressed and of the type reported at Arikamedu, are identified as 'un type bien caractéristique des productions du sud de l'Inde' (Collinet 2015, pp. 166–167, Figures 170.1–6). These are the oldest well-identified Indian ceramics at Sharma, occurring in late tenth/early eleventh century deposits, and although the published images are small, the line drawings in particular (Collinet 2015, Figure 170.3–6) suggest commonalities with the 'waffle' and 'linear paddle' categories from Kinolhas. Pavan and Schenk (2012, p. 197, Figure 1.5) also report the recovery of paddle-impressed sherds at Sumhuram (Oman) and at Berenike and Myos Hormos on the Red Sea coast of Egypt (see for example Tomber 2000, Figure 4), all in contexts dating to approximately 2000 years ago and thus evidencing connections between southern India, Arabia, and Egypt at that time.

Returning to the Kinolhas finds, some of the rarer decorations can also be related to published materials.

The decoration coded 'CP3' ('Carved Paddle 3') is a group of 12 sherds with crisp, neat impressions in a herringbone pattern. Two retain the lower part of the neck, showing that the impressed pattern reached up to the upper body. These items come from several trenches and evidence a range of fabrics, and at least one shows apparent tamper marks on the inside. This material resembles 8 non-conjoining sherds from Arikamedu reported by Begley (1996, Figures 4.216–4.218). Featuring continuous geometric motifs, they are included within the paddle-impressed 'Motif 6'. They are thought to date to around 2000 years ago but are paralleled in museum holdings of archaeological materials from other parts of southern India (Begley 1996, Figures 4.193, 4.219–4.222).

Two further carved paddle motifs also stand out within the Kinolhas assemblage (Figure 5.2). CP4 is a group of 19 sherds, with a range of fabrics and from across the site, that feature sinuous lines and sharply demarcated triangular shapes, while CP6 is a small (N=5), relatively miscellaneous group of impressed decorations which include designs with arched lines and circular nodules. Some of the complex CP6 decorations resemble material recovered from various eighth- to sixteenth- century contexts at Sehwān Šarīf, Sind, Pakistan (Collinet 2010, pp. 70–71, 260, Figure 20: 10, Figure 45: 11, 19), but the shapes are very different and in Sind these wares are understood to represent rare and relatively luxurious items. Moreover, some of these Sind wares appear to have been moulded, while in the case of the Kinolhas sherds striations within the impressed decorations (Figure 5.2, top right) and tamper marks on the inner faces of the sherds (Figure 5.3) suggest the use of a tamper and paddle.

A small heterogeneous group of sherds of fine buff fabric, with fine incisions, also stood out in the Kinolhas assemblage (Figure 5.4). No close parallel could be found in the literature, although again the material from Sehwān Šarīf (Collinet 2010, Figure 20, #6) presents some similarities.

A group of sherds featuring impressions of stamped concentric circles formed a varied set, both in the organisation of the decoration and in terms of fabric (Figure 5.5). Some are comparable to sherds from Arikamedu and medieval sites in Tamil Nadu published by Begley (2004, Figures 3.53–3.56), as well as to material from Mantai (Carswell et al. 2013, CD image 2792).

Figure 5.2 Examples of carved paddled wares in Kinolhas assemblage: CP4 (top row) and CP6 (bottom row). Top row: Sherds #610 (Trench 544: Context 4), #584 (Trench 544: 2), #283 (Trench 321: 1), and #320 (Trench 321: 2). Bottom row: refitting sherds #468/470 (Trench 544: 2) and #35 (Trench 443: 2).

Source: Photo by Guilia Nazzaro.

Figure 5.3 Tamper marks evident on reverse side of some of the sherds in Figure 5.2. Top row: Sherds #610 and #584 (both CP4); bottom row: Sherds #468/470 and #35 (both CP6).

Source: Photo by Guilia Nazzaro.

Figure 5.4 Kinolhas—Incised buff wares. Top left: Refitting sherds #171, #172, #173, #189, #190, #191, from Trench 360, Context 2. Top right: Sherds #475, #476, and #479, from Trench 544, Context 2. Bottom left: Sherds #193 and #174 from Trench 360, Contexts 1 and 2 respectively; they do not refit, but are clearly from the same vessel. Bottom right: sherd #305 from Trench 321, Context 2.

Source: Photo by Guilia Nazzaro.

Figure 5.5 Examples of stamped concentric circle decorations in Kinolhas assemblage (coded S6). Top row: sherds #745 and #746, STP 544; sherds #237 and #238, Trench 325, Context 2. Bottom row: sherd #446, Trench 631, Context 3; sherd #16, Trench 449, Context 2.

Source: Photo by Guilia Nazzaro.

Figure 5.6 Chattered ware. Sherd #28, Shovel Test Pit 449.

Source: Photo by Guilia Nazzaro.

The 'cable' decoration defined at Kinolhas is very close to the cable motif defined at Arikamedu by Begley (1996, Figures 4.195–201, 2004, Figures 3.19–3.20), and takes its name from it. Wheeler et al. (1946, Figure 30: 83a) called a comparable decoration 'finger tip ornament'.

Finally, a single sherd of rouletted ware was recovered at Kinolhas (Figure 5.6). This decoration was first defined, again, by Wheeler at Arikamedu (e.g. Wheeler et al. 1946, Plates XXV, XXVI). In her later work at the site, Begley (1996) referred to it as 'Motif 14'. This is a very fine-textured ware, usually a flat-based dish with a beaked rim, decorated with concentric rouletted designs on the base.[6] Rouletted ware 'is wellknown [sic] in Indian Ocean research' (Schenk 2015, p. 153) and has been recorded at over 100 sites on the Indian peninsula alone (Schenk 2006, Figure 3), as well as from sites on the Red Sea, the southern Arabian peninsula, and throughout southeast Asia (Tomber 2000,

Schenk 2006, Figure 4, 2015, Selvakumar 2011, Mohanty 2013, pp. 213–216, Tripati 2017, Figures 5, 6 and references therein). It had also been previously reported in the Maldives: a single fragment was recovered by Carswell from topsoil in a mosque cemetery in Male' (Carswell 1975–1977, p. 157, Figure 8). As the prevalent idea at the time of that work was that such rouletted ware was of late Hellenistic date, Carswell considered this sherd to be the 'most surprising find' recovered from his survey. Since then, however, further work (see e.g. the critical appraisal by Schenk 2006) has suggested that several variants of this type of pottery existed, some of which locally produced.

'Half-glazed' wares

With contributions from Ran Zhang

A corpus of 117 sherds from partly glazed vessels was also recovered (Table 5.5, Figure 5.7). They were characterised by a relatively thick body and a brown or green outer glaze. Drips of glaze often occurred on the inner side, and the fabric differed notably from that of the earthenware finds, being closer to a stoneware and in a range of darker colours. To illustrate the variability of this group, a sample was sorted into classes defined on a visual basis. Types 2 to 4 appear to be on a continuum; sherds are generally over 1 cm thick and their glaze ranges from black to dark olive grey. While the fabric of Type 2 is a rather vivid pink, Type 3 is grey and Type 4 orange/red. Type 5 stands out for the relative thinness of sherds, but it is otherwise equal to Type 3. Type 6, though comparable to Type 5, is of a slightly grittier fabric.

Table 5.5 Kinolhas: half-glazed sherds.

Unit and context	Type	Comments
321: 2	3	Thick sherds (1 cm+). Light to dark grey paste, at times chunky, with air/vegetal holes and orange inclusions visible on inside. Dark olive brown (Munsell 2.5Y 3/3) glaze overall. Four channels on outside
321: 2	3	Thick sherds (1 cm+). Light to dark grey paste, at times chunky, with air/vegetal holes and orange inclusions visible on inside. Black glaze, wholly glazed
321: 2	5	Medium thickness sherds (0.5 cm+). Light to dark grey paste, at times chunky, with air/vegetal holes and orange inclusions visible on inside. Black glaze with traces of dripping on outside. Almost certainly same as Type 3, but a thinner part of the vessel
321: 2	5	Medium thickness sherds (0.5 cm+). Light to dark grey paste, at times chunky, with air/vegetal holes and orange inclusions visible on inside. Black glaze overall on outside and on inner lip. Almost certainly same as Type 3, but a thinner part of the vessel. Eversion
321: 2	5	Medium thickness sherds (0.5 cm+). Light to dark grey paste, at times chunky, with air/vegetal holes and orange inclusions visible on inside. Black glaze overall outside, as well as 2 channels. Almost certainly same as Type 3, but a thinner part of the vessel
321: 2	6	Medium thickness sherds (0.5 cm+). Light to dark grey paste, gritty. Similar to Type 5, except for grittiness. Olive brown (Munsell 2.5Y 4/4) glaze over half of the outside, in a straight line—no drip
321: 2	6	Medium thickness sherds (0.5 cm+). Light to dark grey paste, gritty. Similar to Type 5, except for grittiness. Dark olive brown (Munsell 2.5Y 3/3) shiny glaze overall on outside, eroding away
321: 2		Half-glazed. Not studied in detail
321: 4	1	Fine, well-sorted white paste and clinky feel. Some iron staining
321: 4	1	Fine, well-sorted white paste and clinky feel. Some iron staining
321: 4		Half-glazed. Not studied in detail
325: 2	3	Thick sherds (1 cm+). Light to dark grey paste, at times chunky, with air/vegetal holes and orange inclusions visible on inside. Base. No glaze but otherwise in all respects identical to the rest of this class
325: 2	3	Thick sherds (1 cm+). Light to dark grey paste, at times chunky, with air/vegetal holes and orange inclusions visible on inside. Black glaze, eroding off
325: 2	5	Medium thickness sherds (0.5 cm+). Light to dark grey paste, at times chunky, with air/vegetal holes and orange inclusions visible on inside. Black glaze overall on outside and on inner lip. Almost certainly same as Type 3, but a thinner part of the vessel. Eversion
325: 2	5	Medium thickness sherds (0.5 cm+). Light to dark grey paste, at times chunky, with air/vegetal holes and orange inclusions visible on inside. Black glaze overall outside, crazed and flaking. Almost certainly same as Type 3, but a thinner part of the vessel
325: 2		MTB Ming
325: 2		MTB Ming
325: 2		MTB Ming
325: 2		MTB Ming
325: 2		MTB Ming
325: 2		MTB Ming
325: 2		MTB Ming
325: 2		MTB Ming
325: 2		MTB Ming
360: 2	6	Medium thickness sherds (0.5 cm+). Light to dark grey paste, gritty. Similar to Type 5, except for grittiness, and slip appears lighter-coloured and thinner. Olive brown (Munsell 2.5Y 4/4) glaze overall on outside, eroding away
443: 2	2	Pink fabric, very few inclusions, some air/vegetal inclusion holes, dark olive grey (Munsell 5Y 3/2) glaze on outside, incompletely applied, and splashes inside. Clinky. Apparent flat base

(Continued)

Table 5.5 (Continued)

Unit and context	Type	Comments
443: 2	5	Medium thickness sherds (0.5 cm+). Light to dark grey paste, at times chunky, with air/vegetal holes and orange inclusions visible on inside. Black glaze overall on outside. Almost certainly same as Type 3, but a thinner part of the vessel
449: 2	?	Very fine reddish brown (Munsell 2.5 YR 5/3) paste, no inclusions, dark yellowish brown (Munsell 10YR 3/6) glaze on outside
449: 2	?	Light brown fabric, dark brown lustrous glaze on outside. Wheel turned. Not martaban-like
449: 2		MTB Ming
449: 3	?	Very fine white paste, no inclusions, dark yellowish brown (Munsell 10YR 3/6) glaze on outside
449: 3	?	Very fine white paste, no inclusions, dark yellowish brown (Munsell 10YR 3/6) glaze on outside
544: 1	2	Pink fabric, very few inclusions, some air/vegetal inclusion holes, dark olive grey (Munsell 5Y 3/2) glaze on outside, incompletely applied, and splashes inside. Clinky
544: 1	3	Thick sherds (1 cm+). Light to dark grey paste, at times chunky, with air/vegetal holes and orange inclusions visible on inside. Dark olive brown (2.5Y 3/3) glaze flaking off. Base
544: 1	3	Thick sherds (1 cm+). Light to dark grey paste, at times chunky, with air/vegetal holes and orange inclusions visible on inside. Trace of dark brown glaze. Base
544: 1	4	Thick sherds (1 cm+). Very similar to Type 3, but a more orange/red fabric (rather than grey). Very similar to Type 2, but less vivid pink. Dark glaze overall. Just under 1 cm thick
544: 1	4	Thick sherds (1 cm+). Very similar to Type 3, but a more orange/red fabric (rather than grey). Very similar to Type 2, but less vivid pink. Base. Droplets of glaze
544: 1	5	Medium thickness sherds (0.5 cm+). Light to dark grey paste, at times chunky, with air/vegetal holes and orange inclusions visible on inside. Black glaze over part of outside, and incrustations of some sort on inside. Almost certainly same as Type 3, but a thinner part of the vessel
544: 1	6	Medium thickness sherds (0.5 cm+). Light to dark grey paste, gritty. Similar to Type 5, except for grittiness. Very faint traces of eroded glaze
544: 1	6	Medium thickness sherds (0.5 cm+). Light to dark grey paste, gritty. Similar to Type 5, except for grittiness. Dark greyish brown (Munsell 2.5Y 4/2) glaze overall outside, still shiny but eroding away
544: 1	?	Fine, well-sorted white paste and clinky feel. Very dark greyish brown (Munsell 2.5Y 3/2) glaze on outside
544: 1		Half-glazed. Not studied in detail
544: 1		Half-glazed. Not studied in detail
544: 1		Half-glazed. Not studied in detail
544: 1		Half-glazed. Not studied in detail
544: 1		Half-glazed. Not studied in detail
544: 1		Half-glazed. Not studied in detail
544: 1		MTB Ming. Body sherd #131, appliqué, two channels. See Figure 5.7
544: 1		MTB Ming
544: 1		MTB Ming
544: 1		MTB Ming
544: 1		MTB Ming
544: 1		MTB Ming
544: 1		MTB Ming
544: 1		MTB Ming. Bears Chinese character yu (玉), meaning 'jade'. See Figure 5.9
544: 2	2	Pink fabric, very few inclusions, some air/vegetal inclusion holes, black glaze on outside, olive brown (Munsell 2.5Y 4/3) and shiny inside. Clinky
544: 2	3	Thick sherds (1 cm+). Light to dark grey paste, at times chunky, with air/vegetal holes and orange inclusions visible on inside. Black glaze, eroding off in circular patches
544: 2	3	Thick sherds (1 cm+). Light to dark grey paste, at times chunky, with air/vegetal holes and orange inclusions visible on inside. Olive to black glaze, eroding off
544: 2	4	Thick sherds (1 cm+). Very similar to Type 3, but a more orange/red fabric (rather than grey). Very similar to Type 2, but less vivid pink. Very dark greyish brown (Munsell 2.5Y 3/2) glaze overall, has lost its lustre
544: 2	4	Thick sherds (1 cm+). Very similar to Type 3, but a more orange/red fabric (rather than grey). Very similar to Type 2, but less vivid pink. Very dark greyish brown (Munsell 2.5Y 3/2) glaze overall, has lost its lustre
544: 2	4	Thick sherds (1 cm+). Very similar to Type 3, but a more orange/red fabric (rather than grey). Very similar to Type 2, but less vivid pink. Base. No glaze but otherwise in all respects identical to the rest of this class
544: 2	5	Medium thickness sherds (0.5 cm+). Light to dark grey paste, at times chunky, with air/vegetal holes and orange inclusions visible on inside. Black glaze overall. Almost certainly same as Type 3, but a thinner part of the vessel
544: 2	5	Medium thickness sherds (0.5 cm+). Light to dark grey paste, at times chunky, with air/vegetal holes and orange inclusions visible on inside. Black glaze overall. 4 channels on outside. Almost certainly same as Type 3, but a thinner part of the vessel
544: 2	5	Medium thickness sherds (0.5 cm+). Light to dark grey paste, at times chunky, with air/vegetal holes and orange inclusions visible on inside. Black glaze overall outside. Almost certainly same as Type 3, but a thinner part of the vessel
544: 2	5	Medium thickness sherds (0.5 cm+). Light to dark grey paste, at times chunky, with air/vegetal holes and orange inclusions visible on inside. Black glaze overall outside. Almost certainly same as Type 3, but a thinner part of the vessel
544: 2	6	Medium thickness sherds (0.5 cm+). Light to dark grey paste, gritty. Similar to Type 5, except for grittiness. Very dark greyish brown (Munsell 2.5Y 3/2) glaze overall. Deeply pitted inside
544: 2		Half-glazed. Not studied in detail

(Continued)

Table 5.5 (Continued)

Unit and context	Type	Comments
544: 2		Half-glazed. Not studied in detail
544: 2		Half-glazed. Not studied in detail
544: 2		Half-glazed. Not studied in detail
544: 2		MTB Ming. Handle. Item #276. See Figure 5.7
544: 2		MTB Ming. Rim and upper part of body survive, with a handle attached. One channel. Sherd #186. See Figure 5.7
544: 2		MTB Ming
544: 2		MTB Ming
544: 2		MTB Ming
544: 2		MTB Ming
544: 2		MTB Ming
544: 2		MTB Ming
544: 2		MTB Ming
544: 2		MTB Ming
544: 2		MTB Ming
544: 2		MTB Ming
544: 2		MTB Ming
544: 2		MTB Ming
544: 2		MTB Ming
544: 3	5	Medium thickness sherds (0.5 cm+). Light to dark grey paste, at times chunky, with air/vegetal holes and orange inclusions visible on inside. Black glaze overall outside. Almost certainly same as Type 3, but a thinner part of the vessel
544: 3		MTB Ming
544: 3		MTB Ming
544: 3		MTB Ming
544: 3		MTB Ming
544: 3		MTB Ming
544: 3		MTB Ming
544: 3		MTB Ming
544: 3		MTB Ming
544: 4		MTB Ming
631: 4	?	Light brown (Munsell 7.5 YR 6/4) fabric, dark brown (Munsell 7.5 YR 3/2) lustrous glaze on outside
631: 10	2	Pink fabric, very few inclusions, some air/vegetal inclusion holes, dark olive grey (Munsell 5Y 3/2) glaze on outside, incompletely applied, and splashes inside. Clinky. Apparent flat base
631: 10	5	Medium thickness sherds (0.5 cm+). Light to dark grey paste, at times chunky, with air/vegetal holes and orange inclusions visible on inside. Very eroded black glaze/incrustations over outside. Almost certainly same as Type 3, but a thinner part of the vessel
631: 12	3	Thick sherds (1 cm+). Light to dark grey paste, at times chunky, with air/vegetal holes and orange inclusions visible on inside. Black (Munsell 2.5Y 2.5/1) glaze overall
631: 12	5	Medium thickness sherds (0.5 cm+). Light to dark grey paste, at times chunky, with air/vegetal holes and orange inclusions visible on inside. Black glaze applied thickly and neatly (straight line) over part of outside. Almost certainly same as Type 3, but a thinner part of the vessel
631: 12		Half-glazed. Not studied in detail
631: 12		MTB Ming
631: 13		MTB Ming
631: 14		MTB Ming
631: 16		MTB Ming
631: 20	3	Thick sherds (1 cm+). Light to dark grey paste, at times chunky, with air/vegetal holes and orange inclusions visible on inside. Black glaze, has lost its lustre
631: 20	3	Thick sherds (1 cm+). Light to dark grey paste, at times chunky, with air/vegetal holes and orange inclusions visible on inside. Wholly glazed (black, Munsell 2.5Y 2.5/1)
631: 20	5	Medium thickness sherds (0.5 cm+). Light to dark grey paste, at times chunky, with air/vegetal holes and orange inclusions visible on inside. Black glaze applied thickly and neatly (straight line) over part of outside. Almost certainly same as Type 3, but a thinner part of the vessel
STP 325		Half-glazed. Not studied in detail
STP 449	3	Thick sherds (1 cm+). Light to dark grey paste, at times chunky, with air/vegetal holes and orange inclusions visible on inside. Part glazed with black (Munsell 2.5Y 2.5/1) glaze
STP 449	5	Medium thickness sherds (0.5 cm+). Light to dark grey paste, at times chunky, with air/vegetal holes and orange inclusions visible on inside. Black glaze overall outside. Almost certainly same as Type 3, but a thinner part of the vessel
STP 544	4	Thick sherds (1 cm+). Very similar to Type 3, but a more orange/red fabric (rather than grey). Very similar to Type 2, but less vivid pink. Olive brown (Munsell 2.5Y 4/4) glaze overall, eroding off
STP 544	4	Thick sherds (1 cm+). Very similar to Type 3, but a more orange/red fabric (rather than grey). Very similar to Type 2, but less vivid pink. Base. Heavily weathered (been underwater?) but one drip of black glaze
STP 544		MTB Ming
STP 544		MTB Ming
STP 544		MTB Ming
STP 631		MTB Ming

Figure 5.7 Sherds #131, #186, and #276 from Trench 544, Contexts 1 and 2.

Source: Photo by Guilia Nazzaro.

This half-glazed group clearly encompasses a diverse range of vessels. Rims were rare, but some flat bases were recovered. Shape therefore remains speculative in most cases. However, we can divide the group into two broad classes based on size. The first consists of relatively small vessels, connected via their fabric and shape to a type frequently seen on display in Maldivian resorts as well as at the National Museum in Male'. The second consists of thick, likely very large, vessels.

In his study of Maldivian ceramics, Mikkelsen (1991, p. 200) described a group of pottery featuring a dark red fabric, a large body and a thick everted rim, sometimes with a black glaze, and, citing local historian Mohamed Lutfi, he suggested that large storage urns were brought from the ports of Cochin and Calicut on the Malabar coast of India in the fifteenth and sixteenth centuries, to be used as containers for imported rice and other types of food.

These items also link to the question of large-sized coarse stoneware jars in southeast Asia, often grouped under the term 'martaban' and amply mentioned by early modern historical sources that insist on the quality and desirability of these wares, used for storing water in households and on board ships. Their name derives from the port town of Martaban (Mottama) in Myanmar, and historical sources refer to their large size; a VOC memorandum of AD 1687 provides the weights of five different jars, which ranged between 65.7 and 111.2 kilograms (Seidel 2014, p. 288). Spot dating comes from the seventeenth-century shipwrecks *Santo Antonio de Tanna* in Kenya and *Witte Leeuw* at St Helena in the South Atlantic (Van Der Pijl-Ketel 1982, Piercy et al. 1992, Chandima 2006, p. 99).

These types have been recovered widely, including in southeast Asia, Sri Lanka, the Persian Gulf, and East Africa (Taha 1983, Kennet 1994, Horton et al. 1996, Priestman 2005). In fact, Seidel (2014, pp. 257–258) comments that

> this class of Burmese jars had an astoundingly wide, almost global distribution on board Asian and European ships, in an eastern direction to insular Southeast Asia, Japan, and Mexico, and in a western direction beyond South Asia to the Middle East, the east coast of Africa, and farther into the Atlantic and its shores, even as far as the eastern shore of Canada.

Judging by historical sources, however, the main direction of export was to India, at least in the sixteenth and seventeenth centuries. It is therefore not unexpected to recover some in the Maldives.

However, the definition of the 'martaban' class is problematic. It is certainly known that a major ceramic industry was based in Martaban, but the term has often unhelpfully grouped together several different wares (Moore 1970, Gutman 2001, Seidel 2014). A survey by Moore (1970) of coarse stoneware jars 'of martabani type', some from dated archaeological contexts, in the collections of the Sarawak Museum of Borneo, highlighted the diversity within the group. Her classificatory framework and chronology spans four phases, from before the ninth century to the fifteenth century. The items termed 'Kwantung ware', 'Kalong ware', 'Soo chou ware', and a jarlet from Mukah (Moore 1970, Plates 7bc, 12c, 13ab, 16c and 18b) all offer good parallels with the Kinolhas material, although it is difficult to be definite due to the fragmentary nature of the assemblage. Considerable uncertainty still surrounds this family of ceramic vessels, and there is scope for confusion between types; for example, the Kinolhas material bears some similarity to Bahla ware, of presumed Omani origin (Kennet 2004, pp. 54–55, Ran Zhang, pers. comm.).

The Chinese martabani type jars, for their part, typically have a rolled or wide and thick rim, and the base is coarse and flat. Four or six lugs, vertically or horizontally positioned, are applied to the shoulder. Decoration is rarely found and is limited to a carved floral pattern on the shoulder. It appears that they were fired in Guangdong in China, where the Shiwan kilns (石湾窑) and Xiaxiang kilns (下乡窑) are potential sites of production. They may have been produced in many places across southern China, including the provinces of Zhejiang, Fujian and Guangdong (Harrison-Hall 2001, p. 305). Their height varies from 10 cm to 92 cm (Figure 5.8) (Krahl 1986, p. 899).

One sherd in the Kinolhas assemblage bears an incomplete Chinese character (Figure 5.9). Similar marks can be seen on pieces from the *Witte Leeuw* shipwreck and have been dated to AD 1613 (Van Der Pijl-Ketel 1982) (Figure 5.10). The complete reading of the mark 玉 on the Kinolhas sherd is *yu* ('jade'), or *mei yu* ('beautiful jade'), and it expresses an auspicious meaning wishing fortune and giving a compliment on the quality of the glazes used on these wares, even though similar jars in China were considered to be of lower quality.

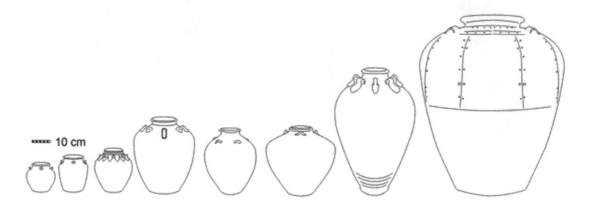

Figure 5.8 Principal shapes of Martaban type jars produced in south China (Shiwan and Xiaxiang kilns in Guangdong Province).
Source: Drawing by Ran Zhang.

Figure 5.9 Mark of *yu* (玉) from a sherd from Kinolhas—#152, from Unit 544, Context 1.
Source: Photo by Guilia Nazzaro.

Figure 5.10 Marks on martaban wares (1: *fu*; 22: *yu*).
Source: Drawing by Ran Zhang.

Rim types

The diagnostics in the Kinolhas assemblage consisted of 459 sherds; 448 recovered from excavations, and 11 from the shovel test pits (Table 5.4). Of these, 374 were in good enough condition to determine morphology and on that basis 42 types of rim (Figure 5.11), seven types of base, and three types of spout were defined (Table 5.6). The following discussion will focus on the rims (N=352), which formed the great majority of the diagnostics.

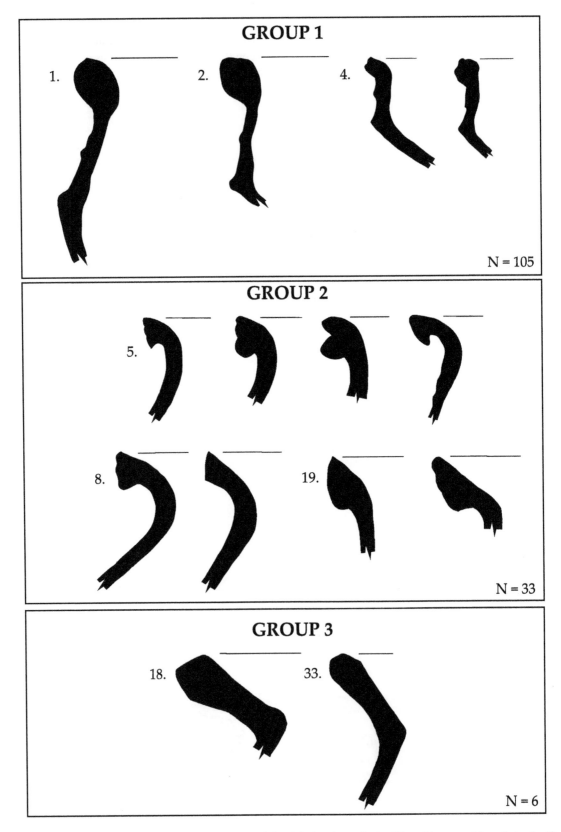

Figure 5.11 Kinolhas rim types. NB: a total of 44 types were defined during the analysis of the wider assemblage, but only 42 of these occurred at Kinolhas (Types 15 and 32 were absent).

Source: Drawing by Susan Anderson, Annalisa Christie, and Giulia Nazzaro.

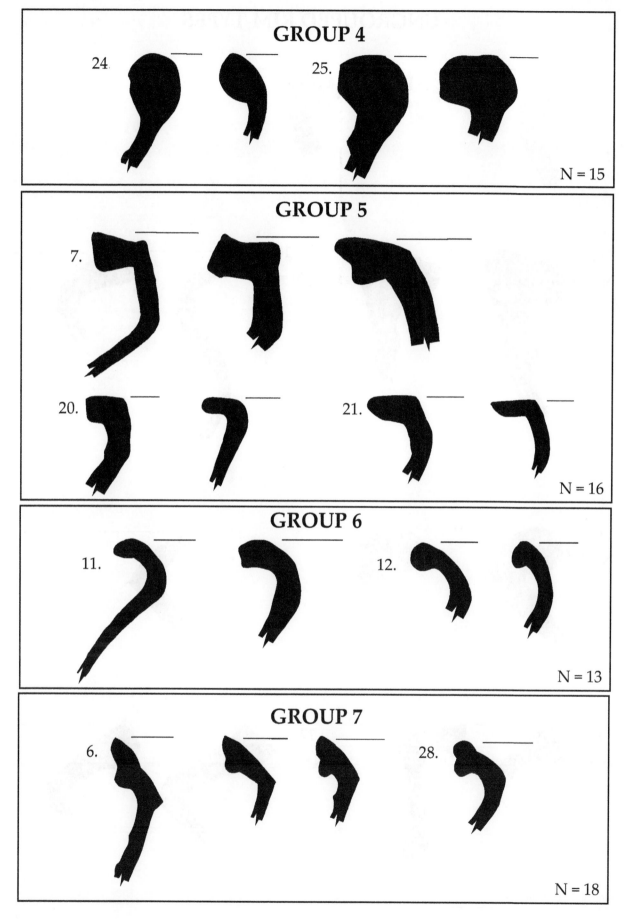

Figure 5.11 (Continued)

UNGROUPED RIM TYPES

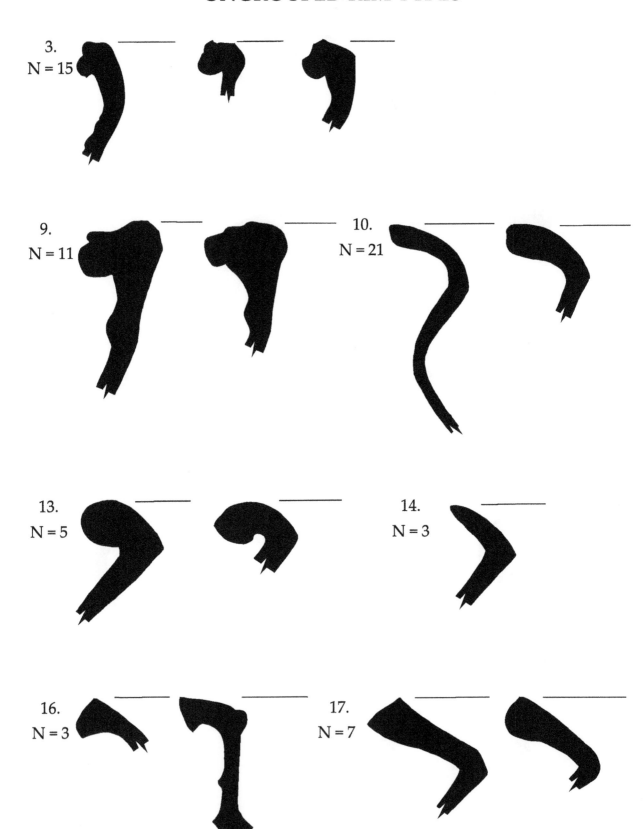

Figure 5.11 (Continued)

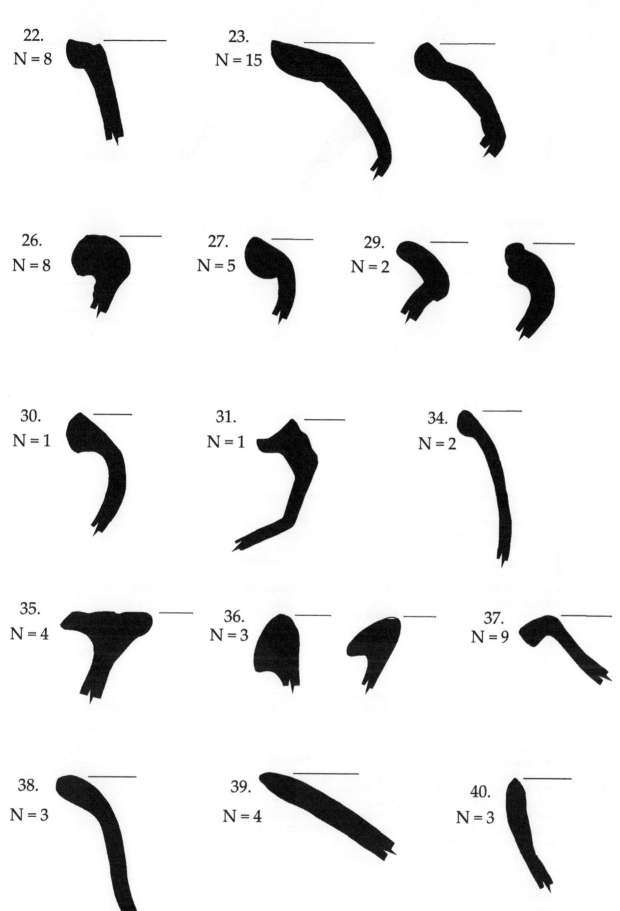

Figure 5.11 (Continued)

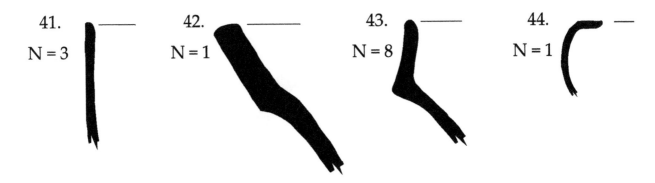

Figure 5.11 (Continued)

Table 5.6 Kinolhas: rim typology; rims are listed in order of frequency.

Rims		Part of group?	Total number
1	Everted, rather round or oval and they thicken towards the lip with a long collar (consisting of external grooves) going slightly outside the vessel and then flaring in below the neck	Group 1	60
2	Everted, similar to Type 1, less rounded but more squarish/ rectangular pointy and somewhat flat on the lip profile. They also thicken towards the lip. Also a long collar (consisting of external grooves) slightly going outside the vessel and then flaring in below the neck	Group 1	35
10	Acutely everted with a curving upper surface and sharp internal angle, generally quite thin rim		21
5	Short wedge with sharp outer edges (sometimes deeply grooved) and slight overhang of lower edge, curving inner edge	Group 2	16
6	Very short wedge/collar with a central groove, appears everted on the inside, usually with an angled inner edge (occasionally slightly rounded)	Group 7	16
3	Squarish bead with grooves externally and on top, slight overhang of exterior lower edge		15
23	Flaring with everted tip		15
9	Slightly sloping everted, acutely angled but rounded internal edge, often grooved or with a raised cordon close to the upper edge		11
24	Rounded bead, some slightly elongated, rounded internally	Group 4	11
4	Squarish bead/short everted with slightly internally sloping top	Group 1	10
8	Similar to Type 5 but longer wedge, sharp outer edges, curving inner edge	Group 2	9
20	Flat-topped everted, rim has parallel top and bottom surfaces, rounded internal edge, upright neck	Group 5	9
37	Hooked rim on bowl/dish		9
19	Short everted rim with wide vertical edge, generally more rounded than Type 5, curving inner edge, appears collared externally	Group 2	8
22	Flaring with short everted or square-beaded tip		8
26	Rounded bead with slight overhang of lower edge		8
43	In-turning; deeply angled collar		8
11	Cavetto with rounded internal angle	Group 6	7
17	Elongated narrow wedge with curving or slightly angled internal edge		7
12	As Type 11 but with a slight rounded bead to the end of the rim	Group 6	6
13	Thick cavetto with rounded underside and sharply angled internal edge		5
21	Flat-topped everted, rim has parallel top and bottom surfaces, sharply angled internal edge, upright neck	Group 5	5
27	Rounded bead with sharp upper edge		5
18	Thickened everted with squared end	Group 3	4
25	Rounded bead, slightly flattened external edge, rounded internally	Group 4	4
35	Flat-topped everted with internal bevel and outer chamfer		4
39	Simple rim on flaring dish/lid forms		4
14	Simple everted with slight internal angle		3
16	Sharply everted with sharp angled inner edge, wedged with slight overhang of lower edge		3
36	Triangular bead with rounded external surface and sharp upper edge		3
38	Flaring rim on bowl/dish		3
40	Simple, sometimes slightly in-turned bowl rims		3
41	Simple upright rim		3
7	Flat-topped everted, squared edge to rim, sharply angled internally, on upright neck	Group 5	2
28	Everted with bifid end	Group 7	2
29	Everted, rounded end, rounded internal edge		2
33	Flaring, slightly thickened end with flat top	Group 3	2
34	Flaring, small round beaded end		2
30	Everted wedge, rounded end with sharp upper and lower edges, rounded internal edge		1

(Continued)

Table 5.6 (Continued)

Rims		Part of group?	Total number
31	Everted, triangular beaded (exaggerated wedge) end		1
42	In-turning; slightly angled; plain collar		1
44	In-turning; sharp		1
Bases			
1	Plain flat		
2	Sagging/rounded		
3	Pedestal with domed centre (subtype 3a concerns concave fragments, possibly part of Type 3)		
4	Tripod?		
5	Hollow baluster?		
6	Small footring?		
7	Footstand?		
Spouts			
1	Simple tapered to narrow pointed end		
2	Tapered with thickened end		
3	Cylindrical with widened/everted end		

Figure 5.12 Refitted vessel from STP 478.

Source: Photo by Giulia Nazzaro.

Simple rims (#39–41) were uncommon, with just ten occurrences, that is, less than 3% of the rim assemblage. They appeared to belong to bowls or dishes, possibly pot-lids, and varied greatly in diameter, between 6 cm and 27 cm. A number shared a characteristic fine grey fabric.

Everted rims constituted the bulk of the assemblage. The closely related Types 1 (N=60) and 2 (N=35) dominated. These are thickened, often bulbous rims, frequently incised on the lip; judging by some whole profiles recovered, they featured a carination at the widest diameter of the vessel. Diameters ranged widely (between 14 cm and 44 cm) but mode, median, and average converge at 24–26 cm. These sherds were never burnished, and only rarely slipped. Associated decorations were incisions (INC), raised band (RB) and square channels (SQCB). The less frequent rim Type 4 (N=10) is related. These three rim types formed Group 1 and make up 29.8% of the assemblage. Given their wide opening and relatively small volume, they likely belong to shallow bowls for serving food. A refitted vessel recovered from one of the shovel test pits (Figure 5.12) illustrates this type.

Some of the small number of earthenware sherds excavated by Carswell in Sultan's Park in Male', which he described as belonging to vessels that were 'often sharply carinated, and [with] overhanging rims' (Carswell 1975–1977, p. 158, Figure 13[7]), are similar to Kinolhas Group 1. The sites of Arikamedu and Vijayanagara in southern India also offer good parallels. The 'flange rim restricted vessels' defined at Vijayanagara are shallow, relatively open vessels with diameters ranging from 23 to 45 cm, likely used for cooking or storage (Sinopoli 1993, p. 57, Figure 4.24, #21, 24, Figure A54, A60, A67). The overall rim shape, the use of channels and stabbed decorations, and the relatively close chronological and regional fit make this a compelling parallel for the Kinolhas material. Some of the material illustrated by Begley (2004, Figures 3.235–242) at Arikamedu is comparable in overall shape to Kinolhas Group 1, and it features grooves and occasional paddle marks. However, these Arikamedu rim profiles are more complex, and their end is less bulbous than at Kinolhas. Related shapes seem to have been geographically wide-ranging. Vessels of comparable morphology, both slipped and unslipped and featuring the same distinct combination of carination and channels as the Kinolhas material, are for example reported from Sumatra, there identified as part of a medieval genre exported to southeast Asia from south Asia (McKinnon 2015, pp. 244–245, Figures 15–16).

Other rims noted at Kinolhas appear closely related to those in Group 1. Group 2 (N=33), formed by merging related Types 5 (N=16), 8 (N=9), and 19 (N=8), constitutes a heterogeneous set in terms of fabric, which includes fine grey, white, pink, and buff, but these rims share a wedge shape and an often sharply curving outer edge. Some appear bifid due to the groove on their lip. Apart from three exceptions, rims in Group 2 are unslipped, and they are either undecorated or marked with channels or incisions. Diameters vary from 15 cm to 35 cm, but median, mode, and average lie at 23–25 cm. This was very fragmented material, and few profiles were recovered, but two instances of carination were observed. The related Group 7, comprising Type 6 (N=16) and Type 28 (N=2), consists of everted rims with a sharp break in the inside line. Again, these often appear bifid due to a central groove on the lip. Average, mode, and median diameter are 22–23 cm. Apart from one doubtful item, perhaps in fact a pedestal base, all Group 7 sherds are decorated with incisions or channels, frequently combined with round or rectangular impressions set in a line.

As was the case with Group 1 rims, Kinolhas Groups 2 and 7 find a good parallel in some of the 'flange rims' at Vijayanagara (Sinopoli 1993, Figure 4.21, especially FN 1–2, FI 1, FE 2) and in ceramics of likely medieval date from Arikamedu (Begley 2004, Figures 3.243–3.247). Tenth/eleventh-century vessels from Sharma, Yemen, are also similar and are indeed described as comparable to the Arikamedu material (Collinet 2015, p. 166 and Figure 174, esp. #7, 8, 13, 14).

Kinolhas Group 5 (N=16), consisting of Types 7, 20, and 21 (N=2, 9, and 5 respectively), are everted rims on an upright neck with a horizontal lip. This flat, horizontal rim, sometimes with a slight dip, finds parallels in material from Sharma (Collinet 2015, Figure 172, #8–20) as well as the representative type of coarse Indian cooking pot (Black Burnished Ware) recovered at Kush, United Arab Emirates (Kennet 2004, Figure 40, 'Type 78'), although in the latter case the fabric appears quite different. Parts of the Vijayanagara and Sind assemblages offer further good parallels (Sinopoli 1993, Figure 4.21, some of the FG, 'flange rim'; Collinet 2010, Figure 145, some of the 'Type 4', 'jarres à col droit').

The emphasis has been placed on Kinolhas Groups 1, 2, 5, and 7 for several reasons. First, and primarily, they emerged as a very distinctive corpus during analysis and together account for almost half of the assemblage from the site (N=172, 48.86%). In addition, they appear related to types reported around the Indian Ocean and linked by researchers with the Indian subcontinent.

The Kinolhas material has some morphological similarities with some relatively early occurrences of so-called Indian ceramics, such as Indian Red Polished ware from the Iranian shore of the Persian Gulf (Whitehouse and Williamson 1973, Figure 5de) and Indian and Indian-style pottery from Berenike (Tomber 2000, Figure 2.3). Within India, notable instances include Wheeler et al.'s (1946, Figures 19–20) Type 24 at Arikamedu, in particular Variants 24 o–t, 'a subclass by themselves' distinguished by a series of ridges at the shoulder, just above a carination (Wheeler et al. 1946, p. 63); Begley's (2004, Figures 3.343–3.356) Form 20 at the same site; and Types 35 and 35a from the Iron Age Megalithic phase at Maski, Karnataka (Thapar 1957, Figure 23). However, beyond a similarity in shape, these materials differ in important respects from the Kinolhas items. Most are coated partly or wholly with red burnished slip, some are of a very fine fabric, and some are stained with soot; none of these features are seen in the Kinolhas material. Moreover, some of the vessel types, in particular Begley's Form 20 and Wheeler et al.'s Type 24, both from Arikamedu, constitute very broad groupings covering a wide range of vessel sizes and shapes, limiting their comparative potential.

While some Indian ceramics, most especially Indian Red Polished ware, once served as a *fossile directeur* of Indo-Roman trade, it has now been recognised that pottery of the same general morphology fits in a longer time-frame, occurring for example in sequences of the Islamic period (Tomber 2000, Kennet 2004, Collinet 2010, Schenk 2015). One subtype warranting further investigation, representing vessels with a ledged outer rim lip, has been reported for medieval periods across India—at Arikamedu, Budhigarh (Odisha), and Sanjan (Gujarat)—and more widely from Qalat al-Bahrain (Bahrain Fort) and from twelfth- and thirteenth- century levels from the vicinity of Tissamaharama (Schenk 2015, p. 162, Figure 12). These vessels, with a ledged outer rim lip and with distinctive carination and channels, present close parallels with many of the Kinolhas sherds.

The remaining rim assemblage from Kinolhas is less easy to qualify. Some types occur in some numbers. Type 3 rims (N=15), grooved and almost square, and with a slight overhang, are all decorated with incisions or channels, and some have the distinctive ledged rim discussed previously. These can probably also be connected to the 'Indian' earthenware group. So too can Type 9 (N=11), a slightly sloping everted rim, acutely angled but with a rounded internal edge, often grooved or with an appliqué strip. Some shapes are less diagnostic: this is the case with Type 10, which are acutely everted rims, occasionally covered with an orange slip but otherwise largely undecorated; the total number is 21, but 6 items, from Trench 631, probably come from the same vessel. Type 23 rims (N=15), flaring with everted tip, stand out for their very fine grey fabric and their association with a decoration consisting of stamped concentric circles ('S6', discussed earlier); all come from Trench 544 and they may represent as few as 6 separate vessels. The remaining rim types occur in relatively small numbers and are not discussed further here.

Conclusion

The Kinolhas assemblage contained a sizable proportion of unglazed earthenware, a situation common, of course, to many sites of the western Indian Ocean. Such materials have sometimes been neglected, but researchers have become increasingly interested in the potential presented by these artefacts. Pavan and Schenk (2012, p. 197; see also Schenk 2015), in an overview of assemblages from the geographically distant sites of Tissamaharama in Sri Lanka and Sumhuram in Oman, highlight the importance of household pottery in identifying commonalities across the western Indian

Ocean. The widely occurring 'Indian' and 'Indian-type wares' in particular raise questions. McKinnon (2015, p. 244) observed that due to a lack of funding, time, and comparative published materials, the Indian ceramics recovered at Kota Cina, northeast Sumatra, were only cursorily recorded—'In retrospect, this was a serious omission'.

A good part of the Kinolhas assemblage is reminiscent of materials commonly described in Indian Ocean studies as having an origin in India. In terms of morphology, over half the rim sherds studied have affinities with material documented in Sri Lanka, India, the Red Sea, and the Persian Gulf, classed as 'Indian' and spanning different times between the last few centuries BC and the medieval period. As well as shape, the decorations identified at Kinolhas, and in particular the paddle impressions, strengthen the idea of a connection with southern India and Sri Lanka. The closest formal parallels are with assemblages recovered from Arikamedu (Begley 1996, Selvakumar 2004) and Tissamaharama (Schenk 2006, Pavan and Schenk 2012), and related occurrences are reported in Yemen, Oman, Egypt, and Indonesia (Tomber 2000, Pavan and Schenk 2012, McKinnon 2015, Collinet 2015).

The sherds of fine fabric recovered at Kinolhas certainly require further study. Small groups of distinctive fine buff, orange, and grey wares stand out within the relatively coarse assemblage. Fine pastes suggestive of Indian Red Polished ware materials, with a very fine, well-levigated, brick-red body covered by a thin orange-red slip (Kennet 2004, p. 88), occur but were very scarce at Kinolhas as elsewhere in the Maldives (Litster 2016, Figure 6.1). The importance of fabric in understanding material from medieval sites across Asia has been repeatedly highlighted. Begley (1996, p. 204) indicated that fabric appeared to be a more reliable indicator of chronology than did decoration in the case of impressed pottery at Arikamedu; Collinet (2015, p. 166) remarked that grey/black wares could serve as important chronological and regional markers as they occur at different times in different parts of India; and Moore (1970) commented that the only adequate basis for classification of 'martabans' was clay, since many kilns used similar glazes and shapes over the centuries. A study of a subgroup of sherds recovered at Tissamaharama, later extended to a much broader region (Schenk 2006, Pavan and Schenk 2012), has presented a particularly instructive example. These sherds were made of a very dense and extremely fine grey clay—a 'high quality paste [that] is eye-catching and completely different among contemporaneous southern Indian and Sri Lankan pottery assemblages' (Schenk 2006, p. 129). The excavators suggest that this represents a product custom-made for South India and Sri Lanka, which did not arrive through ordinary trade but instead constituted the personal belongings of Indian merchants or sailors or served as prestige gifts (Pavan and Schenk 2012, p. 200).[8] Petrographic analysis of the Kinolhas earthenwares was beyond the scope of the present work, which focused on establishing an initial typo-chronology, but such work is planned for the future to provide insights into past connections.[9]

Indeed, in the case of the Maldives, pottery offers very real clues to identity. The wares discussed in this chapter are often cooking pots, quite coarse and likely fragile. The point has been made in other parts of the Indian Ocean world that it is unclear why such utilitarian vessels would have been traded over these great distances (Horton et al. 1996, Horton 2004, Kennet 2004, Collinet 2010). They may have been personal possessions, reflecting the settlement of merchants from afar. All in all, the range of distinctive earthenwares within the Kinolhas assemblage sheds light on the ceramics traded to this Indian Ocean archipelago, be it as containers for some desirable product or in their own right.

Notes

1 Accession numbers EAP. 6229, 6270–6299, 6301–6308, 6751, 6753, 6760–6765, 6766–6801, 6936–7037, 7039, 7041–7046, 7074–7116, 7117–71128, 7144–7292, 7307–7323, 7325–7452, 18270–18416, and 18651–18661. Six boxes were not available to us as their contents were either missing or on display.
2 In addition, since our visit the collection was re-photographed and is in the process of being digitised by the Maldives Heritage Survey team; https://maritimeasiaheritage.cseas.kyoto-u.ac.jp/data/data-sets/carswell-collection/.
3 These are sherds #333–340 in Carswell's classification; their Ashmolean accession numbers are EAP .7235–7242, Box Male' 18.
4 A small number of surface finds are also considered by Litster (2016).
5 See Chapter 2, this volume, for description. 'Havitta' is a term used to refer to ancient Buddhist stupas in the Maldives.
6 As is the case within Europe or the wider Mediterranean world, the term 'roulette' often refers not to fibre or carved wooden roulettes but instead to rolled cylinders or spoked wheels, and this is the way in which Begley uses the term. Using ethnographic comparison, Begley (1988) concluded that the decoration is not in fact the result of the use of roulettes, but rather was 'chattered', probably using sharp-pointed metal strips.
7 The closest parallel in this figure is perhaps with the sherd bottom right, which is from the site of Vankalai in Sri Lanka and which Carswell includes to illustrate the similarity with the Male' material.
8 Some materials, such as rouletted ware sherds, showed signs of repair, suggesting they were carefully curated (Schenk 2006, p. 123, Figure 1c, Pavan and Schenk 2012, p. 200, Schenk 2015, p. 146).
9 An analysis of the spouts recovered at Kinolhas may be of particular interest given the importance of sprinklers and spouted jars in scholarship on Indian Ocean exchange (see e.g. Schenk 2015). A number were characterised by a fine grey fabric (see Table 5.4).

6 The glazed pottery

Asian and Islamic imports

Ran Zhang

Introduction

This chapter aims to provide an understanding of the classification of the glazed ceramics from Kinolhas. In October 2017 and May 2018, the author undertook specialist analysis of the Chinese and southeast Asian ceramics, dated from between the fourteenth and nineteenth centuries, which were imported on a temporary export permit from the site of Kinolhas, Maldives, to the Sainsbury Research Unit for the Arts of Africa, Oceania & the Americas, University of East Anglia. This work involved the identification and classification of the Chinese and southeast Asian ceramic imports. The present author conducted this work. In addition, Professor Wang Guangyao, Deputy Director of the Institute of Archaeology of the Palace Museum, Beijing, very kindly provided suggestions for dating and identifying the Chinese ceramic materials. The Kinolhas assemblage also contains some material originating in the Islamic world. Dr Derek Kennet, Durham University, contributed to identifying these. The assemblage is presented in Table 6.1.

Table 6.1 Glazed ceramic corpus from Kinolhas.

Sherd No	Unit	Context	Class	(Chinese wares only) Dynasty	Dating	Type
444	321	STP	SE CEL	–	15th	SOUTHEAST ASIAN CELADON TYPE 1
445	321	STP	ISLAM	–	–	PERSIA
446	321	STP	SE CEL	–	15th	
447	321	STP	SE CEL	–	15th	
448	321	STP	CBW2–2	Mid Ming	16th	
449	321	STP	CBW2–3	Late Ming	17th	
450	321	1	CBW2–2	Mid Ming	16th	
451	321	1	CBW2–2	Mid Ming	16th	
453	321	2	SE CEL	–	15th	
454	321	2	CBW2–3	Late Ming	17th	
455	321	2	SE CEL	–	15th	
456	321	2	SE CEL	–	15th	
457	321	2	SE CEL	–	15th	SOUTHEAST ASIAN CELADON DIFFERENT TYPE
458	321	2	SE CEL	–	15th	
459	321	2	CBW2–2	Mid Ming	16th	
460	321	2	SE CEL	–	15th	
461	321	2	LQCJDZ	Late Ming	17th	
462	321	2	SE CEL	–	15th	
463	321	2	SE CEL	–	15th	
464	321	2	LQC2	Early Ming	15th	
465	321	2	LQC1	Yuan	14th	
466	321	2	SE CEL	–	15th	
467	321	2	SE CEL	–	15th	
468	321	2	LQC1	Yuan	14th	
469	321	2	SE CEL	–	15th	
470	321	2	SE CEL	–	15th	
479	321	2	CBW2–3	Late Ming	17th	
480	321	2	CBW2–2	Mid Ming	16th	
481	321	2	CBW2–1	Early Ming	15th	EARLY MING CHINESE BLUE AND WHITE
482	321	2	CBW2–3	Late Ming	17th	
483	321	2	CBW2–2	Mid Ming	16th	
484	321	2	CBW2–2	Mid Ming	16th	
485	321	2	CBW2–2	Mid Ming	16th	
486	321	2	CBW2–3	Late Ming	17th	
487	321	2	SE CEL	–	15th	SOUTHEAST ASIAN CELADON TYPE 1
488	321	2	CBW2–2	Mid Ming	16th	MID MING

(Continued)

DOI: 10.4324/9781003166221-6

Table 6.1 (Continued)

Sherd No	Unit	Context	Class	(Chinese wares only) Dynasty	Dating	Type
489	321	2	CBW2–2	Mid Ming	16th	MID MING
490	321	2	SE CEL	–	15th	SOUTHEAST ASIAN CELADON TYPE 2
491	321	2	CBW2–2	Mid Ming	16th	MID MING
492	321	2	CBW2–2	Mid Ming	16th	MID MING
493	321	2	CBW2–3	Late Ming	17th	LATE MING CHINESE BLUE AND WHITE
496	325	STP	CBW2–1	Early Ming	15th	EARLY MING CHINESE BLUE AND WHITE
497	325	STP	SE CEL	–	15th	
498	325	STP	SE CEL	–	15th	
499	325	STP	CBW2–3	Late Ming	17th	
500	325	STP	CBW2–2	Mid Ming	16th	
501	325	STP	CBW2–2	Mid Ming	16th	
502	325	1	CBW2–2	Mid Ming	16th	
503	325	1	CBW2–2	Mid Ming	16th	
504	325	1	LQC2	Early Ming	15th	
505	325	1	LQC1	Yuan	14th	
508	325	2	CBW2–2	Mid Ming	16th	
509	325	2	CBW2–2	Mid Ming	16th	
510	325	2	CBW2–2	Mid Ming	16th	
511	325	2	CBW2–3	Late Ming	17th	
512	325	2	CBW2–2	Mid Ming	16th	
513	325	2	CBW2–2	Mid Ming	16th	
514	325	2	CBW2–2	Mid Ming	16th	
515	325	2	CBW2–2	Mid Ming	16th	
516	325	2	CBW2–2	Mid Ming	16th	
517	325	2	CBW2–2	Mid Ming	16th	
518	325	2	CBW2–3	Late Ming	17th	
519	325	2	No-ID	–	–	UNIDENTIFIED GREEN GLAZED
520	325	2	ISLAM	–	–	PERSIA
522	325	2	CBW2–2	Mid Ming	16th	MID MING
523	325	2	SE CEL	–	15th	SOUTHEAST ASIAN CELADON TYPE 2
524	325	2	LQC1	Yuan	14th	YUAN LONGQUAN CELADON (1276–1368 AD) MONGOLIAN PERIOD
525	325	2	SE CEL	–	15th	SOUTHEAST ASIAN CELADON TYPE 2
526	325	2	LQC2	Early Ming	15th	EARLY–MIDDLE MING LONGQUAN CELADON (ABOUT 1368–1500AD)
527	325	2	LQC2	Early Ming	15th	LONGQUAN CELADON GUANGDONG
528	325	2	ISLAM	–	–	PERSIA
529	325	2	LQC1	Yuan	14th	YUAN LONGQUAN CELADON (1276–1368 AD) MONGOLIAN PERIOD
530	325	2	SE CEL	–	15th	SOUTHEAST ASIAN CELADON TYPE 1
531	325	2	CWP	Mid Ming	16th	MIDDLE–LATE MING CHINESE WHITE PORCELAIN
532	325	2	SE CEL	–	15th	SOUTHEAST ASIAN CELADON TYPE 2
533	325	2	CBW2–3	Late Ming	17th	LATE MING CHINESE BLUE AND WHITE
534	325	2	SE CEL	–	15th	SOUTHEAST ASIAN CELADON TYPE 1
535	325	2	SE CEL	–	15th	SOUTHEAST ASIAN CELADON TYPE 1
536	325	2	SE CEL	–	15th	SOUTHEAST ASIAN CELADON TYPE 1
537	325	2	SE CEL	–	15th	SOUTHEAST ASIAN CELADON TYPE 1
538	325	2	SE CEL	–	15th	SOUTHEAST ASIAN CELADON TYPE 1
539	325	2	CBW2–2	Mid Ming	16th	MID MING
542	325	2	No-ID	–	–	UNIDENTIFIED
551	325	2	No-ID	–	–	UNIDENTIFIED
552	325	2	No-ID	–	–	UNIDENTIFIED
553	325	2	No-ID	–	–	UNIDENTIFIED
554	325	2	LQC1	Yuan	14th	YUAN -LQC. 1276–1368 MONGOLIAN PERIOD
555	325	2	SE CEL	–	15th	SOUTHEAST ASIAN CELADON DIFFERENT TYPE
556	325	2	SE CEL	–	15th	SOUTHEAST ASIAN CELADON TYPE 1
559	325	2	CWP	Mid Ming	16th	MIDDLE–LATE MING CHINESE WHITE PORCELAIN
560	325	2	CBW2–2	Mid Ming	16th	MID MING
561	325	3	No-ID	–	–	UNIDENTIFIED BASE
562	325	5	CBW2–2	Mid Ming	16th	MID MING
563	325	5	CBW2–2	Mid Ming	16th	MID MING
564	325	5	CBW2–2	Mid Ming	16th	MID MING
576	360	1	SE CEL	–	15th	SOUTHEAST ASIAN CELADON TYPE 1? WHITE GLAZE RED BODY
566	360	2	LQC1	Yuan	14th	YUAN LONGQUAN CELADON (1276–1368 AD) MONGOLIAN PERIOD

(Continued)

Table 6.1 (Continued)

Sherd No	Unit	Context	Class	(Chinese wares only) Dynasty	Dating	Type
577	360	2	SE CEL	–	15th	SOUTHEAST ASIAN CELADON TYPE 1
578	360	2	CBW2–1	Early Ming	15th	EARLY MING CHINESE BLUE AND WHITE
579	360	2	LQC1	Yuan	14th	YUAN LONGQUAN CELADON (1276–1368 AD) MONGOLIAN PERIOD
581	360	2	LQC1	Yuan	14th	YUAN LONGQUAN CELADON (1276–1368 AD) MONGOLIAN PERIOD
582	360	2	SE CEL	–	15th	SOUTHEAST ASIAN CELADON TYPE 1
583	360	2	CBW2–2	Mid Ming	16th	MID MING
584	360	2	CBW2–2	Mid Ming	16th	MIDDLE MING CHINESE BLUE AND WHITE
585	360	2	CBW2–2	Mid Ming	16th	MIDDLE MING CHINESE BLUE AND WHITE
586	360	2	SE CEL	–	15th	SOUTHEAST ASIAN CELADON TYPE 1? WHITE GLAZE RED BODY
587	360	2	CBW2–2	Mid Ming	16th	MID MING
390	443	STP	SE CEL	–	15th	
392	443	2	CBW2–2	Mid Ming	16th	
393	443	2	CBW2–1	Early Ming	15th	
394	443	2	SE CEL	–	15th	
395	443	2	SE CEL	–	15th	
396	443	2	ISLAM	–	–	MGPAINT
397	443	2	CBW2–2	Mid Ming	16th	
398	443	2	CBW2–2	Mid Ming	16th	
399	443	2	CBW2–2	Mid Ming	16th	
400	443	2	ISLAM	–	–	MGPAINT
401	443	2	SE CEL	–	15th	
402	443	2	CBW2–3	Late Ming	17th	
403	443	2	CBW2–2	Mid Ming	16th	
404	443	2	CBW2–1	Early Ming	15th	EARLY MING CHINESE BLUE AND WHITE
405	443	2	SE CEL	–	15th	
406	443	2	CBW2–2	Mid Ming	16th	
407	443	2	CBW2–2	Mid Ming	16th	
408	443	2	CBW2–2	Mid Ming	16th	
409	443	2	SE CEL	–	15th	
410	443	2	CBW2–1	Early Ming	15th	
411	443	2	SE CEL	–	15th	SOUTHEAST ASIAN CELADON TYPE 2
412	443	2	SE CEL	–	15th	
437	449	Section Clean	CBW2–3	Late Ming	17th	LATE MING LOW QUALITY
438	449	Section Clean	LQC1	Yuan	14th	
439	449	Section Clean	SE CEL	–	15th	SOUTHEAST ASIAN CELADON TYPE 2
440	449	Section Clean	ISLAM	–	–	PERSIA
441	449	Section Clean	SE CEL	–	15th	SOUTHEAST ASIAN CELADON TYPE 1
590	449	STP	SE CEL	–	15th	SOUTHEAST ASIAN CELADON TYPE 1
591	449	STP	SE CEL	–	15th	SOUTHEAST ASIAN CELADON TYPE 1
592	449	STP	SE CEL	–	15th	SOUTHEAST ASIAN CELADON TYPE 1
414	449	2	SE CEL	–	15th	
415	449	2	SE CEL	–	15th	SOUTHEAST ASIAN CELADON TYPE 1
416	449	2	SE CEL	–	15th	
417	449	2	LQC1	Yuan	14th	
418	449	2	LQC1	Yuan	14th	
419	449	2	SE CEL	–	15th	SOUTHEAST ASIAN CELADON TYPE 2
420	449	2	SE CEL	–	15th	
421	449	2	CBW2–3	Late Ming	17th	LATE MING (LOW QUALITY) CHINESE BLUE AND WHITE
422	449	2	SE CEL	–	15th	SOUTHEAST ASIAN CELADON TYPE 1
423	449	2	CBW1	Yuan	14th	
424	449	2	SE CEL	–	15th	
425	449	2	CBW2–2	Mid Ming	16th	
428	449	2	No-ID	–	–	
429	449	2	CBW2–3	Late Ming	17th	
431	449	2	CBW2–2	Mid Ming	16th	
432	449	2	LQC2	Early Ming	15th	
433	449	2	SE CEL	–	15th	SOUTHEAST ASIAN CELADON DIFFERENT TYPE
434	449	2	ISLAM	–	–	PERSIA
442	449	2	ISLAM	–	–	PERSIA
573	449	2	SE CEL	–	15th	SOUTHEAST ASIAN CELADON TYPE 1
574	449	2	LQC1	Yuan	14th	YUAN LONGQUAN CELADON (1276–1368 AD) MONGOLIAN PERIOD

(*Continued*)

Table 6.1 (Continued)

Sherd No	Unit	Context	Class	(Chinese wares only) Dynasty	Dating	Type
575	449	2	SE CEL	–	15th	SOUTHEAST ASIAN CELADON TYPE 2
97	544	STP	SE CEL	–	15th	SOUTHEAST ASIAN CELADON TYPE 1
100	544	STP	CBW2–3	Late Ming	17th	LATE MING LOW QUALITY
101	544	STP	LQC1	Yuan	14th	YUAN LONGQUAN CELADON (1276–1368 AD) MONGOLIAN PERIOD
102	544	STP	CBW2–2	Mid Ming	16th	MIDDLE MING CHINESE BLUE AND WHITE
104	544	STP	SE CEL	–	15th	SOUTHEAST ASIAN CELADON TYPE 1
105	544	STP	SE CEL	–	15th	SOUTHEAST ASIAN CELADON TYPE 1
106	544	STP	LQC2	Early Ming	15th	LONGQUAN CELADON GUANGDONG
107	544	STP	SE CEL	–	15th	SOUTHEAST ASIAN CELADON TYPE 1
108	544	STP	SE CEL	–	15th	SOUTHEAST ASIAN CELADON DIFFERENT TYPE
109	544	STP	LQC1	Yuan	14th	YUAN LONGQUAN CELADON (1276–1368 AD) MONGOLIAN PERIOD
110	544	STP	SE CEL	–	15th	SOUTHEAST ASIAN CELADON TYPE 1
111	544	STP	SE CEL	–	15th	SOUTHEAST ASIAN CELADON DIFFERENT TYPE
112	544	STP	SE CEL	–	15th	SOUTHEAST ASIAN CELADON TYPE 1
115	544	1	CBW2–3	Late Ming	17th	MIDDLE–LATE MING CHINESE ENAMEL PORCELAIN
116	544	1	CBW2–2	Mid Ming	16th	MID MING
117	544	1	CBW2–2	Mid Ming	16th	MIDDLE MING CHINESE BLUE AND WHITE
122	544	1	CBW2–3	Late Ming	17th	LATE MING LOW QUALITY
123	544	1	SE CEL	–	15th	SOUTHEAST ASIAN CELADON TYPE 2
124	544	1	CBW2–2	Mid Ming	16th	MID MING
125	544	1	CBW2–2	Mid Ming	16th	MID MING
126	544	1	CBW2–2	Mid Ming	16th	MID MING
127	544	1	CBW2–2	Mid Ming	16th	MID MING
128	544	1	LQC1	Yuan	14th	YUAN LONGQUAN CELADON (1276–1368 AD) MONGOLIAN PERIOD
130	544	1	No-ID	–	–	UNIDENTIFIED OPACIFIED GLAZE SAMARRA HORIZON?
132	544	1	CBW2–2	Mid Ming	16th	MIDDLE MING CHINESE BLUE AND WHITE
134	544	1	SE CEL	–	15th	SOUTHEAST ASIAN CELADON DIFFERENT TYPE
135	544	1	SE CEL	–	15th	SOUTH EAST ASIAN CELADON TYPE 2
137	544	1	CBW2–2	Mid Ming	16th	MIDDLE MING CHINESE BLUE AND WHITE
138	544	1	CBW2–2	Mid Ming	16th	MID MING
139	544	1	LQC1	Yuan	14th	YUAN LONGQUAN CELADON (1276–1368 AD) MONGOLIAN PERIOD
141	544	1	SE CEL	–	15th	SOUTHEAST ASIAN CELADON TYPE 1
142	544	1	SE CEL	–	15th	SOUTHEAST ASIAN CELADON TYPE 1
143	544	1	SE CEL	–	15th	SOUTHEAST ASIAN CELADON TYPE 1
144	544	1	SE CEL	–	15th	SOUTHEAST ASIAN CELADON TYPE 2
145	544	1	CBW2–2	Mid Ming	16th	MID MING
146	544	1	CBW2–2	Mid Ming	16th	MID MING
147	544	1	SE CEL	–	15th	SOUTHEAST ASIAN CELADON TYPE 1
148	544	1	LQC2	Early Ming	15th	LONGQUAN CELADON GUANGDONG
149	544	1	SE CEL	–	15th	SOUTHEAST ASIAN CELADON TYPE 1
150	544	1	SE CEL	–	15th	SOUTHEAST ASIAN CELADON TYPE 1
151	544	1	SE CEL	–	15th	SOUTHEAST ASIAN CELADON TYPE 1
156	544	1	CBW2–2	Mid Ming	16th	MIDDLE MING CHINESE BLUE AND WHITE
157	544	1	LQC1	Yuan	14th	YUAN LONGQUAN CELADON (1276–1368 AD) MONGOLIAN PERIOD
158	544	1	CBW2–2	Mid Ming	16th	MIDDLE MING CHINESE BLUE AND WHITE
159	544	1	CBW2–2	Mid Ming	16th	MID MING
160	544	1	SE CEL	–	15th	SOUTHEAST ASIAN CELADON TYPE 1
161	544	1	SE CEL	–	15th	SOUTHEAST ASIAN CELADON TYPE 1
162	544	1	SE CEL	–	15th	SOUTHEAST ASIAN CELADON TYPE 1
163	544	1	SE CEL	–	15th	SOUTHEAST ASIAN CELADON TYPE 1
164	544	1	SE CEL	–	15th	SOUTHEAST ASIAN CELADON TYPE 1
165	544	1	No-ID	?	17th	MID–LATE MING CARP
166	544	1	No-ID	?	17th	MID-LATE MING CARP
167	544	1	CWP	Mid Ming	16th	MIDDLE–LATE MING CHINESE WHITE PORCELAIN
168	544	1	No-ID	?	17th	MI–LATE MING CARP
169	544	1	No-ID	?	17th	MID-LATE MING CARP
170	544	1	No-ID	–	–	NO INFORMATION
171	544	1	CBW2–2	Mid Ming	16th	MIDDLE MING CHINESE BLUE AND WHITE
172	544	1	CBW2–2	Mid Ming	16th	MID MING
173	544	1	CBW2–2	Mid Ming	16th	MID MING

(Continued)

Table 6.1 (Continued)

Sherd No	Unit	Context	Class	(Chinese wares only) Dynasty	Dating	Type
175	544	1	CBW2–2	Mid Ming	16th	MID MING
176	544	1	CBW2–2	Mid Ming	16th	MIDDLE MING CHINESE BLUE AND WHITE
177	544	1	CBW2–2	Mid Ming	16th	MIDDLE MING CHINESE BLUE AND WHITE
178	544	1	CWP	Mid Ming	16th	MIDDLE–LATE MING CHINESE WHITE PORCELAIN
179	544	1	CWP	Mid Ming	16th	MIDDLE–LATE MING CHINESE WHITE PORCELAIN
180	544	1	CWP	Mid Ming	16th	MIDDLE–LATE MING CHINESE WHITE PORCELAIN
181	544	1	CWP	Mid Ming	16th	MIDDLE–LATE MING CHINESE WHITE PORCELAIN
182	544	1	CWP	Mid Ming	16th	MIDDLE–LATE MING CHINESE WHITE PORCELAIN
183	544	1	CWP	Mid Ming	16th	MIDDLE–LATE MING CHINESE WHITE PORCELAIN
184	544	2	No-ID	–	–	UNIDENTIFIED OPACIFIED GLAZE SAMARRA HORIZON?
187	544	2	LQC1	Yuan	14th	YUAN LONGQUAN CELADON (1276–1368 AD) MONGOLIAN PERIOD
188	544	2	CBW2–1	Early Ming	15th	EARLY MING CHINESE BLUE AND WHITE
189	544	2	No-ID	–	–	UNIDENTIFIED BASE
190	544	2	LQC2	Early Ming	15th	EARLY–MIDDLE MING LONGQUAN CELADON (ABOUT 1368–1500AD)
192	544	2	LQC2	Early Ming	15th	EARLY–MIDDLE MING LONGQUAN CELADON (ABOUT 1368–1500AD)
193	544	2	SE CEL	–	15th	SOUTHEAST ASIAN CELADON TYPE 2
195	544	2	SE CEL	–	15th	SOUTHEAST ASIAN CELADON TYPE 1
196	544	2	SE CEL	–	15th	SOUTHEAST ASIAN CELADON TYPE 1
198	544	2	CBW2–3	Late Ming	17th	LATE MING LOW QUALITY
201	544	2	SE CEL	–	15th	SOUTHEAST ASIAN CELADON TYPE 1
202	544	2	CBW2–3	Late Ming	17th	LATE MING (LOW QUALITY) CHINESE BLUE AND WHITE
203	544	2	CBW2–2	Mid Ming	16th	MID MING
204	544	2	ISLAM	–	–	PERSIA
205	544	2	CBW2–2	Mid Ming	16th	MIDDLE MING CHINESE BLUE AND WHITE
208	544	2	LQC1	Yuan	14th	YUAN LONGQUAN CELADON (1276–1368 AD) MONGOLIAN PERIOD
209	544	2	CBW2–2	Mid Ming	16th	MID MING
210	544	2	CBW2–3	Late Ming	17th	MIDDLE–LATE MING CHINESE ENAMEL PORCELAIN
211	544	2	IMPERIAL	Early Ming	15th	IMPERIAL QUALITY
212	544	2	SE CEL	–	15th	SOUTHEAST ASIAN CELADON TYPE 2
213	544	2	SE CEL	–	15th	SOUTHEAST ASIAN CELADON TYPE 1
214	544	2	SE CEL	–	15th	SOUTHEAST ASIAN CELADON TYPE 1
215	544	2	SE CEL	–	15th	SOUTHEAST ASIAN CELADON TYPE 1
216	544	2	CBW2–2	Mid Ming	16th	MID MING
217	544	2	CBW2–3	Late Ming	17th	LATE MING LOW QUALITY
218	544	2	No-ID	–	–	UNIDENTIFIED OPACIFIED GLAZE SAMARRA HORIZON?
219	544	2	CBW2–2	Mid Ming	16th	MIDDLE MING CHINESE BLUE AND WHITE
222	544	2	CBW2–1	Early Ming	15th	EARLY MING CHINESE BLUE AND WHITE
223	544	2	SE CEL	–	15th	SOUTHEAST ASIAN CELADON TYPE 1
224	544	2	SE CEL	–	15th	SOUTHEAST ASIAN CELADON TYPE 1
225	544	2	SE CEL	–	15th	SOUTHEAST ASIAN CELADON TYPE 2
226	544	2	LQC1	Yuan	14th	YUAN LONGQUAN CELADON (1276–1368 AD) MONGOLIAN PERIOD
227	544	2	SE CEL	–	15th	SOUTHEAST ASIAN CELADON DIFFERENT TYPE
228	544	2	LQC1	Yuan	14th	YUAN LONGQUAN CELADON (1276–1368 AD) MONGOLIAN PERIOD
229	544	2	SE CEL	–	15th	SOUTHEAST ASIAN CELADON TYPE 2
230	544	2	CBW2–2	Mid Ming	16th	MID MING
231	544	2	CBW2–2	Mid Ming	16th	MID MING
233	544	2	LQC1	Yuan	14th	YUAN LONGQUAN CELADON (1276–1368 AD) MONGOLIAN PERIOD
234	544	2	SE CEL	–	15th	SOUTHEAST ASIAN CELADON DIFFERENT TYPE
235	544	2	SE CEL	–	15th	SOUTHEAST ASIAN CELADON TYPE 2
237	544	2	SE CEL	–	15th	SOUTHEAST ASIAN CELADON TYPE 1
239	544	2	SE CEL	–	15th	SOUTHEAST ASIAN CELADON TYPE 1
244	544	2	SE CEL	–	15th	SOUTHEAST ASIAN CELADON TYPE 2
245	544	2	CBW2–3	Late Ming	17th	MIDDLE MING CHINESE BLUE AND WHITE
246	544	2	CBW2–3	Late Ming	17th	LATE MING (LOW QUALITY) CHINESE BLUE AND WHITE
247	544	2	CBW2–2	Mid Ming	16th	MIDDLE MING CHINESE BLUE AND WHITE

(*Continued*)

Table 6.1 (Continued)

Sherd No	Unit	Context	Class	(Chinese wares only) Dynasty	Dating	Type
248	544	2	CBW2–2	Mid Ming	16th	MID MING
249	544	2	SE CEL	–	15th	SOUTHEAST ASIAN CELADON TYPE 2
250	544	2	CBW2–1	Early Ming	15th	EARLY MING CHINESE BLUE AND WHITE
251	544	2	CBW2–2	Mid Ming	16th	MIDDLE MING CHINESE BLUE AND WHITE
252	544	2	CBW2–2	Mid Ming	16th	MIDDLE MING CHINESE BLUE AND WHITE
253	544	2	SE CEL	–	15th	SOUTHEAST ASIAN CELADON TYPE 1
254	544	2	SE CEL	–	15th	SOUTHEAST ASIAN CELADON TYPE 2
256	544	2	LQC1	Yuan	14th	YUAN LONGQUAN CELADON (1276–1368 AD) MONGOLIAN PERIOD
257	544	2	CWP	Mid Ming	16th	MIDDLE–LATE MING CHINESE WHITE PORCELAIN
258	544	2	SE CEL	–	15th	SOUTHEAST ASIAN CELADON TYPE 1
260	544	2	LQC2	Early Ming	15th	EARLY–MIDDLE MING LONGQUAN CELADON (ABOUT 1368–1500AD)
261	544	2	SE CEL	–	15th	SOUTHEAST ASIAN CELADON TYPE 1
262	544	2	CBW2–2	Mid Ming	16th	MIDDLE MING CHINESE BLUE AND WHITE
263	544	2	SE CEL	–	15th	SOUTHEAST ASIAN CELADON TYPE 1
264	544	2	ISLAM	–	–	PERSIA
265	544	2	CWP	Mid Ming	16th	MIDDLE–LATE MING CHINESE WHITE PORCELAIN
266	544	2	CWP	Mid Ming	16th	MIDDLE–LATE MING CHINESE WHITE PORCELAIN
267	544	2	CBW2–2	Mid Ming	16th	MID MING
268	544	2	CBW2–2	Mid Ming	16th	MID MING
269	544	2	CBW2–3	Late Ming	17th	LATE MING LOW QUALITY
270	544	2	LQC1	Yuan	14th	YUAN LONGQUAN CELADON (1276–1368 AD) MONGOLIAN PERIOD
271	544	2	CBW2–2	Mid Ming	16th	MID MING
272	544	2	ISLAM	–	–	PERSIA
273	544	2	ISLAM	–	–	
274	544	2	SE CEL	–	15th	
275	544	2	CBW2–2	Mid Ming	16th	MIDDLE MING CHINESE BLUE AND WHITE
277	544	2	SE CEL	–	15th	SOUTHEAST ASIAN CELADON DIFFERENT TYPE
278	544	2	SE CEL	–	15th	
280	544	2	SE CEL	–	15th	
281	544	2	CBW2–2	Mid Ming	16th	
282	544	2	No-ID	–	–	
283	544	2	CBW2–1	Early Ming	15th	EARLY MING CHINESE BLUE AND WHITE
284	544	2	SE CEL	–	15th	SOUTHEAST ASIAN CELADON TYPE 2
285	544	2	ISLAM	–	–	PERSIA
286	544	2	ISLAM	–	–	UNIDENTIFIED OPACIFIED GLAZE SAMARRA HORIZON?
287	544	2	CBW2–2	Mid Ming	16th	MID MING
288	544	2	ISLAM	–	–	PERSIA
289	544	2	No-ID	–	–	UNIDENTIFIED OPACIFIED GLAZE SAMARRA HORIZON?
290	544	2	No-ID	–	–	UNIDENTIFIED OPACIFIED GLAZE SAMARRA HORIZON?
291	544	2	No-ID	–	–	UNIDENTIFIED OPACIFIED GLAZE SAMARRA HORIZON?
292	544	2	CBW2–2	Mid Ming	16th	MID MING
293	544	2	SE CEL	–	15th	SOUTHEAST ASIAN CELADON TYPE 1
294	544	2	SE CEL	–	15th	SOUTHEAST ASIAN CELADON TYPE 2
295	544	2	LQC1	Yuan	14th	YUAN LONGQUAN CELADON (1276–1368 AD) MONGOLIAN PERIOD
297	544	2	CWP	Mid Ming	16th	MIDDLE–LATE MING CHINESE WHITE PORCELAIN
299	544	2	CBW2–3	Late Ming	17th	LATE MING LOW QUALITY
300	544	2	SE CEL	–	15th	SOUTHEAST ASIAN CELADON TYPE 1
302	544	2	CBW2–3	Late Ming	17th	LATE MING LOW QUALITY
303	544	2	CBW2–2	Mid Ming	16th	MIDDLE MING CHINESE BLUE AND WHITE
304	544	2	CBW2–3	Late Ming	17th	LATE MING (LOW QUALITY) CHINESE BLUE AND WHITE
305	544	2	CBW2–3	Late Ming	17th	LATE MING LOW QUALITY
306	544	2	CBW2–3	Late Ming	17th	LATE MING LOW QUALITY
568	544	2	No-ID	–	–	UNIDENTIFIED GREEN GLAZED ORANGE BODY
569	544	2	CBW2–2	Mid Ming	16th	MID MING
310	544	3	CBW2–2	Mid Ming	16th	MID MING
311	544	3	CBW2–1	Early Ming	15th	EARLY MING CHINESE BLUE AND WHITE
312	544	3	SE CEL	–	15th	SOUTHEAST ASIAN CELADON TYPE 2

(Continued)

Table 6.1 (Continued)

Sherd No	Unit	Context	Class	(Chinese wares only) Dynasty	Dating	Type
315	544	3	ISLAM	–	–	MGPAINT
316	544	3	ISLAM	–	–	PERSIA
317	544	3	ISLAM	–	–	PERSIA
318	544	3	LQC1	Yuan	14th	
321	544	3	No-ID	–	–	
322	544	3	CBW2–2	Mid Ming	16th	
323	544	3	SE CEL	–	15th	
324	544	3	SE CEL	–	15th	
325	544	3	CBW2–2	Mid Ming	16th	
326	544	3	LQC1	Yuan	14th	SOUTHEAST ASIAN CELADON TYPE 1
327	544	3	SE CEL	–	15th	
328	544	3	CWP	Mid Ming	16th	MIDDLE–LATE MING CHINESE WHITE PORCELAIN
329	544	3	CBW2–3	Late Ming	17th	LATE MING (LOW QUALITY) CHINESE BLUE AND WHITE
330	544	3	ISLAM	–	–	PERSIA
331	544	3	ISLAM	–	–	PERSIA
332	544	3	No-ID	–	–	
333	544	3	SE CEL	–	15th	
334	544	3	CBW2–2	Mid Ming	16th	MIDDLE MING CHINESE BLUE AND WHITE
335	544	3	SE CEL	–	15th	
338	544	3	SE CEL	–	15th	SOUTHEAST ASIAN CELADON DIFFERENT TYPE
339	544	3	ISLAM	–	–	
340	544	3	SE CEL	–	15th	
341	544	3	LQC1	Yuan	14th	
342	544	3	LQC2	Early Ming	15th	
343	544	3	LQC2	Early Ming	15th	
344	544	3	LQC2	Early Ming	15th	
345	544	3	LQC1	Yuan	14th	
346	544	3	LQC1	Yuan	14th	
347	544	3	LQC1	Yuan	14th	
348	544	3	LQC1	Yuan	14th	
349	544	3	LQC1	Yuan	14th	
350	544	3	LQC1	Yuan	14th	
351	544	3	LQC2	Early Ming	15th	
352	544	3	LQC1	Yuan	14th	
353	544	3	LQC1	Yuan	14th	
354	544	3	LQC1	Yuan	14th	
355	544	3	LQC1	Yuan	14th	
356	544	3	LQC1	Yuan	14th	
357	544	3	LQC1	Yuan	14th	
358	544	3	LQC1	Yuan	14th	
359	544	3	LQC1	Yuan	14th	
360	544	3	LQC1	Yuan	14th	
361	544	3	LQC1	Yuan	14th	
362	544	3	LQC1	Yuan	14th	
363	544	3	LQC1	Yuan	14th	
370	544	4	CBW2–2	Mid Ming	16th	
371	544	4	SE CEL	–	15th	
372	544	4	CBW2–3	Late Ming	17th	
373	544	4	No-ID	–	–	
374	544	4	LQC1	Yuan	14th	
375	544	4	LQC1	Yuan	14th	
376	544	4	LQC1	Yuan	14th	YUAN LONGQUAN CELADON (1276–1368 AD) MONGOLIAN PERIOD
377	544	4	SE CEL	–	15th	
378	544	4	SE CEL	–	15th	
379	544	4	SE CEL	–	15th	SOUTHEAST ASIAN CELADON TYPE 1
380	544	4	SE CEL	–	15th	SOUTHEAST ASIAN CELADON TYPE 2
381	544	4	SE CEL	–	15th	
382	544	4	CBW2–3	Late Ming	17th	LATE MING (LOW QUALITY) CHINESE BLUE AND WHITE
383	544	4	SE CEL	–	15th	
384	544	4	SE CEL	–	15th	SOUTHEAST ASIAN CELADON TYPE 1
385	544	4	SE CEL	–	15th	
387	544	4	CBW2–2	Mid Ming	16th	
388	544	4	SE CEL	–	15th	SOUTHEAST ASIAN CELADON TYPE 1

(Continued)

Table 6.1 (Continued)

Sherd No	Unit	Context	Class	(Chinese wares only) Dynasty	Dating	Type
364	544	4	SE CEL	–	15th	SOUTHEAST ASIAN CELADON DIFFERENT TYPE
365	544	4	LQC1	Yuan	14th	YUAN LONGQUAN CELADON (1276–1368 AD) MONGOLIAN PERIOD
366	544	4	SE CEL	–	15th	SOUTHEAST ASIAN CELADON TYPE 2
367	544	4	SE CEL	–	15th	
368	544	4	SE CEL	–	15th	SOUTHEAST ASIAN CELADON TYPE 2
369	544	4	SE CEL	–	15th	
23	631	4	CBW2–3	Late Ming	17th	
24	631	4	CBW2–3	Late Ming	17th	LATE MING (LOW QUALITY) CHINESE BLUE AND WHITE
25	631	4	SE CEL	–	15th	SOUTHEAST ASIAN CELADON TYPE 1
26	631	4	SE CEL	–	15th	SOUTHEAST ASIAN CELADON TYPE 1? WHITE GLAZE RED BODY
27	631	4	SE CEL	–	15th	SOUTHEAST ASIAN CELADON TYPE 1? WHITE GLAZE RED BODY
571	631	5	CBW2–2	Mid Ming	16th	MID MING
572	631	5	SE CEL	–	15th	SOUTHEAST ASIAN CELADON TYPE 1
28	631	10	SE CEL	–	15th	SOUTHEAST ASIAN CELADON TYPE 1
29	631	10	SE CEL	–	15th	SOUTHEAST ASIAN CELADON TYPE 1
30	631	10	SE CEL	–	15th	SOUTHEAST ASIAN CELADON TYPE 1
31	631	10	CBW2–2	Mid Ming	16th	LATE MING (LOW QUALITY) CHINESE BLUE AND WHITE
32	631	10	CBW2–2	Mid Ming	16th	MIDDLE MING CHINESE BLUE AND WHITE
33	631	10	CBW2–2	Mid Ming	16th	MIDDLE MING CHINESE BLUE AND WHITE
36	631	10	LQC2	Early Ming	15th	GROUP 1 LONGQUAN CELADON GUANGDONG
37	631	12	SE CEL	–	15th	SOUTHEAST ASIAN CELADON TYPE 1
38	631	12	SE CEL	–	15th	SOUTHEAST ASIAN CELADON TYPE 2
40	631	12	SE CEL	–	15th	SOUTHEAST ASIAN CELADON TYPE 1
41	631	12	SE CEL	–	15th	SOUTHEAST ASIAN CELADON TYPE 1
42	631	12	CBW2–3	Late Ming	17th	LATE MING LOW QUALITY
43	631	12	SE CEL	–	15th	SOUTHEAST ASIAN CELADON TYPE 1? WHITE GLAZE RED BODY
44	631	12	SE CEL	–	15th	SOUTHEAST ASIAN CELADON TYPE 1
45	631	12	SE CEL	–	15th	SOUTHEAST ASIAN CELADON TYPE 1? WHITE GLAZE RED BODY
46	631	12	SE CEL	–	15th	SOUTHEAST ASIAN CELADON TYPE 1? WHITE GLAZE RED BODY
47	631	12	SE CEL	–	15th	SOUTHEAST ASIAN CELADON TYPE 1? WHITE GLAZE RED BODY
48	631	12	SE CEL	–	15th	SOUTHEAST ASIAN CELADON TYPE 2
49	631	12	SE CEL	–	15th	SOUTHEAST ASIAN CELADON TYPE 1
50	631	12	SE CEL	–	15th	SE ASIAN CELADON DIFF TYPE?
53	631	12	SE CEL	–	15th	SOUTHEAST ASIAN CELADON TYPE 2
54	631	12	SE CEL	–	15th	SOUTHEAST ASIAN CELADON TYPE 2
55	631	12	LQC1	Yuan	14th	LONGQUAN CELADON GUANGDONG
56	631	12	LQC2	Early Ming	15th	EARLY–MIDDLE MING LONGQUAN CELADON (ABOUT 1368–1500AD)
58	631	13	CBW2–2	Mid Ming	16th	MIDDLE MING CHINESE BLUE AND WHITE
59	631	14	SE CEL	–	15th	SOUTHEAST ASIAN CELADON TYPE 1
61	631	14	ISLAM	–	–	PERSIA
62	631	14	CBW2–2	Mid Ming	16th	MIDDLE MING CHINESE BLUE AND WHITE
63	631	16	SE CEL	–	15th	SOUTHEAST ASIAN CELADON TYPE 1
65	631	16	SE CEL	–	15th	SOUTHEAST ASIAN CELADON TYPE 1
66	631	16	ISLAM	–	–	YB TIN SAMARRAN 9TH CENTURY BASRA (ISLAMIC)
67	631	16	ISLAM	–	–	YB TIN SAMARRAN 9TH CENTURY BASRA (ISLAMIC)
68	631	16	ISLAM	–	–	YB TIN SAMARRAN 9TH CENTURY BASRA (ISLAMIC)
69	631	16	ISLAM	–	–	YB TIN SAMARRAN 9TH CENTURY BASRA (ISLAMIC)
70	631	16	ISLAM	–	–	YB TIN SAMARRAN 9TH CENTURY BASRA (ISLAMIC)
71	631	16	ISLAM	–	–	YB TIN SAMARRAN 9TH CENTURY BASRA (ISLAMIC)

(Continued)

Table 6.1 (Continued)

Sherd No	Unit	Context	Class	(Chinese wares only) Dynasty	Dating	Type
72	631	16	ISLAM	–	–	YB TIN SAMARRAN 9TH CENTURY BASRA (ISLAMIC)
73	631	16	ISLAM	–	–	YB TIN SAMARRAN 9TH CENTURY BASRA (ISLAMIC)
74	631	16	ISLAM	–	–	YB TIN SAMARRAN 9TH CENTURY BASRA (ISLAMIC)
90	631	16	CBW2–3	Late Ming	17th	LATE MING (LOW QUALITY) CHINESE BLUE AND WHITE
91	631	16	CBW2–3	Late Ming	17th	LATE MING (LOW QUALITY) CHINESE BLUE AND WHITE
92	631	16	SE CEL	–	15th	SOUTHEAST ASIAN CELADON TYPE 1
93	631	16	SE CEL	–	15th	SOUTHEAST ASIAN CELADON TYPE 1
94	631	16	SE CEL	–	15th	SOUTHEAST ASIAN CELADON TYPE 1
76	631	20	CBW2–2	Mid Ming	16th	MID MING
77	631	20	CBW2–2	Mid Ming	16th	MID MING
78	631	20	No-ID	–	–	POT BASED UNIDENTIFIED
81	631	20	SE CEL	–	15th	SOUTHEAST ASIAN CELADON TYPE 2
82	631	20	SE CEL	–	15th	SOUTHEAST ASIAN CELADON TYPE 1
83	631	20	SE CEL	–	15th	SOUTHEAST ASIAN CELADON TYPE 1? WHITE GLAZE RED BODY
84	631	20	SE CEL	–	15th	SOUTHEAST ASIAN CELADON TYPE 1? WHITE GLAZE RED BODY
85	631	22	CBW2–2	Mid Ming	16th	MID MING
86	631	22	CBW2–2	Mid Ming	16th	MID MING
87	631	22	SE CEL	–	15th	SOUTHEAST ASIAN CELADON TYPE 1
88	631	22	ISLAM	–	–	PERSIA
89	631	22	SE CEL	–	15th	SOUTHEAST ASIAN CELADON TYPE 1
565	631	22	CBW2–2	Mid Ming	16th	MID MING
443	?	?	No-ID	–	–	

The western Indian Ocean has a very wide distribution of such finds, with similar types of Chinese ceramic imports systematically collected since the 1930s (cf. Mikami 1969). According to earlier work by the present author on the combined assemblages of Chinese ceramic finds from the western Indian Ocean, over 100 archaeological sites have been identified as yielding similar Chinese ceramic finds (cf. Zhang 2016). In the Maldives, the presence of Chinese ceramic imports was first reported by John Carswell during his archaeological surveys in Male' (Carswell 1975–1977). Further insights can be gained from recent doctoral research by Litster (2016) and Jaufar (2019). These projects also considered Chinese ceramic finds in the Maldives, with the latter conducting a statistical analysis of these materials recovered from the excavations in Male', Utheemu, and Veyvah (Jaufar 2019), on which the present author also advised.

Based on the findings of Chinese ceramics published by Carswell (1975–1977) and Litster (2016), there is no clear evidence of early Chinese ceramic imports to the Maldives before the thirteenth century AD, although few sherds are identified to the Qingbai or celadon wares as the late Chinese Southern Song dynasty's products. According to the almost fully illustrated 500 pieces of Chinese ceramic finds from Carswell's work, as well as the few illustrations provided in Litster's thesis, no single sherd can be securely identified to the period from the ninth to twelfth centuries AD. Among them, about 140 pieces are identical to be the Longquan celadon. Blue and white porcelain and white porcelain sherds are well distinguished from both Kinolhas and Carswell's work. Otherwise, nearly 170 sherds from the previous research are dated to the eighteenth to nineteenth centuries as South China made blue and white porcelain wares. This, together with the so-called Batavia porcelain sherds, Qing dynasty enamel wares, and monochrome blue porcelain sherds, was not observed in the material excavated at Kinolhas. In the work on excavated materials from the Kinolhas, it must be noted that Chinese ceramic findings are sometimes substantially younger than the deposits with radiocarbon dating tested samples, suggesting that sites may be quite disturbed.

Methodology

In terms of methodologies, the materials in this case study were recorded using Excel, cataloguing the late Chinese ceramic finds by fabric, form, decoration, and sherd count. This methodology is mainly based on British ceramic studies (Orton and Hughes 2013); however, because Chinese ceramics have their own unique features, such as fine glaze, different qualities of cobalt decoration, marks, and high-fired fabrics, standard terms from Chinese ceramic archaeological traditions were also applied.

Derek Kennet (2004) produced a general classification of Chinese ceramic imports, with contributions from Regina Krahl. This classification covered Chinese ceramic imports from the thirteenth to nineteenth centuries; however, key archaeological evidence for dating and identification was generally missed. Seth Priestman followed Kennet's classification in his master's thesis on the Williamson Collection from South Iran, and his PhD on a wider area in the western Indian Ocean (Priestman 2013) produced a full range of ceramic classifications, including Chinese and Far Eastern ceramics, Islamic pottery, and other locally produced pottery. Bing Zhao's classification offers an excellent understanding of Chinese ceramic materials from Sharma, Yemen, and is well linked to Chinese archaeology. However, it cannot easily be applied to other archaeological sites, as the groups defined only focus on detailed fabric descriptions and features of the sherds. She does not attempt to fit these into a coherent picture of the development of the Chinese trade in ceramics (Zhao 2006). Ran Zhang's work covered the most Chinese ceramic imports from the ninth to the sixteenth centuries in the western Indian Ocean; however, some classes present in the Kinolhas were not included in this research (Zhang 2016). The present chapter therefore aims to standardise classification of the Chinese ceramics from Kinolhas.

General description of the Chinese ceramic imports from Kinolhas

The Chinese ceramic imports from Kinolhas included 237 sherds, representing a fairly good proportion of the overall site assemblage, from 1.1% in Trench 631 to 14% in Trench 325 (Table 6.2).

The lower Chinese ceramic proportion in Trench 631 may be because of its funerary context, and it yields some large fragments. Numbers of Chinese ceramic finds were higher than those from other archaeological sites in the Indian Ocean; and on Islamic archaeological sites in the western Indian Ocean, Chinese ceramic numbers are usually very low, from about 1% to 4% (Scanlon 1971, Rougeulle 1996, pp. 175-176, 2005, p. 226, Kennet 2004, p. 60). For example, at Kush in Ras al-Khaimah, United Arab Emirates (UAE), the proportion of Chinese ceramics ranged between 0.31% and 2.39% (Kennet 2004, p. 98), and at Siraf (South Iran) and Shanga (Kenya), the proportion was below 1% (Horton et al. 1996, Rougeulle 1991, p. 542).

The various class categories of Chinese ceramic imports are listed in Table 6.3. There were 169 pieces of southeast Asian celadon (SE CEL) which can be dated to the fifteenth century. The chronological research and classification is mainly based on the work previously undertaken by Roxanna Brown (Brown 2009).

Table 6.2 Summary of the ceramics assemblages from the seven units excavated at Kinolhas.

Unit	Chinese ceramics	SE Asian Ceramics	Earthenware	N_1	P_1
321	23	17	241	281	8.19%
325	33	13	236	282	11.70%
360	8	4	85	97	8.25%
443	12	8	102	122	9.84%
449	11	15	97	123	8.94%
544	131	79	1679	1889	6.93%
631	19	33	1669	1721	1.10%

Source: N_1=total ceramic finds from each unit.

P_1=percentage of Chinese ceramic finds within the assemblage from each unit

Table 6.3 Classification of Chinese ceramic imports at Kinolhas.

Class	Name	Dating	Quantity	Fabrics	Manufacture kilns	Figure
CBW1	Chinese blue and white porcelain	Fourteenth century	1	Porcelain	Jingdezhen	–
LQC1	Longquan celadon	Fourteenth century	52	Stoneware	Longquan	Figure 6.1
LQC2	Longquan celadon	Fifteenth century	16	Stoneware	Longquan	Figure 6.2
IMPERIAL	Imperial white porcelain	Fifteenth century	1	Porcelain	Jingdezhen	Figure 6.3
SE CEL	Southeast Asian celadon	Fifteenth to sixteenth century	169	Stoneware	Southeast Asia	
CBW2–1	Chinese blue and white porcelain	Fifteenth to seventeenth century	11	Porcelain	Jingdezhen	Figure 6.6
CBW2–2	Chinese blue and white porcelain	Fifteenth to seventeenth century	104	Porcelain	Jingdezhen	Figure 6.7
CBW2–3	Chinese blue and white porcelain	Fifteenth to seventeenth century	37	Porcelain	Jingdezhen	Figure 6.8
CWP	Chinese white porcelain	Seventeenth century	14	Porcelain	Jingdezhen	Figure 6.9
JDZ CEL	Jingdezhen celadon	Seventeenth century	1	Porcelain	Jingdezhen	Figure 6.10
ISLAM	Islamic potteries		32	Stoneware		Figure 6.11 and 6.12
No-ID	Not identifiable sherds	N/A	26	N/A	N/A	

Classification of the Chinese ceramic finds

This section aims to produce an outline classification of the Chinese materials, which can be divided into seven different classes:

CBW1 (Chinese blue and white porcelain of fourteenth-century date)

Only one sherd can be identified as belonging to Class CBW1, coming from unit 449. CWB1 wares were high quality ceramics, normally large in size (Feng 2009). This class has been regarded as the official type of high luxury objects, some of which were produced for the *Fuliang* Porcelain Bureau, in the area now known as Jingdezhen in China, for the Yuan dynasty central court in the middle of the fourteenth century (Liu 1981). Some were produced not only for the Chinese/Mongol rulers, but also circulated for more common use in trading markets (Chen 2012). One typical example comes from the inscriptions on the so-called David Vases (housed in the British Museum), which date to 1351 AD and suggest that they are offering objects rather than for official use. In general, there is no doubt that these wares were produced for central court and high-class individuals (Chen 2012, Li 1994).

Body, glaze, and pigment

Class CBW1 had a heavy and thick porcelain body, which was normally mould-formed and well polished. It normally had a transparent and thin glaze in a very light bluish green. Between the body and glaze, cobalt blue could be found, which was painted onto the body and was dark blue or blackish blue. This imported cobalt ore had a high percentage of inclusions of iron and manganese oxides (Kerr and Wood 2004, pp. 676–682). Small metal black points could be seen on the blue patterns when the sherds were examined in bright sunlight, mainly because of the high percentage of iron giving a metal-black appearance to the pigment. These black points often occurred on the cross-point of painting strokes or areas filled with cobalt pigment (Lv 2004, Sun 1966).

Dating

It can be confirmed that these classes were fired during the fourteenth century (Feng 2009, Medley 1989, Pope 1952), based on their decoration and forming quality. In Chinese ceramic studies, this type can be called the '*Zhizheng* Type (至正型)' blue and white porcelains. The name '*Zhizheng*' comes from the inscriptions on a pair of blue and white vases in the Percival David Foundation, which shows their manufacture date of (至正十一年: the eleventh year of the *Zhizheng* Reign, 1351 AD) (Harrison-Hall and Krahl 2009, pp. 52–53). Similarly decorated blue and white wares are therefore called Zhizheng type blue and white porcelain, and also the 'Fourteenth-Century Group'.

LQC1 (Longquan celadon of fourteenth-century date)

A total of 52 pieces of LQC1 were discovered from almost all trench units, excluding 433. These can be dated to approximately the middle of the Yuan dynasty (the middle of the fourteenth century). During this period celadon wares became larger and thicker and were of a slightly lower quality. This lower quality is represented by the poorly polished, unglazed footring and thinner glaze (Figure 6.1).

Figure 6.1 Longquan celadon, LQC1.

Source: Photo by Guilia Nazzaro.

Body and glaze

The key feature of class LQC1 is a thicker body with thinner glaze, which has a heavy, relatively loose and light greyish white body. The glaze shows some variation in colour, for example light bluish green, bean green, olive green, greyish green, and yellow. The thickness of the glaze is no thicker than 1 mm. Crackles are very common and, where exposed at the base or footring, the body is orange yellow or red.

Dating

Class LQC1 can be dated to the middle of the Yuan dynasty based on the dating evidence summarised below (Table 6.4), which concerns similar objects recovered from well dated archaeological discoveries.

LQC2 (Longquan celadon of fifteenth/sixteenth-century date)

The total number of LQC2 (Figure 6.2) is just 16 pieces, but they were discovered in five units (321,325, 449, 544, and 631) in Kinolhas. Normally LQC2 included both high and low qualities of Longquan celadon, some of which may be connected to the imperial-type celadon ware. Both can be dated to the early to middle Ming dynasty (the late fourteenth century to the mid-fifteenth century). Fine quality celadon includes imperial celadon products, and it has been shown archaeologically that these were produced at the Dayao Fengdongyan kiln site in Zhejiang Province of China and they can be dated precisely to the Yongle period (1403–1424 AD) of the Chinese Ming dynasty. The imperial-type class is only recovered in very small quantities in western Indian Ocean sites, due to the fact that it is imperial or imperial-type celadon; it is reported from Hormuz island, Iran (Lin and Zhang 2015), Ras al-Khaimah, United Arab Emirates (GGBWY et al. 2020), and at Gedi, Kenya (Liu et al. 2012).

The quality of some Ming-dated Longquan celadon sherds (LQC 2) from Kinolhas all have a high fabric quality with fine glazing techniques (see description), following but the missing parts of their bases are difficult to provide strong evidence to classify them to the imperial-quality Longquan celadon of early Ming China. This may suggest that the manufacturing of these high-quality celadon sherds was in the Dayao Fengdongyan kilns of Longquan, but they are not

Table 6.4 Class LQC1 tomb evidence.

Sites	Locations	Findings	Dating	Reference
Ren Shi tomb	Shanghai	Vase	1338–1353 AD	(SHBWG 1982:53)
Cellar	Yecheng, Hubei	Inscription on vase	1345 AD	(Zhang 1996)
Shipwreck	Cixian, Hebei	Shipwreck	1352 AD	(Kim 2012)
Tomb	Zhangshu, Jiangxi	A set of celadon	1353 AD	(Huang 1996)

Figure 6.2 Longquan celadon, LQC2.

Source: Photo by Guilia Nazzaro.

identified as imperial celadon wares. Otherwise, the lower quality early Ming Longquan celadon sherds can be also seen from Kinolhas.

Body and glaze

For the higher quality sherds from Kinolhas, they have a very thick glaze (1 mm to 2 mm) in bean green or light green. The colour of the glaze firing technique has been very well controlled. The lower quality sherds have a glass-like, thinner glaze in different shades of green. The body is loose compared to the higher quality Longquan sherds, and black inclusions can be seen by the naked eye.

Dating

LQC2 can be dated to the early to middle Ming dynasty (from the late fourteenth to the mid-fifteenth centuries AD) based on tomb site excavations in China. Four tomb sites with similar objects to LQC2 have been found in present-day Nanjing City in Jiangsu Province, which was the capital during the early period of the Ming dynasty (the Ming capital moved to Beijing after 1412 AD), and which have been separately dated to AD 1387 (NJSBWG 2005), AD 1395 (NJSBWG 2005), AD 1407 (Li 1962), and AD 1418 (Li 1962). Other examples are provided by the Ge Shi Tomb (戈氏墓) in Shangdong Province of northern China, which can be dated to AD 1441 based on the inscription 'Zheng Tong Liu Nian (正统六年, the sixth year of the Zhengtong Reign)', and which yielded two vases, and the Wei Yuan Tomb (魏源墓) in Jiangxi Province of southern China, which dates to AD 1444 based on the inscription 'Zheng Tong Jiu Nian (正统九年, the ninth year of the Zhengtong Reign)', and which produced a group of celadon plates and vases similar to this class (Zhu 1998, pp. 272–284).

Imperial white porcelain

A single sherd was discovered at Kinolhas, from Unit 544, with a very fine quality porcelain body that is hard, smooth, white, and pure (Figure 6.3). It is covered with an evenly applied transparent glaze with a very slight greyish white shade. A very thin and finely incised pattern is decorated on the body, and this decoration is only visible when held up to the light. This is a unique discovery. Similar archaeological finds are only evidenced from the Julfar site of Ras al-Khaimah, excavated by a Japanese team in the early 1990s, and from South Iran during a survey conducted by Andrew Williamson in 1970s (these datasets are currently under study by the present author and will be published in future).

Vessels of similar quality and complete can be found in museum collections and archaeological excavations of the Jingdezhen site in China. A stem cup with a fine and incised decoration is held in the collections of the British Museum. This incised decoration is called *anhua* (暗花) in Chinese, meaning the secret decoration, because it is only visible when held up to the light. The transparent glaze is called *tianbai* (甜白), meaning sweet-white because the glaze looks like a thin layer of icing sugar. This stem cup is marked with incised writing, and this seal-script characters read *Yongle nian zhi* (永乐年制) [Made in the Yongle reign] (AD 1402–1424). Similar objects with this mark were excavated in 1984 from the Yongle stratum of the imperial kiln site where a deposit of the disqualified and destructed *tianbai* porcelain sherds was discovered (Figure 6.4). This deposit demonstrates that the production and examination of the imperial

Figure 6.3 Imperial ware.

Source: Photo by Guilia Nazzaro.

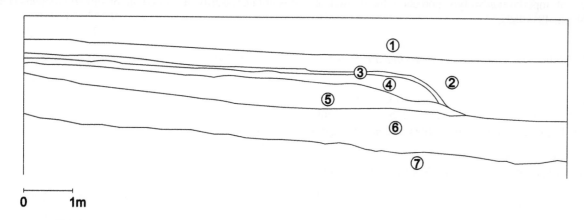

1: topsoil
2: Xuande period porcelain deposite (1426–1435AD)
3: porcelain clay waste
4: sandy red clay
5: *tianbai* porcelain waste sherds deposite
6: a pavement dated to the Song to Yuan dynasties (about the thirteenth to the middle fourteenth centuries)
7: natural earth

Figure 6.4 Section of the excavation at Zhushan imperial kiln site of Jingdezhen.

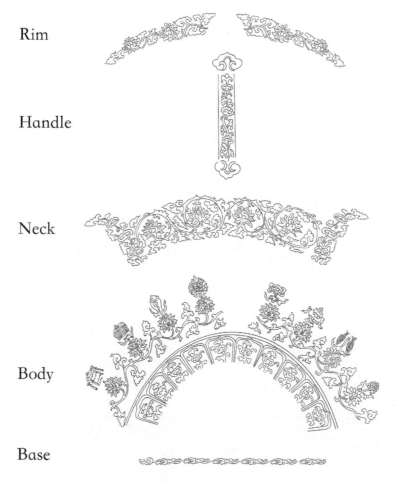

Rim

Handle

Neck

Body

Base

Figure 6.5 Sketch of the incised *anhua* decoration featured on an imperial white porcelain ewer in the Percival David Collection.
Source: Drawn by Ran Zhang.

ceramic products was very strict. No similar disqualified porcelain sherd burial deposits were discovered at any common kiln sites in Jingdezhen (BJDXKGWBXY et al. 2009, pp. 13–15), but some were discovered inside the Forbidden City (imperial residence of Ming and Qing dynasties) in Beijing (Ji 2016).

A similarly decorated and *tianbai* glazed ewer can also be found in the collections of Percival David in the British Museum (Figure 6.5) (Harrison-Hall 2001, pp. 98–99). In general, the shapes featured in the imperial white porcelain collection (*tianbai* type) mainly consist of stem cups, ewers, bowls, vases, jars, saucers, and candle-sticks. For some pieces of imperial *tianbai* type porcelain, the incised pattern is not necessarily decorated on the imperial objects (Feng 2009, pp. 481–482).

CBW2 (blue and white porcelain of fifteenth- to seventeenth-century date)

A total of 152 pieces of Ming dynasty blue and white porcelain were found from all seven units in Kinolhas. This is a group of blue and white porcelain made in the Jingdezhen kilns, which can be called CBW2 and dated to the Ming dynasty (approximately the late fifteenth to the seventeenth century), and can be divided into three subgroups: early Ming (11 pieces), middle Ming (104), and late Ming groups (37 pieces).

Early Ming blue and white porcelain (CBW2–1: 11 sherds)

BODY, GLAZE, AND COBALT

Similar to CBW1, Yuan blue and white ceramics, CBW 2–1 (Figure 6.6) has a heavy and thick porcelain body which is dense and hard. These sherds are a little thinner and their fabric is purer than those Yuan blue and white examples, and they are covered by a transparent and thin glaze in very light bluish green (Feng 2009, p. 461).

The cobalt blue has been painted between the body and the glaze and is dark blue or blackish blue. Small metal black points can also be seen in the blue patterns when examining sherds in bright sunlight, and again this is due to the cobalt ore containing a high percentage of iron, which gives a metal-black appearance to the pigment.

DATING

Similar fabric ceramics can be found in imperial blue and white plate with Wucai-enamelled painting and decorative Tibetan letters, which can be dated to the Xuande period (AD 1426–1435) based on the cobalt blue reign mark '*Da Ming Xuan De Nian Zhi* (大明宣德年制, made in the Xuande Reign of the Great Ming dynasty)' and the legible Tibetan alphabet decoration which was common in the early Ming period (TJIOCA and TFPSM 1992, pp. 141–143). In the western Indian Ocean, a similar type of blue and white porcelain was also found in Julfar in the UAE, and dating by Pirazzoli-T'Serstevens (2003, pp. 3–10) suggests it comes from the early fifteenth century. A similar date is accepted for finds from Fustat in Egypt dated by Tadanori Yuba (2014, pp. 10–11). A recent example came from the excavation at al-Mataf at Julfar, also in the UAE (GGBWY et al. 2020).

Figure 6.6 Early Ming dated blue and white porcelain (CBW2–1).

Source: Photo by Guilia Nazzaro.

Figure 6.7 Middle Ming dated blue and white porcelain (CBW2–2).
Source: Photo by Guilia Nazzaro.

Middle Ming blue and white porcelain (CBW2–2: 104 sherds)

BODY, GLAZE, AND COBALT

The body and glaze of CBW 2–2 group is dense and pure (Figure 6.7). The body is much thinner than that of the material in class CBW1 and the glaze is normally slightly bluish white or similar in colour to an egg white. From the end of the sixteenth century, Chinese native cobalt ore had been successfully and extensively mined (Kerr and Wood 2004, pp. 684–685); it was named 'Po Tang Qing' (陂塘青) or 'Ping Deng Qing' (平等青) and results in a much lighter blue colour with a bit of grey to blue and white porcelain. In the middle and late Ming dynasty, this cobalt ore was gradually replaced by another blue called 'Shi Zi Qing' (石子青), which gave an even more greyish blue.

DATING

According to a tomb dated to the twenty-fifth year of the Jiajing reign (AD 1546), objects similar to CBW2 may have originally occurred in a tomb dated to the sixth year of the Jiajing period (嘉靖六年: AD 1527) (Yang 1983, p. 90). However, according to research on shipwrecks and excavations in the Indian Ocean (McElney 1979, Van Der Pijl-Ketel 1982, p. 50) this date can be extended to the period from between the 1550s to 1570s.

Late Ming blue and white porcelain (CBW2–3: 37 sherds)

BODY, GLAZE, AND COBALT

CBW 2–3 was produced in the late Ming dynasty, which can be dated to the period from the 1570s to the 1620s AD (Figure 6.8). The most representative type in this group is called Kraak porcelain and comes from the blue and white porcelain wares that were found in the cargo of the Portuguese merchant ship called 'Kraken (carracks)' in Dutch. This ship was captured in the seventeenth century by sailors from Holland and Zeeland (Van Der Pijl-Ketel 1982, p. 46). Kraak porcelain is a convenient name for a type which is distinctive but curiously difficult to describe with any precision (Medley 1989, p. 226).

The cobalt blue painting on this group of porcelain is distinguished by the purplish blue cobalt ore. The painting methods are normally outlined with thin strokes and then filled with different shades of blue. The most distinguished characteristic of this group is that they may have panel patterns.

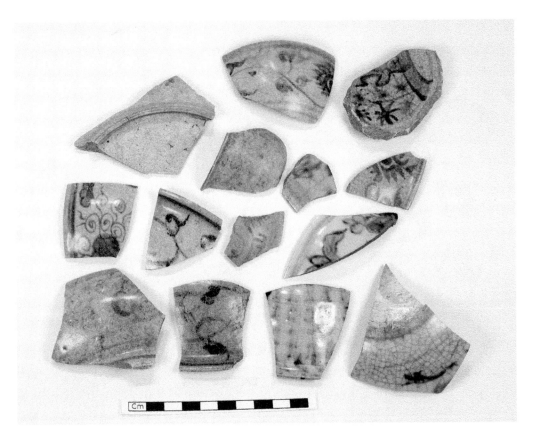

Figure 6.8 Late Ming dated blue and white porcelain (CBW2–3).

Source: Photo by Guilia Nazzaro.

DATING

McElney (1979) suggests that Kraak blue and white porcelain initially started between 1550 and 1570, based on his research on shipwrecks and excavations in the Indian Ocean. However, at this stage, no panel-patterned porcelain has been found (McElney 1979, Van Der Pijl-Ketel 1982, p. 50).

Finds similar to this group were recovered from the cargo of Drake's Bay shipwreck, California (AD 1595), which yielded a group of blue and white porcelain without panel patterns with reliable marks of the Jiajing reign (1522–1566 AD).

Van der Pijl-Ketel discussed the porcelain found in the Witte Leeuw shipwreck (St Helena, dated to AD 1613) and demonstrated that the panel patterns first occurred around AD 1595 and were popular until at least AD 1613 (McElney 1979, p. 50, Van Der Pijl-Ketel 1982).

CWP (Chinese white porcelain) (Figure 6.9)

Fourteen pieces of Chinese white porcelain (CWP) were found, 12 of them from Unit 544. CWP refers to the fine white porcelain body covered with a clear white or light blue tinted glaze. Vessels include a wide mix of cups, bowls, and dishes which mostly share the same vessel forms within the class of enamel (see later). A mark of a Chinese character *fu* (福) with a square outline can be found at the outside of the base. Some pieces have an unglazed ring at the interior of the base.

Dating

The sherds in the white porcelain group are difficult to date as they were mostly undecorated, and their shapes could not be reconstructed. Without form and shape, the fabrics of body and glaze provide very limited information for dating and identification. Moreover, white porcelain production in China has a very long tradition. Similar examples came from the Maojiawan excavation in Beijing, which yielded a large amount of white porcelain manufactured in the Jingdezhen kilns and dated to the middle Ming dynasty (BJSWWYJS 2007, pp. 126–155).

JDZCEL (Jiangxi celadon)

Definition and dating

Only one piece of Jingdezhen made celadon was found, coming from Unit 321 (Figure 6.10). Traditionally, it is believed that imitations of Longquan wares produced in Jiangxi Province in the Jingdezhen kilns, and production here dates to

Figure 6.9 CWP (Chinese white porcelain).
Source: Photo by Guilia Nazzaro.

Figure 6.10 JDZCEL (Jiangxi celadon) sherd.
Source: Photo by Guilia Nazzaro.

the middle Ming dynasty (Yu 1995, pp. 272–273). The imperial kilns from the Ming dynasty at Jingdezhen City yielded many sherds which feature the celadon glaze, although these are regarded as bean green celadon (a term for monochrome green wares during the Ming dynasty) rather than celadon. However, some of the sherds resemble Longquan imitations (Liu et al. 1982, Xue 1965, Yang 1981, Yu 1973, 2011, pp. 475–476).

During the Ming dynasty, Jingdezhen imitations of Longquan celadon wares in Jiangxi Province were called bean green celadon, and was sometimes marked with cobalt blue. Wares were glazed with both celadon and white; the wares were glazed with green but the base had a white glaze (Yu 2011, pp. 478–480).

Body and glaze

Jingdezhen celadon has a fine stoneware body in greyish white, but it is greyer than Longquan celadon. The glaze is thick with small crackles and is greyish green, and is therefore distinguishable from the bean green or olive green glaze of Longquan celadon.

Other glazed ceramic finds from the Persian Gulf

Islamic ware (ISLAM)

The assemblage from Kinolhas yielded 32 sherds which can be attributed to an origin in the Islamic world. They were examined by Derek Kennet of Durham University.

MG Paint (Kennet 2004, pp. 51–53, Priestman 2013, pp. 620–622)

This group consists of bowls with manganese painted decoration under a clear or green-yellow tinted glaze on a thick pale yellow body. These have been defined at Kush, UAE, as being closely related to MG Paint 2. A total of 3 sherds (2 of which refit) were recovered from the assemblage, and they have been identified as dating to between the fifteenth and eighteenth centuries. They may be identified with a production in South Iran.

Persia (Kennet 2004, pp. 53–54, Priestman 2013, pp. 632–635)

This group consists of sherds of blue speckled-reddish earthenware body covered inside and over the rim with a mottled glaze ranging in colour from dark green to light grey but most commonly dark blue (Figure 6.11). Kennet (2004, p. 54) compares this type with that termed 'Standard Monochrome' by Chittick (1974) and 'Blue monochrome' by Horton et al. (1996) at Kilwa Kisiwani and Shanga on the East African coast. Seth Priestman termed this type of pottery

Figure 6.11 PERSIA (Persian blue-speckled) sherds.
Source: Photo by Guilia Nazzaro.

Figure 6.12 YBTIN (plain opaque white glaze) sherds.
Source: Photo by Guilia Nazzaro.

Speckled Glaze Ware, and they may be identified as products from South Iran (Priestman 2013, p. 633). A total of 17 sherds from this group were recovered from the assemblage and have been identified as dating to between the fourteenth and sixteenth centuries and are very worn.

YBTIN (Kennet 2004, p. 39 and Colour Plate 1)

Nine sherds, all of which were from Trench 631, Context 16, and most of which refit, were of very finely levigated and fired white clay, with a grey glaze on both inner and outer surface (Figure 6.12), and were identified as possibly YBTIN (plain opaque white glaze) per Kennet (2004, p. 39). The forms are always thin-walled bowls with flaring rims. It appears datable to the ninth/tenth centuries (Kennet 2004, p. 39). Seth Priestman termed this type of ceramics as monochrome white opaque-glazed ware, and they may be identified as products from South Iraq (Priestman 2013, pp. 558–559).

The four remaining sherds identified as possibly Islamic cannot be classified more closely.

Unidentified ceramics

Twenty-five sherds were noted as possibly having been manufactured in southeast Asia as well as unknown origins, but it is not possible to provide further details due to a lack of comparative data.

One category among this group includes three sherds with a red/orangey body, covered in a non-transparent turquoise green glaze. These may originate from southeast Asia and likely date to the sixteenth century; they are definitely neither Chinese or Islamic. As far as the other sherds in this group are concerned, a definitive comment cannot be made, due to the lack of comparative data or the fact they are too indistinct, too small, or too eroded.

Conclusion

In closing, three potentially interesting aspects emerge for further studies. First, a comparison of the general trading pattern of Chinese ceramics in the western Indian Ocean (excluding Kinolhas; cf. Zhang 2016) and of Kinolhas is shown by Table 6.5 and Figure 6.13.

The site data (N_1 and P_1 in Table 6.5) indicate how many (N_1) and what percentage (P_1) of the 129 sites in the wider assemblage studied returned material of each class. This shows geographical distribution of each class in the western Indian Ocean, and a high proportion means a wider distribution. The sherd data (N_2 and P_2 in Table 6.5) show how many (N_2) and what percentage (P_2) of the 26949 sherds studied from these sites were from each class. These values provide insight into the popularity of these classes in the trade, where a high proportion indicates a greater popularity. The classes of CBW1, LQC1, and CBW2–2 were widely distributed and very popular in the western Indian Ocean (Zhang 2016). In comparison, the Chinese ceramic imports from Kinolhas (N_3 and P_3 in Table 6.5, where N_3 represents the

Table 6.5 Summary comparison for sherd numbers of different Chinese ceramic classes produced in the western Indian Ocean and Kinolhas.

Class	Dating	Western Indian Ocean				Kinolhas	
		N_1	P_1	N_2	P_2	N_3	P_3
LQC1	Fourteenth century	63	48.84%	5568	20.66%	52	21.94%
CBW1		20	15.50%	645	2.39%	1	0.42%
LQC2	Fifteenth century	10	7.75%	910	3.38%	16	6.75%
IMPERIAL		2	1.55%	4	0.01%	1	0.42%
CBW2–1		7	5.43%	150	0.56%	11	4.64%
CBW2–2&3	Sixteenth to seventeenth century	33	25.58%	4457	16.54%	141	59.49%
JDZ CEL		1	0.78%	1	0.01%	1	0.42%
CWP		4	3.10%	28	0.10%	14	5.91%

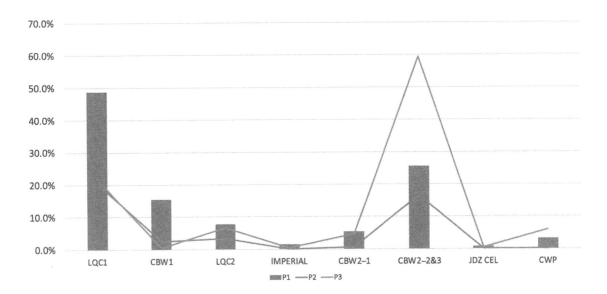

Figure 6.13 Comparison of Chinese ceramic trading patterns between the western Indian Ocean and Kinolhas.

number of sherds from each class recovered from Kinolhas, and P_3 represents this as a proportion of the total assemblage of 237 pieces from Kinolhas) may have a slightly different pattern (Figure 6.13).

From Figure 6.13, it can clearly be seen that CBW1, LQC1, IMPERIAL, LQC2, CBW2–1, JDZ CEL, and CWP from the Maldives all match the Chinese ceramic trading patterns in the western Indian Ocean. However, class CBW2–2 is clearly showing a different situation, in comparison with the similar findings from the western Indian Ocean. At Kinolhas, CBW2–2 has a much higher proportion of this class of ceramics than average in the western Indian Ocean. This may suggest that the trade between China and the Maldives dated between the sixteenth and seventeenth centuries experienced a boom period in comparison with the earlier and later periods. However, Chinese ceramics were absent from the seventeenth century onwards and may show that Chinese ceramic imports declined from the seventeenth century. This is very different from observations in the Persian Gulf and southeast Asia, which showed a sharp increase in late Chinese ceramics (cf. Power 2015, Tai et al. 2020). Otherwise, some Iranian manufactured ceramics were consistently imported to Kinolhas from the fourteenth to the eighteenth centuries. This may suggest that Kinolhas was involved in the Indian Ocean trade during this period.

Second, although only one single sherd in the imperial class was recovered within the assemblage from Kinolhas, it is highly likely it can be linked to the visits of Zheng He's fleets from China, which established a high level of communication and trade between early Ming China and the Maldives, especially as it is well known that the imperial porcelain was not allowed to be used by the common markets outside of the imperial court.

Historical records show that the voyages of Zheng He (郑和) to the Indian Ocean comprised approximately 27000 men and 64 treasure ships (宝船), all supported by 160 smaller boats. The treasure ships were decorated with vibrant colours and the hulls painted with giant seabirds, which must have been an impressive image that expressed wealth and power to the locals (Finlay 2008, pp. 336–337). The fundamental ideology behind the expeditions was to expand the Ming tribute system overseas. The tribute system was established to form alliances with other nations without including them as part of the Ming territory. In this way, the Ming court would gain exotic goods from these nations as part of the tributes.

Seven expeditions were made in the period AD 1405–1433, and Zheng He's fleets officially visited the Maldives for trade between AD 1413 and 1422. As a result, the government in Male' sent gifts to China separately in AD 1416, 1421,

Table 6.6 Far Eastern ceramic statistics from Kinolhas.

Unit		321	325	360	433	449	544	631	
Class	Dating	□	□	□	□	□	□	□	N_1
CBW1	14th	–	–	–	–	1	–	–	1
LQC1		2	4	3	–	4	38	1	52
LQC2	15–17th	1	3	–	–	1	9	2	16
IMPERIAL		–	–	–	–	–	1	–	1
SE CEL		17	13	4	8	15	79	33	169
JDZ CEL		1	–	–	–	–	–	–	1
CBW2		19	24	5	12	5	71	16	152
CWP		–	2	–	–	–	12	–	14
UN-ID		–	6	–	–	1	17	1	25
Earthenware	□	241	236	85	102	97	1679	1669	4109
	N_2	23	33	8	12	11	131	19	237
□	P_1	8.19%	11.46%	8.25%	9.84%	8.87%	6.87%	1.10%	□

Note: N_1 represents the total number from each group of ceramics that was yielded from the same unit. N_2 shows the total number of Chinese ceramics (excluding SE CEL and UN-ID) from the same units. P_1 indicates the percentage of Chinese ceramic findings among all ceramic materials in each unit (N_2/Quantities of Earthenware). Green-marked cells refer to higher quantity and red-marked cells refer to lower quantity.

and 1423 (Ptak 1987, pp. 680–681). It is interesting that Kinolhas is about 80–100 km away from the capital Male'. The sherds recovered from Kinolhas, which include some fine quality pieces from the class LQC2 and the imperial porcelain, may suggest that the visiting fleets stopped in different places of the Maldives—or that Chinese ceramics were traded through commercial networks internal to the Maldives.

Third, according to Table 6.5 and Table 6.6, LQC2 and CBW2–1, dated to the early Ming dynasty (fifteenth century), show a lower frequency at Kinolhas, and this reflects the so-called Ming Gap (late fourteenth to early fifteenth centuries): there was little or no Chinese participation in the Indian Ocean trade during the early Ming dynasty.

Tom Harrisson was the first to promote this idea in 1958 when he observed an absence of early Ming ceramics from the site of Sarawak, East Malaysia (Harrisson 1958). Also, Roxanne Brown examined the pottery deposits from 15 shipwrecks from the East Indian Ocean, and she concluded that the proportion of Chinese ceramics around southeastern Asia decreased from 50% to 5% during and after Zheng He's expedition. After AD 1573, Chinese ceramics recovered to their former dominance, which was almost 100% (Brown 2009). The small proportions of LQC2 and CBW2–1 and the large proportion of SE CEL may show that, because of the Ming Gap, southeast Asian celadon became popular at that time, and was filling this Chinese ceramic market gap in the Indian Ocean. The entry of Islamic ceramics (dated from the fourteenth to sixteenth century) may also show that there was an international diversity of ceramic imports.

The limitation in the interpretation of the Chinese ceramic materials from Kinolhas is mainly due to the small quantities recovered. In Units 321, 325, 449, and 631 in particular, sherd numbers are all fewer than 50 pieces. This may produce a biased pattern when comparing them to larger trends in the western Indian Ocean. Unit 544 is more reliable due to its larger assemblage and, as mentioned earlier, the imperial white porcelain from this unit shows a very positive and important clue for research into Zheng He's voyages to the Maldives and the western Indian Ocean.

By providing general data from other excavations in the Maldives and comparing them with the larger picture in the western Indian Ocean, further research can certainly provide new evidence of the ancient, long-distance trade between the Maldives, the western Indian Ocean, and China.

7 The fauna

Annalisa Christie

Introduction

This chapter presents the faunal remains recovered from the open area excavations in the trenches discussed in Chapter 4. These assemblages are described and examined spatially and stratigraphically. While here the focus is on the material from Kinolhas, in Chapter 9 the discussion will be broadened with further comparisons to the faunal assemblages excavated by members of the team in 2016 at the sites of Utheemu (Haa Alifu atoll), Male', and Veyvah (Meemu atoll).

Methods and recording strategy

All faunal remains, whether marine shell, marine, or terrestrial animal bones, recovered from the excavations were sorted, counted, and recorded individually (Figure 7.1).

For consistency, the recording strategy adopted for the excavation units was the same as that used to assess the faunal remains recovered from the Shovel Test Pit (STP) surveys, outlined in Chapter 3. Fauna were grouped according to the following categories:

- Cowrie shells—identified to species where possible
- Other marine invertebrates (OMI)—comprising all remaining marine molluscs identified to species
- Marine vertebrates (MV)—including fish cranial and post-cranial elements (vertebrae and fin spines) as well as cartilaginous fish (shark or ray) vertebrae
- Terrestrial vertebrates comprising rodents, bird, and ungulate remains
- Unknown—comprising remains that could not be allocated to other categories

Species-level identification of the fish and ungulate remains was not attempted due to the generally fragmented condition of the bones and the absence of comparative samples. However, examination of the bird bones would seem to indicate that all the archaeological bird remains are chicken (*Gallus gallus*).

As noted in Chapter 3, evidence of anthropogenic modification was recorded. For shells, this included any evidence of deliberate modification (e.g. removal of the dorsum for cowries) and evidence for burning; in the case of bones, this also included any evidence of butchery such as cut marks, chop marks, or scraping.

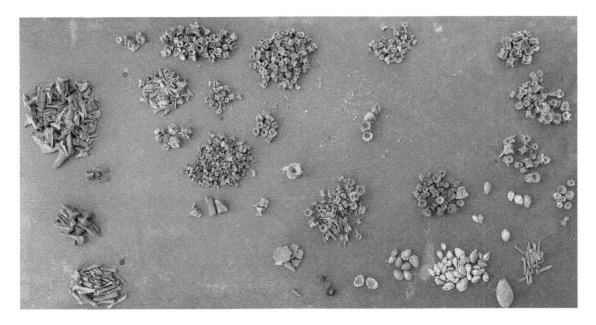

Figure 7.1 Sorted faunal remains from Kinolhas.

DOI: 10.4324/9781003166221-7

Results

Eight thousand, seven hundred, and seventy-four specimens, comprising 1,239 shells and 7,535 bone fragments, were recovered from the open area excavations at Kinolhas (Table 7.1). Of these, 79% (n=6968) were classified to species or category, with the remaining 21% (n=1806) too fragmented to be identified conclusively. While the shells, particularly the cowrie shells, were generally well preserved and showed very little degradation or modification, the bones were much more friable. The fauna, like other material culture, was in general most abundant in Context 2, unless otherwise stated. This highlights the uniformity of the archaeological layer across the site overall. Material recovered from the individual trenches is presented below.

Table 7.1 Overview of faunal remains recovered from Kinolhas.

	T321	*T325*	*T360*	*T443*	*T449*	*T544*	*T631*
Cowries	124	29	237	73	283	308	56
Other marine invertebrates (OMI)	31	33	1	1	12	48	3
Marine vertebrates (MV)	36	46	150	89	649	3942	20
Terrestrial vertebrates (TV)	9	14	28	7	129	606	4
Unknown	6	4	24	15	245	1507	5
Total	**206**	**126**	**440**	**185**	**1318**	**6411**	**88**
% of overall assemblage	**2.35**	**1.44**	**5.01**	**2.11**	**14.92**	**73.07**	**1.00**

Trench 321

From T321, 206 specimens were recovered, of which 75% (n=155) were shells. While most of these (80%, n=124) were cowries, other shells, including 15 *Atactodea striata* and 1 *Nerita sp.*, were recovered alongside 15 shell fragments that could not be identified to family or species level (Table 7.2). These included four unidentifiable gastropods and 11 unidentifiable bivalve fragments. The diversity of shell species is notable here given the high proportion of molluscs in the assemblage overall. In terms of the remaining 51 bones from this trench, 71% (n=36) represented marine fauna, and they were relatively evenly split between cranial and post-cranial element (Table 7.2).

Table 7.2 Faunal remains from T321.

		1	*2*	*3*	*Totals*
Cowries	*M. moneta*	9	90	0	**99**
	M. annulus	1	0	0	**1**
	Naria helvola helvola (Linnaeus, 1758)	1	6	0	**7**
	Cypraea Sp.	1	16	0	**17**
OMI	*Atactodea striata* (Gmelin, 1791)	0	15	0	**15**
	Nerita sp.	0	1	0	**1**
	Unidentified shell	5	10	0	**15**
MV	Fish cranial	3	17	0	**20**
	Fish post-cranial	1	14	1	**16**
TV	Bird	1	7	0	**8**
	Ungulate	0	0	0	**0**
	Rodent	0	1	0	**1**
	Unknown	0	6	0	**6**
	Totals	**22**	**183**	**1**	**206**

Trench 325

T325 returned just 126 specimens, comprising 62 shells and 64 bones (Table 7.3). The shells here showed similar diversity in species with more than half the mollusc assemblage consisting of non-cowrie species.

Trench 360

From T360 issued 440 specimens, comprising 238 shells and 202 bones (Table 7.4). Cowrie shells, primarily *M. moneta*, represented 53% (n=233) of the total assemblage from this trench. This is significant since one of the reasons this trench was selected for further investigation was the high proportion of cowrie shells noted in the STP assemblage (Table 3.2). Of these, 44 were burnt. These were not all issued from the same context (with 23, 10, and 11 burnt *M. moneta* from Contexts 2, 3, and 4 respectively). This suggests these burnt shells were not deposited at the same time. From the

Table 7.3 Faunal remains from T325.

		1	2	3	4	Total
		6	11	0	1	18
Cowries	M. moneta					
	M. annulus	0	0	0	0	0
	Naria helvola helvola	0	2	0	0	2
	Cypraea Sp.	0	7	0	2	9
OMI	Atactodea striata	1	3	0	1	5
	Unidentified shell	1	25	2	0	28
MV	Fish cranial	1	9	1	2	13
	Fish post-cranial	4	29	0	0	33
TV	Bird	1	10	2	0	13
	Ungulate	0	0	0	0	0
	Rodent	0	1	0	0	1
	Unknown	1	3	0	0	4
	Total	**16**	**99**	**5**	**6**	**126**

Table 7.4 Faunal remains from T360.

	Context	*1*	*2*	*3*	*4*	*5*	*Totals*
Cowries	M. moneta	5	150	64	14	0	233
	M. annulus	0	0	0	0	0	0
	Palmadusta asellus (Linnaeus, 1758)	0	2	1	0	0	3
	Cypraea Sp.	0	0	0	1	0	1
OMI	Unidentified shell	0	1	0	0	0	1
MV	Fish cranial	1	31	9	0	1	42
	Fish post-cranial	1	81	21	1	1	105
	Shark/ray vertebra	0	3	0	0	0	3
TV	Bird	1	18	2	2	0	23
	Ungulate	0	0	0	0	0	0
	Rodent	1	3	1	0	0	5
	Unknown	5	18	1	0	0	24
	Totals	**14**	**307**	**99**	**18**	**2**	**440**

perspective of the bones recovered, 74% (n=150) of the remains were fish, with a predominance of vertebrae (72%, n=108) rather than cranial remains (28%, n=42). Of these, three were from a cartilaginous fish such as shark or ray.

Trench 443

T443 returned 185 specimens, comprising 111 bones and 74 shells (Table 7.5). Unlike T321, which yielded a comparatively high proportion of non-cowrie molluscs, T443 only returned a single non-cowrie shell—*Atactodea striata*. The majority of the bone assemblage (80%, n=89) comprised fish bones. These were predominantly vertebrae, including two specimens from cartilaginous fish.

Table 7.5 Faunal remains from T443.

		1	*2*	*4*	*11*	*14*	*Total*
Cowries	M. moneta	0	43	1	0	2	46
	M. annulus	0	3	0	0	0	3
	Cypraea Sp.	0	24	0	0	0	24
OMI	Atactodea striata	0	1	0	0	0	1
MV	Fish cranial	0	18	0	0	0	18
	Fish post-cranial	0	67	1	1	0	69
	Shark/ray vertebra	0	1	0	1	0	2
TV	Bird	0	5	0	0	0	5
	Ungulate	0	1	0	0	0	1
	Rodent	0	1	0	0	0	1
	Unknown	0	5	6	4	0	15
	Totals	**0**	**169**	**8**	**6**	**2**	**185**

Trench 449

T449 was the second most productive trench excavated (Table 7.6). It yielded 22% (n=295) molluscs and 78% (n=1023) bones from marine and terrestrial fauna. Fish bones, including 3 vertebrae from cartilaginous species, formed the bulk of the assemblage recovered from the main archaeological layer.

Most of the shells recovered from this trench were cowries (n=283). While 117 of these were dispersed through the deposits of Context 2, a further 116 were observed in two discrete concentrated deposits (Contexts 12 and 13, returning 17 and 99 shells respectively). The 99 shells recovered from Context 13 were associated with a small ceramic vessel within which a small electrum pendant and six minute glass beads were recovered (see Chapter 8 for further details).

Trench 544

Mirroring what was observed in the STP surveys (Table 4.2), T544 showed a high abundance of faunal remains and in fact represented the largest assemblage excavated (Table 7.7). Just 6% (n=356) of the remains were shells, the majority of which (n=308) were cowries with very few other species present. In terms of bones, 65% (n=3942) were fish remains, with post-cranial elements particularly abundant (n=3068). These included 173 vertebrae of varying size belonging from cartilaginous fish species. This trench also returned a comparatively high proportion of bird bones (n=533), 11% (n=59) of which were burnt. Forty-nine bones from ungulates (likely goat) were also recovered in T544. While these only account for 0.8% of the fauna from this trench, this represents a 60% increase in the number of ungulate remains from T443 and T449 (which contributed 0.5% of each).

Table 7.6 Faunal remains from T449.

		1	2	3	7	9	11	12	13	16	Section	Totals
Cowries	Monetaria moneta	2	117	7	0	2	0	17	99	5	19	**268**
	Monetaria annulus	0	3	0	0	0	0	0	0	0	0	**3**
	Naria helvola helvola	0	2	0	0	0	0	0	0	0	0	**2**
	Ipsa childreni	0	1	2	0	0	0	0	0	0	0	**3**
	Cypraea Sp.	0	6	1	0	0	0	0	0	0	0	**8**
OMI	Atactodea striata	0	9	0	0	0	0	0	0	0	1	**10**
	Unidentified shell	0	0	0	1	0	0	0	0	0	1	**2**
MV	Fish cranial	0	100	15	0	0	0	0	0	7	16	**138**
	Fish post-cranial	2	405	23	0	1	1	0	0	28	46	**506**
	Shark/ray vertebra	0	3	0	0	0	0	0	0	0	2	**5**
TV	Bird	2	82	4	0	0	0	0	0	3	2	**93**
	Ungulate	0	3	0	0	0	1	0	0	0	2	**6**
	Rodent	0	25	1	0	0	0	0	0	1	3	**30**
	Unknown	0	126	22	3	0	0	0	0	69	25	**245**
	Total	**6**	**882**	**74**	**4**	**3**	**2**	**17**	**99**	**113**	**117**	**1318**

Table 7.7 Faunal remains from T544.

		1	2	3	4	6	Total
Cowries	Monetaria moneta	31	128	20	28	0	**207**
	Monetaria annulus	0	0	0	0	0	**0**
	Cypraea Sp.	3	83	13	2	0	**101**
OMI	Atactodea striata	12	25	1	1	0	**39**
	Unidentified shell	7	0	0	2	0	**9**
MV	Fish cranial	56	496	81	241	0	**874**
	Fish post-cranial	121	1749	545	480	0	**2894**
	Shark/ray vertebrae	1	73	62	36	1	**173**
TV	Bird	35	354	25	119	0	**533**
	Ungulate	1	28	2	18	0	**49**
	Rodent	2	2	5	15	0	**24**
	Unknown	99	967	128	311	2	**1507**
	Total	**368**	**3905**	**882**	**1253**	**3**	**6411**

Trench 631

As a predominantly mortuary context, this unit presented a very different picture to that of the other units excavated at Kinolhas. Faunal remains were, unsurprisingly, scarce, with just 88 specimens. Of these, 64% (n=56) were cowrie shells

(Table 7.8). Most of the material was recovered from Contexts 20 and 22, representing deposits below the mound of rubble. Context 20 referred to the northeast corner of the trench, north of Structure 1, while Context 22 designated the entire area north of Structure 1 (Table 4.7). The cowries recovered in Contexts 22 and 25 represent possible caches. In the case of those from Context 22, these were primarily found adjacent to the north face of standing tombstone 27e (Table 4.9). However, as the concentration of shells was only noted once they had been recovered, it is not possible to delineate the boundaries of this possible cache. The nine *M. moneta* from Context 25, on the other hand, were more spatially circumscribed and were found adjacent to the south face of standing tombstone 27b. Given the proximity of the two deposits to standing tombstones, they may represent some form of offering to the deceased. Data from the ethnographic surveys conducted as part of the wider project suggest cowries were often as offerings at mausolea and shrines.

Most of the remaining 29 bones recovered in the assemblage issued from Context 22 and these consisted primarily of fish vertebrae (n=16).

The faunal remains: a comparative analysis

The assemblages from each trench were compared to determine whether any variations were apparent. Three factors were considered. First, evidence of modification was evaluated. Second, the relative proportions of different types of resources (specifically, cowries, other marine molluscs, fish, bird, and ungulates) were examined. As cowries were not exploited for food, the relative proportions of consumable marine and terrestrial fauna (comprising fish, bird, and ungulates) were also assessed. These aimed to identify any differences in use or patterns of consumption across the site. Third, although it was not possible to identify fish species from the post-cranial remains, vertebrae were measured and grouped according to size, providing a proxy indicator for average fish size.

Table 7.8 Faunal remains from T631.

		1	3	10	11	12	15	18	20	21	22	25	26	27	28	Total
Cowries	*M. moneta*	2	0	2		1			24	2	12	9	1			54
	M. annulus	0	0	0		0			0	0	0	0	0			0
	Palmadusta asellus	0	0	0		0			0	1	0	0	0			1
	Ipsa children (Grey 1825)	0	0	0	Veligaa/Hirigaa mound	0	Veligaa/Hirigaa mound		0	0	0	0	0			1
OMI	*Atactodea striata*	0	0	0		0			0	1	0	0	0			1
	Unidentified shell	0	1	0		0			1	0	0	0	0			2
MV	Fish cranial	1	0	0		0		Skeleton	0	0	0	0	0	Standing Tombstones		Structure 1	1
	Fish post-cranial	3	0	0		0			0	0	15	0	0			18
	Shark/ray vertebra	0	0	0		0			0	0	1	0	0			1
TV	Bird	1	0	1		0			0	0	0	0	0			2
	Ungulate	0	0	0		0			0	0	0	0	0			0
	Rodent	2	0	0		0			0	0	0	0	0			2
	Unknown	0	0	0		0			0	5	0	0	0			5
	Total	**9**	**1**	**3**		**1**			**25**	**9**	**28**	**9**	**1**			**88**

Modification

Burning was the primary modification observed across the assemblage. This was noted in only 4% (n=351) of cases, with burnt remains recovered from six of the seven trenches excavated (Table 7.9). None of the material from T325 was burnt.

While the proportion of burnt remains as a percentage of their respective assemblage was generally consistent across four of the six trenches (5%, n=9 from T443; 3%, n=7 from T321; 3%, n=41 from T449; and 4%, n=240 from T544), the figure was noticeably higher in the cases of T360 and T631, where they represented 11% (n=47) and 8% (n=7) respectively.

The higher proportion of burnt remains in T631 is probably a factor of the small overall assemblage size. However, the burnt remains from T360 is interesting Of the 47 specimens recovered from this trench showing evidence of burning, 44 were cowries. A similar pattern was noted in the assemblage issuing from the associated test pit (STP360) during the

Table 7.9 Burnt remains from Kinolhas.

	T321	T325	T360	T443	T449	T544	T631	Total
Cowries	6	0	44	3	10	8	0	71
Fish bones	1	0	3	5	24	172	5	210
Bird bones	0	0	0	1	4	59	1	65
Rodent	0	0	0	0	3	1	1	5
Total	**7**	**0**	**47**	**9**	**41**	**240**	**7**	**351**
% of trench assemblage	**3.40**	**0**	**10.68**	**4.86**	**3.11**	**3.74**	**7.95**	

STP surveys (Chapter 3). The deposits from both the trench and associated STP showed no evidence of burning—no ashy deposits or features resembling a hearth were identified. Additionally, the burnt shells were not found together. This suggests that the shells were burnt before they were deposited. Ethnographic surveys conducted by the author to elucidate of the collection, processing and use of cowries indicates the shells were never deliberately modified. The most common processing strategy involved burying the shells within the domestic compounds, each collection (3000–6000 shells) being buried separately and in sequence. Shells were left for 7–14 days before being excavated, washed in the sea or rinsed in well water, and left to dry in the shade. Other processing strategies included boiling the shells in salt water, then rinsing them, and leaving them to dry in the sun; leaving them soaking in a slow draining drum on water to allow the flesh to drain out; or placing them in a pot with white sand. This suggests the shells recovered from T360 are unlikely to have been burnt as a result of deliberate action - and instead is likely the incidental result of another anthropogenic or natural process.

In the other trenches, most of the burnt remains were fish vertebrae, the majority of which (n=172 of 210) were recovered from T544. This trench also returned 90% (59 of 65) of the burnt bird bones—which is not unexpected given that 83% (533 of the 664) bird bone fragments issued from this trench.

Other forms of modification were much less frequent. As far as the cowrie shells are concerned, only two of the 1078 cowries recovered were missing their dorsa. This is unlikely to have been the result of deliberate anthropogenic modification; these cowries were also worn and pitted, and it is likely that they were perforated naturally.

Patterns of resource use

Figure 7.2 shows the relative abundance of all identifiable fauna from trenches excavated. The first observation to be made here concerns the relative absence of non-cowrie marine molluscs. The material from Trenches 321 and 325, which are situated at the northern edge of the core archaeological area (see Chapter 3), are notable exceptions to this, with both returning higher numbers of *Atactodea striata* (Table 7.2 and Table 7.3 respectively). These bivalves are very small and are unlikely to have been eaten.

Despite the presence of the two cowrie caches in T449, the proportion of cowries from this trench relative to other types of fauna was quite low, representing just 26% of the identifiable remains. Similarly, low proportions of cowrie shells were observed in T544 and T325.

When considering only consumable fauna, patterns across the trenches become more consistent, with a clear dominance for fish across the board (Figure 7.3). A slight difference exists in terms of proportions of bird remains recovered, but these are within the 10–20% range. As expected, ungulate remains were minimal.

Vertebrae

The fish vertebrae recovered were dived into five size categories—very small (<5 mm), small (5–7.5 mm), medium (7.5–10 mm), large (10–15 mm), and very large (>15 mm). The proportions of different sizes were then compared across the

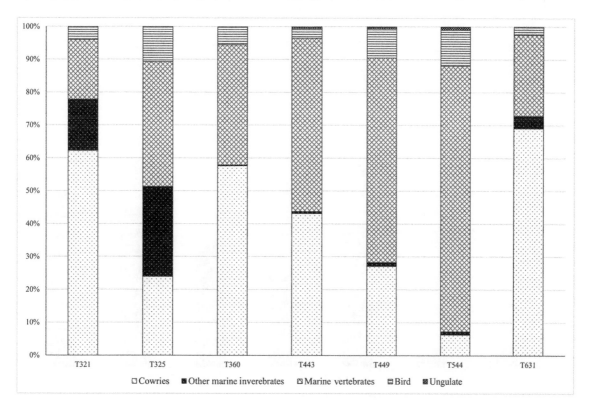

Figure 7.2 Proportions of different resources across the site.

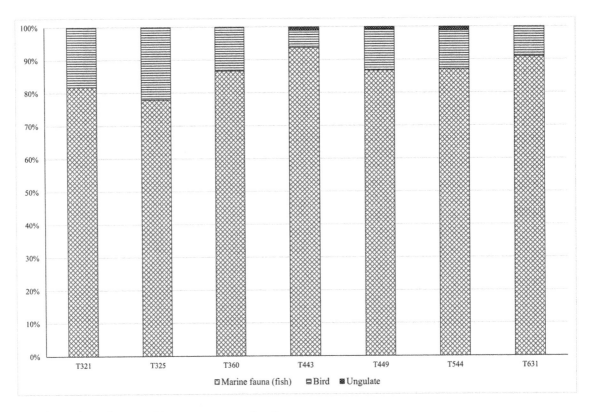

Figure 7.3 Proportions of consumable resources across the site.

trenches (Figure 7.4). Morphometric analysis can be used as an indicator of the size and weight of fish using published regression data; however, as Colley (1990, p. 219) notes, it can be sufficient to consider relative fish sizes depending on the questions being asked. In this case, comparisons aimed to determine whether the proportions of different sized vertebrae were similar or different across the excavations and, in the case of Trench 544 where sample size was adequate, across the stratigraphy. In in most cases, very small, small, and medium vertebrae were dominant, making up 80–90% of the material. While T631 and T325 featured a higher proportion of large vertebrae, this may be a product of the small overall sample size (T631 n=15, T325 n=34). The same issue may skew the data for T321, where only 15 specimens were counted.

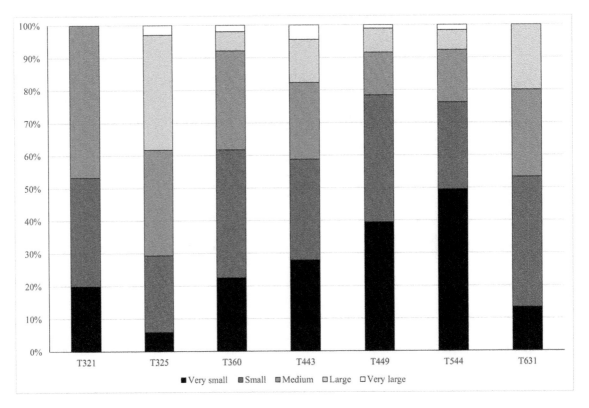

Figure 7.4 Proportions of different vertebrae sizes.

The size of the fish matching the small and medium vertebrae that dominate most of the assemblage depends on species. Ethnographic and historical accounts suggest that tuna was the main species targeted. Were this the case in our assemblages (which seems highly likely), rachidian profiles presented in Marrast and Béarez (2019, p. 193) suggest fish of between 263 mm/305 g (average vertebrae size 5 mm) and 489 mm/2102 g (average vertebrae size 10 mm).

Stratigraphic analysis

Stratigraphic analysis was only conducted for the material from T544, in which a larger quantity of material, issuing from more than one context, was available. This assessment was conducted for the relative abundance of different types of resources (Figure 7.5) and for different vertebrae sizes (Figure 7.6). Very little difference is visible in proportions of resources and vertebrae size throughout the sequence. The marginally higher dominance of non-cowrie molluscs in Context 1 (Figure 7.5) may reflect a greater number of shell inclusions in the topsoil. Given the short time period covered by these strata (which two radiocarbon dates place in the long fourteenth century; see Chapter 4, Table 4.10), the continuity over time is not surprising.

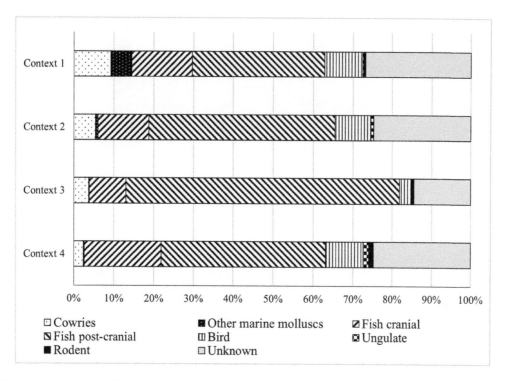

Figure 7.5 Stratigraphic analysis of faunal remains from T544.

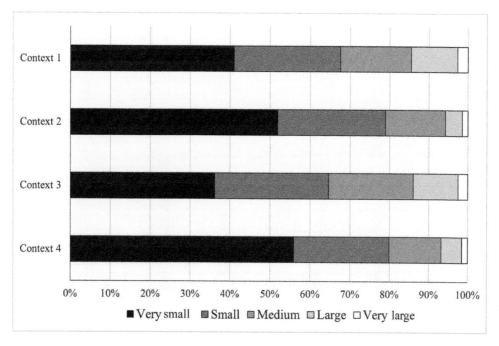

Figure 7.6 Stratigraphic analysis of vertebrae sizes from T544.

Discussion

The fauna recovered from Kinolhas is consistent with the idea that Maldivian communities were largely reliant on the sea for their subsistence, with fish remains being dominant across assemblages. This, and the comparatively small representation of chicken and other terrestrial fauna, is reflective of patterns observed in other assemblages across the Maldives, discussed in more detail in Chapter 9.

8 The small finds

Introduction

Anne Haour

A total of 110 small finds were recovered from the research carried out at Kinolhas. This chapter will discuss these, including material from all shovel test pits—not solely those subsequently extended into full-size excavation units. Each item was given a unique object number (SF number), and objects were photographed and bagged individually. Where artefacts were fragmented into several pieces which clearly belonged together, a single SF number was allocated and they were bagged together.

Where possible, the likely nature and function of the find is suggested, falling into several categories. These included items relating to food preparation, storage, or consumption (including fragments of glass bottles); weaponry; tools (within this category are all artefacts related to crafts, including slag); hardware (items related to building structures, but also implements for fishing, for example); adornment (not just jewellery and clothing accessories, but also fragments of very small glass bottles, suggestive of perfume); and lastly indeterminate.

The first two sections concern glass finds. Chapter 8.1 will discuss the beads, while Chapter 8.2 will discuss the fragments of bracelets and other items.

The material was tabulated in a summary way in a preliminary report (Haour et al. 2017), and the information has been refined and expanded on since. Chapter 9, this volume, offers an overview of the Kinolhas small finds in relation to several other islands of the Maldives that were sampled by the present team.

8.1 The glass beads

Marilee Wood and Laure Dussubieux

Introduction

This chapter presents the results of visual and elemental analyses on eight glass beads from excavations at the site of Kinolhas (Figure 8.1.1)—one from Trench 544, and the remainder from Trench 449, six of which came from the fill of a small vessel recovered in that unit.

Cataloguing the Kinolhas beads (Table 8.1.1) began with establishing whether the sample was glass and, if so, determining the method of manufacture—in this case, six beads are drawn and the remaining two are wound. Drawn beads are basically mass manufactured while wound ones, which are usually easier but more time-consuming to produce, are individually created. Other features recorded included how the ends of drawn beads were finished, the diameter and length of each bead (where fragments were complete enough to allow accurate measurement), and the bead shape. Next, diaphaneity of the glass (transparent, translucent, or opaque) was noted, then the general colour family followed by a more precise colour designation using the Munsell number. Glass quality was recorded by noting the surface condition (dull, shiny etc.). Finally, remarks that include other observations of note were recorded. After the completion of chemical analysis, the glass type was recorded.

Chemical analyses were carried out at the Field Museum of Natural History in Chicago, USA, with a Thermo ICAP Q Inductively Coupled Plasma–Mass Spectrometer (ICP–MS) connected to a New Wave UP213 laser for direct introduction of solid samples. The parameters of the ICP–MS are optimised to ensure a stable signal with a maximum intensity over the full range of masses of the elements and to minimise oxides and double ionised species formation (XO^+/X^+ and X^{++}/X^+ < 1 to 2 %). For that purpose, the argon flows, the RF power, the torch position, the lenses, the mirror, and the detector voltages are adjusted using an auto-optimisation procedure.

For better sensitivity, helium is used as a gas carrier in the laser. The choice of the parameters of the laser ablation will not only have an effect on the sensitivity of the method and the reproducibility of the measurement, but also on the damage to the sample. To be able to determine elements with concentrations in the range of ppm and below while leaving a trace on the surface of the sample invisible to the naked eye, the single point analysis mode with a laser beam diameter of 100 μm is used, operating at 80% of the laser energy (0.1 mJ) and at a pulse frequency of 20 Hz. A pre-ablation time of 20 s is set in order, first, to eliminate the transient part of the signal and, second,

DOI: 10.4324/9781003166221-8

1 cm

Figure 8.1.1 The Kinolhas beads. From left to right and top to bottom: Samples 82d, 82e, 82f, 82g, 82b, 82c, 45, and 90

Table 8.1.1 Morphological features of the beads recovered from excavations on the island of Kinolhas, Raa atoll. The dimension of 82f and g are not provided as the beads were fragmentary.

Unit	Cont.	ID	Qty	Qty frags	How made	Shape	End treat	Diam (mm)	Lgth (mm)	Diaph	Munsell #	Colour	Patination	Surf.	Series	Remarks
T449	2	45	1		Wound	Barrel		10.1	8.4	op	2.5B 6/4	Blue-green	Light		Dull	v-Na-Al	Slightly tapered perforation
	20	82b	1		Drawn	Cylinder	Heat treated	1.9	1.6	op		Black			Dull	m-Na-Al 6	
	20	82c	1		Drawn	Oblate	Heat treated	2	1.4	op		Black			Dull	m-Na-Al 6	
	20	82d	1		Drawn	Oblate	Heat treated	1.5	0.9	tsl	7.5R 5/6	Amber/ violet			Dull	m-Na-Al 2	Colour is pale and difficult to describe
	20	82e	1		Drawn	Cylinder	Heat treated	1.3	1	tsl	7.5R 5/6	Amber/ violet			Dull	m-Na-Al 2	Colour is pale and difficult to describe
	20	82f		1	Drawn	Cylinder	Heat treated			tsl	7.5R 5/6	Amber/ violet			Dull	m-Na-Al 2	Colour is pale and difficult to describe
	20	82g		1	Drawn	Cylinder	Heat treated			tsl	7.5R 5/6	Amber/ violet			Dull	m-Na-Al 2	Colour is pale and difficult to describe
T544	4	90		1	Wound	Sphere		8.1	7.4	op	10B 6/8	Turquoise	Light		Dull	PbO low Li	

Source: Items 82b–g were recovered in the fill of a small ceramic vessel (SF 81) together with an electrum pendant (SF 82a).

to be sure that a possible surface contamination or corrosion does not affect the results of the analysis. For each glass sample, the average of four measurements corrected from the blank is considered for the calculation of concentrations.

To improve reproducibility of measurements, the use of an internal standard is required to correct possible instrumental drifts or changes in the ablation efficiency. The element chosen as internal standard has to be present in relatively high concentrations so its measurement is as accurate as possible. In order to obtain absolute concentrations for the analysed elements, the concentration of the internal standard has to be known. The isotope Si29 was used for internal standardisation. Concentrations for major elements, including silica, are calculated assuming that the sum of their concentrations in weight percent in glass is equal to 100% (Gratuze 1999).

Fully quantitative analyses are possible by using external standards. To prevent matrix effects, the composition of standards must be as close as possible to that of the samples. Two different series of standards are used to measure major, minor, and trace elements. The first series of external standards are standard reference materials (SRM) manufactured by NIST: SRM 610 and SRM 612. Both of these standards are soda–lime–silica glass doped with trace elements in the range of 500 ppm (SRM 610) and 50 ppm (SRM 612). Certified values are available for a very limited number of elements. Concentrations from Pearce et al. (1997) will be used for the other elements. The second series of standards was manufactured by Corning. Their glasses B and D, used here, were produced to match the compositions of ancient glass (Brill 1999, vol. 2, p. 544).

Results

The chemical compositions of the beads are summarised in Table 8.1.2. In terms of elemental analysis, three different glass types were identified:

1 High lead–potash glass (Si-Pb-K low Li)
2 Soda plant ash–high alumina glass (v-Na-Al)
3 Mineral soda–high alumina glass (m-Na-Al)

Table 8.1.2 Kinolhas beads: full elemental results.

	v-Na-Al	m-Na-Al	m-Na-Al	m-Na-Al	m-N a-Al	m-Na-Al	m-Na-Al	Not glass	Pb-K
	SF45	SF82b	SF82c	SF82d	SF82e	SF82f	SF82g	SF82h	SF90
SiO_2	60.5%	59.2%	57.9%	63.4%	63.5%	63.1%	63.1%	0.05%	41.8%
Na_2O	16.3%	19.6%	18.3%	21.4%	21.4%	21.5%	21.6%	0.47%	2.53%
MgO	4.06%	1.05%	1.39%	0.71%	0.70%	0.72%	0.71%	9.67%	0.06%
Al_2O_3	5.42%	9.43%	10.0%	6.27%	6.30%	6.39%	6.32%	0.003%	0.30%
P_2O_5	0.28%	0.21%	0.21%	0.07%	0.07%	0.07%	0.07%	0.17%	0.01%
Cl	0.71%	1.22%	1.04%	1.10%	1.10%	1.16%	1.12%	0.06%	0.48%
K_2O	3.10%	2.25%	2.43%	1.90%	1.87%	1.93%	1.96%	0.05%	9.58%
CaO	3.92%	3.46%	4.25%	2.15%	2.15%	2.20%	2.14%	89.4%	4.89%
MnO	0.05%	0.15%	0.10%	1.00%	0.99%	0.99%	0.99%	0.0005%	0.002%
Fe_2O_3	0.99%	3.09%	4.05%	1.92%	1.90%	1.92%	1.90%	0.10%	0.16%
CuO	0.93%	0.06%	0.06%	0.01%	0.01%	0.01%	0.01%	0.001%	1.16%
SnO_2	2.88%	0.07%	0.06%	0.002%	0.002%	0.002%	0.002%	0.0001%	0.16%
PbO	0.73%	0.17%	0.15%	0.01%	0.01%	0.01%	0.01%	0.02%	38.8%
Li	8	19	20	24	24	24	24	2	8
Be	0.6	1.1	1.2	0.9	0.9	0.9	0.9	0.03	0.1
B	144	117	104	97	97	96	97	36	2
Sc	5	9	11	7	7	7	7	0.1	2
Ti	929	2738	3496	1963	1939	1953	1941	2	61
V	14	115	137	76	75	77	75	2	2
Cr	20	42	61	9	9	9	9	25	2
Ni	18	28	21	18	18	18	18	2	10
Co	6	25	16	9	9	9	9	0.3	2
Zn	44	104	87	28	28	29	30	2	26
As	28	9	6	6	6	6	6	1.2	75
Rb	34	60	67	47	46	47	46	0.2	8
Sr	287	229	285	150	148	155	149	4361	20
Zr	54	179	246	132	130	135	132	0.1	4
Nb	4	10	12	8	8	8	8	0.01	0.27
Ag	2	14	5	0.2	0.3	0.2	0.2	0.6	77
In	81	2	2	0.1	0.1	0.1	0.1	0.01	5
Sb	49	4	2	0.7	0.7	0.6	0.8	0.4	105
Cs	0.3	0.9	1.1	0.5	0.5	0.6	0.6	0.005	0.09
Ba	367	423	441	403	399	413	408	7.7	10
La	5	39	41	25	24	25	25	0.5	1.2
Ce	11	73	77	58	57	59	59	0.3	2
Pr	1.4	8	9	5	5	6	5	0.09	0.3
Ta	0.3	0.8	0.9	0.7	0.7	0.7	0.7	0.001	0.02
Au	0.3	0.9	2	0.09	0.1	0.07	0.5	0.2	0.3
Y	5	15	20	13	13	13	13	6	2
Bi	7	0.2	0.1	0.1	0.1	0.1	0.3	0.03	8
U	0.4	75	87	121	121	121	123	1.5	0.2
W	0.03	0.3	0.5	0.2	0.1	0.2	0.2	0.1	0.03
Mo	0.3	3.2	3.3	0.9	0.9	1.1	1.0	0.05	0.3
Nd	5	26	29	18	18	18	18	0.4	1.0
Sm	1.0	5	6	3	3	3	3	0.1	0.2
Eu	0.4	1.0	1.2	0.7	0.7	0.7	0.7	0.04	0.04
Gd	0.9	4	4	3	3	3	3	0.2	0.2
Tb	0.2	0.5	0.7	0.4	0.4	0.4	0.4	0.05	0.03
Dy	0.9	3	4	2	2	2	2	0.4	0.2

(Continued)

Table 8.1.2 (Continued)

	v-Na-Al	m-Na-Al	m-Na-Al	m-Na-Al	m-N a-Al	m-Na-Al	m-Na-Al	Not glass	Pb-K
	SF45	SF82b	SF82c	SF82d	SF82e	SF82f	SF82g	SF82h	SF90
Ho	0.2	0.6	0.8	0.5	0.5	0.5	0.5	0.1	0.04
Er	0.5	2	2	1.3	1.3	1.3	1.3	0.4	0.1
Tm	0.08	0.2	0.3	0.2	0.2	0.2	0.2	0.05	0.02
Yb	0.5	1.5	2	1.3	1.3	1.3	1.3	0.3	0.1
Lu	0.09	0.2	0.3	0.2	0.2	0.2	0.2	0.05	0.02
Hf	2	5	7	4	4	4	4	0.003	0.1
Th	1.3	25	46	20	21	21	21	0.06	0.4

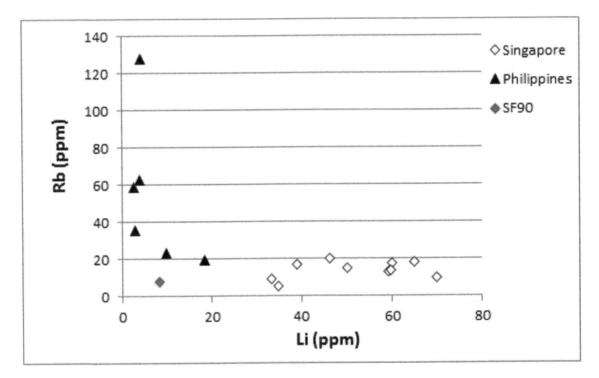

Figure 8.1.2 Li–Rb scatterplot for some beads from Singapore (Dussubieux 2010) and from the Philippines (unpublished data) and for SF 90.

HIGH LEAD–POTASH GLASS

Bead SF90, the sole bead from Trench 544, is a wound spherical bead, 8.1 x 7.4 mm in size, with a high lead composition (39% PbO). The only other constituents present in significant concentrations are silica (41–42%) and potash (9.6%). Glass beads with high lead compositions are characteristic of China, where such beads were manufactured starting from around the second century AD (Fuxi 2009). This glass tradition continued until very recently (Burgess and Dussubieux 2008), but it is possible to distinguish different trace element signatures depending on time periods. The composition of the Maldives high lead bead was compared to that of two sets of beads with an assumed Chinese origin. The first group was excavated in Singapore at the site of Fort Canning Hill and dates to the fourteenth century (Borell 2010, Dussubieux 2010). The second group of beads is from a burial excavated by Karl Hutterer at Tanjay in the Philippines, which was dated to the late fifteenth to early sixteenth century based on associated porcelain ceramics (Laura Junker, personal communication). Bead SF90 has rather low lithium and rubidium concentrations and is similar to the group of beads recovered in the Philippines.[1] It is turquoise blue and owes its colour to copper (1.2%wt) (Figure 8.1.2).

SODA PLANT ASH–HIGH ALUMINA GLASS

Two types of soda plant ash glass were identified, depending on whether alumina concentrations are below or above 4%. Bead SF45, like the bead just discussed, is a large (10.1 x 8.4 mm) wound bead but has a very different composition with low lead (0.7–0.8%) and high soda concentrations (15–16%). High concentrations of sodium in a glass are generally due to the addition of soda, found either in mineral form or produced using the ashes from burnt halophytic plants (which grow in salt-rich soils). SF45's magnesia and potash concentrations are higher than 1.5%, suggesting that soda

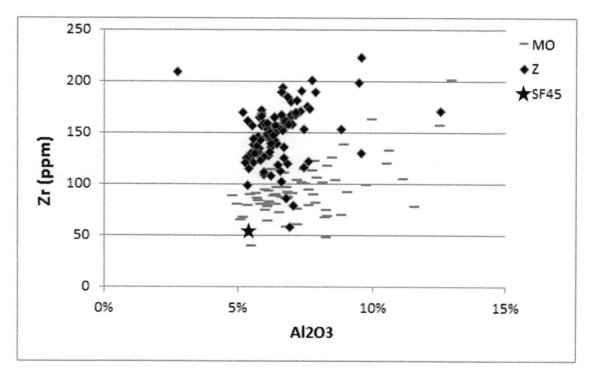

Figure 8.1.3 Bi-plot for the Al_2O_3 and Zr concentrations of MO and Z bead series (Robertshaw et al. 2010) and the SF 45 bead.

plant ashes were used as the flux. This bead, with 5.4% alumina, belongs to the high alumina soda plant ash (v-Na-Al) glass group. The greenish-blue colour of the bead is due to the presence of copper (1.0% as CuO). In addition, it contains 2.9% tin (expressed as SnO_2), an element that might play a role in the opacity of the glass. The provenance of this kind of glass is uncertain. Soda plant ash glasses with high alumina are fairly common in a region that includes Afghanistan (Brill 1999), Uzbekistan (Abdurazakov 2009, Rehren et al. 2010), and Pakistan (Dussubieux and Gratuze 2003) over a wide time period ranging from the second century BC to the fourteenth century AD. The glass from Pakistan is fairly early (200 BC–200 AD) and has a very different trace element pattern, including fairly high trace elements—such as uranium—compared to SF45, so can therefore be excluded. However, comparisons with glasses from the other regions are difficult because trace elements are not included in published compositions.[2]

This type of glass was described by Robertshaw et al. (2010) for glass beads found in southern Africa. Two subgroups were identified: the Mapungubwe Oblate (MO), 1240–1300 AD, and the Zimbabwe (Z), 1300–1430 AD, bead series. The MO v-Na-Al glass has lower zirconium concentrations than the Z v-Na-Al glass type. As Figure 8.1.3 shows, SF45 appears to belong to the Mapungubwe Oblate subtype.

MINERAL SODA–HIGH ALUMINA GLASS

The six remaining samples (SF82b to g) belong to the mineral soda–high alumina (m-Na-Al) glass group. M-Na-Al glass was manufactured in India and its composition can be explained by the use of rather immature sands, with compositions very close to that of the granite from which it derives, containing a relatively high proportion of feldspar. These sands also contain high concentrations of a range of trace elements, including titanium, zirconium, the rare earth elements, uranium, etc. Ethnographic data as well as scientific experiments (Kock and Sode 1995, Brill 2003, Gill 2017) indicate that in several parts of India, glass makers were using a sand naturally mixed to sodic efflorescence called reh which contains large amounts of sodium salts (carbonate, bi-carbonate, and sulfate) and varying proportions of calcium and magnesium salts. This sand occurs in areas where river-draining mountains contain dissolved salts that percolate through the subsoil until saturation. Rains dissolve these salts, which travel upward through the soil by capillary action during the dry season and form white efflorescence on the surface (Wadia 1975, pp. 489, 501, 502). They are present in arid or semi-arid regions. Five subgroups of m-Na-Al glass from India (m-Na-Al 1, 2, 3, 4, and 6) have been recognised based on variations in the concentrations of a number of constituents: Mg, Ca, Sr, Zr, Ba, Cs, and U (Dussubieux et al. 2010, Dussubieux and Wood 2021).

With relatively low U concentrations (75 and 87 ppm) and slightly high Cs concentrations (0.9 and 1.1 ppm), SF82b and c have compositions that fit into the m-Na-Al 6 group, while SF82d to g, with U concentrations in the range of 120 ppm and Cs concentration in the range of 0.6 ppm, are more in line with m-Na-Al 2 glass (Figure 8.1.4 and Table 8.1.3). The compositions of SF82d to g are so similar, with relative standard deviations for the concentrations of most of the elements below 2%, that they were certainly manufactured from the same batch of raw glass. These four beads appear as a single point on Figure 8.1.4. SF82b and c are tiny black beads containing fairly high

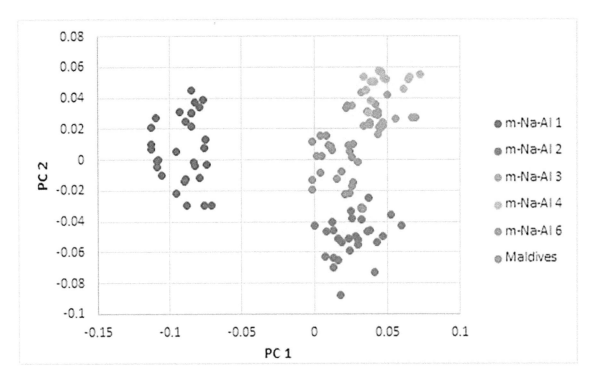

Figure 8.1.4 Bi-plot representing PC1 and PC2 obtained using the concentrations of MgO, CaO, Sr, Zr, Cs, Ba, and U from the m-Na-Al beads from the Maldives and from samples belonging to glass groups m-Na-Al 1, m-Na-Al 2 (Dussubieux et al. 2008), m-Na-Al 3 (Dussubieux and Kanungo 2013), m-Na-Al 4 (Dussubieux 2009), and m-Na-Al 6 (Dussubieux and Wood 2021).

Table 8.1.3 Average concentrations with standard deviations (below) for the elements used in the PCA for glass groups m-Na-Al 2 (Dussubieux et al. 2008) and 6 (Dussubieux and Wood 2021).

	MgO	*CaO*	*Sr*	*Zr*	*Cs*	*Ba*	*U*
m-Na-Al 2	1.0%	4.8%	233	153	0.6	353	110
	0.2%	0.9%	52	66	0.3	87	41
m-Na-Al 6	0.8%	2.5%	235	216	1.5	402	57
	0.2%	0.7%	88	35	0.4	166	22

iron concentrations (3 and 4%). SF82d to g are rather amber in reflected light and pale violet in transmitted light and contain 1% manganese.

M-Na-Al 2 glass beads have been identified at many sites dating from the fourteenth to the nineteenth century AD located on the west coast of India, in southern Africa (e.g. Robertshaw et al. 2010, Wood et al. 2009), and the east coast of Africa (Dussubieux et al. 2008). The site of Chaul, a port in Maharashtra, yielded m-Na-Al 2 glass beads and could have been a point of departure for these beads for distribution around the Indian Ocean. The possibility of bead production at Chaul is proposed by evidence found at the site (although details about what that evidence actually consists of is lacking) (Gogte et al. 2006), as well as by the mention of bead production at a site called 'Chawle' by a Venetian merchant, named Caesar Frederick, who travelled through the west coast of India, including Chaul, in 1563 (Federeci and Hickock 1588).

The m-Na-Al 6 glass type was identified initially at Juani Primary School on Mafia island (Crowther et al. 2016), subsequently at other East African sites that date between the mid-ninth and thirteenth centuries AD. It is also present in southern Africa between the mid-tenth and early thirteenth centuries. No such glass has been identified in India to date, although the similarity between this glass type and the other m-Na-Al glass types suggests that they all come from the Indian subcontinent (Dussubieux and Wood, 2021).

Summary

The eight beads came from three separate contexts within the archaeological site of Kinolhas. All but one came from Trench 449.

Two large wound beads—one from Trench 544, one from Trench 449—have distinct compositions. SF90, the only bead from Trench 544, is made of a high lead glass, assumed to be of Chinese origin where such glass was common. It is consistent with beads excavated in a burial from the Philippines that dates to the late fifteenth/early sixteenth century.

Beads of this type are also present at Songo Mnara, Tanzania, where they are found in association with the earliest type of European bead occurring in East Africa and are recognised as first being produced in about AD 1600, pp. 72–73). The second, SF 45, is made of glass in which soda plant ashes were likely used as the flux and which features a high alumina concentration. This type of glass is the same as that used to make the thirteenth-century Mapungubwe Oblate series beads defined by Robertshaw et al. (2010). But it is interesting to note that many of the v-Na-Al beads that have been identified in East Africa are large, wound, and usually rather crudely made, while those in southern Africa are almost all drawn, small, and well made. The few beads in that region that are wound include eight blue-green well-made sub-spheres, all recovered from Mapungubwe-period burials at K2 (seven came from one infant's grave). As has been suggested, they might have been made locally from imported drawn v-Na-Al beads (Wood 2005). The origins of this glass are still uncertain. A central Asian origin is possible, as discussed earlier.

Six beads made from mineral soda–high alumina glass were recovered inside a small ceramic vessel of indeterminate origin, possibly southeast Asian, which also contained an electrum pendant (SF82a) and was surrounded by cowrie shells. As discussed, these fall into two distinct groups: two of these beads are very small black beads (about 2 mm in diameter) made from m-Na-Al 6 glass, while the remaining four are even smaller (1.3 to 1.5 m in diameter), pale-coloured amber/violet (7.5R 5/6 to 5/8), and made of m-Na-Al 2 glass. The presence of both m-Na-Al 6 (SF 82b and c) and m-Na-Al 2 (SF 82d to g) beads in the same small vessel could be explained in two ways. Perhaps they represent beads from the period when the switch from one type to the other was taking place, which would place them approximately in the early fourteenth century. Alternatively, they could be from a later time, in which case the m-Na-Al 6 beads would represent heirlooms that had been carefully curated. Given that m-Na-Al 6 beads are rare or absent after the thirteenth century and that they were found secreted away in a small pot surrounded by cowries, the second alternative seems more likely. It has been difficult to find other examples of the tiny black beads at East African sites, but that is most likely due to the fact that beads that measure 2 mm or less would seldom be recovered since 3 mm mesh is normally the smallest screen used for sieving. The same observation could be made concerning the translucent amber/violet beads, which are not only very small but are a very unusual colour that appears pale amber in reflected light and pale violet in transmitted light.

Table 8.1.4 summarises the results of the beads from the Maldives.

Table 8.1.4 Recapitulation of the different glass types represented among the beads from the Maldives.

Glass type	Period	Samples
Mineral soda–high alumina, m-Na-Al 6	Ninth to thirteenth centuries AD	SF82b and c
Soda plant ash–high alumina glass, v-Na-Al	Thirteenth to fourteenth centuries AD	SF45
High lead–potash (low Li)	Late fifteenth to early sixteenth centuries AD	SF90
Mineral soda–high alumina, m-Na-Al 2	Fourteenth to nineteenth centuries AD	SF82d to g

8.2 The glass remains

St John Simpson

The bangles

A total of 27 bangles were recovered, one shell, two shell/stone, and the remainder glass, from the site of Kinolhas (Table 8.2.1). Single bangles were found in Trenches 321 (Context 2), 631 (Context 1), and 449 (Context 2); two were found in Trench 360 (Contexts 2, 4); five were found in Trench 325 (Contexts 2, 3, 5); six were found in Trench 449 (Context 2); and 11 were found in Trench 544 (Contexts 2, 3, 4). Bangle size varied from 1.6 to 5.5 cm in length and up to 50% of the original diameters. The internal diameters could be measured in all but seven cases (74.7%) and proved to be small, between 4 and 7 cm across.

The shell bangle (SF 70) had been painted red, the pigment now appearing a dull reddish brown colour. Two other fragments, SF 78 and 79, of shell or stone, possibly belong to the same bangle and do not appear to have been decorated. Little more can be said of these other than the fact that shell bangles have a very long history of manufacture in India, already common by the Harappan period in the third millennium BC when they were cut from *Turbinella pyrum* shells (Kenoyer 1984, cf. Marshall 1931, vol. II, pp. 563–564), and it is likely that this example was brought from the mainland as a finished product.

The glass bangles are a mixture of drawn and moulded types, mostly with D or flattened rectangular sections. They are catalogued in detail in Table 8.2.1 and a selection is shown in Figure 8.2.1. Nine are plain monochrome and include blue and dark green colours (SF 20, 24, 31, 42, 44, 46–47, 77, 91). The remainder are more elaborate, and all appear to have been made by moulding. Five have dark or yellow cores overlaid along the outer edge with glass of a contrasting colour and decorated along the same edge with low raised coloured borders with fine coloured lines between (SF 19b, 27, 53, 75, 84). One was dark with a single white trail (SF 19a), three other dark bangles were decorated with a pair of white ribs along the outer edge (SF 86, 89, 95), and another dark blue piece with a pronounced B section was decorated with white ribs (SF 38). One example with a circular section was made of twisted yellow and green glass (SF

Table 8.2.1 The bangles from Kinolhas.

SF	Description	Int D (% present)	L	W	H	Wgt	Trench	Context
70	Shell bangle; white with traces of reddish brown pigment	4 (50%)	4.9	0.7	0.4	23.2	419	2
78	Shell/stone bangle; grey-brown	?	3.4	0.65	0.55	8.8	544	2
79	Shell (?) bangle; white	4 (20%)	2.7	0.5	0.3	5.8	544	2
19a	Glass bangle; drawn; dark with lopsided D section with white trail added along the dorsal edge	5 (24%)	3.6	0.4	0.3	5	325	2
19b	Glass bangle; moulded; light green with lopsided rectangular section with thin brownish red layer applied along the top, decorated with narrow white lines along the centre and low braided yellow and brownish red ridges along the edges. Sampled using p-XRF (see Table 8.2.2)	?	2.65	0.6	0.4	5.1	325	2
20	Glass bangle; dark plain with almost circular section. Sampled using p-XRF (see Table 8.2.2)	4 (35%)	3.7	0.25	0.25	3.3	325	2
24	Glass bangle; dark plain with D section	6 (12.5%)	2.75	0.4	0.7	5.7	321	2
27	Glass bangle; moulded; dark with rectangular section, decorated with two light green ridges along the upper edges	5.5 (27.5%)	4.6	0.5	0.3	9.9	325	3
31	Glass bangle; dark with almost circular section; similar to SF20	4.5 (27.5%)	3.7	0.3	0.3	3	325	5
35	Glass bangle; dark green with yellowish green spiral design. Sampled using p-XRF (see Table 8.2.2)	6 (19%)	3.5	0.3	0.3	3	631	16
38	Glass bangle; dark blue with B section resembling two parallel ribs, decorated along the top of each with equidistant elongated whitish blobs with brownish 'eyes'	6 (12%)	2.3	0.6	0.4	4.9	449	2
42	Glass bangle; dark with D section; similar to SF20	?	1.7	0.25	0.3	1.4	449	2
44	Glass bangle; blue with D section	?	1.6	0.3	0.3	1.4	449	2
46	Glass bangle; blue with D section; similar to SF44. Sampled using p-XRF (see Table 8.2.2)	4.5 (32.5%)	4.25	0.3	0.3	4.8	449	2
47	Glass bangle; dark blue with D section; two fragments	?	0.8, 2.2	0.3	0.4	3.2	449	2
53	Glass bangle; moulded; dark with rectangular section, decorated with two light green ridges along the upper edges with elongated white lines between; similar to SF27	?	1.65	0.45	0.3	1.9	449	2
75	Glass bangle; moulded; dark with rectangular section with thin yellow layer applied along the top, decorated with brownish red rib along one upper edge and short lines near the centre	?	1.7	0.75	0.45	6.2	544	2
76	Glass bangle; moulded; white with dark blue upper layer and rectangular section, decorated with clusters of fine white dots	5 (17.5%)	3	0.35	0.25	2.6	544	2
77	Glass bangle; drawn; dark green with D section	5 (20%)	3.2	0.55	0.3	4.5	544	2
84	Glass bangle; moulded; dark with rectangular section with thin yellow layer applied along the top, decorated with brownish red ribs along each upper edge and short lines along the centre; same bangle as SF 75	5 (45%)	5.5	0.75	0.4	28	544	2
86	Glass bangle; dark with two white ribs along the upper edges	6 (22.5%)	4.4	0.45	0.4	7.3	544	2
89	Glass bangle; dark with two white ribs along the upper edges; very similar to and possibly same bangle as SF 86	6 (25%)	4.55	0.4	0.35	8.2	544	2
93	Glass bangle; dark with lopsided D section	4.5 (30%)	3.8	0.55	0.3	6.2	544	3
95	Glass bangle; moulded; dark with two white ribs along the upper edges	?	2.3	0.5	0.3	2.8	544	4
98	Glass bangle; drawn; dark with lopsided D section	c.6 (17.5%)	3.6	0.4–0.55	0.25–0.3	4.3	360	4
99	Glass bangle; dark blue with D section. Sampled using p-XRF (see Table 8.2.2)	6 (24%)	4.5	0.4	0.4	6.2	360	2
102	Glass bangle; moulded; yellow with rectangular section, decorated with two light greenish ribs along the upper edges with a braided yellow and brownish red stripe along the centre	7 (10%)	2.5	0.5	0.35	4.6	544	3

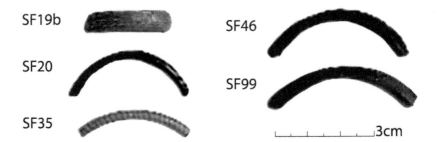

Figure 8.2.1 Sample of bangles from Kinolhas (SF is indicated).

35). Another was dark blue and decorated along the outer edge with clusters of fine white dots (SF 76). All but one was opaque, the exception being a green spiral-twisted fragment (SF 35).

Glass bangles have a long history of production and circulation, first appearing in Europe in La Tène burials of the late first millennium BC (Vellani 1995, Nicolas 2012). Within the Middle East, the earliest glass bangles were rod-formed and monochrome, with green or blue spiral-twisted and simple decorated types beginning to appear in the fourth and fifth centuries in Anatolia, and more elaborately decorated types gradually appearing from the medieval period onwards. Spaer tentatively suggested that Byzantine production might have influenced Islamic bangle production (Spaer 1992). However, thus far there is no evidence to support this, and a detailed comparative analysis of bangles excavated in Anatolia and the Levant instead concluded that Byzantine and Islamic bangles had their own circulation patterns (Zanon 2013, pp. 193–195), and the cold-painted examples found in the former region belong to a class which is distributed across the Black Sea from Bulgaria and southern Russia and the Caucasus (Djingov 1978). Looking east, excavated data from Persian Gulf sites such as Kush (Simpson et al. forthcoming), Bahrain (Insoll et al. 2005, pp. 287–289, Figures 7.6–7, appendix 7.3), Siraf (Whitehouse 1968, p. 19, Semple forthcoming), and Julfar (al-Mataf) (Hansman 1985, pp. 80–81, Figure 19.i) indicate bangles of any variety are rare until the eleventh century when they then begin to steadily increase in frequency. Within the Red Sea region, plain blue and other monochrome bangles were frequent in Mamluk contexts at the sites of Quseir al-Qadim and al-Tur (Whitcomb and Johnson 1982, pp. 237–240, Meyer 1992, p. 91, Shindo 1996). They continued to be common there in the post-medieval period and are found with sixteenth century or later Chinese porcelain and local coarsewares at sites in the eastern province of Saudi Arabia (Burkholder 1984, p. 217, Whitcomb 1978, p. 113, pl. 84.29–33). Excavations at al-Shihr in Yemen also produced a small number from thirteenth- and fourteenth-century contexts, but the majority there again date to the sixteenth to seventeenth centuries (Boulogne and Hardy-Guilbert 2010). It was during this period that polychrome glass bangles with patched, trailed, and/or blobbed prunts became popular along the Persian Gulf, in southern Iran, and along the Red Sea into Egypt and Palestine (Spaer 1992, Shindo 1996). Glass bangles have been reported from many sites of this period, and a number of these assemblages are receiving further study, for instance those from sites in Bahrain (Simpson forthcoming), Qatar,[3] the United Arab Emirates,[4] and Oman.[5] In the case of Kush, the final occupation of the site falls between the late sixteenth or early seventeenth and eighteenth centuries and is marked by a dramatic increase in the number of fragments and variety of colours of glass bangles, including small numbers of monochrome blue-green, black, blue, dark blue, dark green, green, pale green, and yellowish green bangles, a huge number of yellowish brown bangles, and the first polychrome fragments found at that site. The quality of many of these suggests that 'the finished products, in today's terms, qualify as good costume jewelry rather than cheap trinkets' (Spaer 1992, p. 56). The excavated sequence from the pearling town of Fuwairit in northeast Qatar also indicates that they stop abruptly there at the end of the eighteenth or beginning of the nineteenth century, although it is unclear whether this was due to a break in supply or a fall in demand.

The question of where all these bangles were made is an important one. The late David Whitehouse reported a factory site at Bida Khar, 16 km north of Siraf on the plain of Jamm, where surface finds include scraps of Ming dynasty or later porcelain and Islamic pottery decorated in black under a clear turquoise glaze (Whitehouse 1968, p. 19), and Hansman describes finding manufacturing waste of opaque and multi-coloured bangles at eighteenth-century sites in Khuzestan, southwestern Iran (Hansman 1985, p. 81). However, none of these sites have been investigated further and the types have neither been recorded in detail or analysed scientifically. Other glass bangles were made in newly established workshops along the southern Arabian coast near Aden, of which the most famous sites are Kawd am-Saila (where brief excavations revealed a walled compound containing a central building and furnaces around the perimeter); and Habil and Zinjibar, which are dated by the associated pottery to the fourteenth to sixteenth centuries (Reveil 1883, Lane and Serjeant 1948, Doe 1971, pp. 134–137, Figures 9–10, Monod 1978, Whitcomb 1988, pp. 188–191, 201–202, Figure 21). The market for these may have been restricted to the Yemeni hinterland, neighbouring East Africa, and western Indian Ocean as they have not been recognised from sites in the northern Red Sea.[6] If correct, this has important implications for understanding the trade patterns as Indian glass bangles begin to appear at northern Red Sea ports in the sixteenth century, i.e. after the end of the Yemeni industries. Moreover, scientific analyses of others—mostly translucent dark brown, blue, or emerald green monochrome—found in Mamluk and Ottoman contexts at Tell Abu Sarbut and Khirbet Faris in Jordan suggest these may also have an Indian origin as they had distinctive high-alumina compositions resembling some glasses with that origin (Shindo 1996, cf. Boulogne and Henderson 2009). Scientific analysis of glass bangles excavated at Hisn al-Tinat in southern Turkey proved that they had a distinctive high-boron, high-alumina composition, which suggests a separate Anatolian centre of production (Swan et al. 2018). Other bangles from Tell Abu Sarbut and Khirbet Faris in Jordan were found to have plant-ash compositions and were therefore made somewhere within that region (Boulogne and Henderson 2009). Bangles are known to have been produced in Cairo during the Mamluk and later periods (Shindo 1996), and in Palestine the town of Hebron was certainly producing monochrome and mosaic types by the late Ottoman period (Simpson 2001, Steiner and van der Steen 2008). Interestingly, writing in the late eighteenth century, Volney describes how the Hebron workshops produced 'a great quantity of coloured rings, bracelets for the wrists and legs, and for the arms above the elbows, besides a variety of other trinkets, which are even sent to Constantinople' (Volney 1793, pp. 452–453): this point is significant in view of the scientific results reported in what follows, which suggests that some bangles have the same composition as beads and, rather than being made from recycled glass, could have been made in the same workshops, as has been demonstrated from Jalasar in northern India (Kock and Sode [1995], pp. 7–9). Some 70 years after Volney, the Russian traveller P. Uspenskii visited the Hebron workshops and noted

> several large and small ovens installed in sooty and dirty cellars. . . . I was in two works . . . one produces only glasses and jugs of a dark-blue shade, the other bracelets. . . . The number of workers in workshops of this kind probably did not exceed five to ten.
>
> (Quoted by Issawi 1966, p. 243)

Following his own visit in April 1806, Seetzen reported that there were 26 functioning glass kilns employing about 150 people, with 12 workshops making jewellery, 10 making beads, and 4 specialising in making green glass lamps (Seetzen 1854, vol. II, p. 49). These descriptions show different modes of organisation: some produced different ranges in different workshops, yet in others members of the same family could congregate and sit simultaneously on different sides of a small furnace, a practice also paralleled from Nepal (Gaborieau 1977), and beadmakers' workshops in Izmir and Purdalpur (Sode 1995, 1996). In India, the finishing of bangles could also be done in separate workshops (Kock and Sode [1995], p. 15), and this probably also applies to the cold-painted tradition noted earlier from Anatolia.

The exact date and development of the Indian industry are not yet closely defined, and some scholars have attributed its origins to immigrants arriving after the Muslim conquest of India in the fourteenth century (Sankalia 1977, p. 228). However, the excavated sequence at Anuradhapura, Sri Lanka, confirms the Near Eastern evidence that plain or spiral-twisted dark monochrome glass bangles pre-date the polychrome bangles, and they mainly occur in early medieval contexts at that site (Coningham et al. 2006, pp. 349–352). Nevertheless, in India the tendency of these to imitate bangles of other materials hints at the underlying reasons behind the development in styles of decoration:

> The various shapes and styles are no doubt suggested by the then existing fashions in lac, conch-shell, gold and pearl, just as the modern bangles in plastic are exact imitations of those in glass and other material. For instance, type IIID is really an imitation of the one in bone or conch-shell, often coloured red for use in marriage, and further ornamented with gold or pearl rims; whereas in type IIIE, the prototype seems to be the bone or conch-shell bangles decorated with gold or silver wires. In IIIC or IX it is intended to give the effect of inset diamonds or pearls.
>
> (Sankalia and Dikshit 1952, pp. 151–152)

These observations demonstrate another dimension to glass bangles: they are heavily laden with social symbolism and economic aspiration. Winifred Blackman recorded the preference by Egyptian villagers for glass bangles to be worn by the less wealthy, for newly wedded girls to wear 'such a number of glass bangles of various colours that they completely cover both arms from wrist to elbow', and for dark blue or black bangles to be worn by widows (Blackman 1968, pp. 47–50); in northern India, green bangles are restricted to brides-to-be or the newly wed (Kock and Sode [1995], p. 14). A nineteenth-century source also refers to women in Palestine wearing 'bracelets and anklets . . . the commonest being of coloured glass such as is manufactured at Hebron, or of bad silver' (Conder 1879, vol. II, p. 245), and the exceptionally large number (some 530) found in Mary's Well in Nazareth may be explained by the fact that they were lost during the drawing of water from the well (Alexandre 2012, pp. 100–101). The loss or breaking of a bangle in India is considered deeply unlucky, and there is a widespread custom from India to Egypt of breaking and discarding them on the loss of a husband (Kock and Sode [1995], p. 14, Simpson 1995, p. 248), a practice which might account for their occasional presence near Late Islamic graves at some sites recorded in Iraq and Jordan (Simpson 1995, p. 248, with references).

Data recovered from surveys or the excavation of settlement sites are ambiguous as to how exactly they were worn or by whom, but finds from post-medieval graves in the southern Levant and other parts of the Middle East confirm that they were worn in varying combinations on either or both wrists, as anklets, and possibly attached to head scarves or woven into the hair: these items therefore should be described as bangles, rather than bracelets as they are often referred to in the archaeological literature (Simpson 1995, pp. 246, 251, Steiner 1995). The bangles found at Kinolhas ranged in size from 4 to 7 cm across on the inner diameter, making most too small to pass over an adult hand. There is no evidence that the bangles were other than circular in shape, hence it suggests that many—if not all—were worn by children or girls. Looking at comparative data, exactly the same internal diameter range was noted at Fuwairit and Huwailah (Ogutu et al. 2018 (although the authors caution that some were lopsided), Garlake 1978, p. 177); a sample illustrated from Yemeni sites average 5–6 cm with two reconstructed as 4 or 4.5 cm in diameter (Whitcomb 1988, Figure 21), although at the Qala'at al-Bahrain they were found to be 'generally 6–7 cm, occasionally 9 cm and in a small strong one, obviously meant for a child, hardly 2.5 cm' (Frifelt 2001, p. 163).

Bangles could also be worn for their effect of sound as well as colour, as multiple glass bangles clink with every move and, although fragile and easily broken, could be easily replaced in the bazaar (Frifelt 2001, p. 163). On the Indian subcontinent, this continues a pattern which began millennia before when bangles were cut from conch shells and, judging by the representation on a single famous copper statuette of a young dancer excavated at Mohenjo-daro, worn in large numbers on the left arm only (Marshall 1931, vol. I, p. 345, vol. II, pp. 507, 509, vol. III, pl. CXLIV.6–8 (before conservation)). They are also depicted being worn on fired clay figurines of this and later periods, and on representations of women shown on first-century Kushan furniture found hidden in a storeroom at the site of Begram, Afghanistan (Ambers et al. 2014). However, funerary finds from Byzantine sites in Anatolia point to glass bangles being worn there as single specimens (Zanon 2013, p. 195): just as with beads, some individuals or societies therefore may have valued mass whereas others favoured selectivity. Although it is difficult to prove archaeologically, it is possible that bangles of particular types had further symbolism according to their colour or origin: for instance, monochrome black bangles dominate some Persian Gulf assemblages—sometimes to the exclusion of almost any other types—as at Fuwairit (Ogutu et al. 2018) and possibly Huwailah in Qatar,[7] and surface collections from Maqaba and Ruqa'a in Bahrain (Simpson forthcoming; none have been scientifically analysed). Within the Levant, as in Yemen and Iran, glass bangles continued to be worn by women and children into the twentieth century, and they have frequently been found in Bedouin graves excavated in Israel/Palestine, Jordan, and Syria (Simpson 1995, Steiner 1995, Steiner and van der Steen 2008, Michèle Daviau 2014). Although early archaeological reports lack stratigraphic control and should be used cautiously, as some are unstratified surface fragments,[8] a number of more recent excavations—for instance at Jaffa (De Vincenz 2017, pp. 126–127) and Nazareth (Alexandre 2012)—offer better dated examples from the Ottoman period, whereas more recent examples from Bahrain and al-Tur were described as red, dark purple, or green with faceted and/or gold-painted designs (Frifelt 2001, p. 163, Kawatoko 1995, p. 11, pl. 23.13–18, col. pl. 3.14–15, Kawatoko 1996, pp. 13, 38, pls 10.15–16, 30.9).

Further typological analysis is required to conclusively indicate the origins of the bangles from the site of Kinolhas. However, the evidence suggests India for at least some, as the scientific analyses of a small subset of monochrome cobalt blue, monochrome dark, twisted green and yellow, and polychrome decorated bangles indicate these to have a high alumina composition consistent with a South Asian origin (SF 19b, 20, 35, 46, 99), and this is also the probable source of the painted shell bangle (SF 70). Interestingly, none closely resemble examples known from the contemporary production centre of Kawd am-Saila, near Aden, or others from the Levant.

The glass bangles: scientific analysis
Yoshinari Abe (Tokyo Denki University)

The chemical composition of five glass bangles from four different trenches at the site of Kinolhas was quantified using a portable X-ray fluorescence (XRF) spectrometer. The samples analysed were SF 19b, 20, 35, 46, and 99, which come from four different trenches (325, 360, 449, and 631).

The portable XRF spectrometer, 100FA-IIL, was developed collaboratively with Ourstex Co. Ltd., with the aim of archaeological application. Both sodium and magnesium, which are necessary to characterise chemical composition of historical glass artefacts, can be quantified with use of a ring-shaped sample chamber connected to a small vacuum pump. Two excitation modes are available: a monochromatic X-ray excitation mode utilising a built-in monochromator for the analysis of trace amount (~1 ppm) of medium to heavy elements with a K-edge energy of 8~20 keV; and a white X-ray excitation mode for analysis of both light and heavier elements. In this study, two XRF spectra were acquired by two excitation modes for each specimen. Integration time of each spectrum was set to 200 seconds (in live time). The following 24 elements were quantified by a calibration curve method: sodium (Na), magnesium (Mg), aluminium (Al), silicon (Si), potassium (K), calcium (Ca), titanium (Ti), manganese (Mn), iron (Fe), cobalt (Co), nickel (Ni), copper (Cu), zinc (Zn), arsenic (As), rubidium (Rb), strontium (Sr), yttrium (Y), zirconium (Zr), molybdenum (Mo), tin (Sn), antimony (Sb), barium (Ba), lead (Pb), and uranium (U). Quantified values were calculated as typical oxide form for 12 elements detected by white X-ray excitation mode, and elemental form for 12 elements detected by monochromatic X-ray excitation mode. It must be noted that oxidation numbers of metal elements in our quantification results do not necessarily correspond to their actual forms in the glass.

Prior to the XRF analysis, the specimens were observed carefully by naked eye and through a loupe to choose the measurement spot. Glossy spots on each sample were analysed in order to minimise the influence of surface weathering. Whereas two bangles (SF 19b and 35) are polychrome, only one spot was measured within the individual specimen. All measurements were applied in a non-destructive manner. Further information on the 100FA-IIL spectrometer and quantification methods can be found in the author's previous applications for historical glass artefacts (e.g., Abe et al. 2012, Abe, Shikaku, and Nakai 2018, Abe, Shikaku, Yamamoto, et al. 2018, Abe and Shikaku 2020). The chemical composition of five pieces of the Maldivian glass bangles is presented in Table 8.2.2.

Theoretical lower limits of detection (LLD) of each element are also listed in the table. All specimens analysed in the present study contain silica (SiO_2: 55.6~73.9 wt%), soda (Na_2O: 9.1~15.0 wt%), and lime (CaO: 1.20~4.07 wt%) as major components, i.e. soda–lime silicate (Na_2O-CaO-SiO_2) glass. Although our XRF analyses were conducted non-destructively, the quantified value of Na_2O seems not to have been seriously affected by surface weathering. In addition, the chemical composition of all the bangles is characterised by high content of alumina (Al_2O_3: > 6 wt%); such high-Al_2O_3 soda–lime glass, so-called mineral-soda alumina glass, is commonly associated with the Indian subcontinent and Africa. Dussubieux et al. (2010) have pointed out that there are several compositional types of mineral-soda alumina glass, corresponding to differences in the regional distribution, chronology, colour, and use, as summarised in Table 8.2.3.

Table 8.2.2 Chemical composition of a sample of Maldivian glass bangles.

Sample no.	Concentration/wt%											
	Na_2O	MgO	Al_2O_3	SiO_2	K_2O	CaO	TiO_2	MnO	Fe_2O_3	SnO_2	Sb_2O_3	BaO
LLD	0.5	0.15	0.07	0.07	0.02	0.01	0.01	0.003	0.003	0.006	0.01	0.01
SF 99	11.2	0.86	6.21	73.1	1.76	1.88	0.39	0.133	4.109	(0.006)	(0.01)	0.05
SF 46	12.5	1.05	6.80	68.6	2.72	3.15	0.45	0.229	4.178	(0.018)	(0.01)	0.04
SF 20	15.0	0.52	6.19	55.6	2.68	1.20	0.44	0.164	17.93	(0.015)	(0.02)	0.09
SF 19b (opaque yellow)	11.7	0.88	8.78	63.0	1.97	4.07	0.48	2.159	3.526	0.805	(0.01)	0.05
SF 35 (opaque green)	9.1	0.67	7.85	73.9	2.40	1.59	0.50	0.331	2.785	0.137	(0.01)	0.04

Sample no.	Concentration/ppm											
	Co	Ni	Cu	Zn	As	Rb	Sr	Y	Zr	Mo	Pb	U
LLD	17	9.5	7.6	6.6	4.8	2	1.8	1.7	1.8	2	4.4	23
SF 99	1,250	n.d.	70	22	1419	57	65	13	228	n.d.	(13)	(46)
SF 46	330	n.d.	600	32	282	68	156	18	194	(2)	156	(67)
SF 20	440	(20)	110	31	n.d.	77	90	16	240	(4)	144	96
SF 19b (opaque yellow)	140	(10)	70	248	n.d.	57	201	16	237	n.d.	24,650	74
SF 35 (opaque green)	70	30	5140	40	n.d.	76	66	25	315	(3)	1,205	124

Note: n.d.: not detected/lower than detection limit ( ): values lower than quantification limit

Table 8.2.3 Relationship between compositional types of mineral-soda and alumina glass and its distribution, chronology, colour, and use application.

Types	Region	Chronology	Colour	Use application
m-Na-Al 1	South Asia—Sri Lanka Southeast Asia	Fourth century BC—fifth century AD Fourth century BC—tenth century AD	Translucent turquoise blue, opaque red, opaque green, orange, yellow, black, more rarely white	Beads and bangles
m-Na-Al 2	Africa and west coast of India	Fourth to third centuries BC	Translucent turquoise or dark blue, opaque red, opaque green, yellow, black, white	Beads
m-Na-Al 3	Southeast Asia	Fourth to third centuries. BC	Opaque red, black, and translucent green	Beads and bangles
m-Na-Al 4	Southeast Asia, Kenya	Fourteenth to nineteenth centuries AD	Translucent dark blue and turquoise blue, black, opaque red, yellow, white	Beads, bangles, vessels

To characterise the chemical compositional features of the Maldivian glass bangles, the quantified data were compared with published data on four compositional types of mineral-soda alumina glass (m-Na-Al 1~4 types). It should also be noted that some recent scientific investigations suggested the possibility of the glass manufacturing, including the primary production process, of Al_2O_3-rich soda-lime glass in eastern Anatolia (Dussubieux et al. 2010, Schibille 2011, Rehren et al. 2015, Swan et al. 2018) and the Caucasus (Abe and Shikaku 2020) during the mid-first to early second millennium AD. However, this type of Al_2O_3-rich glass is not referred to here because of the strong difference in composition compared to the Maldivian glass bangles.

Figure 8.2.2 shows three bi-plots focusing on some characteristic elements—Figure 8.2.2 (a) for Al_2O_3 vs. U, Figure 8.2.2 (b) for titanium oxide (TiO_2) vs. Zr, and Figure 8.2.2 (c) for CaO vs. Sr—in order to compare the chemical composition of the Maldivian glass bangles with the four types of mineral-soda alumina glass previously reported. As shown in Figure 8.2.2 (a), a trace amount of U (46~124 ppm) was detected in all five bangles; such a compositional feature contrasts with that of m-Na-Al 1 type. The Maldivian glass bangles also differ from the m-Na-Al 1 type of glass in terms of their amount of TiO_2 and Zr (see Figure 8.2.2 (b)). In Figure 8.2.2(c), the Maldivian glass bangles could be divided into two subgroups on the basis of concentrations of CaO and Sr. Furthermore, these two subgroups, two bangles with higher CaO–Sr composition (SF 19b and 46) and three bangles with lower CaO–Sr composition (SF 20, 35, and 99), seem to match m-Na-Al 2 and m-Na-Al 4 types, respectively. As presented in Table 8.2.3, these two types of mineral-soda alumina glass were distributed over a wide area from south and southeast Asia to Africa. The dates of these types also correspond to the chronology of the site of Kinolhas. However, the m-Na-Al 2 type of glass has only been found previously in beads, not bangles. It is therefore possible that two Maldivian bangles, SF19b and 46, were produced by recycling glass beads of the m-Na-Al 2 type.

In order to provide further compositional characterisation of the Maldivian glass bangles, their colouring agents were estimated on the basis of the chemical data. Two kinds of blue colourant were identified: Co (1,250 ppm) from SF 99 and Cu (600 ppm) from SF 46. These metal elements offer vibrant blue colourants when they exist as divalent cation in silicate

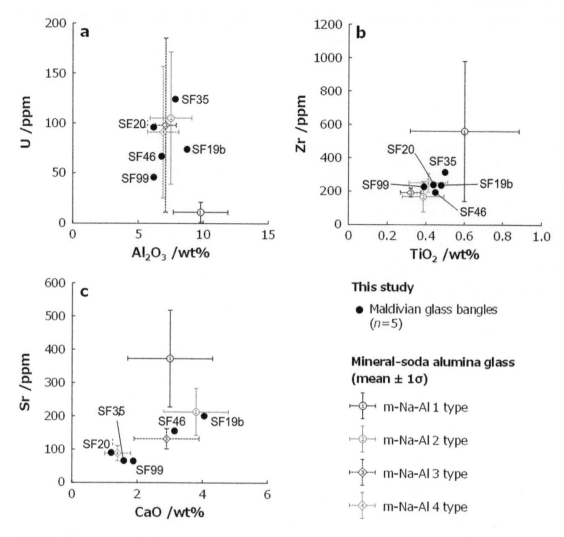

Figure 8.2.2 Bi-plots showing (a) Al₂O₃ vs. U content; (b) TiO₂ vs. Zr content; and (c) CaO vs. Sr content of the Maldivian glass bangles, compared to published data on four compositional types of mineral-soda alumina glass.

glass, whereas Cu^{2+} tends to provide a lighter blue colour compared to Co^{2+}. In addition, a significant amount of As (1419 ppm) was detected in SF 99 coloured by Co-blue colourant. It is thus possible that some arsenical cobalt minerals, such as erythrite ($Co_3(AsO_4)_2 \cdot 8H_2O$) or cobaltite (CoAsS), were used as a raw material for the Co-blue colourant. In SF 20, a black-coloured bangle, high concentration of iron over 17% wt as iron oxide (Fe_2O_3) was detected. Iron gives a blue-green (Fe^{2+}) or yellow-brown colour (Fe^{3+}) to silicate glass, but it can be a black colourant when concentrated. In the case of the opaque yellow part of SF 19b and green part of SF 35, it is considered that lead-tin oxide ($PbSnO_3$) was added as a yellow colourant into the glass. This compound is well known as lead-tin yellow, synthesised inorganic yellow pigment which has been used for ceramic, glassware, and oil painting since the first millennium AD (e.g., Kühn 1968). All the colourants identified in the present study are typical for historical glass, including mineral-soda alumina glasses.

In conclusion, the chemical composition of five fragmentary glass bangles excavated in the Maldives were analysed by means of non-destructive X-ray fluorescence analysis. All have a mineral-soda alumina glass composition, which is one of the major composition groups of historical glass distributed widely around the Pacific and Indian oceans since antiquity. The chemical compositional features of the Maldivian glass bangles correspond well with two previously reported compositional types of mineral-soda alumina glass.

The vessel glass

A total of some 17 sherds of vessel glass (total weight 61.4 g) were recovered. One was found in Trench 321 (Context 2), one in Trench 360 (Context 2), three found in Trench 449 (Contexts 2, 16), and nine found in Trench 544 (Contexts 1–4). A further four issued from the shovel test pit (STP) excavations and were therefore un-contexted—one each from STP 174, 363, and 544 (Table 8.2.4). Sherd size was generally small, averaging 1.6 cm across and no more than 4.3 cm across. Macroscopic examination indicates that there were six fabrics (Fabrics A—F), described in Table 8.2.5. Most were lightly stained by their burial environment and two were lightly weathered (SF 5, 64).

Table 8.2.4 Vessel glass from Kinolhas.

SF	Description	H	W	Average	Th	Wgt	Trench/STP	Context
4	Vessel; body; plain; Fabric A	0.9	0.9	0.9	0.05	0.2	363	–
5	Bottle; rim; blown; Fabric B; flat everted lip, narrow cylindrical neck (aperture 0.45 cm)	1.2	2.1 (rim)	1.6	0.1 (wall) 0.2 (rim)	9.2	174	–
17	Vessel; body; blown; Fabric B with numerous small bubbles; two joining sherds	2.1	3	2.5	0.1	7.5	544	–
25	Vessel; cylindrical neck; blown; Fabric B	3.05	1.5	2.2	0.05	2.2	321	2
32	Vessel; body; blown; Fabric A; several small joining sherds	1.4 (max)	1.3 (max)	1.3	0.05	1.4	544	1
43	Vessel; body; blown; Fabric C	1.4	0.9	1.1	0.15	1.8	449	2
50	Vessel; body; blown; blown; Fabric A; closed vessel with pushed-in wall	3.1	1.2	2.1	0.05	1.9	449	2
54	Bottle; cylindrical neck; blown; Fabric E	1.8	1.25	1.5	0.1	2.2	544	1
64	Closed vessel; base with high push-up (over 0.5 cm); blown; Fabric D	0.8	3	1.9	0.2	4.8	544	3
72	Closed vessel; base with high push-up (over 1.2 cm) and circular pontil (D 1.4 cm) with traces of a pad; blown; Fabric B	1.2	4.3	2.7	0.05	15.4	544	2
73	Vessel; body; blown; Fabric A	1.6	0.5	1	0.05	0.4	544	2
88	Vessel; body; blown; Fabric A; two joining sherds	2.8	1.9	2.3	0.05	1.9	544	2
92	Vessel; body; blown; Fabric A	2.7	0.8	1.7	0.05	0.9	544	4
94	Vessel; body; blown; Fabric A	1.5	1.25	1.3	0.05	0.9	544	3
97	Vessel; body; blown; Fabric F	0.6	0.9	0.7	0.15	–	449	16
101	Vessel; body; blown; Fabric B; four sherds	2.8 (max)	2.1 (max)	2.4	0.05	5.4	360	2
103	Bottle; rim, folded over on the interior (RD 1.5, 50% preserved); blown; Fabric C	0.8	2.3	1.5	0.2 (wall) 0.45 (rim)	6.2	544	3

Table 8.2.5 Fabrics of vessel glass at Kinolhas.

Fabric	Description	Forms	SF
A	Transparent or semi-transparent colourless	Closed vessel with pushed-in wall; uncertain	4, 32, 50, 73, 88, 92, 94
B	Semi-transparent yellowish, sometimes with numerous fine bubbles	Bottle; cylindrical neck; bottle base with high push-up; uncertain	5, 17, 25, 72, 101
C	Semi-transparent light green	Bottle; uncertain	43, 103
D	Light green with weathering layer	Bottle base with high push-up	64
E	Semi-transparent light greenish tinge with elongated bubbles	Cylindrical neck	54
F	Semi-transparent light blue with fine bubbles	Uncertain	97

Most sherds were plain body sherds, and diagnostic feature sherds were limited to the rims of two small bottles with flat rims and cylindrical necks (SF 5, 103: Fabrics B, C), two cylindrical necks of small bottles (SF 25, 54: Fabrics B, E), two fragments of bases with high push-ups which probably belong to the same forms (SF 64, 72: Fabrics B, C), and the wall of a small closed vessel which had been pushed in at the hot-working stage (SF 50: Fabric A). With the exception of a bottle neck and rim (SF 103), a sherd of modern bottle glass (SF 43) and another of uncertain date (SF 97), all of the glass was very thin-walled, usually only 0.5 cm thick. This suggests that most of the vessels were small in size, and this is consistent with the small diameters of the rims and bases present in the assemblage. There were no fragments of vessels with applied, cut, or moulded decoration, and the absence of strongly coloured glass suggests that the glassware was the product of one or more workshops focused on making items for everyday use. Although the number of diagnostic fragments is small, reflecting the limited size of the assemblage, there is no evidence for open tableware forms such as bowls or goblets, and the few diagnostic fragments instead belong to small closed containers. It is likely that these were brought to the Maldives as sealed containers with liquid contents and their limited size suggest perfume or a similar substance.

Most of this glass derives from a deposit excavated in Trench 544 which also yielded large amounts of pottery, animal bone, and shell, thought to reflect a refuse dumping episode dated by the associated finds between the fourteenth and seventeenth centuries, most likely to the earlier part of that date range. The same date range applies to the relevant contexts in Trenches 321, 360, and 449.

There has been a long history of circulation of glassware in the western Indian Ocean, beginning as early as the first century as part of Roman trade along the Red Sea to South Arabia and beyond, and bowls and bottles are found in graves and settlement sites in southern Arabia, the Persian Gulf, and South Asia (e.g. During Caspers 1980 (Bahrain), Andersen

2007 (Bahrain), Whitehouse 1998 (ed-Dur), Van Ham-Meert et al. 2018 (Dibba)). This continues in Late Antiquity, but during the early medieval period there is an increase in the number and range of shapes of vessel, including the addition of small containers for oil and perfume, judging by finds from Raya (Shindo 2004, 2005, 2007, 2008), Quseir al-Qadim (Meyer 1992), Sharma (Foy 2015), Shanga (Horton et al. 1996, pp. 311–322), Bahrain (Frifelt 2001, p. 156, Insoll et al. 2005, pp. 281–287), and Sir Bani Yas (Phelps et al. 2018). The Mamluks and Rasulids maintained close relations because of their shared commercial interests in Red Sea and western Indian Ocean trade, and some 50 Mamluk inlaid metal and enamelled glass objects made as diplomatic gifts or Rasulid commissions are known, bearing a five-petalled rosette as the dynastic emblem (Porter 1987).

The glassware found in the present excavations comes from contexts dated to this period or a little later. It is not the sort of glass exchanged these elites but instead belongs to the category of mass-produced container glassware and to about the period of a Rasulid customs declaration from the port of Aden which is dated to September/October 1412. This lists the various imports and exports flowing through the port: these are dominated by large quantities of textiles and spices, but there are occasional references to perfume, including imports from Egypt and Abyssinia (Smith 2006, pp. 50, 58, 61), rosewater (Smith 2006, p. 47), and 'Aleppan glass' (Smith 2006, p. 48). The possibility that these vessels therefore come from Egypt or the Levant should be considered, and future scientific analysis of their composition would undoubtedly help determine their place of origin.

8.3 The metal, slag, stone, and ceramic small finds

Anne Haour

Introduction

A total of 57 non-glass objects (or groups of objects in the case of heavily fragmented items) were recovered at Kinolhas (Table 8.3.1). This section presents the results of the visual analysis of this assemblage. Eight items came from shovel test pits and one item had an unknown provenance. The rest of the assemblage was issued from the excavation units and all but one unit, Trench 443, yielded material. Trenches 321, 449, and 544 were the most productive, with 12–14 items each, while Trench 631 yielded very few items.

The first step was to divide the objects into groups based on their constituent material. Most (N=35) fell into the category of metallic objects, including slag. There were 15 lithics and 7 ceramic objects.

Table 8.3.1 Non-glass Kinolhas small finds.

Number	Unit	Context	Description	Metal (slag), lithic, ceramic
1	STP325	N/A	Triangular stone piece with green glazed surface. Worn sides. Length 4.5 cm. See Figure 8.3.6	C
2	T321	1	Pebble with polish marks (Type A/B)	L
6a	STP507	N/A	Piece of metal, apparently ferruginous, indefinite shape. Max length 1.5 cm	M
6b	STP507	N/A	Piece of metal, apparently ferruginous, indefinite shape. Max length 1.5 cm	M
7	STP507	N/A	Thin, flat piece of green metal. Length 2 cm	M
8	STP629	N/A	Wedge-shaped ceramic piece, earthy-red, with dark glaze and a line on top surface. Worn sides. Length 8 cm. See Figure 8.3.6	C
9	STP482	N/A	Fragments of a green-hued dark metal piece, globular. Max diameter 2.5 cm	M
10	STP257	N/A	Small piece of metal slag, weight 16 gr	M (S)
11	T325	2	Large metal piece in shape of a diamond. Length 14 cm. See Figure 8.3.2	M
12	T321	2	Small piece of metal slag, weight 9 gr	M (S)
13a	T321	1	Medium piece metal slag, weight 45 gr	M (S)
13b	T321	1	Small piece metal slag, weight 25 gr	M (S)
14	T321	2	Medium piece metal slag, weight 53 gr	M (S)
15a	T321	2	Medium piece metal slag, weight 52 gr	M (S)
15b	T321	2	Small piece metal slag, weight 31 gr	M (S)
16	T325	2	Fragment of a grindstone. Type D stone (quartz?)	L
22	T325	2	Circular ceramic item pierced in centre. ?Spindle whorl. Diameter 3.5 cm. See Figure 8.3.6	C
26	T325	2	Trapezium shaped ceramic piece, rather worn at sides, grey in colour. Length <4 cm	C
28a–i	T321	2	9 assorted pieces of metal slag, total weight 535 gr	M (S)
34	T544	1	Thin, curved metal fragment, 3 cm long, cracked, jagged	M
36a	T544	2	Metal fragment, trapezium in shape. Length 3 cm	M
36b	T544	2	Metal fragment in the shape of an elongated triangle. Length 4.5 cm	M
39	T449	2	Metal rod. Length 4 cm	M
40	T449	2	Slag rope, weight <1 gr	M (S)
41	T449	2	Metal piece. Relatively flat on one side, bulbous protrusions on the other. Length 4.5 cm	M

(Continued)

Table 8.3.1 (Continued)

Number	Unit	Context	Description	Metal (slag), lithic, ceramic
48	T449	2	Triangular metal piece, rough surfaced and jagged, but roughly equilateral with side of 1.5 cm. Exhibits a lip and green in colour—cuprous? Rim on one edge, and slightly curved shape	M
49	T449	2	Thin curving rod of corroded metal. Length 5.5 cm	M
55a-f	T321	2	6 slag pieces of various sizes, total weight 447 gr	M (S)
56	STP363	N/A	Cylindrical grindstone. Micaceous sandstone, cemented with calcite (Type G)	L
58a	T321	2	Small, weighty, ferruginous stone. Very dark in colour with green and orange hues. Weight 10 gr	L
58b	T321	2	Small, weighty, ferruginous stone. Very dark in colour with green and orange hues. Weight 10 gr	L
59	T544	2	Small stone grinder fragment, with possible trace of pigment. Light grey in colour	L
60	T544	2	Stone artefact, irregular shape, exhibiting multiple channels of rectangular section, approx. 10 x 6 cm in size. See Figure 8.3.3	L
63	T325	2	Small, droplet-shaped piece of metal slag. Weight 6 gr	M (S)
65	T544	2	Fragments of a long (15 cm) thin metal flat-sectioned piece, resembling a knife blade, but very corroded and broken in two (likely during transit)	M
66a	T544	2	Small, green-coloured metal fragment of indefinite shape, roughly square with 1 cm sides. Possible rim on one edge, and slightly curved shape. Cuprous?	M
66b	T544	2	Small, green-coloured metal fragment of indefinite shape, 1.5 cm at its longest. Cuprous?	M
67	T544	2	Small, long, spearhead-shaped metal fragment. Very corroded. Approx. length 9 cm. See Figure 8.3.2	M
68a	T544	2	Small metal fragment, irregular in shape and corroded. Max length 2 cm	M
68b	T544	2	Flat metal fragment, jagged sides, thicker on one side than the other. Max length 4 cm	M
69	T449	7	Metal rod with a pointed end, corroded. Length 1.5 cm	M
71	T449	3	Thick rectangular-shaped piece of metal, likely ferruginous, appears narrower towards one side. Length 3 cm	M
74	T449	3	Long, corroded metal piece, bulbous on one side, diminishing to a point on the other. Length 4 cm	M
81	T449	13	Intact pot, small and squat, green glazed with a flat base. 7 cm wide, 6 cm tall. See Figure 8.3.5	C
82a	T449	20	Small yellow electrum artefact, seemingly a pendant, hammered, crushed. Length 1.1 cm. See Figure 8.3.1	M
82h	T449	20	Very small orange fleck found in the fill of SF81. Seemingly stone; natural flake, agate?	L
91	T544	4	Metal piece, seemingly ferruginous. Both ends curved, bulbous protrusion at centre. Length 6 cm. See Figure 8.3.2	M
96	T449	3	Thick metal piece, seemingly ferruginous, thicker at one end than the other, narrowing to a point while one side remains flat. Length 6 cm	M
100	T360	2	Very small grey stone. Exposed purple filaments that break off in very small amounts on touch	L
105	T544	3	Small, Y-shaped ceramic piece. Orange in colour. Possibly a decorative item. 1.5 x 3 cm	C
107	T544	4	Pierced pot sherd, five uneven and rough sides. Orange in colour, very regular hole. Sherd is curved in diagonal axis, making it inconsistent with a pendant. Length 4 cm	C
108	T631	15	Fragment of inscribed tombstone made of coral stone. Potentially belongs to Gravestone 27e (see Chapter 4). See Figure 8.3.4	L
109	T631	11	Decorative, inscribed tombstone piece. Cross-section has flower-like shape along the length of the stone. Potentially belongs to Gravestone 27a (see Chapter 4). See Figure 8.3.4	L
111	T321	4	Grindstone fragment. Grey in colour with black inclusions (Type M)	L
112	?		Grindstone fragment. Grey in colour with small, reflective inclusions (Type N)	L
118	T325	2	Grindstone fragment. Thin fragment of a grey and white stone. Very smooth, rounded outer surface. The inside exhibits some reflective inclusions (Type F)	L
119	T321	2	Grindstone fragment of rough, coarse grey stone. Many small stone inclusions with some reflective material. Piece is rounded on one side and broken on the other (Type K)	L

Metals and slag

The metal finds formed the largest group of artefacts. They are generally in a medium state of preservation. Oxidation had affected the finds in various ways, probably a factor of both the nature of the metal and the size of the object, but also influenced by its use and the context of recovery. All the material is fragmentary. The objects appear to be mostly ferrous with a small number of possible copper objects. A number of slag remains were also recovered.

SF82a (Figure 8.3.1) is a yellow metal artefact recovered from the fill of a small glazed ceramic vessel (SF 81; see Figure 8.3.5) in Trench 449. Portable X-ray fluorescence (pXRF) analysis conducted by Marcos Martinón-Torres in October 2017 at University College London indicated an average composition of 3.6% copper, 42.2% silver, and 54.1%

gold. As levels of copper higher than 1% are very unlikely to occur in natural gold, this must have been added as a separate metal. Similarly, even though natural gold can contain silver as an impurity, levels higher than 30% are very unusual, and hence it is more likely that at least some of the silver in this object was added as a separate component. Thus, the composition indicates an artificial alloy involving all three metals. It is not possible to say whether the metals were deliberately mixed in those proportions, for instance to obtain a particularly 'lime-coloured' metal, or whether the composition reflects the result of somewhat indiscriminate recycling of metals.

Scanning electron microscope work indicated that the item was made not by casting, but by joining of several pieces of metal, with an obvious join between hammered metal sheets in the wider hemisphere. At one of the ends, the aperture was decorated with a collar consisting of two wires: one twisted and one plain. With the presence of soil incrustations and limited time, it was not possible to analyse the joins in detail, but it is likely that remnants of solder would be detected.

Ten entries relate to pieces of slag, and in some cases, such as SF28 and SF55, a single number related to a group of fragments from a single piece. All but two of these objects come from Trench 321. These primarily represent smelting slag (Caroline Robion-Brunner, Université Toulouse II Jean Jaurès, pers. comm.).

The remaining objects in the metals category are fragmentary and are either ferruginous or cuprous. Some are large and of relatively distinctive shape, which allows them to be connected to food preparation, weaponry, or tools in the case of long blades (such as SF 67, which is about 9 cm long); other items, such as SF 91, with two curved ends and a bulbous centre, probably fall into the category of adornment, tools, or hardware (Figure 8.3.2). Metal bracelets and finger rings have been reported from other sites in the Maldives, such as Kaashidhoo and Dhadimagi Havitta on Fuvahmulah island (Litster 2016), and are known from ethnographic, archival, museological, and historical sources (Jaufar 2019, p. 242). However, in the case of Kinolhas, most of the metallic objects are rather undiagnostic pieces that appear to be fragments of sheet metal or small rods, the latter sometimes pointed and consistent with an identification as nails or other building materials.

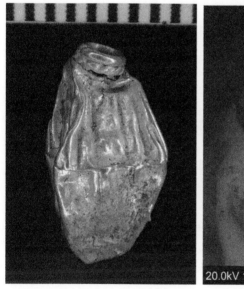 

20.0kV 17.6mm x42 BSECOMP 80Pa   1.00mm

Figure 8.3.1 Electrum pendant, SF 82a.

Source: Images courtesy of Marcos Martinón-Torres.

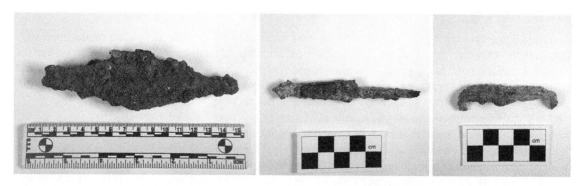

Figure 8.3.2 Some of the iron objects. Left to right: SF 11 (from T325), 67 (from T544), and 91 (from T544).

Figure 8.3.3 Whetstone, SF 60, from T544.

Figure 8.3.4 Gravestone fragments SF 108 (left) and 109 (right), both from T631.

Stone

Fifteen fragments of stone or stone artefacts were recovered. Some can be readily allocated a function. Among these are a whetstone (SF 60) (Figure 8.3.3), several grinders (SF 16, 56, 59, 111, 112, 118, 119) and a smoother (SF 2), and two fragments of gravestones from Trench 631 (SF 108 and 109) (Figure 8.3.4) that are likely be connected to some of the tombstones exposed during excavation (Table 4.9). Fragments of shaped coral stone were also encountered but are not recorded as small finds. Non-local stone fragments are likewise not classed as small finds but are nonetheless briefly discussed at the end of this chapter.

Ceramics

Seven ceramic items were reported. The most striking is SF 81 (Figure 8.3.5), an intact glazed miniature vessel recovered from Trench 449, which contained the glass beads and electrum pendant discussed earlier. The vessel itself is about 7 cm wide at its widest point and 6 cm tall. Its provenance is unclear, but one suggestion is that it is a copy of one of the long-running jarlet forms produced at many Longquan kilns from the late thirteenth to the fifteenth centuries, with a possible Thai source (Nigel Wood, University of Oxford, pers. comm.).

SF 105, a Y-shaped ceramic piece, may be a decorative item, or may once have been attached to a vessel. SF 107 is an otherwise unremarkable earthenware sherd with a small hole drilled into it. The purpose of this drilling is unknown. The sherd's irregular shape and curvature would suggest it probably did not serve as a pendant, and its unspectacular nature make it an unlikely candidate for riveting of the kind documented on material from other regional sites (see e.g. Schenk 2006 , pp. 123–124). SF 22 is a rough ceramic disk, 3.5 cm in diameter, pierced in its centre (Figure 8.3.6). It may have been a spindle whorl, or a bead, thus falling into either tool or adornment categories.

Figure 8.3.5 Miniature vessel recovered in Trench 449, Context 13 (SF 81).

Figure 8.3.6 Ceramic small finds. Left to right: shaped sherds (SF 1 from STP325 and SF 8 from STP629) and possible spindle whorl (SF 22, from T325).

The other three artefacts in the ceramic group appear to be repurposed potsherds. Given the paucity of stone in the Maldives, it is in fact a little surprising that a greater number of shaped sherds were not recovered. SF 1 and SF 8 are two similar ceramic pieces, both triangular in shape (Figure 8.3.6). These were clearly manufactured from potsherds and, in view of the colour and the presence of a glaze, they probably came from partly glazed vessels of likely Far Eastern or southeast Asian origin (see Chapter 5, this volume). SF 26 is a similar piece, but trapezoid in shape and altogether less regular. None of these are pierced. These items may have been used as smoothers in some sort of craft activity; in another context than the Maldives, these would readily be interpreted as scrapers used in the process of building a pot.

Other lithic and ceramic non-small finds

We do not classify as small finds the fragments of imported stone since, despite the fact that they were brought from far afield, they are unworked. Stones were not sampled systematically during excavation, but at least 50 pieces were recovered from Trench 321, close to 30 from Trench 325, and a dozen from Trenches 449 and 544. These varied greatly in morphology, but the best defined included a reddish black pitted stone, probably a microcrystalline quartz (Type C); a hard, fine-grained, metamorphosed sandstone (Type E); and a reddish limestone with occasional black inclusions (Type L). Though this lies outside the scope of the present research, there is an important study to be made on the diversity of engagements with stone among a community lacking all but coral stone (*hirigaa*) and consolidated coral sand (*veligaa*). It is known that unusual and exotic stone objects and materials can be used and re-used for a variety of purposes, and that the rarity of stone might in some contexts lead to it becoming the focus of ritual attention, accumulation, or curation (see e.g. Insoll 2015). On a more prosaic note, stones were likely used as ballast in Indian Ocean shipping.

Although they are not technically small finds and were not recorded systematically, possible architectural fragments deserve a final mention. Several pieces of what appeared to be baked clay were recovered in Trench 321, in Context 1 as well as 2, the main archaeological layer. These would necessarily have been imported to the Maldives. At least one piece evidenced square indentations, perhaps the result of use in an architectural structure of a wattle and daub type.

8.4 The small finds - Concluding remarks

Anne Haour

The methodology employed for the recovery of small finds was consistently applied across units, enabling a comparative analysis. The prevalence of glass items is noteworthy. Almost half the finds recovered were made of glass: beads, bracelets, or other fragments. This is perhaps to be expected in a landscape devoid of clay, metal ore, and non-coralline stone. The other small finds were primarily metal, with smaller showings of lithics and ceramics, in the latter case often repurposed potsherds.

Notes

1 Another high lead bead was recovered during a previous field season by the team at the site of Veyvah (see Jaufar 2019, Chapter 9, this volume). Made of translucent ruby-red glass coloured with copper (0.25% wt CuO), it was found to have elevated levels of lithium. Similar beads of this glass type have been found at Fort Canning Hill (Singapore) and in East Africa, where they have been recorded in small numbers (from one to four items) at several sites, including Lamu, Shaka, Manda, and Gedi in northern Kenya and at Chwaka, Mafia, and Kaole Village in Tanzania. In addition, 33 have been recorded at Kilwa Kisiwani and 15 at Songo Mnara, southern Tanzania. One or two were also found at Great Zimbabwe (Wood 2017). All these sites have early fifteenth-century components, which may be significant in that it has been reported (but not confirmed) that the fleet of the Chinese admiral, Zheng He, visited East Africa during his 1421–1422 voyage (Dreyer 2007, Levathes 1994). Because these beads are rare and occur only in this time period in East Africa, it appears likely that they were gifts rather than trade items. A fifteenth-century date for the Veyvah bead aligns well with a radiocarbon date from its context of recovery to sometime between AD 1435 and 1615 (410 ± 30 BP; Beta 438194) (Laure Dussubieux and Marilee Wood, pers. comm. to Shiura Jaufar, November 2018; Jaufar 2019, Appendix 6).

2 Another bead of soda plant ash-high alumina glass was recovered during a previous field season by the team at the site of Veyvah (Jaufar 2019, Chapter 9, this volume). It was wound and its blue colour was due to the presence of copper (1.0% as CuO). Like SF 45, that bead seemed to belong to the Mapungubwe Oblate v-Na-Al subtype as found in southern Africa in the thirteenth century. In East and West Africa, many beads of this glass are large and wound; they have been recorded from Songo Mnara (both wound and drawn types), Unguja Ukuu (Zanzibar), Mahilaka (Madagascar), Essouk (Mali), Igbo Ukwu (Nigeria), Gao (Mali), and al-Basra (Morocco). It appears likely that the wound varieties have a longer time span than the small drawn types found in southern Africa. Indeed, the context of recovery of the Veyvah bead dates it to sometime between AD 1435 and 1615 (410 ± 30 BP; Beta 438194) (Marilee Wood, Laure Dussubieux, pers. comm. to Shiura Jaufar, November 2018; Jaufar 2019, Appendix 6).

3 Sites include Fuwairit (excavations: Ogutu et al. 2018), Huwailah (survey: Garlake 1978, pp. 176–178), Ras Uwainat Ali, and Zubarah.

4 These are being studied by Dr Stéphanie Boulogne (CNRS) and Charlotte Nash (AHRC Collaborative Doctoral Award student, University of Kent) with scientific analyses by Prof. J. Henderson (University of Nottingham).

5 They were reportedly found 'in abundance' in late medieval and later contexts at al-Balid (Newton and Zarins 2019, pp. 114–115). Others found in excavations directed by Prof. Krista Lewis (University of Arkansas) are undergoing further study.

6 Cf. Shindo 1996. Hunter (1877, pp. 41–429) describes how this trade operated in Aden in the late nineteenth century:
"They [the Habr Awal tribes] bring from Harrar and the Galla country, coffee, saffron (bastard), tusks, and feathers, taking away in return zinc, brass, broad cloth, and piece goods. They remain in Aden for about twenty days at a time during the trading season, which lasts about nine months, making four trips. During their residence they hire a house, and are accompanied by their own domestics. Somalis of the Habr Gerhajis tribe arrive from Ogadain [Ogaden] with feathers, myrrh, gum, sheep, cattle, and ghee, carrying away in exchange piece goods; they also make four trips in the season; they remain for less than a month, and during their stay reside with fellow tribesmen, taking their meals in the *mokhbazah* or eating-house. Somalis of the Habr Tuljaala and Dhulbanta tribes bring similar articles from Ogadain, and trade in the same manner. The Mijjertayn and Warsangli tribes arrive from Ras Hafun, Bunder Morayah, and Las Gori, etc., with frankincense and feathers, etc., taking away in return cotton-piece goods and *jowari* [grain]. They also live with their friends, and take their meals at the *mokhbazah*. These latter tribes only make two trips in the season. . . . The members of this [Dankali] tribe, who visit Aden, are mostly traders or boat-owners. They live, when in the Settlement, in the same manner as the Somalis, sleeping and messing in their boats. They come from Zaila and Tajurrah during the months of August, September, October, and November, bringing sheep, goats, hides and skins, mats and *jowlees*, ostrich eggs and feathers, and take away grain (*jowari*), black cotton cloth, broad cloth, iron and brass. They remain about fifteen days, returning in the same boat they have arrived in. The Dankalis make three or four trips in the season. They are never accompanied by their families, but an occasional woman finds her way to Aden, via Mokha."

7 Although the relative numbers are not given, these are listed first of the four types (Garlake 1978, p. 177).

8 There is a common conflation of Mamluk and Ottoman finds in some early reports, a point first noted by the author when disentangling Ottoman smoking pipes from literature which had dated them before the discovery of the New World and the introduction of tobacco from there (Simpson 1990).

9 The archaeology of the Maldives in the medieval period

A comparative study

Annalisa Christie and Shiura Jaufar

Introduction

This chapter aims to contextualise the archaeological findings at Kinolhas and to assess how representative they are of medieval archaeology in the Maldives. To achieve this, it situates the data from the Kinolhas excavations within a wider body of archaeological work at Maldivian sites from the medieval period examining the nature of—and possible explanations for—the similarities and difference observed between the assemblages. The comparative datasets are drawn from excavations that were conducted at three different locations in 2016 by members of the team: Utheemu island in Haa Alifu to the north, Male' island in Kaafu atoll in the central Maldives, and Veyvah island in Meemu atoll in south-central region (Figure 1.2). These excavations aimed to characterise archaeology from the medieval period over a range of locations and settings. The findings were first presented in detail in a doctoral thesis discussing how they illuminate the role of the Maldives in the medieval Indian Ocean trade system (Jaufar 2019). The combined excavations from the seasons of 2016 and 2017 seasons represent the largest systematic examination of medieval period Maldivian sub-surface archaeology to date.

The present contribution also draws on material from substantive ethnographic surveys conducted by one of the two authors (ACC). This comprised 74 interviews and three focus groups (identified through purposive sampling (Palinkas et al. 2015, p. 534)), with cowrie collectors, fishers, coir makers, boatbuilders, and island elders on 27 islands across eight atolls. A detailed account of this strand of work, which is beyond the scope of the present chapter, will be published elsewhere (Christie, in prep). However, some of the findings are certainly relevant.

To frame the archaeology of Kinolhas, this chapter begins with an overview of the rationale, strategy, and results of the excavations carried out in 2016. In effect, this is a summary of the work behind Jaufar's doctoral thesis, and the reader is referred to it for more detailed coverage, including a first characterisation of medieval Maldivian ceramic assemblages. But, for the purposes of the present argument, this summary underpins the subsequent section by providing a basis for comparison. Then follows a thorough investigation of the similarities and differences between the excavations from 2016 and the work at Kinolhas the following year, focusing on the ceramic, faunal, and small finds assemblages and drawing, where necessary, on data collected during the ethnographic surveys. Finally, the chapter concludes with a brief statement of insights that these data offer on life in the medieval Maldives and with some proposals for further work.

Summary: archaeological excavations during 2016 and 2017

This section provides a brief overview of the excavations conducted in 2016 on three different islands. It outlines the rationale for selecting excavation areas as well as the contextual information necessary for understanding the subsequent results. Further details can be found in Jaufar (2019) and Haour et al. (2016).

Utheemu

The island of Utheemu is home to a satellite of the Heritage Department, established to maintain Utheemu palace (or *Utheemu Gan'duvaru*). The palace is constructed from wood and stone and contains replica artefacts and traditional items that would have been used when it was occupied (Mohamed 2014a, pp. 98–101). This made the island an ideal candidate for further excavations. Though the palace and the historic mosque are from a more recent period (both are usually dated to the early sixteenth century; Riyan 2011, Mohamed 2014a, pp. 98–100), other remains of interest had been reported during development works. Specifically, two cowrie hoards had been recovered, one from within the palace, the other from a nearby field. The latter also included a number of intact glass vessels and ceramics, which the team were able to view, but for which no contextual data were available.

Five trenches of varying sizes were excavated in Utheemu. Two were located within an open-air compound surrounding the palace buildings—one (UTH16–04, hereafter Trench 4) was close to the current northern entrance (1 x 3 m) and one (UTH16–05, hereafter Trench 5) bisected the reported location of the area reported to have been the palace kitchen (1 x 2 m) within the historically attested 'women's quarter'. Both of these trenches revealed a complex stratigraphy, while Trench 5 encompassed in situ structural remains as well as a number of possible hearth features (see Jaufar 2019, pp. 105–117). The unexpected feature of this trench was the discovery of a human burial, discussed in more detail next.

DOI: 10.4324/9781003166221-9

Outside of the palace, one trench (UTH16–01, hereafter Trench 1) sampled the area where the abovementioned chance finds of glassware and ceramics were recovered. Here, there had clearly once been substantial archaeological deposits, but they were heavily disturbed by the creation of a football pitch. The second of these trenches was located to the northwest of the palace, examining a small rise in topography close to a possible medieval landing site, but it yielded few results.

The final trench (Trench 3) was located in an area to the west of the island where pedestrian surveys had identified surface finds including pottery and shell. In 2016, during initial investigations of the area, nine test pits of 0.5 x 0.5 m were dug along a transect (see Haour et al. 2016, pp. 70, 72). Excavated to a depth of about 30 cm, they exposed evidence of continuous archaeological deposits and a large worked coral stone (*hirigaa*) slab in Test Pit 8. To investigate this slab further, the baulk between Test Pits 7 and 8 was removed and the area expanded to a trench measuring 1.5 x 2 m. This completely exposed the slab and also partially revealed a second worked *hirigaa* slab, Slab B, with evidence of a 'groove' for tongue and groove construction (Haour et al. 2016, Figure 2). Due to time constraints during that first field season, the stones were left in situ and covered with the intention of resuming work the following year.

When the site was revisited in 2017, the excavation area was extended to create a trench of 5.5 x 3.5 m. The excavations of 2017 aimed to expose Slab B completely and further contextualise the two visible slabs. Deposits were initially excavated by hoe, with trowelling limited to the areas around the exposed slabs and other features of interest. Although areas of the trench were differentiated for the purposes of finds recovery, stratigraphic contexts were similar throughout the trench, matching the stratigraphy recorded in the test pits of 2016. In addition to the complete exposure of Slab B, three smaller worked *hirigaa* stones were found. Two of these (Slabs C and D) were along the eastern edge of the trench while the other, Slab E, was in the southwest corner. Slab A was removed during the excavations. Exposure of Slab B showed that it was fractured and a section, though articulated, had broken off, most likely in antiquity.

Male'

Once described as the King's Island (Moresby et al. 1838–1839), Male' is (and was) the capital of the Maldives. It is described as the location of the 'residence of the Sultan and Government' (Moresby et al. 1838–1839) and is where the royal palace was constructed. It is also reported in historical accounts, from at least the early seventeenth century, to have been the focal point for trading activities with the wider region, with all ships visiting the islands required to dock in Male' to complete their business (Gray and Bell 1887, Hogendorn and Johnson 2003 [1986], Mohamed 2014b, Romero-Frias 2016). Male' was a priority for excavation because of its long-term historical and economic importance. However, as the modern city covers almost the entirety of the island, locations for excavation were extremely limited.

One of few remaining open areas is Sultan's Park, formally the site of the Sultan's palace, built in the sixteenth century. Though most of the structures within the palace were destroyed in the late twentieth century (Maniku 1982, Riyan 2011, p. 54), the park was retained. It is also one of the few locations where remains from the medieval period had been encountered previously, through small-scale excavations conducted by Carswell (1975–1977) and discussed in detail in Chapters 2 and 5.

Our own excavations in Male' focused on the northwest corner of the park, and historic plans of the palace suggest this area was probably residential (Maniku 1982). Six test pits of 0.5 x 0.5 m were sunk along two transects, with a seventh, referred to as N12, subsequently extended to 1 x 1 m (Jaufar 2019, Figure 58). Most of the test pits were excavated to a depth of about 80 cm and revealed a similar stratigraphy. This consisted of a layer of white beach sand associated with modern debris; five or six layers of deposits containing archaeological remains; followed by a fine yellow-white sand sterile layer that was usually quite moist due to the proximity of the water table (see Jaufar 2019, pp. 119–140 for detailed stratigraphic descriptions). Few in situ features were identified, probably unsurprisingly given the small size of the test pits as well as the well-reported disturbance of the site, not least through the historic destruction of the palace buildings. Notable exceptions to this included a possible hearth (Jaufar 2019, p. 127), evidence of collapsed structural debris (Jaufar 2019, p. 131) and a cowrie cache (Christie and Haour 2018a, Jaufar 2019).

Veyvah

The third island to be investigated, Veyvah, was selected because of the historical significance of the island, including the presence of a coral stone mosque reported in the Heritage Inventory as being more than 400 years old (Riyan 2011, p. 56). Several other islands are reported to feature mosques from this period (Riyan 2011), but the attraction of Veyvah was that satellite imagery, examined on Google Earth, showed the presence of unbuilt areas around and to the south of the historical mosque, with the potential to reveal undisturbed archaeological remains. Another factor of interest was that Veyvah neighbours the island of Mulah, also known as *Boli Mulah*, often mentioned as rich in cowrie shells (Luthufee 1995, p. 31, Ragupathy and Mohamed 2008, p. 11).

The very heavy vegetation in the areas targeted for excavation impeded visibility and required pedestrian surveys guided by the island councillors. Five trenches of 1 x 1 m were opened, informed by the presence of surface remains (Jaufar 2019, Figure 68). With one exception, these trenches returned few, if any, finds (see Jaufar 2019, pp. 142–152 for full stratigraphic analysis). The remaining trench, VEY16–05 (hereafter Unit 5), was more productive and featured a complex stratigraphy, including two pits (see Haour et al. 2016, pp. 79–80 and Jaufar 2019, pp. 147–150).

Chronology

Dates were run on seven charcoal samples across the excavated sites (Table 9.1).

Four dates were run from Utheemu, all of which were on samples from the trenches situated within the current palace compound. Sample 19 was recovered from the fill of a ditch exposed in Trench 4. The remaining three samples dated all issued from Trench 5. Sample 76 was recovered from one of the hearth features identified, while sample 81 was recovered from a feature identified as a burnt floor—possibly associated with a kitchen. Both samples appear to be contemporary with the palace itself, postdating AD 1665. The remaining sample (sample 87) was recovered from the context above the grave fill, which seals the inhumation. The dates returned by this sample provide a *terminus post quem* for the burial. In Male', sample 49 was taken from a proposed hearth feature while sample 37 was recovered from deposits associated with collapsed structural debris. The early date returned by sample 49 suggest that the area of the park was occupied shortly after the reported conversion to Islam in the twelfth century. The second sample, recovered from the mid-layers of the test pit, where finds were abundant, suggests there was intensive occupation in the first half of the fifteenth century. Both samples predate the historically reported construction of the former palace and grounds in the sixteenth century. In Veyvah, sample 57 was recovered from a pit fill in Unit 5 that was rich in faunal remains and ceramics—suggesting an active period of occupation. This deposit also returned two beads. These were analysed by Laure Dussubieux (Field Museum of Natural History in Chicago, USA), who suggests that they have a narrow chronology between the thirteenth and fourteenth centuries. These predate the radiocarbon sample, which could suggest that they were retained for some time before they were finally deposited.

Table 9.1 Radiocarbon dates from the excavations in 2016—calibrated by Beta Analytic, Inc. using the curve INTCAL13 (Jaufar 2019, p. 154).

Sample	Site	Lab #	BP date	Calibrated date
19	Utheemu Trench 4	Beta 438192	450 ± 30	Cal AD 1420–1465 (Cal BP 53–485)
76	Utheemu Trench 5	Beta 438868	70 ± 30	Cal AD 1690–1730 (Cal BP 260–220_ Cal AD1810–1920 (Cal BP 140–30) ¯ Post AD1950 (Post BP 0)
81	Utheemu Trench 5	Beta 438869	150 ± 30	Cal AD1665–1785 (Cal BP 285–165) Cal AD 1795–1890 (Cal BP 155–60) Cal AD1905–1950 (Cal BP45—post 0)
87	Utheemu Trench 5	Beta 438890	820 ± 30	Cal AD 1165–1265 (Cal BP 785–685)
37	Male' N2	Beta 438193	470 ± 30	Cal AD1415–1450 (Cal BP 535–500)
49	Male' E14	Beta 438195	830 ± 30	Cal AD 1160–1265 (Cal BP 790–685)
57	Veyvah Unit 5	Beta 438194	410 ± 30	Cal AD 1434–1510 (Cal BP 515–440) Cal AD 1600–1615 (Cal BP 250–335)

Sampling

The excavation strategies employed by the team during the excavations of 2016 were comparable to those used at Kinolhas in 2017, as described in Chapter 3. As far as possible, deposits were sieved though either a 2 mm or, more often, a 1 cm mesh. The only exception to this were the deposits from Unit 5 in Veyvah, which were wet-sieved as poor weather made regular screening difficult.

The scale of excavations on each of the three islands was quite different. In terms of volumes excavated, Kinolhas is by far the largest, with a cumulative volume of 20.92 m^3 removed, as it was the main focus of the field season of 2017. The remaining work was on a much smaller scale, with a cumulative volume of 7.51 m^3 removed during work at Utheemu in 2017 and 6.31 m^3, 2.3 m^3, and 1.93 m^3, respectively, for the excavations at Utheemu, Veyvah, and Male' in 2016. In light of this, throughout this chapter it is densities of material per m^3 that are discussed in order to make comparisons possible. Similarly, in the case of some artefact categories, sample sizes are sufficient to enable comparisons: for instance, there is a proportional representation of different categories of ceramics (earthenware vs. glazed) and of different faunal resources.

A defining factor with a likely impact on interpretation relates to the location and chronology of the excavation areas. The excavations in Sultan's Park in Male' and of the two trenches within Utheemu palace were all within explicitly high-status areas. However, as highlighted earlier, the radiocarbon dates from Male' and Utheemu suggest that at least some of the deposits predate the construction of these palaces. Thus, the materials issuing from these deposits may not have been associated with higher status occupation.

The other excavations (outwith the current confines of the palace compound in Utheemu, and on Veyvah) were undertaken in places where historical documentation was largely absent and which may therefore sample a whole range of potential contexts. Nonetheless, the data from Utheemu, Male', and Veyvah offer a valuable broader framing for the work conducted at Kinolhas, serving as a basis for significant comparisons.

Results: similarities and differences

The overall suite of archaeological materials recovered from the excavations in Male', Veyvah, Utheemu, and Kinolhas is broadly similar, both quantitatively and qualitatively. It comprises earthenware and glazed ceramics, cowries and other marine invertebrates, terrestrial vertebrates, and small finds including metals, glass, and stone. The following sections discuss the distribution of materials.

Ceramics

During the excavations of 2016, 4890 sherds of pottery (comprising 4688 earthenware and 202 glazed ceramics) were recovered. A further 1103 were recovered from the excavations at Utheemu in 2017 (comprising 1085 earthenware and just 18 glazed ceramics) (Table 9.2). While earthenware sherds were sampled, all glazed sherds were kept due to the small sample size. Sampling was designed to be systematic and straightforward—whereby sherds smaller than 3 cm^2 were counted and discarded. This offered an objective means to reduce the amount of material for study, while incurring minimal loss of information since analysis of variables such as decoration can be very unreliable on smaller items. As a result, the total assemblage subjected to detailed analysis consisted of 2552 sherds, and the discussion that follows focuses on these.

Twelve classes of glazed wares were observed in the assemblages from the excavations in 2016 (see Jaufar 2019, p. 194). This includes seven classes imported from various parts of China (n=147), four from southeast Asia (n=30), and one from Europe associated with Victorian period (nineteenth/twentieth centuries) (Jaufar 2019, p. 202) (n=2). A further 16 sherds could not be identified.

In terms of earthenware, decorated pottery accounted for approximately half the assemblage (n=942 against n=988 undecorated) for the material from 2016. The proportions of undecorated to decorated sherds were the same in Male' and Utheemu—returning 48% undecorated (n=516 from Utheemu, n=308 from Male) vs. 52% decorated sherds (n=551 from Utheemu, n=333 from Male). In contrast, most of the sherds from Veyvah were undecorated (74%, n=164 undecorated vs. 26%, n=58 decorated). The earthenware pottery from the excavations at Utheemu in 2017 showed a similar pattern to Veyvah, with decorated sherds comprising just 34% (n=138) of the assemblage against 66% (n=264) undecorated (Table 9.1).

The decorated earthenware assemblage was homogenous across the various excavated trenches (see Jaufar 2019, pp. 177–192 for full discussion). Impressed sherds were the most common form of decoration, falling into five types, of which linear paddled impressions were the most frequent (Jaufar 2019, Table 24 and Figure 81). 'Waffle'—a term adopted from Mikkelsen (1991)—and 'linear paddle' decorations were defined at this point (Jaufar 2019, pp. 179–180). Incised and slipped sherds were also common. Sixteen types of rim were identified, mainly taking the form of *handi* or large storage or cooking vessels.

As shown in Table 9.2 of all the assemblages from 2016, Utheemu returned the highest number of ceramics overall, particularly earthenware ceramics. The majority of these were recovered from the two test pits situated in the palace compound. However, just 3% (n=36 of 1103) of the Utheemu assemblage excavated in 2016 comprised glazed wares. Given the possible association with a higher status structure (Utheemu palace), one might have expected most of the 36 glazed wares to have issued from Trenches 4 and 5 within the palace compound—yet this was not the case. Glazed wares comprised 3.45% (n=23 of 667) from Trench 4, 3.06% (n=8 of 261) from Trench 5. This compares with a contribution of 3.47% (n=5 of 144) from Trench 1 and 4.2% (n=18 of 420) recovered from the excavations of Trench 3 in 2017.

In contrast, Male' returned both the highest proportion of glazed wares (representing 19% (n=153 of 794) of the assemblage) and the highest sherd density overall (Table 9.2). Of the ceramic assemblage from Male', 45% (n=335) issued from N12, which returned a slightly higher proportion of glazed to earthenware ceramics (26%, n=87 glazed vs. 74% n=248 earthenware).

Veyvah returned both the lowest number of sherds and the lowest density of sherds for the volume of material excavated (Table 9.2). However, the majority (85%, n=200 of 235) were recovered from Unit 5. The overall representation of glazed sherds from Veyvah, 5.53% (n=13), is slightly higher than but still comparable with the proportion of glazed wares from Utheemu.

In summary, the ceramic analysis is based on an assemblage of 5993 sherds recovered over two seasons—of which 2552 were subjected to detailed analysis. The assessment suggests the earthenware assemblages from the three islands

Table 9.2 Ceramics recovered from the excavations of 2016 and 2017.

Location	Earthenware Retained	Earthenware Discarded	Glazed ceramics	Total	Volume excavated	Sherd density/m3
Utheemu 2016	1067	1438	36	2541	6.31	402.85
Utheemu 2017	402	683	18	1103	7.51	146.87
Male	641	927	153	1721	1.93	890.37
Veyvah	222	393	13	628	2.30	273.04
Kinolhas	4109	3485	406	8000	20.92	382.41

were generally homogenous with similar forms and decorative motifs represented in all excavation areas. Decorated sherds account for between 26% and 52% of the assemblage from each island. Glazed sherds account for between 3% and 19% of the ceramics recovered, with the highest percentage issuing from Male'. The excavations at Male' yielded the highest density of ceramics with a sherd density of 890.37 sherds per m³. Densities from the other excavations were much lower. The combined density of ceramics from the 2016 and 2017 excavations in Utheemu is 263.94 sherds per m³—comparable with 273.04 per m³ at Veyvah.

Fauna

In 2016 and 2017, 5220 remains of molluscs and 3012 fish and animal bones were recovered from the excavations at Utheemu, Male and Veyvah, 7% (n=595) of which could not be identified (Table 9.3).

At Utheemu in 2016, most of the remains were recovered from the palace, with the assemblage from Trench 4 (n=1578) representing the largest on the island. This offers some valuable insights into discard patterns. It would seem reasonable to expect more food waste in the area that is reported to have been the location of a kitchen rather than in a space immediately before one of the current main entries to the palace. This is particularly so because, at least in terms of the most recent design of the palace enclosure, the two trenches are separated by a wall (see Jaufar 2019, Figure 50). When the types of marine vertebrate remains are considered, a higher percentage of the fish bones recovered from Trench 5 were cranial elements (63%, n=114). This compares with just 23% (n=148) of the fish bones from Trench 4. This could suggest different discard patterns, with the fish head removed and processed in the kitchen area and the remaining carcasses discarded elsewhere.

The Male' assemblage is dominated by cowrie shells, particularly *M. moneta*. Of these, 82% (n=1445) were recovered from a single deposit. This cache inflates the density of fauna at this site (Table 9.3)[1]. When the cowrie cache is excluded from the Male' material, density decreases to a broadly comparable 687.56 specimens per m³. Few other vertebrate remains were recovered—with marine vertebrates and terrestrial vertebrates representing just 2% (n=55) and 1.1% (n=30) of the total assemblages respectively. It is striking that Male' is the only island of the 2016 excavations to return ungulate remains. Though only present in extremely small numbers (n=5), they likely speak to the status of the palace occupants. As Jaufar (2019, p. 274) notes, 'land mammals were considered a delicacy consumed by the wealthy or on rare occasions'. Regarding vertebrate fauna only, the density of finds from Male' drops significantly from 1436.27 specimens per m³ to just 86.01 specimens per m³ (Table 9.3), consistent with the hypothesis that the trenches sampled a residential space rather than a kitchen or midden area.

In a detailed analysis of the cowrie cache from Male', part of a comparative study of the size, species composition, and modification of three Maldivian and one East African cowrie assemblages (Christie and Haour 2018a), it was observed that the shells from Male' were generally unmodified, with the dorsum intact, but that 40% of them were burnt. This was probably associated with the destruction of the palace rather than deliberate action. As observed in Chapter 7, informants interviewed during the ethnographic surveys were clear that none of the processing strategies involved placing shells in direct contact with fire.

The material from Veyvah was generally well preserved and predominantly issued from Unit 5, representing 61% (n=909) of the total assemblage from the island. This was dominated by fish bones, particularly post-cranial elements. Many of the cranial elements appeared to come from reef fish, including parrotfish, grouper, and emperors. Unlike the pole and line tuna fishery—which is and was a major export commodity—reef fishing nowadays mainly services domestic consumption, though excess fish might be processed and sold. The ethnographic data suggests that the main species caught included snappers (e.g. *Lutjanus bohar, Lutjanus monostigma,* and *Lutjanus gibbus* (particularly during night fishing)), emperor fish (e.g. *Lethrinus conchyliatus* and *Rastrelliger kanagurta* (particularly in northern atolls)), sea-bream (e.g. *Gymnocranius griseus*), trevally (e.g. *Carangoides caeruleopinnatus* and *Gnathodon speciosus*), and

Table 9.3 Fauna recovered from the excavations of 2016 and 2017. Figures in brackets for Male reflect the number of cowries excluding the cache, and the corresponding impact these have on the density of fauna from the site.

Category	Utheemu 2016	Utheemu 2017	Male	Veyvah	Kinolhas
Cowries	431	98	1764 (319)*	182	1110
Other marine invertebrates	1138	162	842	603	129
Marine vertebrates	964	682	55	644	4932
Terrestrial vertebrates	12	30	30	0	733
Unknown	142	330	81	42	1870
TOTAL	**3989**	**1302**	**2772 (1327)**	**1471**	**8774**
Densities of material/ m³					
Volume excavated	6.31	7.51	1.93	2.3	20.92
All fauna	632.17	173.37	1436.27 (687.56)	639.57	419.41
Invertebrate	248.65	34.62	1350.26 (601.55)	341.30	59.23
Vertebrate	177.18	138.75	86.01	298.26	360.18

Figure 9.1 Fish smoking in Raa Alifushi.

Source: Photo by Annalisa Christie, February 2016

groupers (e.g. *Aethaloperca rogaa*) (see also MRC 2003). These are normally caught with handlines, with the bait attached directly to a hook.

The Veyvah assemblage also returned greater quantities of different cowrie species, particularly *Eurosaria helvola argella* (Melvill 1888) (n=31) and *Palmadusta asellus* (n=21).

The dominance of post-cranial elements in the assemblages from all the islands can be explored with reference to the ethnographic interviews. These suggested that the most common processing strategy for fish products was smoking, particularly for tuna. Once landed and divided, fish were initially gutted and filleted and the fish heads often discarded in the sea. The fillets were then boiled, smoked, and dried, and the bones and remaining carcass boiled down to make fish sauce or dried and ground up into a powder. This would leave a clear archaeological signature in the form of hearths. Observations of this process on a household scale (rather than the commercial-scale processing currently practiced) suggest this could have been carried out in a kitchen space (Figure 9.1).

Fire is used to heat the pots in which fillets and carcasses are boiled, or to smoke the fish, but there is no direct contact. Only 1% (n=30) of the marine vertebrate remains recovered from all the assemblages were burnt (13 from the excavation in Utheemu in 2017, 11 from Veyvah, five from Utheemu in 2016, and one from Male'). These were all vertebrae rather than cranial elements and are likely to have been burnt incidentally rather than as a result of deliberate action.

In summary, the analysis presented here is based on the assessment of 8232 shell and bone specimens recovered from Utheemu, Male', and Veyvah in 2016 and 2017. These assemblages were dominated by marine resources: particularly cowries (n=2475) and fish bones (n=2345). Apart from Trench 5, which had a higher proportion of cranial elements, the marine vertebrate assemblages were dominated by vertebrae and other post-cranial bones, providing potential insight into fish processing strategies. Male' returned the highest density of remains, though this was inflated by the recovery of a cowrie cache in test pit N12. This was also the only site where ungulate remains (n=5) were recovered.

Small finds

A total of 114 items were recovered from the excavations at Male', Veyvah, and Utheemu in 2016, with a further 12 items from the work at Utheemu in 2017. Collectively, these comprised 33 glass items, 3 beads, 61 identifiable metal pieces (excluding over 200 unidentifiable metal fragments that were too degraded or fragmented to identify), 23 pieces of worked or imported stone, and 6 ceramic small finds (Table 9.4). Of the small finds, 56% were recovered from Male'. This site also returned the highest density of small finds—35.7 finds per m³, which was considerably richer than other islands where find density was between 1.6 and 5.23 finds per m³ (Table 9.4). At Male, these mostly consisted of metal and glass fragments.

Thirteen of the glass objects recovered (11 from Male', one from Veyvah, and one from the excavations at Utheemu during 2017) were long, thin, and curved. St John Simpson (the British Museum) suggests these were fragments of bracelets (Simpson pers. comm. to SJ; see Jaufar 2019, p. 240, and Chapter 8.2, this volume). Bracelets were an important part of historical Maldivian adornment, as also attested in historical and ethnographic sources (Gray and Bell 1887, p. 163, Bell 1921, and Romero-Frias 2012). For instance, ibn Battuta states that the jewellery of the Maldivian women consists of bracelets which are worn from the elbow up to the wrists (Husain 1976, p. 51).

Table 9.4 Small finds recovered from the excavations of 2016 and 2017.

Location	Glass	Metal	Stone	Ceramic	Beads	Total	Finds/m³
Utheemu 2016	7	21	5	5	0	38	5.23
Utheemu 2017	3	7	2	0	0	12	1.6
Male	22	33	14	1	0	70	35.7
Veyvah	1	1	2	0	2	6	2.61
Kinolhas	45	35	15	7	8	110	4.92

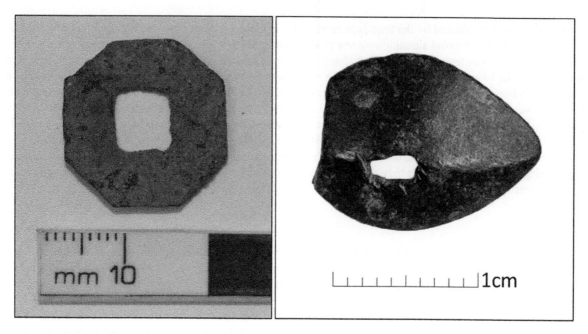

Figure 9.2 Left: octagonal metal object (SF 04) from Male', excavated in 2016. Right: worked metal object (SF 02) from Utheemu, excavated in 2017.

Source: Photos by Maria Ledinskaya (left) and Giulia Nazzaro (right).

The remaining 20 glass items appear to be fragments of glass bottles of varying colours. Only five of these (three from Male' and two from Utheemu) were diagnostic, representing a rim, base, and lidded mouth-piece and two neck fragments respectively (Jaufar 2019, Figures 166, 167, and 168). Glass fragments are commonly recovered in archaeological deposits across the country. Fragments of glass bottles and jars were recovered in archaeological deposits from Nilandhoo (Litster 2016, p. 207), while intact bottles and jars were recovered from deposits disturbed by development in Utheemu (see Jaufar 2019, Figure 170) and more recently at Rasgetheemu in Raa atoll (Zunaam 2021).

Although only two beads were recovered from the excavations in 2016, this is unlikely to be representative of the use of beads overall, resulting instead from differences in sieving strategy. While one bead was recovered during the excavation, the other was identified when the deposits were wet sieved though a finer mesh. At 0.8 cm and 0.5 cm in diameter, under normal circumstances both would have passed through the mesh and thus remained undiscovered. Laure Dussubieux (Field Museum of Natural History in Chicago, USA) suggested an origin in China for one and central Asia for the other (Report in Jaufar 2019, pp. CXVII–CXXV).

The metal remains were the most common category of small find recovered from Utheemu (n=28 identifiable, n=150+ fragments) and Male' (n=33 identifiable, 12 fragments). Only one fragment was recovered from Veyvah. The metal finds were made from either iron or copper alloy (Jaufar 2019, p. 249). With few exceptions, the pieces are highly fragmented or corroded and their function therefore impossible to identify. Those items that were diagnostic included 4 bolts (Male') and 9 nails (Utheemu) likely used in construction. An octagonal object with a central square perforation was also recovered in Male' (Figure 9.2, left). Given its unusual shape, we had hoped that the object might be a coin; however, it had a high level of corrosion which made further visual assessment challenging. The object was therefore examined and conserved by the Norfolk Museums Service to determine whether there was any evidence of markings beneath the corrosion. X-radiography indicated the piece was unmarked and undecorated. It seems the object is of a high tin or lead content alloy (Jaufar 2019, p. 249). Another pierced worked metal item with a small perforation was also recovered from the excavations at Utheemu in 2017 (Figure 9.2, right).

The stone objects presented here are restricted to worked coral stone and possible imported stones (n=2 both from Utheemu). A further 40 fragments of broken plaster (both painted and unpainted) were also recovered, primarily from Male', and their nature is consistent with an identification as rubble resulting from the destruction of the palace structures.

In summary, the small finds assemblage comprised items of adornment (including glass bracelets and beads), broken sherds from glass vessels, fragments of iron and copper alloy in varying states of conservation, worked coral stone, and foreign stone. Male' returned the highest densities of these objects by some margin (35.7 finds per m³ compared with 1.6–5.23 finds per m³ elsewhere). The metal objects, dominant in the assemblages from Utheemu and Male', were highly fragmented and with few exceptions were undiagnostic. Diagnostic items included bolts and nails. Two perforated metal objects were also recovered. These included an octagonal piece with square perforation (from Male'), initially thought to be a coin; and a pointed piece with circular perforation, the purpose of which was unclear.

Mortuary remains

The excavation work conducted by the team was carried out in close cooperation with local communities, and a particular effort was made to avoid situating any test pits within areas in which human remains might be encountered. Despite this, a burial was revealed in Trench 5 (Jaufar 2019, p. 116) at a depth of approximately 1 m. These remains were reported to the island council and heritage office in Utheemu, who gave permission to expose and record the inhumation before reburial. The excavations revealed an articulated adult burial placed on its side, oriented north–south and facing to the west (Haour et al. 2016, p. 76). The position is consistent with an Islamic burial. The inhumation rested in a clearly demarcated sub-circular grave pit and was not associated with any grave goods. The grave pit was sealed by a layer dated to 820 ± 30 BP, which calibrates as AD 1165–1265. Although the discovery of human remains in this location was unexpected, informants reported that burials had been identified during the construction of a new mosque on a neighbouring plot to the south. This may suggest the existence of a former cemetery, which once extended to include the area now encompassed by the palace compound.

Structural remains

The only in situ structural remains recovered during the excavations conducted in 2016 were three blocks of *veligaa* (sandstone), one of which was shaped. These were encountered in Trench 5, approximately 0.5 m south of a more recent cement wall that was constructed to show the boundary of the palace kitchen. These *veligaa* blocks are interpreted as demarcating the original wall of the structure.

In 2017, five pieces of worked coral stone (*hirigaa*) were fully exposed and recorded in the investigations of Trench 3. Two of these were particularly large (Slab A: 75 cm x 110 cm; Slab B: 85 cm x 100 cm). Some showed evidence of having been dressed and cut to form the 'tongue' of the 'tongue in groove' construction method (Figure 9.3), which is characteristic of the building techniques employed in the coral stone mosques of the Maldives (Jameel 2012, Müller and Wille 2019, p. 91).

Figure 9.3 Worked *hirigaa* slabs exposed in the excavations at Utheemu during 2017.

As well as being used for the construction of mosques, *hirigaa* was employed in the construction of shrines, cemeteries, and some elite buildings (Riyan 2011, Ahmad and Jameel 2012). Most domestic structures were constructed with coconut wood and thatch (Shafeeg 1989) and would be difficult to identify archaeologically.

Plain and painted plasterwork and the remains of possible collapsed walls were recorded at the site in Male', most likely associated with the destruction of the palace. Similarly, a number of ceramic roof tiles of likely modern date were recovered from the excavations within the Utheemu palace compound.

Comparative analysis

When juxtaposing the materials from excavations at these various sites across the Maldives, there is a striking overall similarity in assemblages, both in terms of type and frequency of materials recovered. The earthenware objects from Utheemu, Veyvah, and Male' are similar in fabric, form, and decoration to those from Kinolhas (Chapter 5, earlier), and there is also parity in the types of glazed wares present (Jaufar 2019, Chapter 6, this volume). The proportions of earthenware to glazed wares are also broadly comparable across the islands (Figure 9.4).

That said, certain differences emerge, perhaps due to distinct status or usage. The ceramic assemblages from Male' have a higher proportion of glazed wares, along with a high density of ceramics generally (Table 9.2). This elevated occurrence of glazed wares, and of pottery generally, may reflect their siting within an elite structure. However, the two trenches excavated within another elite structure, Utheemu palace, do not share a higher representation of glazed materials. There are a number of possible factors to consider when seeking to explain this fact. First, the radiocarbon dates from Utheemu palace suggest that at least some of the deposits from Trench 4 and Trench 5 predate the construction of the palace itself. Thus, these materials may not be associated with higher status occupation. It is also possible that the lower proportions of glazed wares are because 46% of the excavated deposits were associated with the preparation of food. Even so, while Trench 4 had a higher density of ceramics (239.07 sherds per m^3 compared with just 109.21 sherds per m^3) than Trench 5, the proportions of earthenware to glazed wares is similar in both (3.5% (n=23 of 667) at Trench 4 compared with 3.1% (n=8 of 261) from Trench 5).

The small finds assemblages from the four islands were too limited in size to enable quantitative analysis. However, as was the case with the ceramics, the density of all categories of small find recovered was much higher in the case of the trenches excavated in Male' (Table 9.4).

On a qualitative level, a similar suite of items were recovered from each of the assemblages. These included items of adornment (e.g. bracelets and beads), fragments of glass objects, items of iron and copper alloy, and worked stone. It is clear that while these items may not have been equally abundant on other islands when compared with the capital, they were nevertheless present and thus accessible across all the sites.

With regard to the faunal assemblages, similar patterns of consumption can be observed across the islands. This points towards a marine-based subsistence economy dominated by fish (Figure 9.5).

Consumable terrestrial vertebrates (birds and ungulates) only contribute a small percentage of the faunal remains from the excavated assemblages (accounting for 1% or less of those excavated in 2017, 2% from the 2017 excavations at Utheemu, and just 8% from Kinolhas). These are dominated by bird bones rather than ungulate remains. Evidence for the consumption of ungulates was only found at Male' (representing 0.2% of the assemblage, n=5 bones) and at

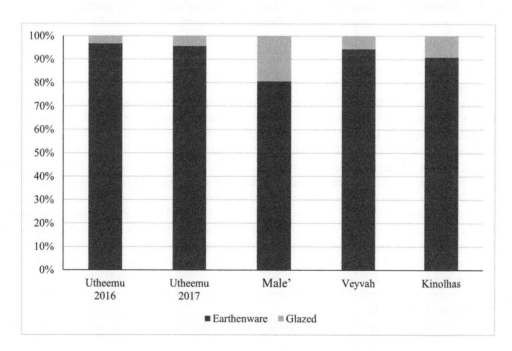

Figure 9.4 Proportions of earthenware and glazed wares in the assemblages from 2016 and 2017.

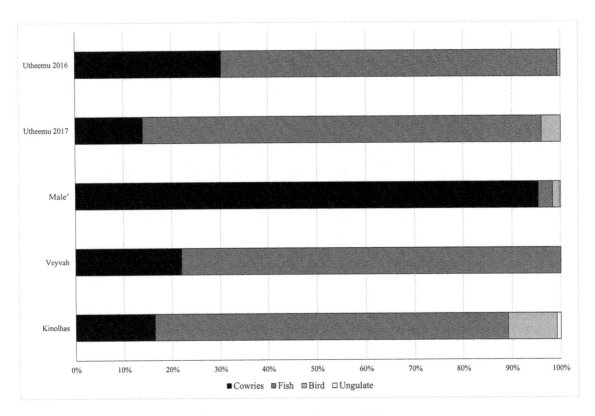

Figure 9.5 Proportion of different resources from the excavations of 2016 and 2017.

Kinolhas (representing 0.6% of the assemblage, n=56) (Figure 9.5). The presence of chickens during the medieval period is attested by ibn Battuta, who reports that they were bartered at a rate of one cooking pot for five or six chickens (Gibb 1929, Husain 1976, p. 45 in Jaufar 2019, p. 162).

The dominance of marine rather than terrestrial vertebrates was also observed in the assessment of an assemblage of 1001 bones from the site of Nilandhoo Foamathi (Litster 2016, pp. 172–188). This site provides a useful point of comparison here as it is the only site with medieval period remains where fish species identification has been attempted. At this site, fish accounted for 99% (n=988) of the vertebrate assemblage, with only 11 bird bone and two rat bones recovered. Of the of the fish remains, 18% (n=178) were identified to family level, with most of these (n=109) identified as belonging to the *Scombridae* (tuna) family (Litster 2016, p. 185). This suggests that while some reef fish (predominantly *Lutjanidae* (n=10), *Lethrinidae* (n=11), and *Scaridae* (n=22) were being caught, offshore fishing, likely using pole and line as described in the ethnographic interviews, would have been the dominant fishing strategy.

Returning to our own excavations, one noticeable difference between the assemblages from the excavations of 2016 and the material from Kinolhas is the lower diversity in other shell species at the latter site (Table 9.2). In the case of Male', the number of other shell species represented may be influenced by the excavation of beach sand in the surface deposits of each of the test pits. This sand was spread around the park to make it look more appealing and contained numerous fragments of naturally broken shells of different species.

The case of *Atactodea striata* is different. Shells of this species became increasingly dominant in deeper contexts, a pattern also observed at Trench 5 in Utheemu. These were not for consumption. Instead, it was suggested during the ethnographic surveys that this species, known locally as *rindhali*, were of particular interest to the *borah* merchants,[2] used for decoration on clothing and as jewellery. The shells were collected from the inter-tidal zone and left in the sun to dry.[3]

As already noted, the assemblage from Male' is markedly different to the others, dominated by cowries. Historically, and in ethnographic sources, cowries collected across the Maldives were cleaned and bought to Male', either as taxes (see Bell 2002 [1940], p. 96 for an example of the rate of taxation for Ishdhoo island, in Laamu atoll, in 1882) or in exchange for goods and produce. These shells are reported to have been stored in warehouses and underground, with one seventeenth-century source suggesting that thousands of tonnes of cowrie shells lay buried in the capital (Hogendorn and Johnson 2003 [1986], p. 83). The recovery of large cowrie caches and hoards is common in the archaeology of the Maldives more generally, often encountered during construction and farming.[4] The largest systematically excavated hoard remains a Buddhist period assemblage from Kaashidhoo that contained over 62000 shells. This hoard, which was dated directly as calibrating to AD165–345 [T-12495], was one of a number of contexts from different phases containing cowrie shells (Mikkelsen 2000, p. 13).

The excavations of 2016 also offer a point of comparison to Kinolhas in terms of medieval mortuary practices. Where the burial at Utheemu was discovered in a clearly defined grave-pit at a depth of 1 m, the inhumation at

Kinolhas that was encountered within the remains of a rectilinear feature (Structure 1) in Trench 631 (see Chapter 4) was encountered just 30 cm below the surface. While the positioning of the remains from both sites was the same, the remains at Kinolhas had been disturbed and damaged after burial. This was evinced by the positioning and condition of the cranium and mandible, which were disarticulated from the post-cranial remains and redeposited at the base of a tombstone. In terms of Structure 1, surveys conducted as part of the Maldives Heritage Survey project have recorded a number of mausolea or shrines from the medieval period, housing the remains of important people. Examples include the *ziyaarat* on Laamu Hithadhoo (LAM-HTD-3) (M. Feener 2021b) or the *kuda ziyaarat* on Kaafu Himnafushi (KFA-HMF-1) (M. Feener 2021c). It may be that Structure 1 is a similar type of feature.

There was little other evidence for structural remains. The *veligaa* foundations observed in Trench 5 and the worked *hirigaa* slabs observed in the excavations at Utheemu in 2017 are notable exceptions. The slabs evince the use of tongue and groove construction, providing insights into how *hirigaa* was worked and used in coral stone buildings (Jameel 2012, Müller and Wille 2019, p. 91). However, it is not clear why the worked slabs were abandoned, nor is it possible to infer the type of structure they might have been used for. As noted, coral stone construction was normally associated with elite structures such as mosques, shrines, and cemeteries. Domestic architecture was made from archaeologically ephemeral wood and thatch.

Discussion

The concept of maritime cultural landscapes has been defined by Westerdahl (1992, p. 5) as 'the human utilisation (economy) of maritime space by boat, settlement, fishing, hunting, shipping and its attendant sub cultures'. This has proved hugely influential within Indian Ocean archaeology and is particularly important within Africanist scholarship (Breen and Lane 2003, Christie 2011, Fleisher et al. 2015, Pollard 2021). While the data presented here remain insufficient to address this concept in all its dimensions, the importance of the sea to Maldivian communities is clear. The faunal assemblages evince a predominantly marine-based subsistence economy. Moreover, the sea provided or played a key role in the creation of the three major long-distance export commodities: cowries, dried fish, and coir (coir is made from used coconut husks, which are buried on the inter-tidal zone to soak, positioned perpendicularly to the shore). It also facilitated connection between the islands and with international trade networks. Given the unique geography of the Maldives, with over 200 inhabited islands spread across several degrees of latitude, there is a natural tendency to think of individual islands in isolation. Yet, as this chapter has shown, the archaeological evidence from the medieval period is remarkably homogeneous.

It is known through historical and ethnographic evidence that the Maldives were reliant on external trade. This was not just for items like earthenware and glazed ceramics, glassware, metals, and other ornaments, which are clearly documented archaeologically, but also for more ephemeral produce including rice, flour, *arica* nuts, and cloth. The historical sources (Gray and Bell 1887) suggest that these commodities were secured in exchange for cowrie shells, fish, and coir, with trade being centralised in Male'.

The evidence presented here makes it impossible to ascertain the mechanisms of who controlled trade in the archaeological past (such as, for example, the politically or religiously prominent, etc.). But it is likely to have been centralised to achieve the level of homogeneity found in our assemblages. Pragmatically, it would not have made sense for visiting merchants to trade with individual islands. Sailing around and between the islands of different atolls would have been time-consuming and potentially hazardous; individual islands are unlikely to have needed substantial quantities of imported items at any given time; nor is it likely that they would have been able to collect or produce the number of cowries, fish, or coir needed to make the exchange worthwhile.

The work presented here also highlights a number of research questions relating to the medieval archaeology of the Maldives. Two specific angles might be suggested. First, and crucially given the rapid pace of expansion and infrastructure development within the capital city, it will be important to test archaeologically areas outside the former location of the royal palace, sampled as part of the present work. Many existing open spaces are now found on reclaimed land, adding to the challenge, but this can be mitigated by carefully considering historical maps. A second question concerns the issue of status on an intra-island scale. While the overall representation of different classes of material culture are similar across the islands, access to these goods probably varied between households and individuals within a given island community. Here, the work at Kinolhas offers a starting point. The archaeological layer was consistent across the site and a similar suite of material culture was recovered in fairly equal proportion in most of the trenches excavated (T631 being the obvious exception). However, to examine the issue of different status on an intra-island scale would require further archaeological refinement in terms of understanding and recognising past settlements. Around the immediate vicinity of the sites excavated at Kinolhas, this could be explored through geoarchaeological sampling across the area to see if it is possible to detect archaeologically ephemeral houses through changes in soil chemistry akin to those used to identify wattle and daub structures within stonetowns along the East African coast (e.g. Sulas et al. 2016, Sulas et al. 2019). A similar strategy could be employed alongside further archaeological reconnaissance in other parts of the island to explore the question raised in Chapter 4; that is, whether the location of core settlement changes during other periods of occupation.

Notes

1 Note that NISP of other categories of fauna from Male' were not affected by the presence of the cowrie cache, which only contained cowrie shells.

2 These merchants were from Sri Lanka and India and were allowed to settle in Male' from the mid-nineteenth century (Phadnis and Luithui 1981, p. 169). They owned shops, particularly along the coast of Male'. Our interviews suggest they monopolised foreign trade until the government store in Male' (the *bodu store*) was founded in 1953 during the presidency of Muhammed Amin Didi (Maloney 1976, p. 657).

3 Interview with Dhonfanu Mohammed Yoosuf, K. Male.

4 Evinced by the two hoards examined at Utheemu, a hoard recovered during the construction of Loama Resort on Raa Maamigilli (Christie and Haour 2018a) and a hoard encountered during development on Alif Alif Omadhoo.

10 Towards an archaeology of the medieval Maldives

Anne Haour

Introduction

Prior to the work presented in this book, a disparate set of data, both historical and archaeological, existed to suggest the importance of the Maldives in medieval trade networks. Historical sources referred to a range of commercial partners across the Indian Ocean and beyond: outsiders have been writing accounts of the Maldives for at least 1000 years, and perhaps far longer. Among these were recurrent mention of exports such as the products of the coconut palm (notably coir), fish, and marine products such as cowrie shells, ambergris, and tortoise shells. The shells of cowries, a small marine mollusc that enjoys the local climate and shallow waters, were among the most frequently discussed commodities, while there were allusions to the import of pottery from India and China. Both these classes of material have the benefit of material durability, yet there had been no archaeological investigation of these accounts. In fact, hardly any archaeological work at all had been undertaken in the Maldives, with the exception of preliminary surveys, test pitting, and amateur excavations, and a single, so far only summarily published scientific excavation, in the 1990s at the site of Kaashidhoo.

The research presented here aimed to close this gap. Following an initial season of excavation and fieldwork at three locations in the Maldives (see Chapter 9), the decision was taken to focus on the island of Kinolhas, in the atoll of Raa. The island was known through historical sources for its association with fourteenth-century traveller ibn Battuta, and initial surveys, both predating and during the visit by the present authors, confirmed the existence of standing remains of likely medieval age.

The research at Kinolhas involved multiple strands of activity. The locations of sites of historical or archaeological importance, including substantial remains possibly predating the medieval period, were identified or re-appraised. A series of shovel test pits located a medieval occupation and confirmed that it lay undisturbed. Seven trenches were excavated, ranging in size from 1 x 2 m to 4.5 x 6 m, totalling 27 m². Most were intended to sample occupation deposits, but the largest, placed over rectilinear stone features interpreted as the remains of domestic structures, in fact exposed a shrine or mausoleum surrounded by gravestones, destruction rubble, and broken pottery. Complementing this extensive horizontal investigation, the other units were consistent in demonstrating the presence of a thin archaeological layer characterised by abundant pottery remains, shell, and other fauna, and a number of imported items such as stone, glass, and metal fragments. One, Trench 544—probably a midden—yielded extremely high volumes of fauna and ceramics, making it suitable for comparative work. This settlement and funerary site was dated, through 13 radiocarbon samples, to the fourteenth/fifteenth centuries, with both earlier and later components. Nine of the dates, spread across the five trenches excavated, fell sometime between AD 1290 and 1440 after calibration, and samples from different trenches returned extremely similar or identical results, allowing a good degree of confidence in the chronology. As such, the main objective of the work—to provide an insight into the medieval occupation of the Maldives—was met.

The broader aim, which was to situate the Maldives within medieval trade networks, required detailed analysis and description of the material culture recovered. This included items originating throughout the Indian Ocean world and beyond, stretching from the Middle East to China. The vast amounts of pottery of likely Indian origin and the cowrie shells provided a compelling confirmation of the historical sources, and indicated participation in a shared Indian Ocean material culture. This picture was strengthened by the recovery of Chinese and southeast Asian ceramics, and of beads and bracelets of types common around the Indian Ocean. The widely occurring presence of similar objects well outside of their production locale, showing that comparable items moved across vast regions, suggests intensified and complex interactions. The archaeological data thereby provide a valuable corrective to the historical sources, which tend to treat the various regional segments in isolation.

Material culture and networks over time

Unglazed earthenwares dominate the Kinolhas assemblage, and they provide unambiguous evidence of a shared membership in a broader sphere of ceramic culture, forming part of a relatively common and geographically widespread 'Indian' and 'Indian-type wares' phenomenon. In morphology and in decoration, the Kinolhas material has affinities with pottery documented at sites in Sri Lanka, India, East Africa, the Red Sea, and the Persian Gulf and that has been considered as 'Indian'. The distinctive paddle impressions strengthen the proposition of a connection with southern India and Sri Lanka, with close formal parallels to assemblages from Arikamedu (Tamil Nadu, east coast of India)

DOI: 10.4324/9781003166221-10

and Tissamaharama (Sri Lanka) and related occurrences reported in Yemen, Oman, Egypt, and Indonesia. Such wares, which are often cooking pots or water jars, and coarse and likely fragile, were probably personal items, and they suggest the existence of trade diasporas of the sort evoked in the historical records.

In terms of Chinese ceramic imports, the Kinolhas assemblage generally matched trading patterns seen across other western Indian Ocean sites, but it also brought in new information (Chapter 6). The earliest ceramics identified date to the fourteenth century and consist mainly of Yuan Longquan celadon. A low frequency of early Ming, fifteenth-century materials reflect a minimal Chinese participation in Indian Ocean trade for a time, and the large proportion of southeast Asian celadon suggests that these wares filled this gap in the market. Following this, middle Ming blue and white porcelain of the sixteenth and seventeenth centuries was unusually common at Kinolhas, perhaps suggesting a boom in trade between China and the Maldives. Incidentally, these later datings run somewhat counter to data from some of the other types of material culture and from radiocarbon dates at Kinolhas, tying into the broader issues of taphonomic disturbances on Maldivian sites, discussed further later. After the seventeenth century, Chinese ceramics were largely absent, in stark contrast with observations from sites in the Persian Gulf, for example. Either Kinolhas was not included in trade networks of the time or—more plausibly—this later evidence lies elsewhere on the island. Data from other islands in the Maldives are limited, but it is known that slightly later Chinese imports were recovered by John Carswell (1975–1977) during surface collections in Male'.

While the glazed materials from eastern and southeastern Asia are present in sufficiently high quantities at Kinolhas to offer helpful chronological pointers, in comparison the number of Islamic materials was much less—they were ten times less common—and they fell within a broad range of dates from the ninth to the eighteenth centuries. Among these were types of likely southern Iranian and Iraqi origin (Chapter 6).

The importation of stone, both as worked items such as grindstones and as unworked fragments, is documented at the site. Whether the stone artefacts were shaped in the Maldives or at their source is, at this stage, unknown. In the exceptional case represented by two high quality gravestones that have been reported from elsewhere on Kinolhas, it has been demonstrated that they were carved in Gujarat before being brought to the island in the fifteenth century. These gravestones were known prior to the work of the present team (Kalus and Guillot 2005), but others may remain to be discovered on Kinolhas, which counts several former, now heavily overgrown, burial areas (Chapter 3). The gravestones documented by the present team were made of local coral stone and the inscriptions that survived point to a range of influences (Chapter 4).

The faunal remains recovered are consistent with a subsistence regime largely reliant on the sea, with fish remains dominant across assemblages (Chapter 7). This, and the small representation of chicken and other terrestrial animals, is in line with the limited data that exist from other assemblages across the Maldives. The demonstration of the local importance of cowries is an important confirmation of the historical data. These shells were recovered throughout various contexts and included several caches.

A generally homogeneous assemblage of small finds was identified across units. These consisted of metal, with smaller showings of lithics and of ceramics, in the latter case often repurposed potsherds. Glass items were dominant, however, and accounted for nearly half of the finds recovered. This includes fragments of small closed containers, possibly used for perfume or a similar substance, curved pieces which appear to be fragments of bangles, and beads (Chapter 8). Chemical analysis of a sample of these finds revealed several glass recipes. Six of the beads, recovered inside a small ceramic vessel in Trench 449, and the five bangles tested, are made of mineral soda–high alumina (m-Na-Al) glass of likely Indian production (Chapter 8). One of the subtypes identified, m-Na-Al 2 glass, has been recognised in beads from sites from the fourteenth to the nineteenth centuries on the west coast of India, in southern Africa, and on the east coast of Africa, with the port of Chaul, Maharashtra, a possible point of distribution around the Indian Ocean (Chapter 8). As noted earlier, these items point to a shared super-regional visual and material culture.

Themes and directions for future work

It is too early, on the present evidence, to answer wide-ranging questions about the cross-cultural interactions of the Maldives over time. Certainly, the nature and direction of connections will have varied, different segments overlapped, and periods of intensity and decline occurred. At the conclusion of the present study, however, the broader backdrop to this fluctuating story is clear. Many models have fostered the assumption that the Maldives were important in medieval trade networks due to the simple fact of their geographical position. This seems evident to whomever opens an atlas, but of course a maritime cultural landscape is defined not solely by latitude and longitude but also by a complex interaction of socio-political and environmental factors. The importance of a shared belief in Islam emerges in some historical sources. The weight of known and trusted routes will have been significant, too. Networks of trusted friends and allies, the presence of a reliable infrastructure which could guarantee a sufficient supply of trade items and essentials (such as water, fish, and coconuts), and a safe harbour would be key concerns. This may also have encouraged centralisation in the diffuse archipelago of the Maldives. Historical sources insist on the existence of government control from Male', for example in storing cowries; but visiting merchants would surely prefer to sail to a central place, taking the opportunity to pay high-level visits and avoid the notoriously treacherous Maldivian reefs.[1] This de facto centralisation would also explain the level of homogeneity observed in the archaeological assemblages studied by the present team.

While charting fluctuations in relationships between regions must await finer-grained studies, the question of connections between the Maldives and various parts of China offers intriguing leads. The maritime routes connecting them appear, on present evidence offered by Chinese ceramics recovered in the Maldives, not to predate the turn of the second millennium or even the twelfth century AD (findings by Carswell 1975–1977, Litster 2016). It may be, however, that an earlier and different set of relationships linked the two areas, perhaps partly through overland routes: certainly Vogel and Hieronymus (1993) and Yang (2004, 2019) have suggested that some or all of the cowries used in Yunnan, southwest China, originated in the Maldives. The detailed assessment carried out on an archaeological cowrie assemblage recovered in Mauritania (Christie and Haour 2018a) shows the value of such work in elucidating provenance and could profitably be applied to the material from Yunnan that is held in museum collections in Kunming and elsewhere.

More broadly, the Maldives may have been a party to two distinct phases of interaction between India and China, of the sort discussed by Sen (2006): one, in the first five or six centuries of the second millennium, primarily through maritime routes and linked to Islam, but preceded by an earlier phase, moderated by Buddhism, in the first millennium AD and mainly overland. After all, it is said that the Buddhist monk and translator Fa Hsien travelled by foot from China to India to spend several years there at the beginning of the fifth century, supposedly mentioning islands near Sri Lanka. Findings from the site of Kaashidhoo may offer important insights: the preliminary account of the work reports the recovery of tens of thousands of cowrie shells, an apparent votive deposit dated to the second part of the first millennium AD, and small finds that include a Chinese coin (Mikkelsen 2000).

The archaeology of the Maldives shows the importance of anthropologically informed examinations of what constitutes value, and how it is created by given individuals and societies. Models such as world systems theory emphasise the categorisation of different types of objects—commodity, raw product, prestige item, and so forth. In the case of the Kinolhas materials, however, such classifications are not straightforward—perhaps partly because of the specific geographical context, which lacked stone, ore, and clay. Ibn Battuta reported that a single pot might cost several chickens, but he also stated that ceramics of Chinese manufacture were widely used, at least within the segment of Maldives society with whom he socialised. The small number of beads recovered during excavation, and the larger number of bangles, appear to be made of glass of Indian origin. The bangles in particular are described as being 'heavily laden with social symbolism and economic aspiration' (Chapter 8) and their small size suggests they may have belonged to children. They were probably worn for their effect of sound as well as colour and would have presumably been complemented by other items of personal adornment made from locally occurring materials. The archaeological assemblage included at least one chank bracelet, and local bivalve shells, recovered in excavations at Kinolhas and other sites (Chapter 9), were described by informants as items for decoration and adornment.

The matters of structured deposition and curation open other lines of enquiry. Some of the beads recovered within the small ceramic vessel, and a bowl of Middle Eastern origin retrieved in the rubble of a funerary monument, predate by some centuries the likely date of their deposition. Other artefacts, such as an electrum pendant and a few extremely high-quality items of Chinese ceramics, probably safely fall into the category of valuables. Ironically, however, a clear insight into construction of value by the past community of Kinolhas comes through a purely local product, in the form of the several caches of cowries that were encountered, some of which in association with funerary monuments. They confirm the value attached locally to these shells, which parallels the economic and symbolic importance that was allocated to them in many marketplaces around the medieval world.

The research presented here offers a first archaeological examination of medieval period contexts in the Maldives. As such, some specifically archaeological directions for future study can now be suggested, particularly in view of the challenges posed by the sandy, shallow stratigraphies of Maldivian sites, the heavy vegetation, and the strong prevalence of perishable materials (wood, fibres) within the suite of traditional material culture.

As regards the island of Kinolhas itself, further survey is important. The dense vegetation on the eastern half of the island impedes archaeological visibility, but a preliminary assessment was begun in 2019—and is particularly relevant as the modern settlement is currently expanding in this direction. The site described in the present book, which lies at the western end of the island, almost certainly represents just a few pages of a longer-term story. One hypothesis to test is that this medieval settlement was replaced by another site elsewhere on the island, possibly in response to changes in shipping technology or shorelines. The patterns of distribution of ceramics of various dates will be fundamental here. As noted in Chapter 6, the units excavated by our team unearthed some later ceramic materials, extending to the seventeenth century, and it may be that some were brought from a later site on the island, as part of an ongoing process of refuse management.

In a more general sense, techniques from archaeological science, so far little deployed in the Maldives, offer promising lines of enquiry. First, the provenancing of cowrie shells through isotopic studies, while it still poses challenges (Leng and Lewis 2016), will offer fundamental insights. Cowries are the iconic export product of the Maldives, and as such the archipelago has almost certainly overshadowed other production locales. Another strand of inquiry should involve geoarchaeological sampling in order to determine whether the archaeologically ephemeral houses of the Maldives can be identified through changes in soil chemistry, as has been achieved on the East African coast (Chapter 9). Third, petrographic studies of potsherds from the extremely varied Kinolhas earthenware assemblage may identify their origin and suggest the functions and values of ceramics: items of commercial trade, personal belongings, prestige gifts, etc. Lastly, geological studies of the variety of imported stone recovered in the Maldives will clarify provenance and perhaps function, both during transit and upon arrival.

Despite, or perhaps because of, the context in which it is being finalised—in the midst of a global pandemic and increasing warnings of a climate emergency—this book has avoided the enormous subjects of the archaeology of disaster and climate change (Witcher 2020). Given this context and the rapid pace of expansion and infrastructure development within the Maldives, the question of archaeological mitigation is, however, pressing. Our hope is that this book will play a role in highlighting the rich historical and cultural foundation on which the modern nation-state, and its tourist industry based on stunning natural beauty, beaches, and marine wildlife, have been built.

Note

1 Such arguments have, of course, been made for the use of certain trans-Saharan routes over time.

Bibliography

Abdurazakov, A. A., 2009. Central Asian glassmaking during the ancient and medieval periods. *In*: G. Fuxi, R. Brill and T. Shouyun, eds. *Ancient glass research along the Silk Road*. Singapore: World Scientific, 201–219.

Abe, Y., et al., 2012. Transition in the use of cobalt-blue colorant in the New Kingdom of Egypt. *Journal of Archaeological Science*, 39, 1793–1808.

Abe, Y., et al., 2018. Ancient glassware travelled the Silk Road: Nondestructive X-ray fluorescence analysis of a fragment of a facet-cut glass vessel collected at Kamigamo Shrine in Kyoto, Japan. *Journal of Archaeological Science: Reports*, 20, 362–368.

Abe, Y. and Shikaku, R., 2020. Report of chemical compositional characterisation of glass fragments excavated from Dariali Fort (Georgia) by non-destructive X-ray fluorescence analysis. *In*: E. W. Sauer, ed. *Dariali: The 'Caspian Gates' in the Caucasus from antiquity to the age of the Huns and the Middle Ages*. Oxford: Oxbow Books, 593–602.

Abe, Y., Shikaku, R., and Nakai, I., 2018. Ancient glassware travelled the Silk Road: Nondestructive X-ray fluorescence analysis of tiny glass fragments believed to be sampled from glassware excavated from Niizawa Senzuka Tumulus No. 126, Japan. *Journal of Archaeological Science: Reports*, 17, 212–219.

Ahmad, Y. and Jameel, M., 2012. *Coral stone mosques of Maldives towards World Heritage Nomination: Phase 1 of preparation for a World Heritage serial nomination Final Report*. Male': Department of Heritage.

Alexandre, Y., 2012. *Mary's well, Nazareth: The late Hellenistic to the Ottoman periods (IAA Reports 49)*. Jerusalem: Israel Antiquities Authority.

Allan, J., 1912. The coinage of the Maldive islands with some notes on the cowrie and larin. *The Numismatic Chronicle and Journal of the Royal Numismatic Society, Fourth Series*, 12, 313–332.

Ambers, J., et al., 2014. *Looted, recovered, returned: Antiquities from Afghanistan*. A detailed scientific and conservation record of a group of ivory and bone furniture overlays excavated at Begram, stolen from the National Museum of Afghanistan, privately acquired on behalf of Kabul, analysed and conserved at the British Museum and returned to the National Museum of Afghanistan in 2012. Oxford: Archaeopress Archaeology.

Andersen, S. F., 2007. *The Tylos period burials in Bahrain, Vol. 1: The glass and pottery vessels*. Manama: Culture and National Heritage, Kingdom of Bahrain, in association with Moesgard Museum and Aarhus University.

Beaujard, P., 2007. East Africa, the Comoros Islands and Madagascar before the sixteenth century: On a neglected part of the world system. *Azania: Archaeological Research in Africa*, 42, 15–35.

Beaujard, P. and Fee, S., 2005. The Indian Ocean in Eurasian and African World-Systems before the sixteenth century. *Journal of World History*, 16 (4), 411–465.

Begley, V., 1988. Rouletted ware at Arikamedu: A new approach. *American Journal of Archaeology*, 92 (3), 427–440.

Begley, V., 1996. Pottery from the northern sector, 1989–1992. *In*: V. Begley, P. Francis Jr., I. Mahadevan, K. V. Raman, S. E. Sidebotham, K. Warner Slane, and E. Lyding Will, eds. *The ancient port of Arikamedu: New excavations and researches 1989–1992*, Vol. 1. Pondichéry: Ecole française d'Extrême-Orient, 115–285.

Begley, V., 2004. Pottery from the 1992 excavations in the southern sector. *In*: V. Begley, P. Francis Jr., N. Karashima, K. V. Raman, S. E. Sidebotham, and E. Lyding Will, eds. *The ancient port of Arikamedu: New excavations and researches 1989–1992*, Vol. 2. Paris: Ecole française d'Extrême-orient, 104–323.

Bell, H. C. P., 1883. *The Maldive Islands: An account of the physical features, climate, history, inhabitants, productions, and trade*. Colombo: Government Printer.

Bell, H. C. P., 1921. *The Maldive Islands: Report on a Visit to Male', Ceylon Sessional Paper No. 15 of 1921*. Colombo: Government Record Office.

Bell, H. C. P., 1924. Excerpta Maldiviana n°3, 'Dives Akuru Gravestone Epitaphs'. *Journal of the Ceylon Branch of the Royal Asiatic Society*, XXIX (77), 283–303.

Bell, H. C. P., 1925. Excerpta Maldiviana: No. 4: A description of the Maldive Islands circa A. C. 1683. *Journal of the Royal Asiatic Society*, 30 (78), 132–145.

Bell, H. C. P., 1931. Excerpta Maldiviana: No. 9: Lomafanu. *JCBRAS*, XXXI (83): 539–578.

Bell, H. C. P., 2002 [1940]. *The Maldive islands: Monograph on this history, archaeology and epigraphy*. Male': Novelty Printers and Publishers (Reprinted from Ceylon Branch of the Royal Asiatic Society, Colombo).

Bertius, P., 1618. *Description de zeilan, et des isles maldives*. Amsterdam: Jodocus Hondius. British Library: BLL01014498551.

BJDXKGWBXY, JXSWWKGYJS, and JDZSTCKGYJS, 2009. 景德镇出土明代御窑瓷器 Jingdezhen Chutu Mingdai Yuyao Ciqi. Beijing: Wenwu Chubanshe.

BJSWWYJS, 2007. 毛家湾明代瓷器坑考古发掘报告 Maojiawan Mingdai Ciqi Keng Kaogu Fajue Baogao. Beijing: Kexue Chubanshe.

Blackman, W. S., 1968. *The Fellahin of Upper Egypt: Their religious, social and industrial life, with special reference to survivals from ancient times*. London: Frank Cass and Co. Ltd.

Borell, B., 2010. Glass from China and from India: Finds of vessel glass from Fourteenth Century Singapore. *Archipel*, 80, 139–196.

Boulogne, S. and Hardy-Guilbert, C., 2010. Glass bangles of Al Shihr, Hadramawt. *Proceedings of the Seminar for Arabian Studies*, 40, 135–148.

Boulogne, S. and Henderson, J., 2009. Indian glass in the Middle East? Medieval and Ottoman glass bangles from Central Jordan. *Journal of Glass Studies*, 59, 53–75.

Bovill, E. W., 1958. *The golden trade of the Moors*. London: Oxford University Press.

Bovill, E. W., 1968. *The golden trade of the Moors*. London: Oxford University Press.

Bramoullé, D., 2012. The Fatimids and the Red Sea 969–1171. *In*: D. A. Agius, J. P. Cooper, A. Trakadas, and C. Zazzaro, eds. *Navigated spaces, connected places: Proceedings of the Red Sea Project V* held at the University of Exeter, 16–19 September 2010. BAR, 127–136.

Breen, C. and Lane, P. J., 2003. Archaeological approaches to East Africa's changing seascapes. *World Archaeology*, 35 (3), 469–489.

Brill, R. H., 1999. *Chemical analyses of early glasses*. 2 vols. New York: The Corning Museum of Glass.

Brill, R. H., 2003. *The glassmakers of Firozabad and the glassmakers of Kapadwanj: Two pilot video projects, Annales du 15e Congrès de l'Association Internationale pour l'histoire du verre, Corning New York, 2001*. Nottingham, UK: AIHV, 267–268.

Brown, R. M., 2009. *The Ming Gap and shipwreck ceramics in Southeast Asia: Towards a chronology of Thai trade ware*. Bangkok: Siam Society.

Burgess, L. and Dussubieux, L., 2008. Chemical composition of late eighteenth and nineteenth century glass beads from North America: Clues to sourcing beads. *Beads*, 19, 58–73.

Burkholder, G., 1984. *An Arabian collection: Artifacts from the Eastern province*. Boulder City, NV: GB Publications.

Carswell, J., 1975–1977. China and Islam in the Maldive Islands. *Transactions of the Oriental Ceramic Society*, 41, 119–198.

Carswell, J., Deraniyagala, S., and Graham, A., 2013. *Mantai: City by the sea*. Aichwald: Linden Soft.

Chakravarti, R., 2015. Indian trade through Jewish geniza letters 1000–1300. *Studies in People's History*, 21, 27–40.

Chandima, A., 2006. 斯里兰卡藏中国古代文物研究—兼谈古代中斯贸易关系 *A critical examination of ancient economic relationships between China and Sri Lanka based on Sri Lankan artifacts*.

Chen, K., 2012. A sixty year's study of Yuan Dynasty Blue-and-White. *In*: Shanghai Museum, ed. *Splendos in Smalt* 幽蓝神采. Shanghai: Shanghai Museum, 12–29.

Chittick, N., 1974. *Kilwa: An Islamic trading city on the East African coast*. 2 vols. Nairobi: British Institute in East Africa.

Chittick, N., 1984. *Manda: Excavations at an island port on the Kenya coast*. British Institute in Eastern Africa Memoir, 9. Nairobi: British Institute in Eastern Africa.

Christie, A. C., 2011. *Exploring the social context of maritime exploitation in the Mafia Archipelago, Tanzania: An archaeological perspective*. Ph.D. Dissertation, University of York.

Christie, A. C., in prep. *Maritime practices in the Maldives: An ethnographic study*.

Christie, A. C., Grant, A., and Haour, A., 2019. Cataloging cowries: A standardized strategy to record six key species of cowrie shell from the West African archaeological record. *African Archaeological Review*, 36 (4), 479–504.

Christie, A. C. and Haour, A., 2018a. The 'Lost Caravan' of Ma'den Ijafen revisited: Re-appraising its cargo of cowries, a medieval global commodity. *Journal of African Archaeology*, 16, 1–20.

Christie, A. C. and Haour, A., 2018b. The cowrie shells. *In*: A. Haour, ed. *Two thousand years in Dendi, Northern Benin: Archaeology, history and memory*. Leiden: Brill/JAAMS, 205–210.

Colley, S., 1990. The analysis and interpretation of archaeological fish remains. *Archaeological Method and Theory*, 2, 207–253.

Collinet, A., 2010. *Au prisme de la céramique: le Sind et l'islam: culture matérielle du sud du Pakistan, IIe-XIIe/VIIIe-XVIIIe siècles*. Ph.D. thesis, Sorbonne.

Collinet, A., 2015. Les céramiques de l'Inde et du Sind. *In*: A. Rougeulle, ed. *Sharma—un entrepôt de commerce médiéval sur la côte du Ḥaḍramawt Yémen, ca 980–1180*. British Foundation for the Study of Arabia Monographs (formerly Society for Arabian Studies Monographs) 17. Oxford: Archaeopress, 165–168.

Conder, C. R., 1879. *Tent work in Palestine: A record of discovery and adventure*. 2 vols. London: Richard Bentley and Son.

Coningham, R., et al., 2006. *Anuradhapura: The British-Sri Lankan excavations at Anuradhapura Salgaha Watta 2, Vol. II: The artefacts* (BAR International Series 1508 / Society for South Asian Studies Monographs 4). Oxford: Archaeopress.

Cooper, J., 2014. *The medieval Nile: Route, navigation, and landscape in Islamic Egypt*. Cairo: American University in Cairo Press.

Crowther, A., Faulkner, P., Prendergast, M.E., Quintana Morales, E.M., Horton, M., Wilmsen, E., Kotarba-Morley, A.M., Christie, A., Petek, N., Tibesasa, R., Douka, K., Picornell-Gelabert, L., Carah, X., Boivin, N., 2016. Coastal Subsistence, Maritime Trade, and the Colonization of Small Offshore Islands in Eastern African Prehistory, The Journal of Island and Coastal Archaeology, 11: 211–237.

Denemark, R. A., et al., 2000, eds. *World system history: The social science of long-term change*. London: Routledge.

De Vincenz, A., 2017. Ottoman pottery and glass bracelets from Yafo (Jaffa), Jerusalem boulevard and its vicinity. *'Atiqot*, 88, 115–129.

Deyell, J. S., 2010. Cowries and coins: The dual monetary system of the Bengal Sultanate. *Indian Economic and Social History Review*, 47 (1), 63–106.

Didi, M. I., 1995. Maldives through Pyrard's pen. *Malas*, 55, 1–457.

Djingov, G., 1978. Bracelets en verre à décor peint de la Bulgarie mediévale. *Annales du 7e Congres International d'Etude Historique du Verre, Berlin—Leipzig 15–21 août 1977*, 149–157. Liège.

Doe, B., 1971. *Southern Arabia*. London: Thames and Hudson.

Dreyer, E., 2007. *Zheng He: China and the oceans in the early Ming dynasty, 1403–1433*. New York: Pearson/Longman.

Duarte, R. T., 1993. *Northern Mozambique in the Swahili World: An archaeological approach*. Studies in African Archaeology 4. Stockholm, Maputo, Uppsala: Central Board of National Antiquities.

Duarte, R. T., 2012. Maritime history in Mozambique and East Africa: The urgent need for the proper study and preservation of endangered underwater cultural heritage. *Journal of Maritime Archaeology*, 7, 63–86.

Duckworth, C. N., et al., 2016. End of line? Glass bangles, technology, recycling, and trade in Islamic North Africa. *Journal of Glass Studies*, 58, 135–169.

During Caspers, E. C. L., 1980. *The Bahrain tumuli*. An illustrated catalogue of two important collections. Leiden: Nederlands Historisch—Archaeologisch Instituut—te Istanbul.

Dussubieux, L., 2009. Compositional analysis of ancient glass fragments from North Sumatra, Indonesia. *In*: D. Perret and H. Surachman, eds. *Histoire de Barus III: Regards sur une place marchande de l'océan Indien XIIe—milieu du XVIIe s*. Paris: Association Archipel/EFEO, 385–417.

Dussubieux, L., 2010. Glass material from Singapore. *Archipel*, 80, 197–209.

Dussubieux, L., et al., 2008. The trading of ancient glass beads: New analytical data from South Asian and East African soda—alumina glass beads. *Archaeometry*, 50 (5), 797–821.

Dussubieux, L. and Gratuze, B., 2003. Nature et origine des objets en verre retrouvés à Begram Afghanistan et à Bara Pakistan. *In*: O. Bopearachchi, C. Landes, and C. Sachs, eds. *De l'Indus à l'Oxus: Archéologie de l'Asie Centrale*. Lattes: Association Imago, Musée de Lattes, 315–323.

Dussubieux, L., Gratuze, B., and Blet-Lemarquand, M., 2010. Mineral soda alumina glass: Occurrence and meaning. *Journal of Archaeological Science*, 37, 1646–1655.

Dussubieux, L. and Kanungo, A., 2013. Trace element analysis of glass from Kopia. *In*: A. Kanungo, ed. *Glass in ancient India: Excavations at Kopia*. Triruvananthapuram: KCHR, 360–366.

Dussubieux, L., Wood, M., 2021. Indian glass: chronology and distribution in Eastern Africa, in: Kanungo, A.K. and Dussubieux, L, eds. *Ancient Glass of South Asia—Archaeology, Ethnography and Global Connections*. Singapore: Springer Nature and Gandhinagar: IIT Gandhinagar, 511–532.

Edwards, A. J., n.d. Sea-level rise and the Maldives, Indian Ocean. Unpublished Manuscript.

Egami, N., 1974. Migration of the cowrie-shell culture in East Asia. *Acta asiatica*, 26, 1–52.

Einzig, P. 1949. *Primitive money in its ethnological, historical and economic aspects*. London: Eyre & Spottiswoode.

Federeci, C. and Hickock, T., 1588. *The voyage and travaile: Of M. Caesar frederick, merchant of Venice, into the East India, the Indies, and beyond, wherein are contained very pleasant and rare matters, with the customes and rites of those countries. Also, herein are discovered the merchandises and commodities of those countreyes, aswell the aboundance of goulde and silver, as spices, drugges, pearles, and other jewelles*. London: Richard Jones and Edward White. Available from: https://quod.lib.umich.edu/e/eebo/A00611.0001.001?rgn=main;view=fulltext

Feener, M., 2018. *Maldives heritage survey* [Online]. Available from: http://maldivesheritage.oxcis.ac.uk/ [Accessed 8 March 2021].

Feener, M., 2019. New documentation at Kuruhinna Tharaagadu. *In*: M. Feener, ed. *Maldives heritage survey*. Available from: https://maldivesheritage.oxcis.ac.uk [Accessed 23 October 2020].

Feener, M., 2021a. Maldives. *In*: K. Fleet, G. Krämer, D. Matringe, J. Nawas, and E. Rowson, eds. *The encyclopedia of Islam, III*. Leiden: Brill.

Feener M., 2021b. *Ziyaarat on Hithadhoo: Maldives heritage survey database entry LAM-HTD-3*. Available from: https://maldivesheritage.oxcis.ac.uk/index.php/3d-models/mosques-cemeteries-and-muslim-funerary-monuments/ziyaarat-on-hithadhoo/ [Accessed 22 March 2021].

Feener M., 2021c. *Kuda Ziyaarat, Kaafu: Maldives heritage survey database entry KFA-HMF-1*. Available from: https://maldivesheritage.oxcis.ac.uk/index.php/3d-models/mosques-cemeteries-and-muslim-funerary-monuments/kuda-ziyaarat-kaafu [Accessed 22 March 2021].

Feener, M. and Daly, P., 2018. Maldives heritage survey. Unpublished proposal to the Department of Heritage, Male'.

Feener, M., et al., 2021. The Maldives heritage survey. Antiquity Project Gallery.

Feng, Xianming, 2009. 中国陶瓷 *Zhongguo Taoci* [*Chinese Ceramics*]. Shanghai: Shanghai Guji Chubanshe.

Finlay, R., 2008. The voyages of Zheng He: Ideology, state power, and maritime trade in Ming China. *Journal of the Historical Society*, 8 (3), 327–347.

Fleisher, J., et al., 2015. When did the Swahili become maritime? *American Anthropologist*, 117 (1), 100–115.

Fleisher, J. and LaViolette, A., 1999. Elusive wattle-and-daub: Finding the hidden majority in the archaeology of the Swahili, AZANIA. *Journal of the British Institute in Eastern Africa*, 34, 1

Forbes, A. D. W., 1980. Archives and resources for Maldivian history. *Journal of South Asian Studies III*, 1, 70–82.

Forbes, A. D. W., 1981. Southern Arabia and the Islamicisation of the Central Indian Ocean Archipelagoes. *Archipel*, 21, 55–92.

Forbes, A. D. W., 1983. The Mosque in the Maldive Islands: A preliminary historical survey. *Archipel*, 26, 43–74.

Forbes, A. D. W., 1984. A Roman Republican denarius of c. 90 B.C., from the Maldive Islands, Indian Ocean. *Archipel*, 28, 53–60.

Forbes, A. D. W., 1987. The 'Čīn-Hǫ' Yunnanese Chinese caravan trade with North Thailand during the late nineteenth and early twentieth centuries. *Journal of Asian History*, 21, 1–47.

Forbes, A. D. W. and Henley, D., 2011. *China's ancient Tea Horse Road*. 2nd ed. Los Gatos, CA: Cognoscenti Books.

Forrest, I. and Haour, A., 2018. Trust in long-distance relationships, 1000–1600 CE. *Past & Present*, 238 (13), 190–213.

Foy, D., 2015. Les verres. *In*: A. Rougeulle, ed. *Sharma: un entrepôt de commerce médiéval sur la côte du Hadramawt (Yémen, ca 980–1180)* (British Foundation for the Study of Arabia Monographs, 17). Oxford: Archaeopress Archaeology, 323–367.

Francis Jr., P., 2002. *Asia's maritime bead trade: 300 B.C. to the present*. Honolulu, HI: University of Hawai'i Press.

Frifelt, K., 2001. *Islamic remains in Bahrain*. Moesgaard: Jutland Archaeological Society.

Fuxi, G., 2009. Origin and evolution of ancient Chinese glass. *In*: G. Fuxi, R. H. Brill, and T. Shouyun, eds. *Ancient glass research along the Silk Road*. Singapore: World Scientific, 1–40.

Gaborieau, M., 1977. Bracelets et grosses perles de verre: Fabrication en verte en Indie et au Népal. *Objets et Mondes*, 17, 112–117.

Garlake, P. S., 1978. Fieldwork at al-Huwailah, site 23. *In*: B. de Cardi, ed. *Qatar Archaeological Report: Excavations 1973*. Oxford: Oxford University Press/Qatar National Museum, 172–179, pls XXIX–XXX.

GGBWY, Department of Antiquities and Museums of Ras al-Khaimah, Department of Archaeology of Durham University, and JLDXKGX, 2020 Archaeological findings from al-Mataf, excavation 2019 in Ras al-Khaimah, the UAE [拉丝海马阿尔玛塔夫遗址 2019 年考古收获]. *Journal of the Palace Museum* [故宫博物院院刊].

Gibb, H. A. R., 1929. *Ibn Battuta: Travels in Asia and Africa 1325–1354*. London: Routledge and Kegan Paul LTD Broadway House.

Gill, M. S., 2017. A single ingredient for primary glass production: Reassessing traditional glass manufacture in Northern India. *Journal of Glass Studies*, 59, 249–259.

Gogte, V., et al., 2006. The ancient port at Chaul. *Journal of Indian Ocean Archaeology*, 3, 62–80.

Goitein, S. D., 1973. *Letters of medieval Jewish traders*. Princeton, NJ: Princeton University Press.

Goitein, S. D. and Friedman, M. A. 2008. India Traders of the Middle Ages: Documents from the Cairo Geniza ('India Book'). Leiden: Brill.

Graham, A., 2013. Pottery from the excavated sequence in Trenches H and G. *In*: J. Carswell, S. Deraniyagala, and A. Graham, eds. *Mantai: City by the sea*. Aichwald: Linden Soft, 191–212.

Gratuze, B., 1999. Obsidian characterization by laser ablation ICP–MS and its application to prehistoric trade in the Mediterranean and the Near East: Sources and distribution of obsidian within the Aegean and Anatolia. *Journal of Archaeological Science*, 26, 869–881.

Gray, A. and Bell, H. C. P., 1887. *The voyage of François Pyrard of Laval to the East Indies, the Maldives, the Moluccas and Brazil*. London: Hakluyt Society.

Guo, L., 2004. *Commerce, culture, and community in a Red Sea port in the thirteenth century: The Arabic documents from Quseir*. Leiden: Brill.

Gutman, P., 2001. The Martaban trade: An examination of the literature from the seventh century until the eighteenth century. *Asian Perspectives*, 40 (1), 108–118.

Hansman, J., 1985. *Julfar, an Arabian port: Its settlement and far Eastern ceramic trade from the 14th to the 18th centuries*. London: The Royal Asiatic Society of Great Britain and Ireland.

Haour, A., 2013. *Outsiders and strangers: An archaeology of liminality in West Africa*. Oxford: Oxford University Press.

Haour, A., 2017. What made Islamic trade distinctive—as compared to pre-Islamic trade? *In*: D. J. Mattingly, V. Leitch, C. N. Duckworth, A. Cuénod, M. Sterry, and F. Cole, eds. *Trade in the ancient Sahara and beyond: Trans-Saharan archaeology*, Vol. I, Series editor D. J. Mattingly. Cambridge: Cambridge University Press and The Society for Libyan Studies, 80–100.

Haour, A. and Christie, A., 2019. Cowries in the archaeology of West Africa: The present picture. *Azania*, 54, 287–321.

Haour, A., Christie, A., and Jaufar, S., 2016. Tracking the cowrie shell: Excavations in the Maldives, 2016. *Nyame Akuma*, 85, 69–77.

Haour, A., et al., 2017. Back to Ibn Battuta's island—Excavations in the Maldives, 2017. *Nyame Akuma*, 88, 33–40.

Harrison-Hall, J., 2001. *Ming ceramics in the British Museum*. London: The British Museum Press.

Harrison-Hall, J. and Krahl, R., 2009. *Chinese ceramics: Highlights of the Sir Percival David Collection*. London: British Museum Press.

Harrisson, T., 1958. The Ming Gap and Kota Batu, Brunei. *Sarawak Museum Journal*, 8 (11), 273–277.

Hawkes, J. D. and Wynne-Jones, S., 2015. India in Africa: Trade goods and connections of the late first millennium. *Afriques: débats, méthodes et terrains d'histoire*, 6. Available from: https://afriques.revues.org/1752

Heimann, J., 1980. Small change and ballast: Cowry trade and usage as an example of Indian Ocean economic history. *Journal of South Asian Studies*, 3 (1), 48–69.

Heyerdahl, T., 1986. *The Maldive mystery*. Chevy Chase, MD: Adler and Adler Publishers Inc.

Higham, C., 1996. *The Bronze Age of southeast Asia*. Cambridge: Cambridge University Press.

Hiskett, M. 1966. Materials relating to the cowry currency of the Western Sudan--II: Reflections on the provenance and diffusion of the cowry in the Sahara and the Sudan. *Bulletin of the School of Oriental and African Studies, University of London*, 29(2), 339–366.

Hogendorn, J. and Johnson, M., 2003 [1986]. *The Shell money of the slave trade*. Cambridge: Cambridge University Press.

Horton, M., 1996. *Shanga: The archaeology of a Muslim trading community on the coast of East Africa*. London: British Institute in East Africa (BIEA Memoirs, 14).

Horton, M., 2004. Artisans, communities, and commodities: Medieval exchanges between Northwestern India and East Africa. *Ars Orientalis: Communities and Commodities: Western India and the Indian Ocean, Eleventh-Fifteenth Centuries*, 34, 62–80.

Horton, M., Brown, H. W., and Mudida, N., 1996. *Shanga: The archaeology of a Muslim trading community on the coast of East Africa*. London: British Institute in Eastern Africa.

Hourani, G. F., 1995 [1951]. *Arab seafaring in the Indian Ocean in ancient and early medieval times*. Revised and expanded by John Carswell. Princeton, NJ: Princeton University Press.

Hrbek, I., 1977. Egypt, Nubia and the eastern deserts. *In*: R. Oliver, ed. *Cambridge history of Africa, Vol. 3: c. 1050-c. 1600*. Cambridge: Cambridge University Press, 10–97.

Hunt, L. B., 1976. The true story of Purple of Cassius. *The Gold Bulletin*, 9 (4), 134–139.

Hunter, F. M., 1877. *An account of the British settlement of Aden in Arabia*. London: Trübner and Co.

Husain, M., 1976. *The Rehla of Ibn Battuta- India, Maldive Islands and Ceylon- Translation and Commentary*. Baroda: Oriental Institute.

Insoll, T., 2015. *Material explorations in African Archaeology*. Oxford: Oxford University Press.

Insoll, T., 2021. Marine shell working at Harlaa, Ethiopia, and the implications for Red Sea trade. *Journal of African Archaeology*, 19, 1–24.

Insoll, T., et al., 2005. *The land of Enki in the Islamic era: Pearls, palms, and religious identity in Bahrain*. London: Kegan Paul.

Iroko, F., 1987. *Les cauris en Afrique occidentale du Xe au XXe siècle*. Ph.D. thesis, Sorbonne.

Issawi, C., ed., 1966. *The economic history of the Middle East 1800–1914: A book of readings*. Chicago: University of Chicago Press.

Jameel, M., 2012. *Architectural typological study of coral stone mosques of Maldives*. MA Thesis, University of Malaya Kirshenblatt Gimblett, Kuala Lumpur.

Jameel, M. and Ahmad, Y., 2016. *Coral stone mosques of Maldives: The vanishing legacy of the Indian Ocean*. Los Angeles, CA: Gulf Pacific Press.

Jaufar, S., 2012. Excavation of a bathing tank in Ha. Utheemu. Unpublished Report to Department of Heritage, Male'.

Jaufar, S., 2013. Coral stone mosques of Maldives toward World Heritage List. *ACCU Nara International Correspondent: The Twelfth Regular Report*, 12, 21–22. Available from: www.nara.accu.or.jp/img/dissemination/12th.pdf

Jaufar, S., 2014. Test excavations carried out at A. Dh Fenfushi and HA. Ihavandhoo for 'Coral stone mosques of Maldives towards World Heritage List' project. *ACCU Nara International Correspondent: The Thirteenth Regular Report*, 13, 20–21. Available from: www.nara.accu.or.jp/img/dissemination/13th.pdf

Jaufar, S., 2015a. Detailed survey of R. Meedhoo ancient mosque and its boundary for 'Coral stone mosques of Maldives towards World Heritage List' project. *ACCU Nara International Correspondent: The Fourteenth Regular Report*, 14, 28–29. Available from: www.nara.accu.or.jp/img/dissemination/14th.pdf

Jaufar, S., 2015b. Excavation of a bathing tank at Kandhuvalu Mosque in Ha. Utheemu. *ACCU Nara International Correspondent: The Fifteenth Regular Report*, 15, 33–34. Available from: www.nara.accu.or.jp/img/dissemination/15th.pdf

Jaufar, S., 2016. Excavation of a newly discovered ancient structure in Ha. Ihavandhoo. *ACCU Nara International Correspondent: The Sixteenth Regular Report*, 16, 24–27. Available from: www.nara.accu.or.jp/img/dissemination/16th.pdf

Jaufar, S., 2017a. Archaeological research on Buddhism in the Maldives. *In*: S. Garg, ed. *Archaeological of Buddhism: Recent discoveries in South Asia*. New Delhi: Manohar Publishers and Distributors, 207–210.

Jaufar, S., 2017b. Cowrie–An early global commodity: An archaeological research on the Islamic period of the Maldive Islands. *ACCU Nara International Correspondent: The Seventeenth Regular Report*, 17, 30–32. Available from: www.nara.accu.or.jp/img/dissemination/17th.pdf

Jaufar, S., 2017c. Second season of excavation in the Maldives for the 'Cowrie shells: An early global commodity' project, 2017. *ACCU Nara International Correspondent: The eighteenth regular Report*, 18, 27–30. Available from: www.nara.accu.or.jp/img/dissemination/18th.pdf

Jaufar, S., 2018. Documenting the endangered Heritage of the Maldives: Maldives heritage survey project. *ACCU Nara International Correspondent: The Twentieth Regular Report*, 20, 14–15. Available from: www.nara.accu.or.jp/img/dissemination/20th.pdf

Jaufar, S., 2019. *An archaeological study of the Maldive Islands: Investigating the Islamic period settlements*. Ph.D. thesis, University of East Anglia. Available from: https://core.ac.uk/download/pdf/231838599.pdf

Jennings, J., 2011. *Globalizations and the ancient world*. Cambridge: Cambridge University Press.

Ji, L., 2016. Archaeological excavation at inside of the Palace: The excavation of the ceramic burial pit of the Grand South storage in the Forbidden City in 2014 [皇宫大内的考古发掘—2014 年故宫南大库瓷片埋藏坑的考古发掘]. *Forbidden City* [紫禁城], 11 (262), 44–51.

Johnson, M., 1970. The cowrie currencies of West Africa: Part I. *The Journal of African History*, 11 (1), 17–49.

Kalus, L. and Guillot, C., 2005. Inscriptions islamiques en arabe de l'archipel des Maldives. *Archipel*, 70, 15–52.

Kawatoko, M., 1995. *A port city site on the Sinai Peninsula: al-Tur Area: The 11th expedition in 1994 (A summary report)*. Tokyo: The Middle Eastern Culture Center in Japan.

Kawatoko, M., 1996. *A port city site on the Sinai Peninsula: al-Tur Area: The 12th expedition in 1995 (A summary report)*. Tokyo: The Middle Eastern Culture Center in Japan.

Kawatoko, M., 1998. *A port city site on the Sinai Peninsula: al-Tur Area: The 13th expedition in 1996 (A summary report)*. Tokyo: The Middle Eastern Culture Center in Japan.

Kench, P. S. and Brander, R. W. 2006. Response of reef island shorelines to seasonal climate oscillations: South Maalhosmadulu Atoll, Maldives. Journal of Geophysical Research Earth Surface 111(F1). https://doi.org/10.1029/2005JF000323

Kennet, D., 1994. Jazīrat al-Ḥulayla: Early Julfār. *Journal of the Royal Asiatic Society*, 4 (2), 163–212.

Kennet, D., 2004. *Sasanian and Islamic pottery from Ras al-Khaimah: Classification, chronology and analysis of trade in the Western Indian Ocean*. Oxford: Archaeopress, Society for Arabian studies.

Kenoyer, J. M., 1984. Shell-working industries of the Indus Civilization: A summary. *Paléorient*, 10 (1), 49–63.

Kerr, R. and Wood, N., 2004. *Science and civilisation in China, Vol. 5: Chemistry and chemical technology: Part 12, ceramic technology, Vol. 12: Ceramic technology*. Cambridge: Cambridge University Press.

Kock, J. and Sode, T., 1995. *Glass, glassbeads and glassmakers in Northern India*. Vanløse: THOT Print.

Kovács, L., 2008. *Vulvae, eyes, snake heads: Archaeological finds of cowrie amulets*. Archaeopress: BAR International Series.

Krahl, R., 1986. *Chinese Ceramics in the Topkapi Saray Museum Istanbul: A complete catalogue, Vol. II: Yuan and Ming Dynasty Porcelains*. Sotheby's Publications.

Kühn, H., 1968. Lead–tin yellow. *Studies in Conservation*, 13, 7–33.

Lambourn, E., 2008. Tombstones, texts, and typologies: Seeing sources for the early history of Islam in Southeast Asia. *Journal of the Economic and Social History of the Orient*, 51, 252–286.

Lambourn, E., 2018a. *Abraham's luggage–A social life of things in the medieval Indian Ocean world*. Cambridge: Cambridge University Press.

Lambourn, E., 2018b. India in the 'India Book': 12th Century northern Malabar through Geniza documents. *In*: C. Hardy-Guilbert, H. Renel, A. Rougeulle, and E. Vallet, eds. *Sur les chemins d'Onagre—Histoire et archéologie orientales—Hommage à Monik Kervran*. Oxford: Archaeopress, 71–84.

Lane, A. and Serjeant, R. B., 1948. Pottery and glass fragments from the Aden littoral, with historic notes. *Journal of the Royal Asiatic Society*, 2, 108–133.

Leng, M. J. and Lewis, J. P., 2016. Oxygen isotopes in molluscan shell: Applications in environmental archaeology. *Environmental Archaeology*, 21 (3), 295–306.

Levathes, L., 1994. *When China ruled the seas*. Oxford: Oxford University Press.

Li, M., 1994. 浮梁瓷局与御土窑器 Fuliang Ciju Yu Yutu Yaoqi. 南方文物 *Nanfang Wenwu*, 3.

Li, W., 1962. 南京中华门外明墓清理报告 Nanjing Zhonghuamen Wai Mingmu Qingli Baogao. *Kaogu*, 9, 470–478.

Lightfoot, K., 1989. A defense of shovel-test sampling: A reply to Shott. *American Antiquity*, 54 (2), 413–416.

Lin, M. and Zhang, R., 2015. Zheng He's voyages to Hormuz Island: The archaeological evidence. *Antiquity*, 89 (344), 417–432.

Litster, M., 2016. *Cowry shell money and monsoon trade: The Maldives in past globalizations*. Ph.D. thesis, The Australian National University. Available from: http://hdl.handle.net/1885/110238

Liu, L., Jiadong, Y., and Zhifan, X., 1982. 江西南城明益宣王朱翊鈏夫妇合葬墓 Jiangxi Nancheng Ming Yixuan Wang Zhu Yiyin Fufu Hezang Mu. *Wenwu*, 8.

Liu, X., 1981. Yuandai Yaoshi Xiaokao 元代窑事小考 一—兼致约翰· 艾惕思爵士. *Taoci Xuebao*, 1, 008.

Liu, Y., Qin, D., and Kiriama, H., 2012. The Chinese porcelains unearthed at Gedi Ruins in Coast Province, Kenya [肯尼亚滨海省格迪古城遗址出土中国瓷器]. *Wenwu* [文物], 11, 37–60.

Longhurst, A. R. and Pauly, D., eds., 1987. *Ecology of tropical islands*. San Diego: Academic Press.

Luthufee, M. I., 1991. Ibn Batuta in the Maldives. *Malas*, 32, 3–190.

Luthufee, M. I., 1995. *Introduction to the geography of the Maldives*. Vol. 1 and Vol. 2. Male': Department of Public Examination.

Luthufee, M. 1., 1998a. Al-Qazi Hassan Tajuddin. *Faithoora*, 235, 5–10.

Luthufee, M. 1., 1998b. Al-Qazi Hassan Tajuddin. *Faithoora*, 236, 23–39.

Luthufee, M. 1., 1998c. Al-Qazi Hassan Tajuddin. *Faithoora*, 237, 29–32.

Lv, Chenglong, 2004. 元代青花瓷器识鉴 Yuan Dai Qinghua Ciqi Shijian. 故宫博物院院刊 *Gugong Bowuyuan Yuankan*, 2, 20–34.

Majumdar, S. B. and Chatterjee, S., 2014a. Cowries in eastern India: Understanding their role as ritual objects and money. *Journal of Bengal Art*, 19, 39–56.

Majumdar, S. B. and Chatterjee, S., 2014b. The Alagum (Odisha) Garttesvara Siva Temple and the two temple inscriptions. *Pratna Samiksha* (New Series), 5, 97–108.

Maloney, C., 1976. The Maldives: New stresses in an old nation. *Asian Survey*, 16 (7), 654–671.

Maloney, C., 1980. *People of the Maldive Islands*. 1st ed. New Delhi: Orient Blackswan Private Limited.

Maloney, C., 2013. *People of the Maldive Islands*. 2nd ed. New Delhi: Orient Blackswan Private Limited.

Maniku, H. A., 1982. *The royal palace of the Maldives*. Male': National Centre for Linguistic and Historical Research.

Maniku, H. A. and Wijayawardhana, G. D., 1986. *Isdhoo Loamaafaanu*. Colombo: Royal Asiatic Society of Sri Lanka.

Maps, 2016. *Maps of Maldives: The complete guide to the atolls & islands of Maldives*. 2nd ed. Male': Water Solutions Pvt. Ltd.

Margariti, R. E., 2007. *Aden and the Indian Ocean Trade: 150 Years in the life of a medieval Arabian port*. Chapel Hill, NC: University of North Carolina Press.

Marrast, A. and Béarez, P., 2019. Osteometry and size reconstruction of the Indian and Pacific Oceans' Euthynnus species, E. affinis and E. lineatus Scombridae. *Cybium: Revue Internationale d'Ichtyologie*, Paris: Muséum national d'histoire naturelle, 43, 187–198.

Marshall Sir John, ed., 1931. *Mohenjo-daro and the Indus Civilization: Being an official account of Archaeological Excavations at Mohenjo-daro carried out by the Government of India between the years 1922 and 1927*. 3 vols. London: Arthur Probsthain.

Martin, N. and Rougeulle, A., 2015. Les céramiques africaines. In: A. Rougeulle, ed. *Sharma–un entrepôt de commerce médiéval sur la côte du Ḥaḍramawt Yémen, ca 980–1180*. British Foundation for the Study of Arabia Monographs (formerly Society for Arabian Studies Monographs) 17. Oxford: Archaeopress, 168–175.

McElney, B. S., 1979. *The Blue and White Wares post 15th century*. Hong Kong: South East Asian and Chinese Trade Pottery.

McKinnon, E. E., 2015. Medieval South Asian earthenwares in Northern Sumatra: Relevance for contemporary maritime trade. In: S. Tripati, ed. *Maritime contacts of the past: Deciphering connections amongst communities*. New Delhi: Delta Book World, 229–251.

Medley, M., 1989. *The Chinese potter*. Ithaca, NY: Cornell University Press.

Meyer, C., 1992. *Glass from Quseir al-Qadim and the Indian Ocean Trade*. (Studies in Ancient Oriental Civilization 53). Chicago: The Oriental Institute of the University of Chicago.

MHS, 2020. *Maldives heritage survey*. Available from: https://maldivesheritage.oxcis.ac.uk/index.php/3d-models/mosques-cemeteries-and-muslim-funerary-monuments/gni-ddm-1-dhandimago/ [Accessed 4 December 2020].

Michèle Daviau, P. M., 2014. Adorned for death: Glass bracelets for the dead at Khirbat Al-Mudayna (Thamad). *Journal of Islamic Archaeology*, 1 (1), 37–54.

Mikami, T., 1969. 陶磁の道 *Ceramic Road*. Tokyo: Iwanami Shuten Publishers.

Mikkelsen, E., 1991. An archaeological pottery sequence [sic] from Nilandu, the Maldive Islands. In: A. Skjølsvold, ed. *The Kon-Tiki Museum Occasional Papers, Vol. 2: Archaeological test-excavations on the Maldive Islands*. Oslo: Kon-Tiki Museum, 185–202.

Mikkelsen, E., 2000. *Archaeological excavations of a monastery at Kaashidhoo: Cowrie shells and their Buddhist context in the Maldives*. Male': National Centre for Linguistic and Historical Research.

Mitchell, P. J., 2020. Settling Madagascar: When did people first colonize the world's largest island? *The Journal of Island and Coastal Archaeology*, 15 (4), 576–595.

Mohamed, N., 2002. Pre-Islamic Maldive. *Journal of the Indian Society for Prehistoric and Quaternary Studies*, XXVII (1), 1–11.

Mohamed, N., 2005. Note on the early history of the Maldives. *Archipel*, 70, 7–14.

Mohamed, N., 2008. *Essays on early Maldives*. 2nd ed. Male': National Centre for Linguistic and Historical Research.

Mohamed, N., 2014a. Essays of Naseema Mohamed 1. *Malas*, 93, 19–116.

Mohamed, N., 2014b. Maldivian trade. *Maldivian Heritage*, 13, 3–67.

Mohamed, N. and Ragupathy, P., 2005. *Inscriptions of Maldives—no. 1: A gold leaf inscription from Veymandoo Island of Thaa Atoll, Republic of Maldives and a coral stone relic casket with engraved pictures and legends from Nilandhoo Island of Faafu Atoll, Republic of Maldives*. Male': National Centre for Linguistic and Historical Research.

Mohanty, R., 2013. Indian imported pottery. *In*: J. Carswell, S. Deraniyagala, and A. Graham, eds. *Mantai: City by the sea*. Aichwald: Linden Soft, 213–227.

Monod, T., 1978. Sur une site à bracelets de verre des environs d'Aden (République démocratique populaire du Yémen). *Raydan*, 1, 111–124.

Moore, E., 1970. A suggested classification of stonewares of Martabani type. *The Sarawak Museum Journal*, 18 (36–37), 1–78.

Moresby, R., Powell, F. T., and Carless, T. G., 1838–1839. *Trigonometrical survey of the Maldeeve [or Maldiva] Islands: Scale [1:300,000]*. London: John Walker. Available from: https://rgs.koha-ptfs.co.uk/cgi-bin/koha/opac-detail.pl?biblionumber=3917

MRC, 2003. *Fishes of the Maldives*. Maldives: Marine Research Centre, Ministry of Fisheries, Agriculture and Marine Resources Republic of Maldives.

Müller, K. and Wille B., 2019. Materiality and mobility: Comparative notes of heritagization in the Indian Ocean World. *In*: B. Schnepel and T. Sen, eds. *Travelling pasts: The politics of cultural heritage in the Indian Ocean World*. Brill: Washington.

Museum of London, 1994. *Archaeological site manual*. 3rd ed. Romsey: BAS Printers.

Nance, J. and Ball, B., 1986. No surprises? The reliability and validity of test pit sampling. *American Antiquity*, 51 (3), 457–483.

National Centre for Linguistic and Historical Research, 1979. *Radavalhi*. Male': National Centre for Linguistic and Historical Research.

National Centre for Linguistic and Historical Research, 2002. *National museum*. Male': National Centre for Linguistic and Historical Research.

National Centre for Linguistic and Historical Research, 2004. *Heritage sites in the Maldives*. Male': National Centre for Linguistic and Historical Research.

Newton, L. S. and Zarins, J., 2019. *Dhofar through the ages: An ecological, archaeological and historical landscape*. Oxford: Archaeopress Archaeology.

Nicolas, N., 2012. Bijoux celtes et romaines: les bracelets en verre. *In*: P. Cattelain, N. Bozet, and G. V. Di Stazio, eds. *La Parure de Cro-Magnon à Clovis 'Il n'ya pas d'âge(s) pour se faire beau'*. Treignes, Belgium: Cedarc, 71–83.

NJSBWG, 2005 南京市两座明墓的清理简报 Nanjing Shi Liang Zuo Ming Mu De Qingli Jianbao. 华夏考古 *Huaxia Kaogu*, 2, 6–13.

Ogutu, J., Kuzbari, D., and Carter, R., 2018. *Typological and chronological description of glass bangles from Fuwairit, northern Qatar (18th to 19th Century AD)*. Poster presented at the Seminar for Arabian Studies, London.

OpenHeritage 3D. https://openheritage3d.org/news.php?p=digitally-documenting-the-endangered-cultural-history-of-the-maldives [Accessed 23 June 2021].

Orton, C. and Hughes, M., 2013. *Pottery in archaeology*. Cambridge: Cambridge University Press.

Palinkas, L. A., Horwitz, S. M., and Green, C. A., et al., 2015. Purposeful sampling for qualitative data collection and analysis in mixed method implementation research. *Administration and Policy in Mental Health Services Research*, 42 (5), 533–544.

Pavan, A. and Schenk, H., 2012. Crossing the Indian Ocean before the Periplus: A comparison of pottery assemblages at the sites of Sumhuram Oman and Tissamaharama Sri Lanka. *Arabian Archaeology and Epigraphy*, 23, 191–202.

Pearce, N. J. G., et al., 1997. A compilation of new and published major and trace element data for NIST SRM 610 and SRM 612 glass reference materials. *Geostandards Newsletter*, XXI, 114–115.

Peng, K. and Zhu, Y., 1995. *New research on the origins of cowries used in Ancient China*. Sino-Platonic Papers no. 68. Philadelphia: Department of Asian and Middle Eastern Studies, University of Pennsylvania. Available from: www.sino-platonic.org/complete/spp068_cowries_china.pdf

Perry, C. T., et al., 2013. Time scales and modes of reef lagoon infilling in the Maldives and controls on the onset of reef island formation. *Geology*, 41 (10), 1111–1114. Data Repository item 2013308 | doi:10.1130/G34690.1 Available from: geology.gsapubs.org [Accessed 6 February 2016].

Phadnis, U. and Luithui, E. D., 1981. The Maldives enters world politics. *Asian Affairs: An American Review*, 8 (3), 166–179.

Phelps, M., Simpson, St J., and Freestone, I. C., 2018. The early Islamic glass from Sir Bani Yas, UAE. *Proceedings of the Seminar for Arabian Studies*, 48, 249–267.

Piercy, R. C. M., Darroch, A., and Bass, G. F., 1992. The wreck of the Santo Antonio de Tanna. *Archaeology*, 45 (3), 32–35.

Pirazzoli-t'Serstevens, M., 2003. *La Céramique Extrême-Orientale a Julfar Dans l'Emirat de Ra'S Al-Khaimah Xive-Xvie Siècle, Indicateur chronologique, économique et culturel*. Beijing: Centre de Pekin.

Pollard, E. J., 2021. African maritime archaeology. *Oxford Research Encyclopedia of African History*. Available from: https://oxfordre.com/africanhistory/view/10.1093/acrefore/9780190277734.001.0001/acrefore-9780190277734-e-419 [Accessed 30 June 2021].

Pope, J. A., 1952. *Fourteenth-century blue-and-white: A group of Chinese porcelains in the Topkapu Sarayi Mèuzesi, Istanbul*. Freer Gallery of Art.

Porter, V., 1987. Enamelled glass made for the Rasulid Sultans of the Yemen. *In*: R. Ward, ed. *Gilded and enamelled glass from the Middle East*. London: British Museum Press, 91–95.

Pouwels, R. L., 2002. Eastern Africa and the Indian Ocean to 1800: Reviewing relations in historical perspective. *The International Journal of African Historical Studies*, 35 (2–3), 385–425.

Power, T., 2012. *The Red Sea from Byzantium to the Caliphate, AD 500–1000*. Cairo and New York: American University in Cairo.

Power, T., 2015. A first ceramic chronology for the Late Islamic Arabian Gulf. *Journal of Islamic Archaeology*, 2, 1–33.

Pradines, S., 2018. *Buddhism and mosques in the Indian Ocean: Islamic Archaeology in the Maldives*. Paper presented at The Fourth Annual Islamic Archaeology Day hosted by SOAS and UCL, 3rd February 2018.

Pradines, S., n.d. Archaeological Investigations on the coral stone mosques of the Maldives. Available from: https://maxvanberchem.org/en/scientific-activities/projects/archeology/11-archeologie/171-archaeological-investigations-on-the-coral-stone-mosques-of-the-maldives [Accessed 11 March 2021].

Priestman, S., 2005. *Settlement & ceramics in southern Iran: An analysis of the Sasanian & Islamic periods in the Williamson collection*. Master's thesis, Durham University. Available from: http://etheses.dur.ac.uk/2745/

Priestman, S., 2013. *A quantitative archaeological analysis of ceramic exchange in the Persian Gulf and Western Indian Ocean, AD c.400–1275.* Ph.D. Thesis, Archaeology Department, University of Southampton. Available from: http://eprints.soton.ac.uk/id/eprint/370037

Ptak, R., 1987. The Maldive and Laccadive Islands liu-shan 溜 山 in Ming Records. *Journal of the American Oriental Society*, 675–694.

Quiggin, A. H., 1949. *A survey of primitive money.* London: Methuen.

Ragupathy, P. and Mohamed, N., 2008. *An etymological dictionary of Maldivian island names.* Male': National Centre for Linguistic and Historical Research.

Regert, M., et al., 2015. Les résines végétales de type copal et encens: caractérisation, exploitation et circuits commerciaux. *In*: A. Rougeulle, ed. *Sharma–un entrepôt de commerce médiéval sur la côte du Ḥaḍramawt Yémen, ca 980–1180.* British Foundation for the Study of Arabia Monographs (formerly Society for Arabian Studies Monographs) 17. Oxford: Archaeopress, 395–416.

Rehren, T., Osório, A., and Anarbaev, A., 2010. Some notes on early Islamic glass in Eastern Uzbekistan. *In*: B. Zorn and A. Hilgner, eds. *Glass along the Silk Road from 200 BC to AD 1000.* Mainz: Verlag des Römisch–Germanischen Zentralmuseums, 93–103.

Rehren, T., et al., 2015. Changes in glass consumption in Pergamon (Turkey) from Hellenistic to late Byzantine and Islamic times. *Journal of Archaeological Science*, 55, 266–279.

Reimer, P. J., et al., 2013. IntCal13 and Marine13 Radiocarbon age calibration curves 0–50,000 years Cal BP. *Radiocarbon*, 55 (4), 1869–1887.

Reveil, G., 1883. Fours et ateliers d'émailleurs antiques à Cheikh Othman près d'Aden. *Revue d'Ethnographie*, 2.

Risk, M. J. and Sluka, R., 2000. The Maldives: A nation of atolls. *In*: T. R. McClanahan, C. R. C. Sheppard, and D. O. Obura, eds. *Coral reefs of the Indian Ocean—Their ecology and conservation.* Oxford: Oxford University Press, 325–351.

Riyan Ltd., 2011. Preliminary inventory of cultural resources of Maldives and Heritage Action Plan. Draft Unpublished Report to the Department of Heritage, Ministry of Tourism Arts and Culture. UNESCO funded.

Robertshaw, P., et al., 2010. Southern African glass beads: Chemistry, glass sources and patterns of trade. *Journal of Archaeological Science*, 37 (8), 1898–1912.

Romero-Frias, X., 2012. *Folk tales of the Maldives.* Copenhagen: NIAS Press.

Romero-Frias, X., 2016. Rules for Maldivian trading ships travelling abroad (1925) and a soujourn in southern Ceylon. *Politeja*, 13 (1(40)), 67–84.

Rougeulle, A., 1991. Les importations de céramiques chinoises dans le Golfe arabo-persique VIIIe-XIe siècles. *Archéologie islamique*, 2, 5–46.

Rougeulle, A., 1996. Medieval trade networks in the western Indian Ocean (8–14th centuries): Some reflections from the distribution pattern of Chinese imports in the Islamic world. *Tradition and Archaeology: Early Maritime Contacts in the Indian Ocean*, 159–180.

Rougeulle, A., 2005. The Sharma Horizon: Sgraffiato wares and other glazed ceramics of the Indian Ocean trade (c. AD 980–1140). *Proceedings of the Seminar for Arabian Studies*, 35, 223–246.

Rougeulle, A., Collinet, A., and Martin, N., 2015. Les céramiques non glaçurées. *In*: A. Rougeulle, ed. *Sharma—un entrepôt de commerce médiéval sur la côte du Ḥaḍramawt Yémen, ca 980–1180.* British Foundation for the Study of Arabia Monographs (formerly Society for Arabian Studies Monographs) 17. Oxford: Archaeopress, 157–236.

Sankalia, H. D., 1977. *Aspects of Indian history and archaeology.* Delhi: Indian Society for Prehistoric and Quaternary Studies.

Sankalia, H. D. and Dikshit, M. G., 1952. *Excavations at Brahmapuri (Kolhapur) 1945–46.* Deccan College Monograph Series, 5. Poona: Deccan College Postgraduate and Research Institute.

Saunders, B., 2013. *The trade and distribution of ceramics in the Western Indian Ocean 1250–1550AD: An analysis of current available assemblages from Arabia, Iran and East Africa.* Master's thesis, Durham University. Available from: http://etheses.dur.ac.uk/7316/

Scanlon, G. T., 1971. The Fustat Mounds: A shard count 1968. *Archaeology*, 24(3), 220-233

Schenk, H., 2006. The dating and historical value of Rouletted Ware. *Zeitschrift für Archäologie Außereuropäischer Kulturen*, 1, 123–152.

Schenk, H., 2015. Role of ceramics in the Indian Ocean maritime trade during the Early Historical period. *In*: S. Tripati, ed. *Maritime contacts of the past: Deciphering connections amongst communities.* New Delhi: Delta Book World, 143–181.

Schenk, H. and Weisshaar, H.-J., 2016. The citadel of Tissamaharama: Urban habitat and commercial interrelations. *In*: M.-F. Boussac, J.-F. Salles, and J.-B. Yon, eds. *Ports of the ancient Indian Ocean.* New Delhi: Primus Books, 459–479.

Schibille, N., 2011. Late Byzantine mineral soda high alumina glasses from Asia Minor: A new primary glass production group. *PLoS ONE*, 6, e18970.

Scott, J. C., 2011. *The art of not being governed: An anarchist history of Upland Southeast Asia.* New Haven, CT: Yale University Press.

Seetzen, U. J., 1854. *Reisen durch Syrien, Palästina, Phönizien, die Transjordan Länder, Arabia Petraea und Unter-Aegypten* (Friedrich Kruse, ed.). 2 vols. Berlin: Dietrich Reimer.

Seidel, B., 2014. A true Martaban jar: A Burmese ceramic jar in the Ethnological Museum in Heidelberg Germany. *Artibus asiae*, 74 (2), 257–297.

Seland, H., 2011. The Persian Gulf or the Red Sea? Two axes in ancient Indian Ocean trade, where to go and why. *World Archaeology*, 43 (3), 398–409.

Selvakumar, V., 2004. Appendix B: Impressed pottery from the 1990–1992 excavations. *In*: V. Begley, P. Francis Jr., N. Karashima, K. V. Raman, S. E. Sidebotham, and E. Lyding Will, eds. *The ancient port of Arikamedu: New excavations and researches 1989–1992*, Vol. 2. Paris: Ecole française d'Extrême-orient, 613–621.

Selvakumar, V., 2011. Contacts between India and southeast in ceramics and boat building traditions. *In*: P.-Y. Manguin, A. Mani, and G. Wade, eds. *Early interactions between south and southeast Asia.* Singapore: Institute of southeast Asian studies, 197–220.

Semple, C., forthcoming. The glass bangles. *In*: S. Priestman and St J. Simpson, eds. *A catalogue of the excavated finds from Siraf in the British Museum.* Oxford: Oxbow.

Sen, T., 2006. The formation of Chinese maritime networks to Southern Asia, 1200–1450. *Journal of the Economic and Social History of the Orient*, 49 (4), 421–453.

Shafeeg, M., 1989. *Traditional houses of the Maldive Islands*. Newcastle: University of Newcastle upon Tyne.

Shepherd, G., 1982. The making of the Swahili: A view from the southern end of the East African coast. *Paideuma: Mitteilungen zur Kulturkunde*, 28,129–147.

Shindo, Y., 1996. Islamic Glass Bracelets Found in the Red Sea Region. *Annales du 13e Congrès de l'Association Internationale pour l'Histoire du Verre, Pays Bas 28 août—1 septembre 1995*, 269–276. Lochem: International Association for the History of Glass.

Shindo, Y., 2004. Glassware from the Rāya site. *In*: M. Kawatoko, ed. *Archaeological survey of the Rāya/al-Tur area on the Sinai Peninsula, Egypt 2003*. Tokyo: The Middle Eastern Culture Center in Japan, 51–53.

Shindo, Y., 2005. Glassware from the Residential Quarter of the Rāya Site in 2004. *In*: M. Kawatoko, ed. *Archaeological survey of the Rāya/al-Tur area on the Sinai Peninsula, Egypt 2004*. Tokyo: The Middle Eastern Culture Center in Japan, 57–61.

Shindo, Y., 2007. Islamic glass of the 8th century in Rāya. *In*: M. Kawatoko, ed. *Archaeological survey of the Rāya/al-Tur area on the Sinai Peninsula, Egypt 2005 and 2006: The first Japanese—Kuwaiti archaeological expedition (2006)*. Tokyo: The Middle Eastern Culture Center in Japan/Kuwait: Dar al-Athar al-Islamiyyah, 97–116.

Shindo, Y., 2008. Various aspects of cut decoration glass unearthed in the Rāya site. *In*: M. Kawatoko, ed. *Archaeological survey of the Rāya/al-Tur area on the Sinai Peninsula, Egypt 2007: The second Japanese—Kuwaiti archaeological expedition (2007)*. Tokyo: The Middle Eastern Culture Center in Japan/Kuwait: Dar al-Athar al-Islamiyyah, 55–68.

Simpson, St J., 1990. Ottoman clay pipes from Jerusalem and the Levant: A critical review of the published evidence. *Society for Clay Pipe Research Newsletter*, 28, 6–16.

Simpson, St J., 1995. Death and burial in the late Islamic Near East: Some insights from archaeology and ethnography. *In*: S. Campbell and A. Green, eds. *The archaeology of death in the Ancient Near East*. Oxford: Oxbow, 240–251.

Simpson, St J., 2001. Glass beads from Hebron. *Bead Study Trust Newsletter*, 38 (Winter), 11–12.

Simpson, St J., forthcoming. *Pottering among the palm-groves*. Observations on archaeological sites on Bahrain with a catalogue of casual finds. Al-Rafidan.

Simpson, St J., et al., forthcoming. *Excavations at Kush: A Sasanian and Islamic Site in Ras al-Khaimah, United Arab Emirates, Vol. II: The small finds and glassware*. Catalogue, Discussion and Scientific Analyses. Oxford: Archaeopress Archaeology.

Sinopoli, C. M., 1993. *Pots and palaces: Earthenware ceramics of the Noblemen's Quarters of Vijayanagara*. New Delhi: Manohar Publishers.

Skjølsvold, A., 1991. *The Kon-Tiki Museum Occasional Papers, Vol. 2: Archaeological Test-excavations on the Maldive Islands*. Oslo: The Kon-Tiki Museum.

Smith, G. R., 2006. *A medieval administrative and fiscal treatise from the Yemen: The Rasulid Mulakhkhas al-Fitan of al-Hasan B. 'Alī al-Husaynī*. Oxford: Oxford University Press on behalf of the University of Manchester (Journal of Semitic Studies, Supplement 20).

Sode, T., 1995. Purdalpur, a glass bead-making village in Northern India. *In*: M. Rasmussen, U. Lund Hansen and U. Näsman, eds. *Glass beads: Cultural History, technology, experiment and analogy*. Studies in Technology and Culture, 2. Lejre: Historical-Archaeological Experimental Centre, 103–107.

Sode, T., 1996. *Anatolske glasperler*. Vanløse, DK: Thot.

Spaer, M., 1992. The Islamic glass bracelets of Palestine: Preliminary findings. *Journal of Glass Studies*, 34, 44–62.

Stein, G. J., 2002. From passive to active agents: Emerging perspectives in the archaeology of interregional interaction. *American Anthropological Association*, 104, 903–916.

Steiner, M. L., 1995. Glass bracelets from Tall Abu Sarbut. *Studies in the History and Archaeology of Jordan*, 5, 537–40.

Steiner, M. L., 2008. An analysis of the Islamic glass bracelets found at Tell Abu Sarbut. *In*: M. L. Steiner and E. J. van der Steen, eds. *Sacred and sweet*. Studies in the Material Culture of Tell Deir 'Alla and Tell Abu Sarbut (Ancient Near Eastern Studies Supplement Series 24). Louvain: Peeters, 231–240.

Sulas, F., Fleisher, J., and Wynne-Jones, S., 2016. Geoarchaeology of urban space in tropical island environments: Songo Mnara, Tanzania. *Journal of Archaeological Science*, 77, 52–63.

Sulas, F., Kristiansen, S. M., and Wynne-Jones, S., 2019. Soil geochemistry, phytoliths and artefacts from an early Swahili daub house, Unguja Ukuu, Zanzibar. *Journal of Archaeological Science*, 103, 32–45.

Sun, Yingzhou, 1966. 元明清瓷器的鉴定 续 Yuan Ming Qing Ciqi De Jianding Xu Wenwu, 3, 48–58.

Swan, C. M., et al., 2018. High-boron and High-alumina Middle Byzantine (10th–12th century CE) glass bracelets: A Western Anatolian glass industry. *Archaeometry*, 60 (2) (April), 207–232.

Taha, A. B. H., 1983. Recent archaeological discoveries in Peninsular Malaysia 1976–1982. *Journal of the Malaysian Branch of the Royal Asiatic Society*, 47–63.

Tai, Yew Seng, et al., 2020. The impact of Ming and Qing dynasty maritime bans on trade ceramics recovered from coastal settlements in northern Sumatra, Indonesia. *Archaeological Research in Asia*, 21 (2).

Tajuddin, H., 2010. *The Islamic history of the Maldives Tarikh Islami Diba Mahal*. Male': National Centre for Linguistic and Historical Research.

Tajuddin, H., Muhibbuddin, M., and Sirajuddin, I., 1981. *Dhivehi Tarikh*. Male': National Centre for Linguistic and Historical Research.

Talma, A. S. and Vogel, J. C., 1993. Mathematics used for calibration scenario: A simplified approach to calibrating C14 dates. *Radiocarbon*, 35 (2), 317–322.

Thapar, B. K., 1957. Maski 1954: A Chalcolithic site of the southern Deccan. *Ancient India*, 13, 6–142.

Tibbetts, G. R., 1971. *Arab navigation in the Indian Ocean before the coming of the Portuguese: Being a translation of Kitāb al-Fawā'id fī uṣūl al-baḥr wa'l-qawā'id of Aḥmad b. Mājid al-Najdī*; together with an introduction on the history of Arab navigation, notes on the navigational techniques and on the topography of the Indian Ocean and a glossary of navigational terms. London: Royal Asiatic Society of Great Britain and Ireland, Oriental Translation Fund; new ser., v. 42.

TJIOCA and TFPSM, 1992. *Ceramic finds from Jingdezhen Kilns*. Hong Kong: Hong Kong University & Feng Pingshan Museum.

Tomber, R., 2000. Indo-Roman trade: The ceramic evidence from Egypt. *Antiquity*, 74, 624–631.

Tripati, S., 2017. Seafaring archaeology of the East Coast of India and Southeast Asia during the early historical period. *Ancient Asia*, 8 (7), 1–22. DOI:https://doi.org/10.5334/aa.118

UNESCO, 2013. *Coral stone mosques of Maldives* [Online]. Available from: http://whc.unesco.org/en/tentativelists/5812/ [Accessed 11 March 2021].

Van Der Pijl-Ketel, C., 1982. *The ceramic load of the Witte Leeuw 1613*. Amsterdam: Rijks Museum.

Van Ham-Meert, A., et al., 2018. Glass and glass production in the Oman peninsula in antiquity reconsidered: Chemical and mineralogical investigation of sands. *Arabian Archaeology and Epigraphy*, 29, 93–101.

Vecsei, A., 2000. Database on isolated low-latitude carbonate banks. *Facies*, 43 (1), 205–221.

Vellani, S., 1995. La Tène Glass Bracelets from Emilia Romagna (Italy). *Annales de l'Association Internationale pour l'Histoire du Verre (Pays Bas, the Netherlands, 1995)*, 13, 33–46.

Vogel, H. U. and Hieronymus, S., 1993. Cowry trade and its role in the economy of Yünnan: From the ninth to the mid-seventeenth Century: Part I. *Journal of the Economic and Social History of the Orient*, 36 (3), 211–252.

Volney, C.-F. 1793. Travels Through Syria and Egypt: In the Years 1783, 1784, and 1785. Ireland: Messrs. White, Byrne, W. Porter, Moore, Dornin, and WM. Jones.

Von Dewall, M., 1967. The Tien culture of South-west China. *Antiquity*, 41, 8–21.

Wadia, D. N., 1975. *Geology of India*. 4th ed. New Delhi: Tata McGraw Hill Publishing Co.

Wallerstein, I., 1974. *The modern world system I*. New York: Academic Press.

Weisshaar, J., 2015. Ancient Tissamaharama: the formation of urban structures and growing commerce. *In*: S. Tripati, ed. *Maritime contacts of the past: Deciphering connections amongst communities*. New Delhi: Delta Book World, 208–228.

Westerdahl, C., 1992. The maritime cultural landscape. *The International Journal of Nautical Archaeology*, 21, 5–14.

Wheeler, M., Ghosh, A., and Deva, K., 1946. ARIKAMEDU: An Indo-Roman trading station on the East Coast of India. *Ancient India*, 2, 17–124.

Whitcomb, D, 1978. The Archaeology of al-Hasa Oasis in the Islamic Period. Atlal, Journal of Saudi Arabia Studies, 2, 95–113.

Whitcomb, D. S., 1988. Islamic archaeology in Aden and the Hadhramautin. *In*: D. T. Potts, ed. *Araby the Blest: Studies in Arabian archaeology*. Copenhagen: The Carsten Niebuhr Institute of Ancient Near Eastern Studies (CNI Publications 7), 177–263.

Whitcomb, D. S. and Johnson, J., 1982. *Quseir al-Qadim 1980*. Preliminary Report (American Research Center in Egypt Reports, 7). Malibu: Undena.

Whitehouse, D., 1968. Excavations at Sīrāf: First Interim Report. *Iran*, 6, 1–22, pls I—VIII.

Whitehouse, D., 1998. *Excavations at ed-Dur (Umm al-Qaiwain, United Arab Emirates), Vol. I: The glass vessels*. Leuven: Peeters.

Whitehouse, D. and Williamson, A., 1973. Sasanian maritime trade. *Iran*, 11, 29–49.

Witcher, R., 2020. Editorial. *Antiquity*, 94 (378), 1399–1408.

Wood, M., 2005. *Glass beads and Pre—European trade in the Shashe—Limpopo Region*. MA thesis, University of the Witwatersrand, Faculty of Humanities.

Wood, M., 2015. Divergent patterns in Indian Ocean trade to East Africa and southern Africa between the 7th and 17th centuries CE: The glass bead evidence. *Afriques* [online], 06 | 2015, published 21 December 2015, consulted on 7 February 2021. Available from: http://afriques.revues.org/1782.

Wood, M., 2016. Glass beads from pre-European contact sub-Saharan Africa: Peter Francis's work revisited and updated. *Archaeological Research in Asia*, 6, 65–80.

Wood, M., 2017. Glass beads and Indian Ocean trade. *In*: S. Wynne–Jones and A. LaViolette, eds. *The Swahili world*. London and New York: Routledge, 458–471.

Wood, M., Dussubieux, L., and Wadley, L., 2009. A cache of ~5000 glass beads from the Sibudu Cave Iron Age occupation. *Southern African Humanities*, 21, 239–261.

Xue, Y., 1965. 江西南城、清江和永修的宋墓 Jiangxi Nancheng, Qingjiang He Yongxiu De Song Mu. *Kaogu*, 11.

Yang, B., 2004. Horses, silver, and cowries: Yunnan in global perspective. *Journal of World History*, 15 (3), 281–322.

Yang, B., 2011. The rise and fall of cowrie shells: The Asian Story. *Journal of World History*, 22 (1), 1–25.

Yang, B., 2019. *Cowrie shells and cowrie money: A global history*. London and New York: Routledge.

Yang, H., 1981. 永新县发现元代瓷器 Yongxin Xian Faxian Yuandai Ciqi. 南方文物 *Nanfang Wenwu*, 2.

Yang, H., 1983. Jiangxi Mingdai Jinianmu Chutu De Qinghua Ciqi. *Jiangxi Lishi Wenwu*, 3, 85–95.

Yao, A., 2010. Recent developments in the archaeology of southwestern China. *Journal of Archaeological Research 2010*, 18, 203–239.

Yu, J., 1973. 江西玉山、临川和永修县明墓 Jiangxi Yushan, Linchuan He Yongxiu Xian Mingmu. *Kaogu*, 5.

Yu, J., 1995 江西吉安市临江窑遗址 Jiangxi Ji'an Shi Linjiang Yao Yizhi. 考古学报 *Kaogu Xuebao*, 2, 243–274.

Yu, J., 2011. 江西仿龙泉青瓷与浙江龙泉青瓷之间的相互关系 Jiangxi Fang Longquan Qingci Yu Zhejiang Longquan Qingci Zhijian De Xianghu Guanxi. *In*: ZGGTCYJH, ed. 龙泉窑研究 *Longquan Yao Yanjiu*. Beijing: Gugong Chubanshe, 473–481.

Yuba, T., 2014. Chinese porcelain from Fustat based on research from 1988–2001. *Transactions of the Oriental Ceramic Society*, 76, 1–17.

Zanon, M., 2013. Tyana/Kemerhisar (Niğde): Glass bracelets of the Byzantine and Islamic period. *Anatolia Antiqua*, 21, 181–197.

Zhang, R., 2016. *An exploratory quantitative archaeological analysis and a classification system of Chinese ceramics trade in the Western Indian Ocean, AD c. 800–1500*. Ph.D. thesis, Archaeology Department, University of Durham. Available from: http://etheses.dur.ac.uk/11747/

Zhao, B., 2006 中世纪时期贸易中转港—也门舍尔迈遗址出土的中国瓷片 Zhongshiji Shiqi Maoyi Zhongzhuan Gang-Yemen Sheermai Yizhi Chutu De Zhongguo Cipian. *In*: Xingchan Chen and Michela Bussotti, eds. 考古发掘与历史复原 *Kaogu Fajue Yu Lishi Fuyuan*. Beijing: Zhonghua Shuju, 79–116.

Zhu, B., 1998. 龙泉窑青瓷 Longquanyao QIngci. 艺术家出版社 *Yishujia Chubanshe*.

Zunaam, F., 2021. Archaeological artifacts unearthed by accident in Rasgetheemu. *The Times of Addu*, 16 February 2021. Available from: https://timesofaddu.com/2021/02/16/archaeological-artifacts-unearthed-by-accident-in-rasgetheemu/ [Accessed 22 March 2021].

Index

Page numbers in italics indicate a figure.

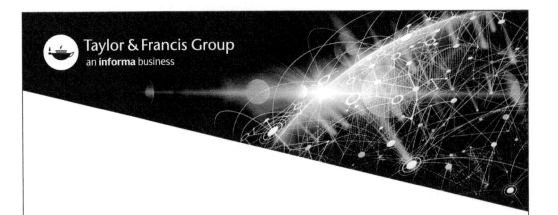

Printed and bound by CPI Group (UK) Ltd, Croydon, CR0 4YY

26/11/2024

01795390-0001